Catholic Education
in Australia
1806-1950

II

CATHOLIC EDUCATION
IN AUSTRALIA
1806-1950

BROTHER RONALD FOGARTY, F.M.S.

B.A., B.Sc., B.Ed., Ph.D. (Melb.)

Master of Scholastics, Marist Brothers' Scholasticate, Sydney
Formerly Research Scholar, University of Melbourne

VOLUME II

Catholic Education under
the Religious Orders

MELBOURNE UNIVERSITY PRESS

FIRST PUBLISHED 1959

PRINTED AND BOUND IN AUSTRALIA BY
MELBOURNE UNIVERSITY PRESS, CARLTON, N.3, VICTORIA

REGISTERED IN AUSTRALIA FOR TRANSMISSION
BY POST AS A BOOK

NIHIL OBSTAT

D. Conquest, *Censor Deputatus*

IMPRIMATUR

D. Mannix, *Archiepiscopus Melbournensis*

23 September 1957

LONDON AND NEW YORK: CAMBRIDGE UNIVERSITY PRESS

Contents

VOLUME II: CATHOLIC EDUCATION UNDER
THE RELIGIOUS ORDERS

7 The Coming of the Religious   257

    *The Quest for Religious, 258; The Response of the Religious,
268; Problems in Adaptation, 286; The Contribution of the
Religious, 297*

8 Catholic Schools under the Religious Orders   304

    *The Parochial System, 304; Secondary Schools: Boys', 311;
Secondary Schools: Girls', 342*

9 The Curriculum: Profane Subjects   352

    *The Primary Curriculum, 352; The Secondary Curriculum:
Boys', 358; The Secondary Curriculum: Girls', 376*

10 The Curriculum: Religious Education   383

    *Documents Affecting Religious Education, 383; Parents and
Teachers, 385; Religious Instruction, 389; Moral and Religious
Formation, 402*

11 Reorganization and Reaction   421

    *Improving the System, 421; Expanding the System,
446; Reaction, 457*

12 Retrospect   470

Appendices:

    I *Principal Education Acts, Committees, and
Commissions*   482

    II *Foundation of Catholic Dioceses and Succession
of Bishops*   484

    III *Outline of the Sheil-Woods scheme of Catholic
education in South Australia*   486

    IV *Rules and Regulations of the Catholic Association
for the Promotion of Religion and Education,
New South Wales, 1867*   488

V Regulations of Catholic Education Committee,
    Victoria, 1863   489

VI Regulations for Catholic schools, 1848, attributed
    to Archbishop Polding   490

VII Statements of New South Wales Bishops to
     Legislature in 1866 and 1867   492

VIII Programme and Method followed in the first
      schools of the Sisters of St Joseph   494

Bibliography   496

Index   545

Illustrations

Plates

VOLUME II

5 Archbishop Vaughan's letter to Alderman J. G. O'Connor,
29 October 1881   262 *and* 263

6 The Reverend J. E. Tenison Woods   278

7 Mother Mary of the Cross   294

8 St Mary's College, Lyndhurst, Glebe, in the 1870s   310

9 St Patrick's College, Melbourne, in the 1860s   374

10 All Hallows' Convent. The first building, 1863, and
a later building, 1881   390

Figures

VOLUME II

11 Orders entering dioceses for first time   273

12 Initial foundations from within and from outside Australia 275

13 Spread of Presentation communities from Wagga Wagga,
New South Wales   277

14 Increase in number of religious teachers in Australia   280

15 Dioceses of Australia, 1950, showing the number of Sisters,
Brothers, and priests engaged in teaching   282 *and* 283

16 Replacement of lay teachers by religious in Catholic schools,
archdiocese of Melbourne   281

17 Parishes and parish schools in Australia   307

18 Development of boys' secondary schools, irrespective of
enrolments   332

19 Development of girls' secondary schools, irrespective of
enrolments   343

20 Organization of authority in the Catholic school system   441

Abbreviations

A.C.D.	*Australian Catholic Directory*
B.T.	Bonwick Transcripts
CCCE	Central Council of Catholic Education (South Australia)
CCSA-A	Catholic Church of South Australia Archives
C.O.D.	Colonial Office Despatches
C.S.F.	Colonial Secretary's Files
C.S.O.	Colonial Secretary's Office
Cod. Iur. Can.	*Codex Iuris Canonici*
Conc. Plen.	*Acta et Decreta Concilii Plenarii*
D.S.B.	Denominational Schools Board
H.R.A.	*Historical Records of Australia*
H.R.N.S.W.	*Historical Records of New South Wales*
ML	Mitchell Library, Sydney
Parl. Deb.	*Parliamentary Debates*
P.P.	*Parliamentary Papers.* This includes *Votes and Proceedings, Journals* and *Printed Papers*
Q-A	John Oxley Memorial Library, Brisbane (Queensland State Archives)
SA-A	Archives Department, Public Library of South Australia
S.C. and C.H.	*Southern Cross and Catholic Herald* (South Australia)
T-A	State Archives, Tasmania
V-A	State Archives, Public Library of Victoria
WA-A	Archives Department, Public Library of Western Australia

7

The Coming of the Religious

ARCHBISHOP VAUGHAN had promised his opponents that he would solve the school question, 'in a way that would astonish them'[1] (see Plate 5). Within two years the Archbishop was dead, but the system he established remained. No longer a subject of astonishment—at least to Australians[2]—it had come by the middle of the present century to be taken largely for granted, being regarded more or less as a part of the national system.[3]

As planned, Vaughan's scheme was dependent, almost entirely, on religious; they were essential to it. 'Without the religious teaching orders,' the Australian bishops were to admit seventy years later, 'Catholic schools might gradually have disappeared after the passing of the State Education Acts.'[4] When these Acts were passed there were few such orders in Australia and these were in small and scattered communities. It was one thing to plan a policy, but an entirely different thing to carry it out. Religious had to be sought—in the Catholic countries of Europe; they had to be invited, or rather begged, to interest themselves in Australia. They had to come, to settle, to adapt themselves to Australian conditions, and then stretch their slender resources of personnel as far as they would go. They brought with them, besides the service of their own hands and whatever scholarship they possessed, their own educational systems in which were epitomized not only the many-sided tradition of the Church in her role as educator, but also all that had proved of lasting value in educational development in Europe generally from the sixteenth century to the nineteenth. By this means they considerably enriched the culture of the land of their adoption, and, in return, drew from it all that they needed for their own fuller preparation in the work they had undertaken.[5]

This quest for religious, therefore, their coming, and the process of acculturation that accompanied their dispersal throughout the whole continent constitute an important chapter in the history of Catholic education in Australia.

[1] Letter, Vaughan to O'Connor, 29 October 1881 (ML).
[2] Generally speaking, it is overseas visitors who comment upon the uniqueness of the Catholic system in Australia.   [3] See remaining chapters, especially ch. 10.
[4] Beovich, Archbishop M., 'Catholic Education and Catechetics in Australia'. Catholic Education Office, Melbourne.
[5] Catholic teachers, in increasing numbers, received their training in Australian universities.

THE QUEST FOR RELIGIOUS
Vaughan's Efforts

Vaughan had become Archbishop of Sydney and Metropolitan in 1877. At that time the Church in New South Wales stood in need of just such strong leadership as the new Archbishop could give, especially in education.[6] This was to be the particular object of his energy and genius. In his own mind he had accepted a challenge and he dared not fail; for on its issue depended, to a large degree, the future of the Church in Australia.

The Catholic schools had to be saved. On that point the Archbishop's mind was now perfectly clear; for in every battle, he believed, victory depended on the possession of the key to the situation, and in this battle that key was 'the supreme question of education'.[7] 'If our Catholic people,' he said, 'bring up their children thorough Catholics, that is, educate them in thorough Catholic schools, the victory is ours; if, on the contrary, the State takes possession of them and they are thrown into Public Schools, the victory will eventually be with our opponents.'[8]

But Vaughan felt assured of victory. He saw no reason for Catholics 'to despair or be downhearted'.[9] 'The Church's exuberant life', he believed, would 'furnish [them] with instruments for forming [the] rising generation' to a degree 'far beyond what the State [could] offer'. 'Were we deprived of all assistance to-morrow,' he wrote in September, 1879, 'we might suffer for a moment; but it would not be for long. There is an elasticity in the Catholic body that knows how to respond to a great call in a cause of vital religious interest.'[10]

This theme—the resourcefulness of the Church and its ability to provide education for its children at its own cost—recurs time and time again in Vaughan's speeches over the last months of 1879.[11] It is as though he felt more confidence in the support of his people now that they were closely united in the face of a common danger. 'The faith', he said, that had willingly spent so much blood in the past, that had 'witnessed with life itself to Gospel truth', would 'spring to the front with the old generosity, and spend itself in support of such religious teachers as would serve the great cause of the Catholic Church' —and 'the true interests of the colony'.[12]

---

[6] Vaughan gave up his cathedral income for the cause of Catholic education. Minute Book of Catholic Board of Education, 6 November 1882, p. 11 (St Mary's Cathedral Archives).   [7] Vaughan, Archbishop R. B., *Pastorals and Speeches on Education*, p. 36.
[8] Ibid.   [9] *Pastoral 4* (on Education), 28 September 1879, p. 13.   [10] Ibid.
[11] Speech on education delivered on occasion of laying the foundation stone of the school at Forest Lodge, Sydney, 12 October 1879. Vaughan, *Pastorals and Speeches*, p. 18. 'This much,' said Vaughan, 'we may take for granted, that the Catholic Church in this Archdiocese will be equal to the emergency and will give Catholic children a Catholic education.'
[12] *Pastoral 4*, 28 September 1879, p. 13.

Lay teachers were out of the question for many reasons.[13] First, as has been shown,[14] the Church could not pay salaries for lay teachers— certainly not at the rate paid by the state.[15] Had it tried, the burden imposed on the Catholic people would have been insupportable.[16] The fact was widely and openly admitted. Tenison Woods had made use of it to induce the Catholics of South Australia to respond to the Sisters of St Joseph.[17] Bishop Matthew Quinn had also exploited it successfully in Bathurst.[18]

The second reason was the marked deterioration in the efficiency of the Catholic schools. Owing to the fact that many of their best teachers had swung over to the higher salaried posts in the state department, these schools were left in a seriously weakened condition. New and competent teachers had to be found somewhere, and the only likely source of supply seemed to be the religious. Already they had given proof of their skill[19] and pupils flocked to their schools.[20]

Vaughan was not unaware of the results likely to accrue from the well-tried methods of the new orders. Already he had established several communities;[21] and, if state support were withdrawn, 'more Jesuits, Franciscans, and Marists', he said, 'would be forthcoming at once'. In addition, he would put himself 'into immediate communication with the Christian Brothers, the Xaverian Brothers, and the Premonstratensians'.[22]

The Archbishop was as good as his word. Four years later, on the eve of his departure for Europe, he gave a resumé of developments since his arrival in Sydney in 1875. Over the ensuing nine years the number of Catholic schools had been exactly trebled,[23] and four out of every five were in the hands of religious.[24] Of the 15,200 Catholic children of school age then in the archdiocese, 12,500 were in Catholic schools, over two-thirds of them being in schools taught by religious.[25] Sixty-eight of the eighty establishments in the hands of religious had been

[13] The suggestion that Catholic lay teachers were to be found in sufficient numbers cannot be supported. See Byrne, Rev. F., *History of the Catholic Church in South Australia*, pp. 155, 186. [14] See ch. 6.
[15] Corrigan, Rev. Br Urban, *The Achievements of Catholic Education in Australia*, p. 7. [16] Beovich, 'Catholic Education and Catechetics in Australia', p. 2.
[17] Report of Director-General, meeting of Central Catholic Council of Education, Adelaide, November 1869. *S.C. and C.H.*, 20 November 1868, p. 223.
[18] Quinn, Rt Rev. Matthew, *Pastoral Letter to the Clergy and Laity of the Diocese*, 1882, p. 5.
[19] Report of Royal Commission on Education (Q'ld.), 1875. Minutes of Evidence: evidence of Mr J. Cameron, p. 202.
[20] Letter to Editor, *Freeman's Journal*, 29 March 1873, p. 9, d.
[21] *Pastoral 1*, 10 August 1879, p. 11. [22] Ibid., p. 12.
[23] That is, from 34 to 102; Vaughan's speech at Balmain, 15 April 1883, in Everard Digby (ed.), *Australian Men of Mark*, p. 197.
[24] Of the 102 schools 22 were taught by lay teachers, 11 by religious orders of men, and 69 by religious orders of women. Balmain speech.
[25] Ibid. Number of children in schools taught by lay teachers was 1,564; in schools taught by religious, 10,916.

started, as the Archbishop himself put it, since he had 'troubled the peace of Sleepy Hollow', and forty-five since Parkes had prophesied 'death' to the calling of the clergy.[26] Twenty-seven had been established in the first four months of 1883.[27]

But Vaughan gloried not in numbers. His gaze went beyond them to something that gave him infinitely greater assurance—the fact that the bulk of his teachers were religious. He told the people of Balmain as he bade them farewell in 1883: 'You know what I have said about schools being "holy places". You know I believe in the teaching of men and women who have dedicated their whole beings to God.'[28] Such teachers, he felt, would 'give a tone and thoroughness to the rising generations',[29] and 'hold an attraction which even non-Catholics [would] find difficult to resist'. In them the Church would 'possess an instrument of power . . . of which her opponents little [dreamt]'.

This idea had completely taken hold of the Archbishop. For him, the introduction of religious orders, from being a mere economic necessity, as it had been in the beginning, had become almost a moral necessity.[30]

Efforts of Other Bishops

What Vaughan had come to realize by the beginning of the eighties, however, had already been a principle of activity with many of the other bishops for more than fifty years. The Catholic countries of Europe had been searched over and over again by envoys from Australia, all bent on the same purpose—the securing of teaching orders.[31]

Father Therry, from his first years in the colony, had turned his thoughts towards teachers of this type. In them, he saw a powerful antidote to the virus of immorality and indifference that spread unchecked under the appalling social conditions of his day. In a pamphlet published in 1825, he referred to the possibility of 'a convent or monastery' and hoped that his Protestant friends would 'not be alarmed at the idea'.[32] He was not without hope, even then, of inducing some men who had been trained in a monastery to undertake school work in the colony.[33]

Fathers McEncroe and Ullathorne had carried the same quest a little farther. McEncroe had requested Dr Murray, who then occupied the

[26] Ibid. See also Birt, Rev. Henry Norbert, *Benedictine Pioneers in Australia*, vol. 2, p. 460. Vaughan's words, as reported at any rate, are a little inaccurate. The reference is to Parkes' speech of 23 February 1880: 'Some of the priests of both Churches—and nearly the whole . . . of one Church—are opposed because . . . enlightenment . . . is death to their calling.' *Parl. Deb.* (N.S.W.), 1879-80, 2, p. 1284.

[27] See Balmain speech.

[28] Ibid. The fact that Vaughan was going abroad to secure more teachers was widely circulated. *Express*, 3 February, p. 5.   [29] *Pastoral 1*, 10 August 1879, p. 11.

[30] Balmain speech, 1883. See also lecture on education in the Pro-Cathedral, Sydney, 11 January 1880. Vaughan, *Pastorals and Speeches*, p. 103.

[31] Corrigan, *The Achievements of Catholic Education in Australia*, p. 7.

[32] Quoted in O'Brien, Archbishop E. M., *Life and Letters of Archpriest John Joseph Therry*, p. 82.   [33] Ibid.

see of Dublin, to secure a small group from the newly founded order of Christian Brothers.[34] Could he but establish them in the colony, he would be able to look forward to the time when they could accept Australian recruits and comfortably 'supply all the Catholic schools with proper teachers'.[35] Dr Ullathorne added his weight to the request and wrote asking Polding, who was then still a monk at Downside, to take the matter up directly with the Superiors of the Christian Brothers in Ireland.[36] Seven years later, as Vicar Apostolic of New Holland, Polding was to repeat the request,[37] appealing this time not only to Ireland[38] but direct to Rome itself.[39] As a result three Brothers were sent out;[40] but, as has been shown (p. 245), their sojourn in Sydney was very short.

In his early visits to Europe Polding had himself spent some time seeking religious orders for teaching. But in Europe and on the Continent proper New South Wales was little known and its Bishop even less.[41] Through Dr Ullathorne he had earlier secured the Sisters of Charity and, at the end of the forties, welcomed a community of Benedictine nuns.[42] In the meantime he had set his own Benedictine monks teaching and was engaged upon plans for extending this work.[43] Early in the fifties, too, he had hopes of securing teaching Brothers from Germany. Had they been able to come, he 'would have been able to provide for the support of thirty or forty and', he added, 'give them plenty to do'.[44] But they were not able to come. Later still, he gave approval for the introduction of two communities of Sisters of Mercy: one for Goulburn, the other, originally intended for Bathurst, but diverted at the last moment to Sydney.[45] These, it is to be noted, had not come at the Archbishop's own request; their introduction had been the work of others.[46] He himself appears either to have given up the idea of securing other teaching orders, or to have been extraordinarily unsuccessful in his attempts.

[34] Letter, McEncroe to Dr Murray, Sydney, 2 November 1832. Quoted in Moran, Cardinal P. F., *History of the Catholic Church in Australasia*, p. 142. The Mr Rice's brothers referred to were the Irish Christian Brothers founded by Ignatius Rice, who was then still living. [35] Ibid.

[36] See letter, Br F. Thornton to senior members of the Irish Christian Brothers, 21 November 1833, given in full in *Edmund Ignatius Rice and the Christian Brothers*.

[37] Letter, Polding to Heptonstall, 4 September 1840. Quoted in Birt, *Benedictine Pioneers in Australia*, I, p. 484. [38] Ibid.

[39] Letter, Polding to Propaganda, Rome, praying that some of the Irish Christian Brothers be sent to New South Wales. Quoted in Moran, *History of the Catholic Church in Australasia*, pp. 224-5.

[40] *Edmund Ignatius Rice and the Christian Brothers*, p. 411.

[41] Quoted in 'Rose Bay and District', Australian Historical Society Records, 1944, p. 6. [42] See Table XXXIX, p. 270. [43] See ch. 8.

[44] Letter, Fr Kranewitter (S.J.), to Secretary of Munich Missionary Society, Clare, 24 February 1853 (Archives, St Aloysius' College, Sevenhill, S.A.).

[45] See McMahon, Rev. J. J., 'The History of Catholic Secondary Education in New South Wales'. Australian Catholic Historical Society Records, 1950, p. 9.

[46] Men like Fathers McEncroe and Rigney, for example, were still very active. *Freeman's Journal*, 27 June 1872, p. 10, d; *Sydney Morning Herald*, quoted in Corrigan, op. cit., p. 85; McMahon, op. cit., p. 10.

It was altogether different with his suffragans. Where these bishops did not bring nuns with them when they came to the colony, they sent for them soon after they arrived. Matthew Quinn, as has been seen, brought a group with him to Bathurst. Bishop Murray, by the first mail after his arrival in Maitland, sent home to Ireland for a community, telling them that they were 'wanted very badly'.[47] These were the Dominicans. Later he was to call in three or four other groups.[48] Similarly, Dr Torreggiani, upon his arrival in Armidale, sent home to England for a group of nuns he had known in London.[49] Communities of teaching Brothers were also sought by Quinn, Lanigan, and Murray. Quinn, as has been shown, throughout the seventies had hoped to secure the services of the Marist Brothers.[50] When these failed him he tried the De La Salle Brothers in France[51] and, finally, the Patrician Brothers in Ireland. Not satisfied with an odd group or two, he wanted to establish a mother house for them in Bathurst so that they could spread throughout his whole diocese.[52] Likewise Dr Lanigan, having failed to induce the Marist Brothers to come to Goulburn,[53] announced his intention of establishing communities of Patrician Brothers not only at Goulburn but at Albury and Wagga as well.[54] To secure these men was one of the reasons for his visit to Ireland in 1880, whither he was accompanied by Dr Murray. The latter joined in the search, hoping to find a group for the Maitland diocese.[55]

In Tasmania the situation was a little different. Bishop Willson had afforded a haven to the Sisters of Charity who desired to get away from Sydney; but apparently entertained no idea of using them primarily as teachers in the Catholic schools. They were used mainly for social work among the poor and the convicts.[56] Father John Hall, the Vicar-General, aware of the Christian Brothers' desire to leave Sydney, thought he might be able to induce them also to come to Hobart, but he was not successful.[57]

Thereafter there was no change in policy until Dr Murphy succeeded Bishop Willson twenty years later. The new Bishop immediately sent

[47] Letter, Murray to Kingstown Dominicans in Ireland, East Maitland, 20 November 1866. Quoted in O'Hanlon, Sr M. Assumpta, *Dominican Pioneers in New South Wales*, p. 49.
[48] See p. 276.
[49] McMahon, op. cit., p. 13, quoting from Ursuline Annals in Ursuline Convent, Armidale, N.S.W.
[50] Marist Brothers' Annals, p. 3 (Archives, Marist Brothers' Provincial House, Mittagong, N.S.W.).
[51] Aloysius, Rev. Brother, 'St John Baptist de la Salle and his Institute in Australia', Australian Catholic Historical Society Records, April 1951, p. 8.
[52] *Record* (Bathurst), 15 July 1880, p. 325, a.   [53] Marist Brothers' Annals, p. 26.
[54] Newspaper cutting, undated (Archives, Presentation Convent, Wagga, N.S.W.).
[55] McMahon, op. cit., p. 13.
[56] Letter, Hall to Mother de Sales O'Brien, 23 April 1847. Quoted in Kelsh, Rev. Thomas, *Personal Recollections of the Rt Rev. R. W. Willson*, p. 68.   [57] Ibid.

My dear Alderman O'Connor

Could you

get me a copy of

that Return mentioning

the Number of Catholic

Teachers in Public Schools?

5. ARCHBISHOP VAUGHAN'S LETTER TO
ALDERMAN J. G. O'CONNOR, 29 OCTOBER 1881

From the original in the Mitchell Library, Sydney

5. ARCHBISHOP VAUGHAN'S LETTER TO
ALDERMAN J. G. O'CONNOR, 29 OCTOBER 1881 (cont.)

home to Ireland for Sisters for the schools[58] and then set about procuring a community of Brothers. First, he applied to the Marist Brothers in Sydney;[59] but, when these could not help him, he turned to his own compatriots, the Irish Christian Brothers. For many years he continued to send passage money to Ireland for two or three men, only to have it repeatedly returned—always with expressions of sincere regret that there were no men to spare.[60]

Religious were not so plentiful that they could be had for the asking. Bishop Murphy in Adelaide had realized this. No other pioneer bishop in Australia had made such valiant efforts to obtain religious teachers; no-one was so unsuccessful. Acquainted with the work of the Christian Brothers in Sydney,[61] he begged in person from their Superior-General in Ireland in 1846 for a few men for his Adelaide schools,[62] but he begged in vain.[63] Later he was hopeful of securing Brothers from the same German missionary society that Polding had tried in Munich, but he was no more fortunate than his Archbishop.[64] Through the same society he also sought to secure a community of 'Englische Fräulein' (the Loreto Sisters),[65] but he had little to offer them and they did not come. Thereupon he wrote to Mother Ursula Frayne, one of the Sisters of Mercy brought to Perth by Dr Brady, requesting her 'to send three or four nuns for [his] poor school and boarding school'.[66] But Mother Frayne had already accepted an invitation from Dr Goold to go to Melbourne, and, although she called at Adelaide en route the following year,[67] she could not be induced to leave any Sisters.[68] Accordingly Murphy wrote direct to Bishop Serra in Perth. Eliciting no satisfactory response there, he turned his attention to Goold.[69] But Goold was too preoccupied with his own needs to be able to help South Australia.

Death finally put an end to Dr Murphy's efforts. But his plan for securing religious was prosecuted with equal vigour by his successors. In Ireland in 1862, Dr Geoghegan had put himself 'in earnest communication with religious bodies of men and women for [his] schools';[70] but

[58] See Table XXXIX, p. 270.   [59] Marist Brothers' Annals, p. 26.
[60] Catholic Standard (Hobart), August 1878, p. 127, a; see also Fr Michael Beechinor, Memoir of Archbishop Murphy, p. 67.
[61] Murphy, Bishop Francis, Journal, 1843, 1844 (Catholic Church Archives, S.A.).
[62] Morrison, Rev. R. A., 'The Story of Catholic Education in South Australia', 1844-64 (Catholic Church Archives, S.A.).
[63] Letter, Murphy to Ryan, 1846. Quoted in Byrne, op. cit.
[64] Letter, Kranewitter to Secretary of Munich Missionary Society.
[65] Ibid.   [66] Murphy, Journal, 9 December 1856.
[67] Ibid. This fact is added by way of note to the transcript of Dr Murphy's Journal. See entry for 1 March 1857. The editor of the transcript of Dr Murphy's Journal, evidently unaware of the Melbourne project, is of the opinion that Mother Ursula Frayne had made a special visit from the West just to inspect the situation in Adelaide.
[68] Murphy, Journal, 24 March 1857.
[69] Ibid., 20 January 1858.
[70] Letter, Geoghegan to his Vicar-General, Dublin, 25 December 1862. Quoted from Byrne, op. cit., p. 173.

before he could achieve any success he was appointed to the new see of Goulburn. Dr Sheil continued the quest. Having unsuccessfully approached the Loreto Sisters and the Sisters of Mercy,[71] he secured a promise from the Dominican nuns at Cabra, Dublin.[72] In 1880, his successor, Dr Reynolds, also secured from Ireland a community of Irish Sisters of Mercy who had been obliged to withdraw from South America,[73] but the latter's repeated requests to the Marist Brothers in Sydney for men to staff his boys' schools were unavailing.[74]

In Victoria the same quest for religious had gone on since that colony had been made a bishopric at the end of the 1840s. When Dr Goold was leaving for Europe in 1851 he announced it as his intention to 'procure for this district the valuable services of the Sisters of Charity' and 'to bring out other young ladies who had by vow consecrated their lives to the education of the female portion of the Catholic youth',[75] but he returned without either. It was then that he put himself in touch with the Sisters of Mercy in Western Australia.[76] One community, however, was not enough, for the vast increase in population following upon the gold rush period had put such a severe strain on existing educational facilities that teachers were desperately needed. These increased numbers, together with the threat of the Secular Bill[77] in 1858 drove the Bishop once more to Ireland in search of nuns. His diary reveals the steps he took[78] and the success that eventually crowned his efforts.[79]

Meanwhile the search had continued for religious to provide education for the boys of the colony. Dr Geoghegan had referred to the Christian Brothers in his evidence before the Select Committee on Education in 1852, and trusted that the day was 'not distant' when Victoria would

[71] Morrison, Rev. R. A., 'The Story of Catholic Education in South Australia', 'The Dominican Nuns', p. 21. (Catholic Church Archives, S.A.)

[72] Southern Cross, 20 December 1868, pp. 241, c, 242, a, b, c.

[73] Morrison, 'The Story of Catholic Education in South Australia', 'The Sisters of Mercy', p. 7. A great wave of anti-clericalism had broken out in Buenos Aires, the capital of the Argentine. Life there for religious, especially foreigners, had become impossible. This particular group of Irish nuns, finding it impossible to remain there, had returned to Dublin.

[74] Marist Brothers' Annals, p. 26.   [75] Herald (Melbourne), 22 January 1851.

[76] Mother Ursula Frayne, in July 1856, wrote: 'It was now time for me to urge a matter which had been pending for some months past, namely a foundation of our order in the neighbouring Colony of Victoria. The respected Bishop of Victoria had written to me about a year previous requesting me to come with three other Sisters to found a house in his diocese.' 'Recollections of M. Ursula Frayne', p. 81. (Archives of Convent of Mercy, Victoria Square, Perth.) See also letters, Mother Ursula Frayne to Dr Goold, 29 July 1855 and 24 November 1855 (St Patrick's Cathedral Archives, Melbourne).   [77] The proposal of Sir Alexander Michie. See ch. 2.

[78] Diary of Dr Goold, quoted in Moran, op. cit., p. 763. (During this period Goold assisted as one of the consecrating prelates at the consecration of Dr James Quinn, newly elected Bishop of Brisbane. Diary entry for 29 June 1859.)

[79] Diary of Dr Goold, 13 July 1859, 5 September 1859. The Sisters reached Melbourne on 28 November 1859; see also Sr M. Ignatius, 'The Sisters of Mercy in Victoria' (Archives, Convent of Mercy, Geelong, Victoria).

'have schools under their direction'.[80] This securing of Brothers and priests, too, had evidently been a part of Goold's mission to Europe in 1859; for while in Rome he joined forces with Father McEncroe, and they went searching together. Through McEncroe, Goold appears to have received some hope of getting Jesuits for his St Patrick's College.[81] Besides these men for teaching, he also hoped to induce the Marist Fathers to undertake the work of evangelizing the Chinese who had flocked to the Victorian goldfields.[82]

It was this contact with the Marist Fathers that afforded him a chance to pursue further another plan that had been shaping itself in his mind. Shelving for the moment the idea of securing sufficient Christian Brothers to staff his schools, he conceived the plan of establishing a training school for lay teachers and placing it in the hands of religious 'from the lay institute of teachers under the Marists' rule'.[83] This was the Institute now known as the Marist Brothers. The Marist General, according to Goold, received the proposal 'with delight' and promised to secure an answer for him from the superiors of the Brothers at Lyons. But the Bishop left Rome disappointed: the Brothers were unable to supply the men. Victoria would have to rely solely on lay teachers for boys' schools.

This it continued to do for a few years, but after the Secular Act of 1872[84] even lay teachers were becoming difficult to find. In their distress the bishops and priests of the colony turned once more to Ireland for religious, sending countless imploring letters. One such letter, from Father Corbett, the pastor of St Kilda parish, began: 'Dear Reverend Mother, from the ends of the earth I write to you for help.' Then, explaining the hardships imposed by the Bill that had just been passed, he went on to beg for 'three or four Sisters, to whom [he] would give up [his] house . . . and collect funds to have everything in order on the arrival of the Sisters'.[85] He was also 'directed by the Bishop', he said, 'to ask . . . for four Sisters . . . for Melbourne'. 'His Lordship [would] provide a house and schools in the city'.[86]

The same cry was taken up in the two suffragan sees of Ballarat and Sandhurst when they were established 1874. Both the new bishops looked to Europe for religious to help solve the schools problem: Bishop Crane of Sandhurst to the Sisters of Mercy[87] in Ireland, and to the De

---

[80] Report of Select Committee on Education. Minutes of Evidence: evidence of Dr P. B. Geoghegan, q. 59, P.P.(Vic.), 1852, II, p. 639.

[81] Letter, Goold to Geoghegan, St Maria in Postiesula, 20 January 1859 (Archives, St Mary's Cathedral, Sydney). McEncroe, at this same period, was also seeking a rector for St John's College, University of Sydney.

[82] Ibid.   [83] Diary of Dr Goold, 15 January 1859.

[84] That is, Act, 36 Vic., no. ccccxlvii; see especially clause 12.

[85] Letter, Father J. F. Corbett to Presentation Sisters, Limerick. St Kilda, 28 January 1873 (copy from Archives, Presentation Convent, Windsor, Victoria).

[86] Ibid.   [87] Sr M. Ignatius, op. cit., section on Bendigo, p. 2.

La Salle Brothers in France;[88] and Bishop O'Connor of Ballarat to the Loreto Sisters of Rathfarnham where he had been parish priest.[89] Then, when Goold died in Melbourne, Archbishop Carr pursued the same policy with even greater vigour.[90]

In Queensland, Bishop James Quinn[91] had obviously thought all along in terms of religious teachers.[92] A gifted teacher himself, he believed that the twofold aim of education, the religious and the secular, could best be secured by the aid of the teaching orders.[93] He brought Sisters of Mercy with him to the colony, and, so that all the children of his diocese might be adequately provided for, had arranged for more nuns to follow.[94] His other great concern was the education of the boys. When the French Assumptionists[95] whom he had brought with him failed to establish themselves, he begged for a community of Christian Brothers.[96]

It was the same story in Western Australia. Dr Brady had sought the Sisters of Mercy in Ireland in 1845. In the fifties Bishop Serra had gone to Europe to bring back the first band of Sisters of St Joseph of the Apparition,[97] while his successor, Dr Griver, continued to ask for more of them.[98] In response to representations from the Catholics of Fremantle, Griver also wrote to France for some De La Salle Brothers,[99] but his request could not be met. In the seventies therefore he turned his attention towards the Marist Brothers in Sydney,[1] but with no better results. The Brothers were so committed in the East that they had no men to send to the West. Accordingly Dr Gibney, Griver's successor, made overtures once more to the De La Salle Brothers and even induced Cardinal Moran to speak on his behalf.[2] In the meantime the imminence of the Education Act of 1895 in that colony made it imperative for Bishop Gibney to secure help from somewhere. Accordingly, he turned to the Christian Brothers and, by a munificent gift of land and money, induced them to settle in Perth early in 1895.[3]

---

[88] Aloysius, 'St John Baptist de la Salle and his Institute in Australia'. Australian Catholic Historical Society Records, April 1951, p. 8.   [89] Moran, op. cit., p. 987.

[90] Carr was particularly anxious that the country districts should be supplied with nuns. Ignatius, op. cit., section on Mansfield, p. 2, and *passim*.   [91] See ch. 6.

[92] Report to Propaganda, *Sketch of the Life and Labours of the Rt Rev. Dr O'Quinn, First Bishop of Brisbane*, p. 28.   [93] Moran, op. cit., p. 626.

[94] *Sketch of the Life and Labours of the Rt Rev. Dr O'Quinn*, p. 20.

[95] Rev. Fathers F. Hedebough, F. Tissot, and later Fr Brunn. *Moreton Bay Courier*, 20 April 1861, p. 2, a.

[96] Annals of Gregory Terrace, Christian Brothers' College, Brisbane, p. 2 (Archives, C.B.C., Gregory Terrace, Brisbane). *Brisbane Courier*, 6 July 1875, p. 3, c.

[97] Reilly, J. T., *Reminiscences of Fifty Years' Residence in Australia*, p. 71.

[98] Ibid.   [99] Letter, Griver to Propaganda, 1886 (Cathedral Archives, Perth).

[1] Marist Brothers' Annals, p. 26.

[2] Letter, Moran to Gibney, Albany, 6 February 1887 (Cathedral Archives, Perth). See also Aloysius, op. cit., p. 8.

[3] Speech of Dr Gibney at laying of the foundation stone of Christian Brothers' College, St George's Terrace, Perth. *West Australian Record*, 9 February 1895, p. 10.

In the archdiocese of Sydney, Cardinal Moran had continued the work initiated by Vaughan. At first there had been some doubt about the policy the new Archbishop would pursue. As Bishop of Ossory in Ireland, he had been spokesman of the Irish bishops in a case at Rome against the Christian Brothers. The Brothers won their case, whereupon the bishops appealed; but Rome upheld the decision in favour of the Brothers.[4] As a result, relations between the Brothers and the Hierarchy were momentarily strained; the situation was delicate. Whether or not Moran would invite the Brothers to Sydney was therefore very doubtful. Once in Sydney, however, he made his position clear: in this matter of securing religious, Christian Brothers included, he would follow the pattern already laid down by the other bishops[5] and continue the search. The international reputation, moreover, that he was shortly to acquire as Prince of the Church and the high credit in which he stood in Ireland gave him considerable advantage, especially when it came to approaching superiors of religious orders about new foundations in his archdiocese.

But Moran belongs as much to the twentieth century as he does to the nineteenth. Even before his arrival in Australia the practice of handing the schools over to the teaching orders had become quite general. In some instances, it was already being explicitly stated as a policy.

As early as 1860, for example, the parishioners of Adelaide had resolved 'never to rest until they saw the schools of [that] diocese staffed by nuns and Christian Brothers (monks)'.[6] Such also became the policy of the Central Committee for Catholic Education established later on in the same decade.[7] In Ballarat, two years after the establishment of that diocese, the new Bishop intimated that it was the policy of the diocese to place all schools 'as soon as possible' under religious.[8]

Later the policy was explicitly laid down in the decrees of the diocesan synods. Thus the Maitland Synod of 1888 decreed that convents for nuns should be established everywhere.[9] Likewise, the Sydney Synod

[4] In 1875, the National Synod of the Irish Hierarchy passed a number of decrees binding on 'Brothers who conduct schools'. These decrees, the Christian Brothers considered, were directed against them, since they were the only native congregation of teaching Brothers who had central government under a Superior-General. The Brothers appealed against the decrees and Rome decided in their favour. But the Bishops reopened the case in 1879, selecting as their representative at Rome the capable Dr Moran. Rome upheld the Brothers' case a second time and Moran returned defeated. As a result the Brothers became unpopular in Ireland and their work among the poor suffered eclipse. On the other hand, it meant that men were available in greater numbers for the Australian mission. Moran was not unaware of this (P.J.B., 'A Bit of Forgotten History', *Christian Brothers' Educational Record*, 1919, p. 52).

[5] *Express* (Sydney), 20 September 1884, p. 15.

[6] Resolution proposed by Rev. Father Russell at a meeting of Catholics in Adelaide, 27 September 1860. *Adelaide Observer*, 6 October 1860, p. 5, c.

[7] Director-General's Report, meeting of 9 March 1869. *S.C. and C.H.*, 30 March p. 289, c; see similar policy hinted at by Catholic Education Association, Sydney, *Freeman's Journal*, 13 April 1872, p. 10, a.   [8] *Advocate*, 5 February 1876, p. 7, a.

[9] 'Ut haec bona Catholicae nostrae iuventuti obveniant, enixe in Domino sacerdotes hortamur ut monialium conventus ubique instituantur, quae in hac Diocesi praeclare de

of 1891 exhorted 'the clergy and laity to establish, wherever it might be possible, convents for the Religious Sisters to whom the Australian Church [owed] so much'.[10] Already Moran recognized in this something more than a policy: it was a crusade; and he felt that he could say without exaggeration that 'Catholics would never consider the victory complete until they had schools under purely religious orders'.[11]

Thus, by the end of the nineteenth century, the Catholic people of Australia had come to look upon Catholic education as education of a specific type: that which was imparted not only in Catholic schools but also by teachers who were at the same time religious.

But the development of this concept of Catholic education had not been spontaneous. It was an ideal which some of the bishops and the more zealous of the clergy had laboured half a century to cultivate. Hesitatingly, as has been shown, and with a certain diffidence at first, then later, with greater resolution, the remaining bishops had joined in the quest for religious teachers. Requests went forth and the appeal, which had been faint at first, grew louder until, by the time of the Education Acts of the seventies and eighties, it resounded from every diocese in the land. By then it had grown urgent and, in some cases, frantic: Come, it said to the religious orders; in God's name come and 'aid us to stem the torrent of irreligion against which we must wage war'.[12] And come they did—slowly at first, then in greater numbers. Their response, in the eyes of the Church, was magnificent.[13]

THE RESPONSE OF THE RELIGIOUS

New Communities Arrive

The arrival of the religious orders in response to the bishops' requests for teachers may be likened to a stream. That stream, a mere trickle at first, gradually increased in volume until, in the eighties—under the impulse of men like Vaughan, Moran, and the Quinns—it became a veritable flood. By the middle of the present century the religious in Australia numbered more than 12,000.[14] Five out of every six were engaged in education,[15] the rest being employed in social services of other kinds—orphanages, hospitals, homes for the aged, and so on. The

Ecclesia meritae sunt, quarumque labores in Catholica iuventutis institutione promovenda exantlatos non possumus quin maximis laudibus extollamus.' Statuta Synodi Diocesanae Maitlandensis, 8 August 1888, Section V, De Educatione, 4.
[10] Decree X, Decrees of the Diocesan Synod of Sydney, 29 July 1891.
[11] Speech made at St Joseph's College, 1889, quoted by Rev. Denis O'Haran, 'State Educational System from Catholic Standpoint', Year Book of Australia, 1890.
[12] Words used by Father J. F. Corbett, letter to Presentation Sisters (Ireland), 28 January 1873.   [13] Beovich, 'Catholic Education and Catechetics in Australia'.
[14] A.C.D., 1951, p. 453.
[15] Beovich, 'Catholic Education and Catechetics in Australia'.

influence exerted by these religious can be appreciated from their numbers,[16] and the institutions under their control.[17]

They began to arrive, in small numbers, as early as the 1830s (see Table XXXIX),[18] the first being the Benedictine Fathers and the Irish Sisters of Charity. Thereafter they continued to come in an unbroken stream until the middle of the present century—forty-four orders in all: nine orders of priests, eight of brothers, and twenty-seven of sisters.[19]

The greater number of these were from overseas. The rest—the Good Samaritans, the Sisters of St Joseph, the Sisters of St Joseph of the Sacred Heart (sometimes referred to as the Brown Josephites on account of their brown habit, and to distinguish them from the other Sisters of St Joseph who wear a black habit), the Home Missionary Sisters, the Brothers of the Sacred Heart, and the Brothers of St John the Baptist —were founded in Australia.

Not all these orders came for the specific purpose of teaching. Some were in the country a considerable time before they took up that work. Others began, but later discontinued. One order, the French Assumptionists, did not even start. Brought to Queensland by Dr Quinn in 1861[20] with the intention of taking over the education of the boys of the colony, the Fathers were reluctant to start unless their school could be organized and conducted from the very beginning on the lines of their academies in France.[21] This, obviously, owing to the state of the colony, was impossible. The Fathers, therefore, relinquished the idea of teaching and devoted their attention to pastoral work.

Teaching was not the exclusive occupation of any of the orders of priests; most of their members, in fact, were engaged in other aspects of pastoral work. The Benedictines, for example, did not begin teaching until the end of the 1830s; they withdrew altogether in the seventies.[22] The Marist Fathers were in the country for the greater part of a century before opening a school, the Augustinians for three quarters of a century, and the Missionaries of the Sacred Heart for half a century. The Vincentians and the Jesuits, on the other hand, took up teaching shortly after their arrival—the latter after eight years, the former after four. The last to arrive among the priests, the Holy Ghost Fathers, began teaching immediately they landed but withdrew after about a year.[23]

Some of the orders of Brothers likewise had a very short teaching record in the country. As shown earlier, the Brothers of the Sacred Heart,

[16] See pp. 278, 280.   [17] See ch. 8.
[18] The figures for 1830-60 are compiled from the various sources cited in these notes. Those for the remaining years are compiled from the *Ordo Divini Officii Recitandi*, 1876, 1878, 1881, and from A.C.D. for the years 1888, 1895, 1900, 1910, 1920, 1930, 1940, and 1951 (the *Ordo* and the *Directory* are different parts of the same publication. Earlier it bore the name *Ordo* . . . later the name *Australasian Catholic Directory*).
[19] This does not include orders arriving after 1950. A.C.D., 1958, pp. 561-83.
[20] *Moreton Bay Courier*, 20 April 1861, p. 2, a. *Catholic Leader*, 10 December 1931, p. 13.   [21] Ibid.   [22] See ch. 8.   [23] Ibid.

TABLE XXXIX

Orders Taking up Teaching in Australia

Decade	Order	Destination
1830s	Benedictine Fathers	Sydney
	Sisters of Charity	Sydney
1840s	Christian Brothers (Irish)	Sydney
	Sisters of Mercy	Perth
	Marist Fathers	Sydney
	Benedictine Sisters	Sydney
	Jesuit Fathers	Clare (S.A.)
1850s	Sisters of St Joseph of the Apparition	Fremantle
	Good Samaritan Sisters	Sydney
1860s	Good Shepherd Sisters	Melbourne
	Sisters of St Joseph of Sacred Heart	Penola
	Dominican Sisters	Maitland (N.S.W.)
	Presentation Sisters	Hobart
	Assumptionist Fathers	Brisbane
	De La Salle Brothers	Perth
1870s	Marist Brothers	Sydney
	Sisters of St Joseph	Bathurst
	Brothers of the Sacred Heart	Adelaide
	Augustinian Fathers	Sandhurst (Victoria)
	Loreto Sisters	Ballarat
1880s	Ursulines	Armidale (N.S.W.)
	Dominican Sisters (3rd order)	North Adelaide
	Faithful Companions of Jesus	Melbourne
	Religious of the Sacred Heart	Sydney
	Patrician Brothers	Maitland
	Brigidine Sisters	Coonamble (N.S.W.)
	Poor Clares	Sydney
	Daughters of the Sacred Heart	Sydney
	Vincentian Fathers	Sydney
	Sisters of Nazareth	Ballarat
	Missionaries of the Sacred Heart	Sydney
1890s	Franciscan Brothers	Sydney
	Notre Dame de Sion	Sale (Victoria)
	Sisters of St John of God	Perth
	Notre Dame des Missions	Perth
	Holy Ghost Fathers	Ballarat
1900s	Marist Sisters	Sydney
1910s	Brothers of St John Baptist	Adelaide
1920s	Salesian Fathers	Sunbury (Victoria)
1930s	Missionary Franciscan Sisters of I.C.	Brisbane
1940s	Brothers of St John of God	Morisset (N.S.W.)
	Sisters of Compassion	Broken Hill
	Sisters of St Joseph of California	Sydney
	Home Missionary Sisters	Longford (Tasmania)

founded by Tenison Woods in Adelaide in the early seventies, did not outlive their founder's sojourn in that colony.[24] Monsignor Healy's Brothers of St John the Baptist, also founded in South Australia, gave up teaching in the 1940s after thirty years' work. A third short-lived group in this country, the Franciscan teaching Brothers who settled at Waverley in New South Wales in 1892,[25] abandoned their project after a few years and returned to Brooklyn, U.S.A. The Irish Christian Brothers, as has been indicated, stayed only five years the first time. When they returned to Australia, twenty years later, they came to Melbourne.[26] The De La Salle Brothers (or Christian Brothers as they were called) settled in the West, having come south from Malaya in about 1864.[27] There were only two of them, but each opened a school, one in Fremantle, the other in Perth. This arrangement, however, did not last. Since the Brothers were obliged by rule to live together,[28] the Fremantle man had to close his school and join his confrère in Perth.[29] But what was good for the Brother was bad for the boys: the Fremantle people rose in indignation and petitioned Dr Griver to send him back to them.[30] Within another couple of years, however, both men returned to Europe, but not without having first made a deep impression on those who had been in contact with them.[31]

Among some of the orders of nuns, too, there were certain obstacles and delays hindering them from engaging immediately in the work of education. Not until twenty years after their arrival could the Sisters of Charity take up teaching in the real sense, their hands being fully tied with charitable work among the convicts and other unfortunate victims of colonial society.[32] The Benedictine Sisters who arrived in 1849 also

24 See ch. 6.   25 A.C.D., 1895, p. 65.   26 In the year 1868. A.C.D., 1888, p. 87.

27 The names of these two men were Brother Bothian and Brother Amphion. The writer, on 9 November 1950, interviewed a Mr Michael Mannix, then 98 years of age and living at Wembley, Perth. Mr Mannix actually remembered the two Brothers and recalled their names. These were later verified from the Archives of the De la Salle Brothers in Rome through the courtesy of Brothers Aloysius and Gregory of Oakhill Training College, New South Wales.

28 See later edition of Règles communes des Frères des Ecoles, ch. iii.

29 After the closing of the Fremantle school one of the Brothers, it seems, visited the place each week in order to give religious instruction. This practice was followed from February 1864 on. Letter, parishioners of Fremantle to Bishop Griver, 26 July 1864, pp. 1-2 (1864 volume of correspondence, Cathedral Archives, Perth).

30 The Brothers themselves were blamed. The spokesman of the Fremantle parishioners, Peter Gibbons, wrote protesting against the opening of the school by a Brother for 'one week only', and 'inducing Parents to remove their children from other schools, and which was no sooner done than the teacher takes himself away without explanation or apology'. Such conduct Gibbons declared was 'the means of totally extinguishing the Catholic School' there. He was sorry to say, furthermore, that 'the first start of the Christian Brothers as teachers in this colony has been in every way discreditable to their character as regards their treatment of the Fremantle Catholics'. (Gibbons to Griver, 1 March 1864.) Further letters from Fremantle Catholics were written on 27 July 1864, and 17 March 1865. In 1864 and 1863 (by mistake) volumes of correspondence, Cathedral Archives, Perth.

31 Mr Molloy (Perth), 10 October 1893. Parl. Deb. (W.A.), 5, p. 1118.

32 On leaving Ireland the Sisters understood that their work was to be not only among

waited some years until reinforcements arrived from England before embarking on teaching. In the early 1920s they withdrew from it altogether.

Communities Multiply Throughout Australia

But this account of original foundations fails to convey an adequate idea of the real development that took place. It does not take into account either the subsequent foundations from overseas or the daughter foundations from houses already established in Australia, both of which were much more numerous. For example, after the first foundation of the Sisters of Mercy in Perth, in 1846, there were fourteen others of the same order in other parts of the country: two in the fifties,[33] three in the sixties,[34] four in the seventies,[35] and five in the eighties.[36]

No attempt can be made here to cover all these foundations. It will suffice merely to give an idea of the over-all growth pattern. This can be

TABLE XL

Orders Entering Dioceses for First Time

Decade	Priests	Brothers	Sisters	Total
1830s	1	—	1	2
1840s	3	1	3	7
1850s	—	—	3	3
1860s	2	2	8	12
1870s	2	4	11	17
1880s	3	4	30	37
1890s	1	8	10	19
1900s	—	2	21	23
1910s	—	5	13	18
1920s	1	4	12	17
1930s	4	2	9	15
1940s	3	2	10	15

the convicts but more particularly among the Australian aborigines. For this reason they came provided with black statues, crucifixes, and so on. One large black crucifix still hangs in the parlour of St Joseph's Convent, Hobart, where it has been since 1847.

[33] The first group at Geelong under Mother Xavier Maguire in 1857. Ignatius, Sr M., 'The Sisters of Mercy in Victoria'. (Archives of Convent of Mercy, Geelong, section on Melbourne, pp. 4, 37.) The second group, under Mother Ignatius Murphy, settled at Goulburn. Sisters of Mercy, *Brief History of the Goulburn Foundation*, p. 1.

[34] The first at Brisbane. *Moreton Bay Courier*, 11 May 1861, p. 2, a. The names given in the shipping list were: Miss Whitty, Miss Molony, Miss Morgan, Miss Conlon, Miss McDermott, Miss McAuliffe. The second at Bathurst. See *A.C.D.*, 1900, p. 33. The third group in Sydney (the present Monte St Angelo group).

[35] To Yass, 1875, *A.C.D.*, 1888, p. 39; to Singleton, 1875, *A.C.D.*, 1888, p. 46; to Warrnambool (Vic.), 1874, *Mercy Centenary Record*, p. 45; to Bendigo, 1876, *Mercy Centenary Record*, p. 50; *A.C.D.*, 1900, p. 7.

[36] To Grafton, 1882, *A.C.D.*, 1895, p. 94; to Emmaville, 1885, *A.C.D.*, 1895, p. 83; to Parramatta, 1888, *A.C.D.*, 1895, p. 70; to Adelaide and Mt Gambier, 1880, *A.C.D.*, 1888, p. 104; to Cooktown (Q'ld.), 1888, *A.C.D.*, 1895, p. 146.

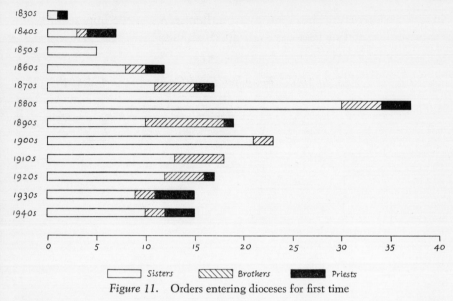

Figure 11.   Orders entering dioceses for first time

seen partly from Table XL.[37] If the first entry of an order into a diocese is regarded as an initial foundation, then the frequency of these foundations will give some idea of the rate of growth (see Table XL and Fig. 11).[38] Table XLI[39] adds to the picture by showing which of these foundations were from abroad and which were from other foundations already established in Australia.[40]

A further glance at Fig. 11 reveals the fact that the growth pattern of these initial foundations was bi-modal, one peak occurring in the 1880s, the other in the 1900s. Both are significant. That in the 1880s corresponds to the period when the main National Education Acts were enacted. This was the hour of the Church's greatest need: if Catholic schools were to be saved, religious would have to be sought in greater numbers. This period marked a significant phase in the development of many of the European orders, especially those founded during the early part of the nineteenth century in Ireland. Having fulfilled the immediate purpose for which they were originally established, many of these Irish congregations had expanded to a point where they had personnel available for missionary work abroad. To this personnel the Australian Hierarchy, clergy, and laity, all predominantly Irish, naturally looked for assistance. On the Continent itself, too, religious were available, but for a different reason. Times of trouble, religious persecution, and even ecclesiastical differences, had compelled a number of religious to seek freedom

[37] See note 18, above.   [38] Based on Table XL.
[39] Based on a rearrangement of data in note 18, above.
[40] Of the total, roughly a third were from overseas and two thirds from within Australia.

in exile. Many were thus glad to avail themselves of the opportunity of a home and a field of useful service in Australia.[41]

TABLE XLI

Countries of Origin of Initial Foundations of Orders in Australia, 1830-1950

Decade	Ireland	France	England	Germany	New Zealand	Italy	America	Malaya	Spain	Australia
1830s	1	—	1	—	—	—	—	—	—	—
1840s	2	1	1	1	—	—	—	—	1	1
1850s	3	1	—	—	—	—	—	—	—	1
1860s	8	1	1	—	—	—	—	1	—	1
1870s	10	1	—	—	—	—	—	—	—	6
1880s	13	5	3	1	—	—	—	—	—	15
1890s	1	1	—	—	1	—	1	—	—	15
1900s	2	1	—	—	—	—	—	—	—	18
1910s	—	—	—	—	—	1	—	—	—	17
1920s	—	—	2	—	—	1	—	—	—	14
1930s	—	—	—	—	—	1	—	—	—	14
1940s	—	—	—	—	1	—	1	—	—	13
	40	11	8	2	2	3	2	1	1	115

The peak in the 1900s (to be observed more clearly in Fig. 12)[42] is to be explained differently. By this time the flood of religious communities from other lands had subsided; henceforth the bulk of Australia's needs would be met by the daughter communities referred to on p. 272. These 'first generation' Australian foundations reached their peak in the first decade of the present century.

The Church, too, was better organized. Australia had, in the meantime, achieved federation and was growing accustomed to thinking as a Commonwealth rather than as separate colonies. The great Plenary Councils, moreover, of 1885, 1895, and 1905, embracing the whole Australian Hierarchy, had had the effect of welding the different provinces of the Church more closely together. Problems which had been considered purely regional or even parochial, could be viewed henceforth against the wider framework of the whole Australian background, and more effective solutions could be reached. Many of the problems, naturally, were common to all dioceses and a uniform policy seemed desirable. Clearly it was time for stock-taking.

The position, educationally speaking, was this: some of the dioceses had as many as five or six religious orders—the larger ones even ten or a dozen—each with one or more schools operating within the diocese.

[41] For example, the Ursulines who came to Armidale had previously taken asylum in London in order to escape the persecution of Bismarck. The Sisters of Mercy who came to Adelaide had been forced to withdraw from the Argentine through anti-clericalism.
[42] Derived from data of Table XLI.

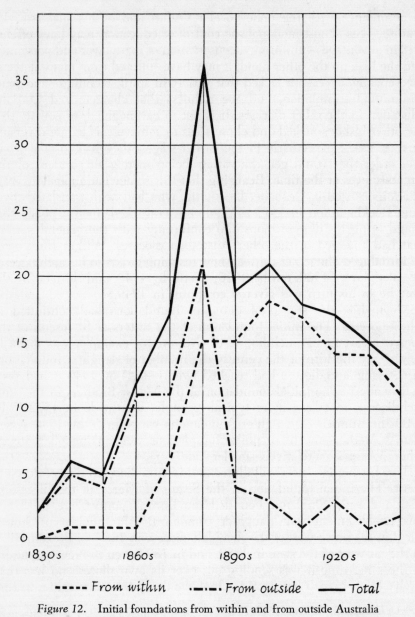

Figure 12. Initial foundations from within and from outside Australia

The archdiocese of Sydney, for example, had eighteen different orders teaching within its boundaries, Melbourne fourteen, but Brisbane only two. Sydney and Melbourne did not have a relatively greater number of schools than Brisbane, but all the Brisbane schools were in the hands of the Christian Brothers and the Sisters of Mercy, which was apparently in accordance with the policy of Dr Quinn and of his successor, Dr Dunne. This almost monopolistic control of education may have offered certain advantages—uniformity, conservation of manpower and personnel, and the like; on the other hand, it may have suffered from many defects: theoretically, at least, it lacked that variety in spirit, technique and tone, the mutual stimulation, and the richness that characterized Catholic education in the other dioceses. It is not to be imagined, of course, that the other bishops picked and chose so as to achieve this happy diversity. In most cases, particularly in the earlier stages, they had to take whatever order they could get, the variety being merely an accident of the circumstances at the time. Realizing that this somewhat anomalous state of affairs existed in Brisbane, Dr Duhig, who had been translated there from Rockhampton in 1912 as coadjutor, embarked upon a policy that would bring his diocese more into conformity with the general pattern that had emerged in the other Australian dioceses. Within forty years he introduced altogether thirteen new teaching orders to his archdiocese: five of them by 1920, ten by 1930, twelve by 1940, and thirteen by the time he in his turn was given a coadjutor in 1949.[43]

Meanwhile the spread of daughter foundations had continued in other dioceses. The initial foundation of the Sisters of St Joseph of the Sacred Heart in the archdiocese of Sydney, for example, was made in 1880:[44] by the turn of the century the number of daughter foundations in the same archdiocese had reached twenty-six,[45] by 1940 it had risen to fifty-one.[46] The initial foundation of the Marist Brothers in the same archdiocese, to take a more typical example, was made in 1872:[47] by 1900 the number of daughter foundations was nine,[48] by 1940 seventeen.[49] At the same time similar foundations were taking place in the other dioceses on a relatively smaller scale.

Two further instances will illustrate this extra-diocesan type of development. The initial foundation of the Sisters of Mercy in the diocese of Maitland was at Singleton. Founded from Ennis, County Clare, in 1875,[50] this establishment sent daughter communities far afield: to Gunnedah[51] in the north-west of the Armidale diocese in 1887, to Broken Hill[52] in the far west of the state in 1889, and in 1897 even to New Zealand;[53] at the same time it was sending out over its own diocese no less than twelve other branch houses.[54] Each of the daughter communities in turn

43 Dr O'Donnell, A.C.D., 1951, p. 349.   44 Ordo Divini Officii Recitandi, 1881, p. 54.
45 A.C.D., 1900, pp. 17-18.   46 Ibid., 1940, pp. 142-3.
47 Freeman's Journal, 13 April 1872, p. 10, b.
48 A.C.D., 1900, p. 13.
49 Ibid., 1940, p. 137. 50 Ibid., 1888, p. 46. 51 Ibid., p. 71. 52 Ibid., 1895, p. 100.
53 Ibid., 1900, p. 117.
54 A.C.D., 1951, pp. 208, 209. Murrurundi 1879, Raymond Terrace 1881, Morpeth 1883, Lambton 1883, Muswellbrook 1883, East Maitland 1885, Branxton 1886, Scone 1887, Campbell's Hill 1910, Stockton 1920, Waratah 1921, Tighe's Hill 1928.

became the mother house of other branches: Gunnedah, of seven,[55] Broken Hill of seven also before it became amalgamated with another group from the eastern part of the diocese;[56] and Dunedin (New Zealand) of ten.[57]

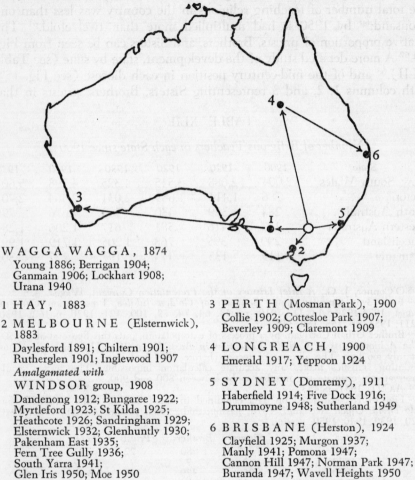

WAGGA WAGGA, 1874
Young 1886; Berrigan 1904;
Ganmain 1906; Lockhart 1908;
Urana 1940

1 HAY, 1883

2 MELBOURNE (Elsternwick), 1883
Daylesford 1891; Chiltern 1901;
Rutherglen 1901; Inglewood 1907
Amalgamated with
WINDSOR group, 1908
Dandenong 1912; Bungaree 1922;
Myrtleford 1923; St Kilda 1925;
Heathcote 1926; Sandringham 1929;
Elsternwick 1932; Glenhuntly 1930;
Pakenham East 1935;
Fern Tree Gully 1936;
South Yarra 1941;
Glen Iris 1950; Moe 1950

3 PERTH (Mosman Park), 1900
Collie 1902; Cottesloe Park 1907;
Beverley 1909; Claremont 1909

4 LONGREACH, 1900
Emerald 1917; Yeppoon 1924

5 SYDNEY (Domremy), 1911
Haberfield 1914; Five Dock 1916;
Drummoyne 1948; Sutherland 1949

6 BRISBANE (Herston), 1924
Clayfield 1925; Murgon 1937;
Manly 1941; Pomona 1947;
Cannon Hill 1947; Norman Park 1947;
Buranda 1947; Wavell Heights 1950

Figure 13. Spread of Presentation communities from Wagga Wagga, New South Wales

The second illustration, dealing with a less numerous community, shows the development that followed upon the initial foundation of the Presentation Sisters at Wagga Wagga. Made from Kildare (Ireland) in

[55] Inverell 1891, Narrabri 1889, Walcha 1911, Armidale 1919, Mungindi 1924, Deepwater. Emmaville (from Ireland) amalgamated with Gunnedah 1919. A.C.D., 1951, p. 184.
[56] Broken Hill South 1900, Parkes 1922, Mathoura 1926, Trundle 1928, Condoblin 1929; and, in the archdiocese of Adelaide, Brighton (1916) and Mt Barker (1902). A.C.D., 1951, pp. 222, 312.   [57] Ibid., p. 433.

1874,[58] this foundation was later responsible for five other daughter foundations each of which became in turn a mother house for further communities (see Fig. 13).[59]

In this way the various groups were soon widely spread. In 1880 the total number of teaching religious in the country was less than one thousand;[60] by 1950 it had multiplied more than twelvefold.[61] The relative proportion of priests, Brothers, and Sisters can be seen from Fig. 14.[62] A more detailed study of the development, state by state (see Table XLII),[63] and of the mid-century position in each diocese (see Fig. 15[64] with columns 1, 2, and 3 representing Sisters, Brothers, priests in that

TABLE XLII

Number of Religious Teachers in each State since 1900

State	1900	1910	1920	1930	1940	1950
New South Wales	2,004	2,688	3,515	4,325	4,798	5,601
Victoria	786	1,414	1,689	2,031	2,564	2,701
South Australia	284	389	430	582	676	796
Western Australia	173	416	581	617	1,206	1,284
Queensland	299	395	763	1,205	1,719	1,993
Tasmania	119	135	174	197	227	302

[58] O'Connor, J. G., A Brief History of the Presentation Convent, Wagga, p. 6.

[59] Fig. 13 is compiled from: Souvenir of Golden Jubilee, Presentation Convent, Wagga, 1874-1924; A.C.D., 1910, pp. 43, 64, 74, 79, 100, 121; 1920, p. 162; 1930, p. 211; 1951, pp. 153, 160, 358.

[60] Brother Urban Corrigan, by a process of extrapolation, puts this figure at about 500 (The Achievements of Catholic Education in Australia, p. 26). That figure is almost certainly too low. The absence of records before 1885 and the lack of uniformity in presenting statistics makes any accurate calculation impossible. The writer would conservatively estimate the number to be between 800 and 900.

[61] A.C.D., 1951, p. 453.

[62] Fig. 14 is constructed on data contained in the following table, compiled from Ordo Divini Officii Recitandi, 1878, passim; ibid., 1881, passim; A.C.D., 1900, 1910, 1920, 1930, 1940, 1950, passim.

Year	Sisters	Brothers	Priests	Totals
1880	815	80	22	917
1890	?	?	?	?
1900	3,059	379	53	3,491
1910	5,081	466	53	5,600
1920	6,571	634	51	7,246
1930	8,277	778	61	9,116
1940	10,149	1,041	84	11,274
1950	11,245	1,532	124	12,901

Between 1,000-2,000 of the nuns included above would be engaged in other social work—orphanages, hospitals, etc. It has been impossible to separate them exactly from the rest.

In some years the Directories summarized the statistics on one table. These, egregiously inaccurate, had to be ignored, and the figures collected from each community individually. With the exception of 1950, the figures for the other years represent the total at the beginning of a year rather than at its close.

[63] See volumes of A.C.D. mentioned in note 62.

[64] Fig. 15 is drawn from the following facts compiled from A.C.D., 1951, passim.

6. THE REVEREND J. E. TENISON WOODS

By courtesy of the Sisters of St Joseph, Sydney

order) reveals a more or less uniform growth throughout the whole of Australia.

Replacement of Lay Teachers

The only significant variations were in the rates at which religious replaced lay teachers. In some of the dioceses, particularly those of Adelaide, Brisbane, and Bathurst, as has been shown,[65] this replacement began at an early date. By the turn of the century it had become more general, teachers in the New South Wales schools at this time being described by Bishop Dwyer of Maitland as 'mostly Religious'.[66]

In Sydney, rapid changes had occurred after 1879. By the end of 1883, the year in which Vaughan left for Europe, two-thirds of the total number of teachers were religious.[67] And the rate of replacement was increasing.[68] When Moran took over, the boys' metropolitan schools, according to a contemporary inspector's report, were 'mainly conducted

State	Diocese	Sisters	Brothers	Priests
Q'ld.	Cairns	108	12	—
	Townsville	176	22	—
	Rockhampton	323	28	—
	Brisbane	1,032	96	6
	Toowoomba	197	27	15
N.S.W.	Lismore	294	13	13
	Armidale	276	17	—
	Maitland	507	23	—
	Bathurst	345	19	13
	Wilcannia-Forbes	237	17	—
	Sydney	2,466	162	30
	Wagga	212	18	—
	Canberra and Goulburn	477	30	—
Vic.	Sale	97	7	—
	Melbourne	1,753	274	35
	Sandhurst	254	10	—
	Ballarat	383	23	—
Tas.	Hobart	282	20	—
W.A.	Perth	967	67	12
	Geraldton	170	20	—
	New Norcia	145	8	2
	Kimberley	29	—	—
S.A.	Adelaide	603	69	—
	Pt Augusta	73	—	—
	Darwin	41	—	—

[65] See ch. 6.

[66] Dwyer, Bishop P. V., *What steps may be taken to advance the interests of our religious primary and higher schools?* p. 10.

[67] Rogers, J. W., Report on Catholic Schools, 1883, p. 1.

[68] As a result of the opening of the Marist Brothers' School at St Patrick's in 1872 a sharp decline in attendance was reported in two adjacent Catholic schools still under the Council of Education, St Mary's and the Kent Street North School. The effect at St Mary's was that 'of drawing away nearly all the most advanced pupils and many others, so that the school suffered greatly as regards both numbers and status' (Report of Inspector Hicks). Of Kent Street it was reported 'that the falling off in this school does not warrant the maintenance of the existing staff, but as it is quite possible that the Marist Brothers will only temporarily depress the attendance, it may be premature to recommend the withdrawal of the assistant teacher'. Council of Education, Inspector's Report (Sydney District), 1873 (ML).

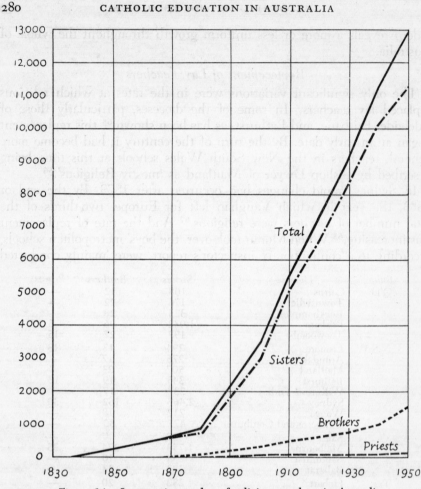

Figure 14. Increase in number of religious teachers in Australia

by the . . . Marist Brothers, the rest chiefly in the hands of five orders of Religious Sisters'. Only 'a small number of lay teachers' remained.[69]

The country dioceses of Goulburn and Maitland were only a little behind Sydney. In Goulburn, the turning point in the change from lay to religious teachers had occurred in 1883, there being twenty religious against seventeen lay teachers by the end of that year.[70] Similarly, in Maitland, the conversion process was being closely watched; the fact that in 1884 'two more lay teachers were replaced by Religious' was sufficiently important to merit a special mention in the Bishop's Pastoral.[71]

[69] Report of the Catholic Schools' Board, Freeman's Journal, 11 October 1884.
[70] Half-Yearly Report of Father Barr, Inspector of Schools, 1883. Record (Bathurst), 15 September 1883, p. 420, b.
[71] These were the two Patrician Brothers at St John's. Pastoral Letter published in the Record (Bathurst), 16 August 1884, p. 473.

In the other dioceses the half-way marks of this change-over occurred at different times. In Western Australia, for example, the period of greatest change was subsequent to the Acts of 1893 and 1895 during the episcopate of Dr Gibney; later the appointment of Dr Prendiville initiated a second great wave of development.[72]

In Melbourne, the movement was more gradual. The number of religious did not surpass the number of lay teachers (see Fig. 16) until after 1900; and not until the middle of the second decade did the number of schools under religious pass the two-thirds mark (see Table XLIII).[73] In Sydney, it will be remembered, this point had been reached in 1883, over thirty years earlier. At the end of the first quarter of the century more than a quarter of the teachers were still laymen (see Table XLIV[74] and Fig. 16), while 19 of the 142 schools then existing were still entirely in their hands. By the middle of the century, however, virtually all the schools had been taken over by the religious and the number of lay teachers reduced to a little below one in five. But even that ratio was

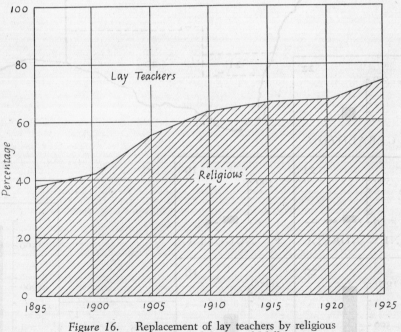

Figure 16. Replacement of lay teachers by religious in Catholic schools, archdiocese of Melbourne

[72] See Table XLII, p. 278.
[73] Table compiled from Annual Reports of the Inspector of Catholic schools. *Advocate*, 9 December 1905, p. 13, a, b; 10 December 1910, p. 19, c, d; 11 December 1915, p. 27; 23 December 1920; 31 December 1925, p. 9, b, c.
[74] Table compiled from Annual Reports listed in note 73 and from that for 1895, *Advocate*, 14 December, p. 10.

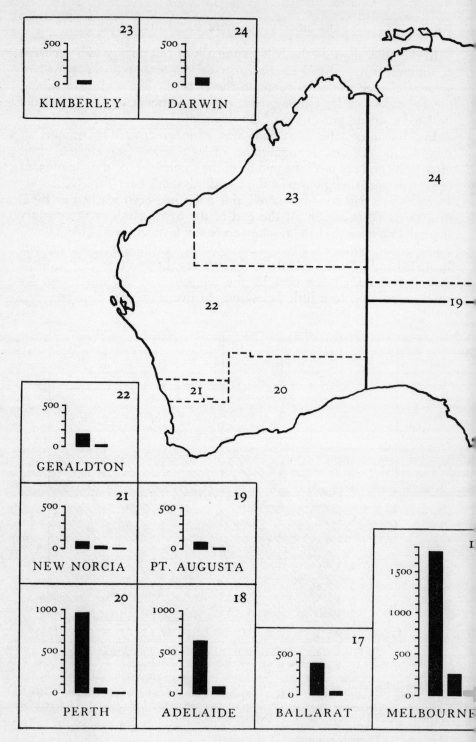

Figure 15. Dioceses of Australia, 1950, showing

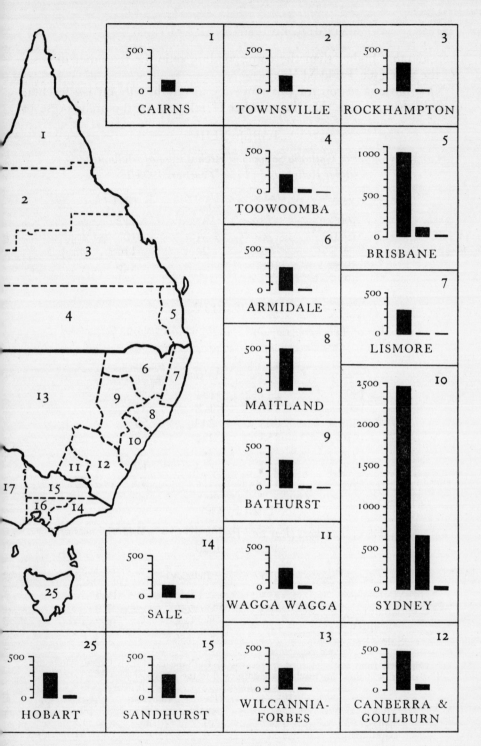

ber of Sisters, Brothers, and priests engaged in teaching

considerably higher than the corresponding ratio for the other dioceses of the state (see Table XLV).[75]

One obvious reason for this tendency to rely heavily on lay teachers was the simple fact that the number of religious in the archdiocese of

TABLE XLIII

Number of Catholic Schools in Archdiocese of Melbourne under Religious and Lay Teachers 1905-25

Year	Under religious	Under lay	Total
1905	75	37	112
1910	76	31	107
1915	92	24	116
1920	108	20	128
1925	123	19	142

TABLE XLIV

Number of Teachers (Lay and Religious) in Catholic Schools of Archdiocese of Melbourne, 1895-1925

Year	Lay	Religious	Percentage of religious
1895	242	151	38
1900	270	178	42
1905	203	249	55
1910	158	274	63
1915	169	328	66
1920	171	354	67
1925	156	418	73

TABLE XLV

Number of Teachers (Lay and Religious) in Catholic Schools of Victoria, 1950

Diocese	Lay	Religious	Percentage of lay
Melbourne	254	1,046	19.5
Ballarat	22	257	7.9
Sandhurst	20	166	10.7
Sale	4	59	6.3

[75] Compiled from statistics filed in records of Catholic Education Office, Melbourne. The majority of these lay teachers are employed in the parochial schools:

Diocese	Secondary Religious	Lay	Primary Religious	Lay
Melbourne	396	94	650	160
Ballarat	124	10	133	12
Sandhurst	100	6	66	14
Sale	22	4	37	—

Melbourne was always relatively lower than it was in the other arch-dioceses. If, for example, the figures for 1900 in Table XLVI[76] be compared, it will be seen that the ratio of religious to children of school

TABLE XLVI

Ratio of Religious to School Population

Archdiocese	Ratio of religious expressed as one religious per so many children	
	1900	1950
Sydney	20	14
Melbourne	37	21
Adelaide	15	13
Brisbane	29	17
Perth	15	13
Hobart	28	15

age in Melbourne was 1 to 37, whereas in Sydney it was 1 to 20, in Adelaide 1 to 15, and so on. On the other hand, despite the fact that this replacement of lay teachers was slower in Melbourne than in other places, it was launched as a part of diocesan policy as early as 1873. The year after the Education Act of 1872 lay teachers in Catholic schools began to receive notice that 'their services [would] not be further required' and that religious would take their place.[77] Significantly, too, the Sisters of Mercy took over the senior diocesan girls' school the same year.[78] The Act, however, had caught the Church authorities unprepared and there were by no means sufficient religious to go round. All they could do was to spread their services as far as they would go. Thus in those orders where custom or constitutions allowed it, schools were opened and conducted by staffs which were almost fifty per cent lay; in some cases the figure was even higher (see Table XLVII).[79] In the Mercy schools of Geelong it was so arranged that at least every second year a pupil was under the care of a religious; the religious instruction, however, was always given by the nuns.[80]

76 The figures (*A.C.D.*, 1900, pp. 162-3; 1950, pp. 421, 423), from which Table XLVI is compiled, are:

	1900		1950	
	Religious	Pupils	Religious	Pupils
Sydney	1,124	21,943	3,249	54,043
Melbourne	585	21,918	2,219	46,098
Adelaide	299	4,501	713	9,394
Brisbane	211	6,713	1,165	18,358
Perth	165	2,500	1,062	13,858
Hobart	119	3,331	310	4,761

77 *Advocate*, 4 January 1873, p. 10, b.

78 Although the Sisters of Mercy had been in Melbourne sixteen years, they did not take over St Francis' school until 1873.

79 Table compiled from Annual Reports of Inspector of Catholic Schools (note 73, above).

80 Sr M. Ignatius, 'The Sisters of Mercy in Victoria', Geelong Primary Schools, p. 4.

TABLE XLVII

Number of Lay Teachers Employed in Schools of Various Orders in Victoria, 1905-25

	Schools and Teachers	Christian Brothers	Loreto	F.C.J.	Mercy	Presen-tation	Charity	Good Samari-tans
	Schools	8	1	5	27	7	7	3
1905	Religious	29	2	14	73	25	28	12
	Lay	23	6	14	37	6	34	7
	Schools	8	1	4	26	7	5	4
1910	Religious	31	4	12	68	25	23	19
	Lay	12	6	12	26	3	22	19
	Schools	8	2	4	29	12	5	5
1915	Religious	30	4	13	91	32	27	28
	Lay	12	8	14	39	7	23	13
	Schools	13	2	4	30	14	5	5
1920	Religious	41	5	11	88	34	25	28
	Lay	24	6	18	41	10	17	15
	Schools	13	1	3	30	20	6	6
1925	Religious	50	5	13	86	40	30	37
	Lay	17	4	11	44	17	13	16

Once started, this system of staffing schools with a staff half lay and half religious tended to perpetuate itself. Instead of using new religious to replace the lay half of the existing staffs, they were used to open new schools. Some orders, too, were slower than others in adapting themselves to Australian conditions and some years were yet to elapse before they would be in a position to train up sufficient Australian subjects to stabilize their staffs and at the same time satisfy the demands for new openings.

PROBLEMS IN ADAPTATION

For the European Orders

The great majority of the thirteen thousand religious in Australia in 1950 were Australians; of the thousand in the country in 1880, however, more than half would have been Irish. A few were French, fewer still German. Some of the larger groups, such as the Christian Brothers and the Sisters of Mercy, continued to receive great numbers of subjects from Ireland until well into the present century.[81] Right from

[81] For example, the *Catholic Leader* (Brisbane), 10 December 1931, p. 9, published full lists of Irish recruits for the Queensland Sisters of Mercy during the sixties and seventies. Even the Australian congregation, the Sisters of St Joseph, have a recruiting house in Ireland. Fact related to writer by Secretary-General of the Sisters of St Joseph, February 1952.

the start, however, it had been recognized that Australian subjects would be desirable, even necessary, if the work was to continue to expand. Young Australians had, moreover, evinced a readiness to join the orders,[82] and within a short time religious communities were admitting to their ranks the products of their own schools.[83]

Notwithstanding this readiness, there were some who doubted whether the colonial youth possessed the qualities requisite for such a vocation.[84] It was feared, for example, that the French ways and customs of the Marist Brothers would deter young Australians from joining them. Despite these misgivings, a novitiate was opened within twelve months of the arrival of the Brothers in Sydney.[85] The result was gratifying and even Dr Vaughan, who had been as sceptical as any at first, 'rejoiced' to find such a promising start.[86] Any apprehensions that may have existed about the suitability of the new subjects were gradually dispelled. The 'excellent dispositions and most satisfactory qualities' which they were found to possess led the French superiors to conclude that 'Providence [had] special views on the Australian youth in reference to Catholic education and the monastic life'.[87] Accordingly Brother Ludovic, the first superior and master of novices, addressed a letter 'to the clergy of Australia and other neighbouring countries', praying that they would 'kindly see whether, in the extent of [their] mission some such young men could not be found and thus directed to [the] Novitiate'.[88] To this, Vaughan appended a covering letter assuring Brother Ludovic that he felt 'the greatest interest in forwarding the Spread of [the] Society', and he expressed the belief that the clergy of the archdiocese entertained 'the same feelings as [himself]'.[89]

This need for fostering vocations to the teaching orders became more and more apparent. Subjects for the orders of women were not wanting;[90] for the teaching brotherhoods they were not so plentiful.[91] For neither were the numbers offering as large as might be desired. Yet on this

---

[82] Letter, Prioress of Princethorpe to Prioress of Stanbrook, relating parts of Scholastica Gregory's letter (copy, St Mary's Cathedral Archives, Sydney).

[83] See Sr M. Ignatius, 'The Sisters of Mercy in Victoria', section on Melbourne, p. 4; section on Geelong, p. 3 (Archives, Convent of Mercy, Geelong).

[84] Corrigan, *The Achievements of Catholic Education in Australia*, p. 4.

[85] Polding was at first opposed to this scheme, but afterwards became its ardent supporter, even writing a special pastoral urging his priests to give the project their support. Marist Brothers' Annals, p. 3 (Archives, Marist Brothers' Provincial House, Mittagong, N.S.W.).

[86] On Christmas Eve, 1873. *Freeman's Journal*, 3 January 1874, p. 10, c.

[87] *Ordo Divini Officii Recitandi*, 1878, p. 43.   [88] Ibid.   [89] Ibid., p. 44.

[90] *Guardian* (Q'ld.), 17 April 1863, p. 5. At the critical period in New South Wales, 1882, the entry into the order of the Sisters of Charity of 'several experienced and highly qualified teachers' enabled the Sisters to take over St Mary's Cathedral School as well as several others. Sr M. Dunstan Wilson, 'The Sisters of Charity in Australia', p. 13. Australian Catholic Historical Society Records.

[91] *Record* (Bathurst), 15 July 1880, p. 325, a. See also *Brisbane Courier*, 6 July 1875, and *Ordo Divini Officii Recitandi*, 1878, p. 48.

very issue the future of Catholic education in Australia largely depended. On that account it came before ecclesiastical notice very early, and the synodal decrees of certain dioceses began to exhort the clergy 'by every means in [their] power [to] secure the success of [their] educational institutions . . . by procuring candidates for the different religious orders'.[92]

But this matter of securing Australian recruits for the European orders was only one aspect of the wider process of adaptation. Another was that of diverting to teaching work orders that had never been intended for it, or at most had envisaged it only as a minor role in their general apostolate.[93] Pressed into the work of teaching on a large scale, therefore, they suddenly found themselves face to face with a major problem.

The Australian order of the Good Samaritans was a case in point. Founded by Archbishop Polding on 2 February 1857,[94] the congregation really grew out of the work of the Pitt Street Refuge, in Sydney.[95] Its functions were only partly concerned with teaching, being directed mainly to the care of penitents and similar charitable work.[96] The Sisters, it is true, gave religious instruction in some of the denominational schools in Sydney and, in the sixties, were themselves conducting a school at Maitland[97] and in a few other places as well.[98] But these constituted a mere handful and absorbed only a small proportion of the order's personnel.[99] With the passing of the 1880 Act, however, and the complete withdrawal of government aid in 1883, all this was changed. Harassed clergy, their schools suddenly left without teachers and with no funds to hire new ones, came to the Sisters begging help. The Sisters could hardly refuse. Residences were quickly acquired, and new school staffs were hurriedly mustered. In this way the schools in

[92] Diocese of Bathurst, Synodal Decrees on Education, Decree IV, *Record* (Bathurst), 16 January 1883, p. 38.

[93] On this matter Inspector Rogers wrote: 'Some others [religious] who, I understand, became Religious originally for other than teaching purposes, and who when the demand for their services arose, applied themselves with much zeal to the work of teaching.' Report on Catholic Schools, 1883.

[94] Scholastica, Sr M., 'Story of the Institute of the Good Samaritan'. Australian Catholic Historical Society Records, p. 1.

[95] Ibid. Three Sisters of Charity had staffed the Refuge. Two died suddenly as a result of a disease contracted while tending others. Sister Scholastica Gibbons alone remained, helped by a few pious young ladies: these became the nucleus of the new order established on the Benedictine Rule.

[96] Journal of Mary Agnes Hart (one of the original members). Quoted by Scholastica, op. cit., p. 8. In the sixties and seventies it was the custom for the Sisters to accompany the Archbishop in his missionary tours of the country, staying at Presbyteries and driving out to bush homes to give instruction during the day (ibid., p. 15).

[97] They were replaced by the Dominican Sisters in 1867. Denominational Schools Board (N.S.W.), Inspectors' Reports, Catholic Schools, 1861-6. Report of Inspector Reilly on Catholic School, Maitland West (ML).

[98] Denominational Schools Board (N.S.W.), Inspectors' Reports, 1856-65. Report on Catholic School, Pitt Street South, October 1886 (ML).

[99] At Glebe, for example; also at Five Dock, St Mary's, Balmain, Wollongong, and Windsor. Pitt Street and Balmain were opened in the sixties; the remainder belong to the seventies. *Ordo Divini Officii Recitandi*, 1876, pp. 69-70. (Pitt Street Infant School had on its roll the Australian poet and scholar, Christopher Brennan.)

the larger centres around Sydney—Rozelle, Surry Hills, Pyrmont, Forest Lodge, and St Benedict's—were taken over by the nuns.[1] Within a short time teaching had become practically the sole occupation of the order.

A minor adaptation of this type was the question of fees. Founded originally for the education of the poor, some orders were strictly forbidden to collect fees or any other remuneration from their pupils.[2] But in Australia, where no other sources of revenue were at hand, these prescriptions, if insisted upon, were likely to stultify the whole plan of the Hierarchy. Some modification was therefore essential. A few orders —the Christian Brothers and the Sisters of Mercy, for example—had already adopted the idea of 'pay' schools[3] or 'pension' schools[4] in Ireland. Others, like the Presentation Sisters[5] and the Sisters of Charity,[6] had to seek special dispensation from Rome to regularize the acceptance of fees in the private schools they set up in Australia.

Several other instances of significant modifications could be cited,[7] but one of great importance, for some of the orders of women especially, was that dealing with the government of communities. Many of the groups settling in Australia, particularly the Mercy and the Presentation Sisters were from strong independent houses in Ireland. The same organization was adopted here. Thus the Mercy foundation at Singleton, which became the central or mother house of the Mercy communities in the diocese of Maitland, was entirely independent of the Mercy Sisters of, say, the Bathurst diocese with their central house at Bathurst, or those in the Goulburn diocese with their central house in Goulburn. The jurisdiction of the superior of each group was limited, generally, to the houses within the diocese. In some dioceses, on the other hand, there were as many as two, or even three, independent groups of the same order, such as the two Presentation groups in Melbourne with their

[1] These belong to the 1880s. Scholastica, op. cit., p. 23.

[2] Règles des Frères des Écoles Chrétiennes, ch. i, articles 1 and 5; ch. vi, article 1.

[3] Letter, Br Rice to Br Joseph, 22 January 1838. Quoted in The Christian Brothers' Educational Record, p. 95. See also Freeman's Journal, 3 August 1872. A certain contributor to this journal contended that, although the Marist Brothers had been intended for middle-class schools, they had, in the emergency that confronted the archdiocese, turned to primary schools. Freeman's Journal, 5 April 1873, p. 9, d.

[4] Burke-Savage, Rev. Roland, Catherine McAuley, p. 269. See also Customs and Directory of the Sisters of Mercy, 1865, p. 22. A mutilated copy of this early Directory exists in the Archives of the Convent of Mercy, Victoria Square, Perth.

[5] Catholic Standard (Tas.), January 1868, p. 112, b. The document relating to the Wagga foundation contained among other requests the clause asking for 'Permission to teach not only the children of the poor, but also those of the wealthier class, and also to receive a suitable pension for the same'. It is signed by Joannes Simeoni, Cardinal Secretary of Propaganda (copy in Archives, Presentation Convent, Wagga). Up to this time the Sisters, in giving their services to the poor, had relied for their own support largely on their dowries.

[6] The rescript reached Australia on 31 January 1881. Annals of St Joseph's Convent, Hobart, p. 64 (Archives, St Joseph's Convent, Hobart).

[7] The case of permission to teach Latin in the Brothers' Schools. Règles des Frères des Écoles Chrétiennes, ch. xxviii.

central houses at Windsor and Gardenvale respectively, or the three Mercy groups in the original Goulburn diocese with their central houses at Goulburn, Yass and Albury.[8]

Opposed to this was a type of central control in which all the houses of the one order in Australia were under the one authority, known generally as the provincial superior. This form of government was found in the orders of Brothers and in certain orders of women such as the Loreto Sisters, and the religious of the Sacred Heart.

The first of these types, the diocesan, was in a way admirably suited to the pioneering stages in Australia. The dioceses themselves were extensive and somewhat isolated from one another, and means of communication between them often slow and difficult. Within the diocese, moreover, there was ample room for expansion, and the shorter distances allowed for the easy circulation of personnel and superiors. The bishops favoured this type of organization for it gave them personally more control and enabled them to plan for expansion and future developments.[9] But as the population spread and new lines of communication opened up, this type of government became redundant and wasteful. Not only did it preserve a certain parochialism in outlook but even became a hindrance in those cases where a strong central policy was required for the efficient and successful prosecution of essential projects such as wider interchange of teachers and broader and more intensive preparation of subjects.

Thus, when legislation[10] in Victoria and Tasmania in the early 1900s demanded a uniformly higher standard in the training of teachers, the three or four groups of Mercy Sisters in those states found it altogether wasteful and in other ways unwise to build and equip three or four different training colleges. Accordingly, an amalgamation of the various groups was effected[11] and, as Dr Carr said in his address to the first novices of the new central novitiate for Victoria in 1907, a 'new generation of Sisters of Mercy' began from that day.[12]

But government legislation was not entirely responsible for this

[8] Similar sub-divisions among the Mercy Sisters were common. In the diocese of Perth, there were two groups, Perth and Bunbury; in the diocese of Adelaide, two groups—Mt Gambier and Adelaide; in Melbourne, two—Fitzroy and Geelong; in the diocese of Sydney, two—Parramatta and North Sydney. Similar groups existed in the Wilcannia-Forbes diocese.

[9] Dr Goold, for example, was opposed to the Christian Brothers he established in Victoria extending their labours to other colonies. *Advocate*, 5 February 1876. See also efforts of Bishops James and Matthew Quinn. *Record* (Bathurst), 15 July 1880, p. 325, a.

[10] See the Registration Acts of 1905 and 1906 respectively.

[11] *Constitutions of the Sisters of Mercy of the Amalgamated Houses of Victoria and Tasmania*. Some stood out at the first amalgamation but sought admission later. Ballarat, however, feeling that it was well able to look after its own affairs, remained a separate group.

[12] *Mercy Centenary Record*, p. 81.

development. Other factors were at work: the bishops in some cases urged it, and certain members within the groups themselves were by no means unaware of the advantages to be derived from a larger, more resourceful and more vital organization. The matter had been discussed by the Hierarchy at the Third Plenary Council of 1905, and Rome agreed that the time was ripe (*opportunum*) for such amalgamations, not only among the Mercy Sisters in Victoria, but among other groups as well. In implementing this recommendation, however, the bishops were forbidden to use pressure; instead they were to use persuasion and exhortation (*prudenter . . . suadere et insinuare*).[13] As a result, further amalgamations followed: Goulburn, Yass and Albury in 1907;[14] then others—Bunbury and Perth, Adelaide and Mt Gambier, the Wilcannia-Forbes groups,[15] and so on. The movement had in the meantime spread to certain groups of the Presentation Sisters.[16] The result was that, by the middle of the century, the restricted diocesan form of government had been almost entirely superseded.[17]

The principle of adaptation seen in these and other modifications must not be considered as novel or peculiar to Australia. It was no more than an extension of that principle underlying the development of all religious orders whereby each new one might be looked upon as a progressive adaptation specially designed to meet contemporary needs. Adaptation of this type was in fact explicitly provided for in the Ursulines (1535), the first order founded expressly for teaching.[18] It was carried further by the Loreto Sisters (1609) and further still in more recent times by such orders as the Presentation Sisters, the Mercy Sisters, or the Sisters of Charity. But the two most thoroughgoing adaptations were the orders of the Sisters of St Joseph and the Home Missionary Sisters of Tasmania.

Adaptation in the Australian Orders

The Sisters of St Joseph were to play a most important role in the development of Catholic education, especially the education of the poor. In the days before government social services the poor were a real problem. To do what he could for their material and spiritual needs, Dr Polding

[13] Letter, Fumasoni-Biondi, Sect. of Propaganda, to Moran, Cardinal Delegate of Third Plenary Council, dated Rome, 27 October 1906. Printed in *Acta et Decreta Concilii Plenarii Tertii Australiensis*, p. vi.

[14] Sisters of Mercy, *Brief History of the Goulburn Foundation*, p. 5.

[15] To each of these amalgamations Rome readily gave its 'ratam habet'. Cf. that for the last-named union, given at Rome, 23 September 1926. Printed in *Australasian Catholic Record*, April 1927, p. 110.

[16] Cf. the Gardenvale and Windsor groups in Victoria.

[17] The best example of this is that of the Sisters of Mercy. The smaller groups that had amalgamated between 1900 and 1920 further amalgamated in 1954 to make one Australian group with different provinces and a Mother-General residing at Canberra. A.C.D., 1955, p. 245.

[18] See Pius X, Motu Proprio to the Ursulines, 9 May 1905. Quoted in Sr M. Monica, *Angela Merici and Her Teaching Idea*, p. 239.

had founded the Sisters of the Good Samaritan.[19] Their educational needs were being adequately provided for, so it was considered, in the denominational schools taught by lay teachers under the Board. Actually, it was the middle and upper classes that, in the eyes of the Archbishop and his clergy, needed an education at the hands of religious. This view was not restricted to New South Wales alone. The schools of the Benedictine priests and nuns in Sydney, for example, and the first schools of the Dominicans in Adelaide,[20] of the Mercy Sisters in Victoria, of the Presentation Sisters in Hobart, as well as many others, were all for the upper classes.[21] Only when aid was withdrawn from the denominational schools in the 1870s and 1880s were these orders asked to supply staffs for the parochial schools as well. Most of them, as has been shown, did so, but the task called for considerable adaptation and adjustment.

The Sisters of St Joseph, on the other hand, had been founded specifically for the Catholic poor. These, according to Mother Mary McKillop, were settled 'in scattered bands all over the colonies'. They had been brought up 'with little or no knowledge of their holy religion' and in total blindness to all that 'concern[ed] the religious education of their children'. To labour among such people required a special order which, although it might seem 'much out of place in Europe', was obviously the only solution for Australia.[22]

Such an order was developed in South Australia. Sprung from the genius of Tenison Woods and the mind and heart of Mary McKillop, the co-foundress (Plates 6, 7), this new congregation was the Sisters of St Joseph of the Sacred Heart. Woods adapted the idea from certain religious orders he had seen working in France,[23] believing that something after this style was required to meet the problems confronting the Church in Australia.[24] But numerous obstacles stood in his way. First he had to break down the prejudice that religious were only for the middle and upper classes and that the poor were to be satisfied with the denominational schools. Then he had to overcome certain erroneous ideas prevalent amongst the laity: that nuns must have elaborate convents provided for them, that to be a nun a young lady must have moved in polite society, that she must have a private fortune of her own, and so on.

[19] These were to take over the work to which, in the Archbishop's estimation, the Sisters of Charity should have devoted their exclusive attention. Clare, Sr M., 'The Story of the Good Samaritans', Australian Catholic Historical Society Records, Sydney, 1945.

[20] Southern Cross (Adelaide), 20 February 1869, p. 274: 'The Sisters of St Dominic opened their convent school on Tuesday, 2nd February. There was a large attendance of pupils from highly respected families, both Catholic and Protestant, and the number has since increased.'

[21] Moran, op. cit., p. 287. Here and there, where a school was intended for the poor, special attention was drawn to the fact.

[22] McKillop, Mother Mary, Statement in Rome (Archives, St Joseph's Convent, Mount Street, North Sydney, pp. 2-4).   [23] Corrigan, op. cit., pp. 9-11.

[24] Memoir of Julian E. T. Woods, quoted in Rev. George O'Neill's Life of the Reverend Julian Edmund Tenison Woods, 1832-1889, pp. 123-4.

Woods' proposal, which he communicated to Mary McKillop and over which he had meditated at great length, was to establish a religious order of teachers whose members should penetrate into the more remote parts of the colony in order to provide a Catholic education for the poorer children. With him it was not merely a question of founding yet another religious order, one that would duplicate the work already being done by others. His idea was to found one that undertook 'to teach poor schools without any aid except alms and what the children [could] themselves afford'. Other orders, he said, could continue doing 'what they [had] to do'; 'their whole rules and spirit would be out of harmony with the change' he proposed.[25]

Eventually, with the advice of Bishop Goold of Melbourne and of Dr Elley, Vicar-Apostolic of Central Oceania,[26] and with the sanction of Dr Sheil of Adelaide, Woods went ahead with his idea, and the new order was launched in a stable-like makeshift of a building at Penola in 1866. The following year Woods brought the Sisters to Adelaide,[27] erected a novitiate,[28] and drew up for them a more formal rule of life.[29]

As already indicated, the undertaking was an immediate success. The Sisters took over all the schools in the city and opened others as well.[30] Within five years they numbered 120[31] and had even opened six schools in the diocese of Brisbane.[32]

Judged by modern standards, the first Sisters of St Joseph were not exceptionally well versed in the theory of pedagogy; in the practice of it, however, their own experience and natural talent combined to make them a competent body of teachers.[33] Mother Mary herself had conducted the school at Penola; before that she had been an assistant in the government school in Portland, Victoria, just across the border. Her writings and letters, moreover, reveal her as a woman of sound judgment and no mean intellectual ability. For that reason Woods insisted that the young Sisters be closely associated with her in school in order that they might be imbued with her ways and learn her method.[34]

[25] Letter, Woods to Mother Mary McKillop. Printed in Sr Chanel's *Life of Mother Mary, Foundress of the Sisterhood of St. Joseph of the Sacred Heart*, pp. 28-9.
[26] Woods, Rev. J. E. T., Statement made by Father Woods on the Institute of the Sisters of St Joseph and his connection with it, para. 1 (copy in Archives, Mother House of Sisters of St Joseph of the Sacred Heart, Mount Street, North Sydney). (On the last page of this document is this statement: 'We certify that this is a correct copy of the original document in Father Woods' own Handwriting.' Signed: Sr Mary Josephine, Sr Mary de Sales, 23 March 1896, Mother House, Sydney.) The document is sometimes referred to as the 'Memoir' of Father Woods. It is also printed in Chanel, op. cit., pp. 47-9.   [27] Ibid., para. 8.   [28] Ibid., para. 9.
[29] Woods, Rev. J. E. T., Rules for the Institute of the Sisters of St Joseph for the Catholic Education of Poor Children (Archives, Mother House of the Sisters of St Joseph, Mount Street, North Sydney).
[30] Woods, Statement on the Institute of the Sisters of St Joseph, para. 8.
[31] Ibid., para. 9.   [32] Ibid., para. 10. Cf. *Ordo Divini Officii Recitandi*, 1876, pp. 73-4.
[33] For educational qualifications of early Sisters of the order see O'Neill, op. cit., pp. 143-4, and O'Neill, Rev. George, *Life of Mother Mary of the Cross*.
[34] O'Neill, *Life of Woods*, p. 143.

Little was left to chance or individual taste. Uniformity of method and organization of class work was enjoined in the *Directory*,[35] wherein were outlined all the practices to be followed. In it theory was eschewed and the emphasis was entirely on the practical. The Little Sister (the name given to the Superior) was, for example, 'to see that each day the Sisters [had] a fresh task on each subject, which they [had to] study in class the evening before, and then be able to impart to their classes the next day'.[36] Then followed more minute instructions on the various types of lessons. The Sisters, for example, who were to give the gallery and object lessons were 'to prepare their subjects the night before, and not give any without the consent and knowledge of the Little Sister of their school'.[37] The Sisters were further directed to 'prepare their parsing sentences the previous night', and in all schools 'immediately taught from the Convent' (presumably the mother house) 'the class lessons, gallery and object lessons, parsing, etc., [were to] be the same . . . in each class'.[38] The details of method and the programme followed in the first schools of the Sisters are given in Appendix VIII.

This type of organization, simple but over-centralized when judged by present-day standards, was well suited to the needs of the times and a distinct advance on contemporary practice. Necessary modifications and adaptations were made from time to time, not only in school work, but also in the organization of the communities; nevertheless, any departures from the essential principles of poverty and simplicity on which the order stood, were strenuously and consistently resisted.

In the matter of government, to take but one instance, the foundress insisted on central government with one general superior and subordinate provincial superiors. Bishop Quinn of Bathurst, however, believed that 'there should be no general superior, but, like the Sisters of Mercy, the Bishop of each diocese where they may be established should be superior',[39] and in this view he was supported by the great majority of the other bishops. But against this judgment of most members of the Australian Hierarchy Mother Mary remained firm. The lives of her Sisters would be fraught with difficulties: the poverty of existence among the city poor, the loneliness of life in the little convents of the bush with their tiny communities of two or three members,[40] days and even weeks without Mass and the sacraments—all these would be real hardships. To support this kind of life, she argued, preparation of a special sort would be needed—training in a large central mother house where a true spirit

---

[35] Sisters of St Joseph of the Sacred Heart, *Directory of Order of Discipline*, c. 1867-9. (See biliographical note, p. 518.)   [36] Ibid., p. 90, para. 2.
[37] Ibid., p. 90, para. 3.   [38] Ibid., p. 90, para. 4.
[39] Letter, Quinn to Mother Mary, Bathurst, 14 April 1873. Printed in Chanel, p. 106.
[40] For example, in Queensland in 1875 there were three communities of two each and two communities of three each. *Ordo Divini Officii Recitandi*, 1876, pp. 73-4.

7. MOTHER MARY OF THE CROSS

By courtesy of the Sisters of St Joseph, Sydney

could be acquired and where it could be renewed from time to time, especially at annual retreats.

But Dr Quinn would have his way. Having received several of Mother Mary's Sisters into his diocese where they were already conducting schools,[41] he induced them to separate from her jurisdiction and allow themselves to be constituted into a diocesan organization under his direction.[42] To distinguish them from the others he was obliged (by Rome) to clothe them in a black habit and, with the assistance of Tenison Woods himself, modified certain of their constitutions.[43]

His brother, James, of Brisbane acted differently. Since the Sisters whom Mother Mary had sent to Queensland would not agree to become diocesan, he allowed them to return to their mother house, churlishly and ungratefully announcing at the same time that the sojourn of these Sisters in the colony 'was only temporary and until such time as other and a higher class of teachers could be obtained'.[44]

But Rome upheld Mother Mary's point of view.[45] Having just sided with the Christian Brothers in Ireland on a similar matter, it could hardly have done otherwise. Besides, with broader vision, Rome could not fail to see the ultimate benefits such an organization would confer on the Church in Australia.

Those benefits were quickly realized. By 1950 there were approximately 1,600 Brown Josephites scattered throughout Australia in all but seven of its twenty-five dioceses.[46] The primitive spirit of the congregation, moreover, continued to animate these Sisters and direct

[41] Byrne, Rev. J. P., Report of Inspector of Catholic Schools. *Record*, 1 January 1878, pp. 122-3.

[42] *Ordo Divini Officii Recitandi*, 1876, p. 78.

[43] Ibid.; this modification was made in 1875.

[44] This was in answer to a friend of the Sisters who dared inquire of the Bishop why the Sisters of St Joseph had been quite overlooked in the school collections. Address of Dr Quinn at meeting of Catholics in St Mary's Church, South Brisbane. *Brisbane Courier*, 13 March 1879, p. 2, e. See also letter to Editor, *Brisbane Courier*, 7 March 1879, p. 3, c.

[45] By approving of her type of government and giving its approbation to the constitutions. See latest edition, Sisters of St Joseph of the Sacred Heart, *Customs and Practices*.

[46] These seven dioceses were Bathurst, Maitland, Darwin, Kimberley, Geraldton, Cairns, Hobart (*A.C.D.*, 1951, *passim*). The position at the end of 1950 was:

State	Diocese	Convents	Sisters
N.S.W.	Sydney	58	550
	Armidale	16	73
	Goulburn	11	41
	Lismore	10	37
	Wagga	9	51
	Wilcannia-Forbes	3	15
Vic.	Melbourne	31	266
	Ballarat	5	19
	Sale	12	46
	Sandhurst	3	9
S.A.	Adelaide	24	201
	Pt Augusta	13	49

their activities.[47] In the manuscript of the rules he drew up in 1867, Tenison Woods had penned on the first page that 'this institute [had] been erected for the pious education of the children whose parents [were] in humble circumstances . . .', that the Sisters were 'principally bound to education and more to the children of the poor than to others'; and, he added, 'they must give place and preference to the religious of other orders'.[48]

For almost a century that spirit has endured. At first the work was restricted solely to primary education, since this was all that the poor could afford; but as the present century advanced the nuns advanced with it. As secondary education became less the preserve and privilege of the rich and became the right also of the poor, the Institute, in order not to curtail its sphere of usefulness, gradually extended its scope and provided, where necessary, secondary education to at least the inter-mediate stage.[49] Where, on the other hand, it was a case of offering a distinctly middle-class type of education, the Sisters demurred. Rather than violate the spirit of their congregation they preferred to withdraw their communities and allow other orders to take over the schools. By means of the staffs thus saved the Sisters were able to multiply their usefulness in parts where their special type of help was most sorely needed.[50] Not social prestige, but social uplift had always been their primary objective.[51] It was certainly so in the days of their lowly origin; it was still so a century later.

W.A.	Perth	16	68
	New Norcia	5	21
Q'ld.	Brisbane	12	80
	Rockhampton	5	23
	Toowoomba	10	40
	Townsville	4	17

[47] Rome, it is true, in approving the constitutions, modified the foundress's original ideas on certain matters. The poverty, for example, that Mother Mary wanted was not allowed. It would, Rome felt, leave the position of the Sisters too utterly dependent and insecure, thus jeopardizing the stability of the congregation. See Mother Mary's remarks on poverty and money in her *Statement in Rome,* pp. 5, 7: The Sisters, she said, shrank 'with positive terror, from the idea of possessing property of their own'. See also letter, Father Tappeiner to Mother Mary, 16 July 1873, on the banishing of accomplishments, music, etc., from the schools of the Sisters. Quoted in O'Neill, *Life of Mother Mary,* p. 152.

[48] Woods, *Rules for the Institute of St. Joseph for the Catholic Education of poor children,* p. 1.

[49] For example, in the archdiocese of Sydney alone, by 1950, at least thirteen of these schools went to the intermediate stage, and nineteen others were classified as post-primary. *A.C.D.,* 1951, pp. 150-1, 156-7.

[50] Thus in 1948, the Sisters gave up two of their finest Sydney schools, Clovelly and Drummoyne. In arriving at this decision the General Council said: 'We must offer something worth offering. These schools are in suburbs where the people ask for a type of education which conflicts with the spirit of our order. Sisters would be released for openings in the remote districts.' Minute of 13 May 1947. Minutes of the General Council (Archives, Sisters of St Joseph, Mount Street, North Sydney. Through the courtesy of Sister Campion).

[51] See Corrigan, *The Achievements of Catholic Education in Australia,* p. 9.

But not even the Josephite adaptation of the religious life could solve the problem of Catholic education in the more scattered parts of the Australian bush. That was to be the achievement of a new order founded in Tasmania by Father John Wallis and Archbishop Tweedy in 1944. Appalled at the spiritual hardships suffered by the scattered, isolated Catholic families in Tasmania, Father Wallis began to dream of the idea of religious who, instead of bringing children into school, would bring the school to the children; religious who would follow the children into their bush homes and instruct them there.[52] The idea received warm support from Archbishop Tweedy, who succeeded to the see of Hobart in 1943. The following year, Wallis's dream became a reality and the Home Missionary Sisters of Our Lady came into being.[53] These religious at once began to engage in those tasks which were to constitute their particular apostolate—catechetical missions, the visitation of homes in the outback, and other social work; in addition they organized correspondence courses in religion and undertook the work of vacation schools.[54]

THE CONTRIBUTION OF THE RELIGIOUS

This more recent adaptation of the Home Missionary Sisters appeared at first quite revolutionary. Relatively speaking, it was no more revolutionary a departure from current practices than the adaptations of seventy or eighty years earlier had been from the practices then in vogue. In some respects the task confronting the older orders was the more difficult: they had to overcome the initial difficulties of settling down among strange people and, not infrequently, of mastering a new tongue. But whether English or Irish, French or German, all had a contribution to make, a fact which was quickly recognized,[55] not only by Catholics but by non-Catholics as well.[56]

The convents came to be regarded as centres of culture.[57] In them the fine arts were highly developed, particularly needlework, painting and music.[58] The great musical traditions early established in many of the larger convents were not approached in any other institutions in

[52] The story of the genesis of this new institute was related by Father Wallis himself as he drove the writer back from a day spent at a centre in the remote parts of southern Tasmania where the Sisters were working.   [53] A.C.D., 1951, p. 477.

[54] Ibid. In their missionary journeys into the interior the convent goes on wheels—a caravan. This, together with the sacristy of the lonely bush church, is the Sisters' temporary home.

[55] This fact was widely attested by both Catholic and non-Catholic authorities alike. For commendation of the work of the nuns see Report of Select Committee on Education (Q'ld.), p. 57, P.P.(Q'ld.), 1861, I, p. 661; Census of the Colony of Western Australia, 1870, p. 12; D.S.B. (N.S.W.), Inspectors' Reports, 1861-6. Report of Inspector Reilly on Sisters of Mercy school at Bathurst; remarks of Thomas Arnold, formerly Inspector of Schools in Tasmania, in Passages in a Wandering Life, p. 135.

[56] For instance, large numbers of Protestant girls attended the convent schools. Sketch of the Life and Labours of the Rt Rev. Dr O'Quinn, First Bishop of Brisbane.

[57] Moran, Cardinal P. F., History of the Catholic Church in Australasia, p. 626.

[58] These were even carried down into the primary parochial schools. The following report shows to what extent this had been done: 'Vocal Music is taught in all the

Australia.[59] The fact that in many cases the nuns depended for their very existence on the fees from music tuition[60] did not detract in any way from the cultural contribution of their work.

A similar situation existed with the diffusion of books: besides the carefully selected books which the pupils annually carried off to their homes as prizes,[61] there were books to be borrowed from the libraries conducted by the nuns. In the early days libraries had been frequently established as adjuncts to the parish churches,[62] but had often languished for want of care and organization. In many cases they were revived under the care of the Sister-librarians.[63] In other cases, the nuns established libraries in their own convents.[64]

---

schools that are in charge of the Nuns. Where attention and care are given to the singing lesson, the results are highly pleasing and very successful.

'Needle-work is taught for a short time to all girls' classes. The permanent results achieved in this subject, in both its branches, plain and fancy, were exhibited in all the schools visited. In several of the schools of the Sisters of Mercy, I noticed needle-work which had been awarded the highest prizes at the shows held annually in Maitland, Singleton and other places.' Dwyer, Rev. P. V., *Report on the Primary Schools*, Maitland Diocese, 1884, p. 7.

[59] The following report of Mr A. Somerwell, an examiner in music about the turn of the century, is significant: 'There is one thing I noticed in the school examinations and that was that the teaching in the Convent Schools was far superior to that of other schools. Why it should be so I do not know, but I have seen it not only here, but also in Sydney, and in some cases the contrast has been wonderful. It was just the same at Sale a few days ago, and wherever I go I notice it.' Quoted by Father John McCarthy in his Report of Inspector of Catholic Schools, archdiocese of Melbourne, 1900. *Advocate*, 8 December 1900, p. 7, a. In the archdiocese for that year twelve matriculated in music, 395 got other distinctions and honours in the examinations of the Royal College of Music. See also music results in Catholic schools of Victoria in the R.A.M. and R.C.M. for 1905. *Advocate*, 4 January 1905, p. 11.

At All Hallows', Brisbane, there were concerts on the first of every month for the non-star musicians. Annals of All-Hallows' (Archives, All Hallows', Brisbane).

All Hallows' also became the musical centre of the city. The programme for the Annual Concert of 1895 reveals the standard of work achieved (*Brisbane Courier*, 13 December 1895, p. 6, g). For similar accounts see, for example, *Brisbane Courier*, 15 December 1893, p. 6, c. For attitude of nuns to music examinations see *Loreto Annual Magazine* (Ballarat), 1901, p. 25. For complete music and art syllabus at All Hallows', Brisbane, in the nineties see *Age* (Brisbane), 16 December 1899, p. 24.

[60] *Mercy Centenary Record*, p. 62.

[61] See account of annual prize distribution at St Vincent's, Nudgee, Queensland. *Catholicism in Queensland*, pp. 155, 156.

[62] Such a library established in Adelaide in 1847 serves as an illustration: 'A circulating library forms part of the school establishment in town, and is intended for the dissemination of knowledge on religious and scientific matters.' *South Australian Almanack and General Directory*, p. 71.

[63] The Sisters of Charity, for example, took over the 'Hobart Town Catholic Library' that had been established by Dr Willson in 1846. Kelsh, *Personal Recollections of the Rt Rev. R. W. Willson*, p. 71.

[64] E.g., the lending library established by the Sisters of Mercy, Geelong. This library contained over 2,000 volumes. On this point, Sr M. Ignatius gives the reminiscences of an old Geelong gentleman: 'When I was a grown boy, I used to go to the Convent Library every Saturday to change the books my parents had finished reading. The room was always crowded, but every one was quiet. We liked going up just because we wanted to see and speak to a nun. "The Lady Sherlock", as everyone used to call her, presided. She took no time to find our names in the Members' Book, and knew exactly where to replace returns or to take down any book called for. She could give information on any subject.' Ignatius, 'The Sisters of Mercy in Victoria', section on Sacred Heart College, Geelong, p. 4.

But there were things of greater moment. Besides the influence they exerted on the Catholic people through instruction[65] and visitation,[66] the early religious made a contribution of another kind, one that was less sensible, perhaps, but no less real—that of their refinement and good breeding. These were not the least of the graces they had to confer on a land where the pioneering conditions of colonial days had robbed its people of what little elegance their forefathers had brought from across the seas. Not only were the daughters of these hardy pioneers to learn whatever the religious had to teach them of art and letters but also those indefinable qualities that are transmitted, as it were, from one soul to another—courtesy in speech, ease in manner and conversation, true simplicity, poise and nobility of carriage; lastly, good taste and judgment.

These influences, as has been said, were noted even by those outside the Church. 'The cultured ladies of the religious sisterhoods,' wrote Sir Henry Parkes, 'and the enthusiasts of religious brotherhoods have been enlisted into the service of the separate schools, and it may be acknowledged with pleasure that in many cases they are excellent teachers.'[67] A similar observation from an anti-Catholic and obviously anti-Irish contributor to *Macmillan's Magazine* ran:

Within the last seven years, churches, schools, colleges, seminaries, nunneries [sic], sisterhoods, and monastic orders have been founded or established in all the Australian colonies, and are—many of them—under the control of Frenchmen, Italians, and Englishmen of exceptional ability, who present a marked contrast to the illiteracy of the ordinary priest.[68]

A few there were who valued the religious, not for their 'ability' but for their vow of poverty: the prospect of securing teachers who besides conducting the school could also be called upon to perform other invaluable services in the parish—all for a very low salary—was most attractive. But the majority preferred them precisely because they were religious, men or women whose mere presence in the parish was calculated to have an uplifting and spiritualizing effect on the lives of their people.

This was acknowledged long before the school question became urgent. From the very beginning Dr Polding had hoped to establish a monastery of monks in the diocese of Sydney, being convinced that he was thereby 'best consulting and providing for the interests of the district'.[69] It was

[65] The country folk round Maitland, for example, gathered at the Dominican Convent on Sunday afternoons for simple instruction in the essential doctrines of the Church. O'Hanlon, Sr A., *Dominican Pioneers in New South Wales*, pp. 63-4.

[66] Visitation of the sick, or poor, or others in need of spiritual help is a part of the Mercy vocation. The Sisters engaged in this work right from the beginning in Australia. *Sketch of the Catholic Mission in Western Australia*, p. 71.

[67] Parkes, Sir Henry, *Fifty Years in the Making of Australian History*, vol. 2, p. 28.

[68] From the pen of a Mr Wise. Cf. article by F. B. Freehill, attacking Wise for his 'know nothing' attitude towards the Irish, *Centennial Magazine*, October 1889.

[69] Letter, Polding to Father President of English Benedictines, 14 August 1834. Quoted in Birt, Rev. Norbert (O.S.B.), *Benedictine Pioneers in Australia*, vol. I, p. 244.

not only that he was ambitious to see his own Benedictines strongly entrenched around him; his mind soared beyond to a broader vision still. 'What a delightful thing it is,' he wrote, 'to contemplate the institute that civilized and christianized the North of Europe more than a thousand years since now taking its flight into the Southern Hemisphere for purposes equally noble and good.'[70] Pope Gregory XVI spoke in the same vein to the Spanish Benedictines, Serra and Salvado, who accompanied Dr Brady to the West in 1846. 'Forget not', he told them, that the Benedictines of old 'not only converted to the faith so many nations and peoples, but likewise instructed them in the ways of civilization and the arts of cultured life, and remember that you are entering on a work like to theirs . . .'[71]

But the same reminder could well have been given to all the other orders. The opening of each new convent or monastery was regarded as a deliberate attempt 'to engraft'[72] on this land the civilizing power of monasticism in which institution Vaughan saw 'the highest form . . . the most perfect meaning of Christian education'.[73] For the Irish-Australian Catholics particularly, the spreading of the religious orders was the epic of their homeland's greatness all over again, that homeland whose 'saints and scholars', the 'Wisdom-sellers of the West', as they called them, had carried back over Europe 'the regenerating idea— Christian education'.[74] That epic they saw being re-enacted on the hill outside Wagga where Vaughan had gone in 1875 to open the new Presentation Convent of Mt Erin. 'From this hill,' they said, 'which has lighted its lamp at "Kildare's Holy Fane",'[75] will shine a light—pure, clear, and bright as that inextinguishable flame from which it springs—and shed blessings on ages yet unborn. Its mission is a holy and patriotic one.'[76]

Despite the obvious enthusiasm of such addresses, the claim made in them is substantially true: the orders then being introduced into this country were in reality adaptations of the older form of monasticism, the achievements of which they were to perpetuate. The links in the chain of tradition were strong and easily discoverable.

[70] Polding to Novices at Benedictine Convent, Princethorpe, England (copy in St Mary's Archives, Sydney).   [71] Quoted in Moran, op. cit., p. 563.
[72] See O'Connor, J. G., *A Brief History of the Sacred Heart Presentation Convent, Wagga*, p. 14.
[73] Ibid., p. 15. Vaughan's ideas on the importance of monasticism as an educational institution are further elaborated in his address at St John's College in the University of Sydney in 1875. 'The schools,' he said, 'which trained the barbarians, and laid the seed of a civilization which grew into a mustard tree in the modern world, sprang from the deep heart of monastic life.' And further, 'Without possessing the high fastidious culture of pagan periods, the monks knew one thing better than any other people, how to master, purify, and cultivate the heart'. Vaughan, R. B., *Higher Education—Inaugural Address at St. John's College within the University of Sydney*.
[74] O'Connor, op. cit., pp. 2, 14.
[75] The Wagga foundation was made from Kildare, Ireland. [76] O'Connor, op. cit., p. 14.

The Sisters of Mercy, to take but one example, were modelled closely on the Presentation Sisters,[77] likewise the Brigidines. The Presentation Sisters in their turn had been formed by Nano Nagle on the lines of the Ursulines,[78] the first order in the Church founded specifically for teaching. But the Ursulines themselves were strongly linked with those that went before. Some years after their foundation, when they were enclosed, they were given the Rule of St Augustine and trained in monastic observance by an Augustinian Abbess.[79] In this way they were linked not only with the monasticism of the Middle Ages but with the thirteenth century and the Dominicans who had themselves been established on an adaptation of the Augustinian Rule at Prouille in 1206.[80]

Working forward instead of back, the same strong links are to be observed. Many of the new ideas introduced by the Ursulines, had had to be abandoned, so strong was the force of convention; but they were taken up again by Mary Ward's Institute, the Sisters of Loreto, and passed on to others in a variety of ways. Mary Aikenhead, for example, the foundress of the Irish Sisters of Charity, spent three years in the famous Loreto Abbey, Bar Convent, at York. The ideas and principles she learnt there were later incorporated in the rule she gave her own nuns.[81] Other orders were even more eclectic in the ideas they absorbed. For instance, the first four members of the Sacred Heart order who gathered around Madeleine Sophie Barat had been educated, one by the Ursulines, a second by the Benedictines, a third at Madame de Maintenon's institution at St Cyr, and the fourth at a Visitation Convent.[82] Sophie Barat assimilated ideas from all four.[83]

The same process of assimilation is observed in Australia: Benedictine influence on the early Church was too profound to have left no trace,[84] its peculiar genius was instilled by Polding himself into the Good Samari-

[77] The only big alterations being the rules for visitation. Burke-Savage, Rev. Roland (S.J.), *Catherine McAuley.*

[78] Nano Nagle established schools for the poor in Dublin and Cork and then decided to confide her work to a religious order. Some of her helpers, therefore, went to Paris to the convent of the Rue St Jacques. There they underwent an Ursuline training and, in fact, returned to Ireland as Ursulines. To these, Nano Nagle confided her schools and her children in 1772, but finding they could not devote attention to the poor, she decided to adapt the constitutions and dress of Ursulines to a new order exclusively for work among the poor. To these she gave the name Sisters of the Presentation. *The Ursulines*, p. 23-4.   [79] McKiernan, Rev. Mother Justin, *The Order of St. Ursula*, p. 21.

[80] See *The Rule of St. Augustine and the Constitutions of the Congregation of Dominican Sisters of New South Wales*, 1941.

[81] Coleridge, Rev. Henry James (ed.), *St. Mary's Convent, Micklegate Bar, York*, p. 284.   [82] Monahan, M., *Saint Madeleine Sophie*, p. 72.

[83] In addition she drew from the Port Royalists, the Oratorians, the Jesuits. See H. C. Barnard's *Little Schools of Port Royal*, and *The Port Royalists on Education*; see also Margaret O'Leary, *Education with a Tradition*, pt. 1, chs. 2, 4, 5, and 6.

[84] The Benedictine monks retired from education in New South Wales with the closing of Lyndhurst in the seventies (see p. 325). The Benedictine nuns closed their sole school at Subiaco in the twenties of the present century.

tan Sisters who remained to carry on its traditions.[85] The Brown Jose-phites likewise drew much from their co-founders, the scholar and mystic, ex-Passionist and Jesuit-trained Tenison Woods and his most illustrious spiritual daughter, Mother Mary of the Cross.[86]

The orders of teaching Brothers stemmed directly from De La Salle who, in his turn, would appear to have been more attuned to the spirit of Cardinal de Berulle and the French Oratorians than to that of the Jesuits.[87] The very close connection between the De La Salles and the Marists is obvious from a comparison of the Rules and Constitutions of the two orders,[88] while some of the early Irish Christian Brothers spent some time in Paris observing practices in De La Salle institutions.

Thus there was no break in the tradition handed down.[89] Nor was it merely a tradition of the unwritten word. The educational lore of the orders became enshrined in their various systems or manuals of educational practice, which incorporated not only the accumulated educational wisdom of the Church but embodied also the accepted contemporary secular practice of the time.[90]

This was a second important contribution of the orders. Its impact was felt immediately. The aged Polding, for example, remembering the Christian Brothers he had lost in the forties, expected much from the 'methods and motives' of the Marist Brothers to whom he accorded a lukewarm welcome in the seventies.[91] The Inspector of Catholic Schools in Sydney also observed a change. 'Several of the orders,' he wrote in 1883, 'now engaged in teaching being essentially scholastic, have with considerable talent and power of organization, developed special systems of training, which yield very good results.' 'To some extent', he added, these results 'are patent to the public'.[92]

[85] Corrigan, The Achievements of Catholic Education in Australia, p. 9.
[86] O'Neill, Rev. George (S.J.), Life of Mother Mary of the Cross.
[87] O'Leary, Margaret, The Catholic Church and Education, pp. 26-7.
[88] Cf. Constitutions et Règles du Gouvernement de l'Institut des Petits Frères de Marie and Règles Communes des Frères des Écoles Chrétiennes.
[89] The sacredness of an order's tradition was generally referred to in specific terms within the constitutions. Cf. I.B.V.M., Constitutions of the Institute of the Blessed Virgin Mary for the Houses Dependent on the General Mother House, Rathfarnham. The members of the institute, according to constitution 224 of chapter xix, 'should eagerly carry on that tradition of the Institute regarding the training and education of girls'.
[90] The Benedictines absorbed most of what was worth salvaging from the Middle Ages; the Dominicans and Franciscans saved what was best from the age of the Scholastics. The best contributions of the Renaissance and Reformation were assimilated by the Jesuits in their Ratio Studiorum, see Ellwood P. Cubberley, The History of Education, p. 339; and Letter of Transmission of Ratio Studiorum, 1599, quoted by Rev. E. A. Fitzpatrick, St. Ignatius and the Ratio Studiorum, p. 119. For some of the more important comments on the draft of the Ratio, see Alan P. Farrell, The Jesuit Code of Liberal Education, p. 13; and Règlements des Religieuses Ursulines de la Congrégation de Paris, quoted in Sister M. Monica, Angela Merici and her Teaching Idea, pp. 362-3; Martin, Marie de Saint Jean (O.S.U.), Ursuline Method of Education, p. ix; O'Leary, op. cit., p. 65.
[91] In speech delivered at public meeting to devise means of raising funds for the Marist Brothers, Sydney, 25 July 1872.   [92] Rogers, Report on Catholic Schools, 1883.

The better known systems were those contained in the *Ratio Studiorum*[93] of the Jesuits, in the *Conduite des Écoles*[94] of the De La Salle Brothers, in the *Guide des Écoles*[95] of the Marist Brothers, in the *Règlements*[96] of the Ursulines and in the *Plan d'Études*[97] of the religious of the Sacred Heart. Those orders which produced no special manuals of school organization generally incorporated their educational system into their Rules or books of Practices and Customs, as in the case of the Loretos[98] and the Dominicans.[99]

From the point of view of education in general and Catholic education in particular the contribution of the teaching orders was a significant one.[1] But the magnitude of their contribution was not to be measured in terms of education alone. The struggle for Catholic education which they had helped to wage had raised the morale of the Church itself to a pitch that was only dreamed of by the early bishops, who had, in the seventies, been called upon to make a momentous decision. They made it—some in the face of intense opposition, all in the midst of doubt and anxiety. Yet, within even a decade of Vaughan's passing, the objects of their hopes and dreams had been realized. 'Time and results [had] vindicated their action.'

These were Archbishop Carr's words in the closing address of the Second Plenary Council of 1895.[2] Vaughan's prophecy that 'the teaching religious orders . . . would give a tone and thoroughness to the rising Catholic generations which the existing system . . . could not give' had, he said, been abundantly fulfilled. 'The Catholic Church [was that] day substantially stronger, more united, and better equipped than if the old school system had been permitted to continue.'[3] That old school system has already been described in chapters 2-3. The system that replaced it is described in the chapters that follow.

[93] Cf. Fitzpatrick, op. cit.
[94] Appearing first in 1695. See W. J. Battersby, *De La Salle, A Pioneer of Modern Education*, p. 78.
[95] *Guide des Écoles* à l'usage des Petits Frères-de-Marie, Redigé d'après les Règles et les Instructions de M. l'abbé Champagnat.
[96] *Règlements des Religieuses Ursulines de la Congrégation de Paris.*
[97] *Plan d'Etudes des Pensionnats de la Société du Sacré Coeur de Jesus; Plan of Studies of Boarding Schools of the Society of the Sacred Heart.*
[98] See *Constitutions of the Institute of the Blessed Virgin Mary for the Houses Dependent on the General Mother House, Rathfarnham*, chs. xviii, xix of Part 1, and ch. xi of Part 2.
[99] See *Rule of St. Augustine and the Constitutions of the Congregations of the Dominican Sisters of New South Wales*, pt. 1, ch. 24.
[1] 'Pastoral Letter of the Cardinal Delegate and the Archbishop and Bishops of the Australian Commonwealth in Plenary Council assembled, to the Clergy and Laity of their charge, 8 September 1905.' *Austral Light*, 1 October 1905, p. 711.
[2] *Record* (W.A.), 2 December 1895, p. 15.
[3] Ibid. 'While we have to complain,' wrote Bishop James Quinn, 'of the gross injury that is inflicted on us, it is our belief that nothing could happen which could conduce more to the prosperity of the Catholic Church in this colony.' Letter, Dr Quinn to Minister of Education, Brisbane, 31 December 1880. It was subsequently published in the *Brisbane Courier*, 6 January 1881, p. 3, f, g.

8

Catholic Schools under the
Religious Orders

THE PAROCHIAL SYSTEM

Extent of Parochial System

THE NEW SYSTEM of Catholic schools developed rapidly. Determined, after the Education Acts of the seventies and eighties, not to allow their children to be drawn into the un-Catholic atmosphere of the state schools, the Catholic community spared no efforts in multiplying the number of Catholic schools. To observers the withdrawal of state aid, instead of proving a death blow, appeared to act as a stimulant.[1] Within two generations the new system numbered over 1,700 institutions, ranging from kindergartens to university and ecclesiastical colleges, and including schools of all types; primary and secondary, schools for the blind and schools for the mentally handicapped (see Table XLVIII).[2] The 1,613 primary and secondary schools, which constituted the backbone of the system, were further diversified into day schools and boarding schools. Of these, 53 were for boys and 201 for girls.[3]

TABLE XLVIII

The Catholic School System, 1950

Type of Institution	Number
Schools, primary and secondary	1,613
Orphanages	53
Ecclesiastical seminaries	29
University colleges	7
Training colleges for teachers	15

Built up over eighty years, the system is important, not only in the history of education, but also in the development of the Church. According to Archbishop Mannix, the Catholic school in this country

[1] *Adelaide Observer*, 30 January 1892, p. 37, a. Report of Inspector of Catholic Schools, archdiocese of Sydney, 1883. See also Pastoral Letter of Bishop Murray of Maitland, 5 October 1884, *Record* (Bathurst), 16 October 1884, p. 473.
[2] *A.C.D.*, 1951, pp. 171-455, *passim*.   [3] Ibid.

constituted the 'ante-chamber of the Church'; without the schools the Churches would have been empty.[4] So important had they become in the eyes of the Catholic community that Archbishop Carr had come to 'regard the building of each new Catholic school as a distinct act of supernatural faith'.[5] Whereas the older denominational system had never appealed to the imagination of the Catholic people, the system that supplanted it had won their support almost from the very start. 'The system of Catholic schools,' reported the Hierarchy in 1948, 'is truly, to-day, the glory of the Catholic Church in Australia.'[6]

The central feature of the whole system is its scheme of parochial schools.[7] In this lie the strength and cohesion, extent and vitality, of the whole organization. Archbishop Panico, a former Apostolic-Delegate to this country, regarded the parochial system as the Church's 'most cherished heritage' in Australia.[8] The system had also been brought to the favourable attention of Pope Pius XII when, as Cardinal Eugenio Pacelli, he served as Papal Secretary of State to Pius XI.[9]

Its influence, from the point of view of numbers alone, was far-reaching. By the middle of the present century eight out of every ten children in the Catholic system were to be found in the parochial schools. In New South Wales, and Tasmania, for example, the ratio was just below eight in ten; in South Australia just above; while in Queensland it was closer to nine out of ten (see Table XLIX).[10] In practice this meant that each parish had built its own parish school, installed a community of religious teachers, and made itself responsible for their support. Such a system was bound to confer many obvious advantages upon the Catholic life of the parish.

TABLE XLIX

Pupils in Primary and Secondary Schools, 1950

State	Primary	Secondary	Total
New South Wales	73,464	22,917	96,381
Victoria	46,443	12,936	59,379
Tasmania	3,927	1,029	4,956
South Australia	8,382	1,952	10,334
Western Australia	—	—	16,144
Queensland	27,077	3,310	30,387

[4] In an address at the opening of St Brendan's School, Flemington. *Argus*, 16 March 1914, p. 7, g.
[5] In address at opening of St Brendan's Primary School, Shepparton, *Austral Light*, 1 December 1916.
[6] Beovich, 'Catholic Education and Catechetics in Australia', p. 2.   [7] Ibid., p. 3.
[8] From address by the Most Rev. Dr Panico at the official opening of the Catholic Education Congress in Adelaide, 1936. *Catholic Education Congress*, p. 28.
[9] Letter, Pacelli to Archbishop Killian of Adelaide, Vatican City, 14 September 1936. *Catholic Education Congress*, p. 30.
[10] Table compiled from *A.C.D.*, 1951, p. 455.

The pattern that emerged was uniform throughout the whole of Australia. It was only the exceptional parish that did not have its parochial school. Even remote and scattered parishes of the bush could boast of their little schools staffed by small religious communities of three and having enrolments no bigger than thirty.[11] Many of the larger parishes in the populous areas of the cities would have several schools, so that in general the parochial schools outnumbered the parishes (see Fig. 17).[12] The actual ratio between the two, however, varied: in 1900 it had averaged approximately two schools to one parish; in 1950 it had fallen to four schools for every three parishes—a reflection of the flight from the land and the tendency towards consolidation of schools, not only in rural areas but in the cities as well.

The actual difference between the rural and urban pattern has always been quite marked, as a comparison between the archdioceses of Sydney and Hobart will show (see Table L).[13] The relative plateau in the Tasmanian development is to be explained partly by the fact that in comparison with Sydney the population of Tasmania is rural and scattered, and partly by the policy of consolidated schools pursued by the Education Department of Tasmania and the greater facilities for school transport thereby provided in the island.[14]

Origin of Parochial System

The Australian parochial system is the result of several factors. In the first place it was a logical development of what is shown to have been

[11] For examples of this see *A.C.D.*, 1951, p. 383.
[12] This figure was drawn up on the data in the following table compiled from: *A.C.D.*, 1888, *passim*; 1900, pp. 162-3; 1910, pp. 194-5; 1920, pp. 246-7; 1930, pp. 312-13; 1940, pp. 489, 491; 1951, pp. 453, 455:

State		1888	1900	1910	1920	1930	1940	1950
N.S.W.	Parishes	117	159	182	233	277	305	351
	Schools	200	310	365	401	426	451	528
Vic.		61	95	119	154	179	188	210
		182	204	205	220	242	249	255
S.A.		28	30	41	45	48	58	70
		46	43	49	53	68	72	85
W.A.		12	23	41	69	57	70	96
		13	30	62	75	67	105	100
Q'ld.		45	50	57	59	121	150	184
		48	100	68	87	122	157	199
Tas.		21	19	20	21	21	26	32
		19	30	25	27	26	31	32
Totals	Parishes	284	376	463	531	703	797	943
	Schools	508	717	774	863	951	1065	1199

[13] Table compiled from *A.C.D.*, 1900, pp. 162-3; 1910, pp. 194-5; 1920, pp. 246-7; 1930, pp. 312-13; 1940, pp. 489, 491; 1951, pp. 453, 455.
[14] This development was contemporary with the establishment of the consolidated or 'area' school system in Tasmania.

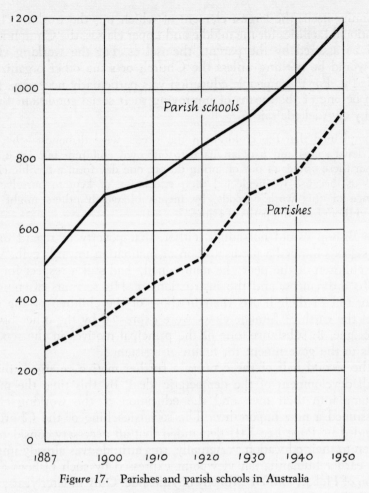

Figure 17.   Parishes and parish schools in Australia

TABLE L

Parochial School Patterns in Urban and Rural Dioceses

Diocese		1900	1910	1920	1930	1940	1950
Sydney	Parishes	68	74	85	111	122	165
	Schools	158	166	144	172	184	230
Hobart	Parishes	19	20	21	21	26	32
	Schools	30	25	27	26	31	32

the traditional practice of the Church in Europe.[15] In the second place it was a direct outcome of the denominational system in vogue throughout Australia in the nineteenth century.[16] Thirdly, Catholic education policy was inevitably influenced by the social composition of the Catholic

[15] See ch. 1.   [16] See ch. 2.

community itself, the largest element of which was the working class.[17] Educational facilities for the middle and upper classes, the Church knew, would be assured by the parents themselves. For the working classes there would be nothing unless the Church or some other organization provided it. For these people education was particularly necessary, for it was to be one of the means of improving their social condition. Bishop Murphy of Adelaide said:

We complained that the children in the streets were dishonest—that they taught lewd songs and bad language to our own children; but let us take care that these crimes of our offspring do not one day form a terrible charge against us, because we neglected their education, or kept to ourselves the substance of this world's goods, by means of which others might have retrieved them from the paths of crime.[18]

The Bishop would not admit, either, that poverty in regard to this world's goods implied a predisposition or inclination towards evil. 'Many of the children of the poor,' he maintained, 'had still a respect for God and His ordinances, and the instructions of His servants often found a better soil in their hearts than in those of the children of the great ones of the earth.'[19] Similar views were expressed by the other bishops and became, in substance, one of the principal motives in the repeated appeals to the government for financial assistance.[20]

In the second half of the century a further motive emerged—that of the full development of the democratic ideal. By this time the masses had come into their own and the education of the working classes had assumed a new importance. The social teaching of the Church as expounded by Pope Leo XIII demanded that all necessary consideration be given to their education.[21] Actually, this attitude was already implicit in the earlier humanitarian viewpoint expressed by such bishops as Dr Willson of Hobart and Dr Murphy of Adelaide. Only in later years, after the encyclicals of Leo XIII, was the socio-political aspect stressed.

This change is apparent in the writings of Cardinal Moran. 'The wealthier classes', he maintained, could 'provide means for having their children trained in religion and piety, independently of scholastic training, but for the great mass of children the only education [was] that afforded in the public schools'. The poorer classes must no longer be regarded as a mere 'element in society', but as 'a governing element'.

[17] See chs. 2, 11.
[18] Sermon preached at opening of a school chapel in Adelaide. *South Australian Register*, 8 October 1945, p.1, e.   [19] Ibid.
[20] Letter to His Excellency in Council from the Rt Rev. Bishop Murphy, 26 July 1875, P.P.(Tas.), 1875, no. 67.
[21] In the encyclicals, *Inscrutabili*, 1878; *Rerum Novarum*, 1891; *Graves de Communi*, 1901; and those of his successors, *Ubi Arcano*, 1922; and *Quadragesimo Anno*, 1931.

People used to speak of the eighteenth century as 'a century of aristo-crats, or of absolute government'. But in the nineteenth century and particularly in the independent colonies of the British Empire 'demo-cracy [was] the ruling power, and if democracy [was] to be allowed to be tainted with irreligion, or socialism, or impiety . . . the future of society [would] be sad indeed'.[22]

The Church therefore had more than one reason for paying particular attention to its primary parochial schools and directing towards them its first care and the bulk of its educational legislation.

Ecclesiastical Legislation for Primary Schools

Even before the Church had been officially constituted in the country Father Therry had believed that an important part of his duty was to provide Catholic schools, and, as has been shown, he made great efforts to put his belief into practice.[23] The Provincial Council of 1844 empha-sized the same principle: so that the children of the lower classes might not be neglected each pastor was to be responsible for erecting schools in his district.[24] The same regulation was set down in the decrees of the various diocesan synods[25] that were held about the time of the First Plenary Council of 1885, but in these cases it was made more explicit: a primary or elementary school was to be established in every mission where there was a priest.[26] The 1885 Council, moreover, extended the obligation, making it binding on the 'laity as well as the clergy'.[27] Later Councils merely repeated the injunctions[28] with the addition, however, of two further regulations: first, that no school, once opened, could be closed or removed without the consent of the bishop;[29] second, that if a pastor refused to support the parish school or build a new one, he could be removed from his benefice.[30]

Such sanctions were evidently called for, otherwise they would not have been established. For most of the clergy, however, thoroughly aware, as they were, of the enormous potentialities of the parochial school,[31] they were unnecessary. By that period, too, the clergy on the whole had grown accustomed, as the Second Plenary Council urged they

[22] *Advocate,* 28 July 1894, p. 8, a.   [23] See ch. 1.
[24] Cf. in the First Provincial Council, in 1844: 'Omnis sit missionarii cura Scholas in suo districtu erigere.' *Acta et Decreta* concilii primi provinciae Australiensis. See section 'De verbi praedicatione', p. 25.
[25] Decrees of Diocesan Synod, Bathurst, 1883, decr. 1, 3. *Conc. Plen.,* IV, 1937, decr. 606.   [26] *Conc. Plen.,* I, 1885, decr. 240.
[27] 'Omnes Catholici potissimum vero pastores.' *Conc. Plen.,* I, 1885, decr. 239; II, 1895, decr. 302; IV, 1937, decr. 606.
[28] See *Conc. Plen.,* II, 1895, decr. 302; IV, 1937, decr. 606.
[29] 'Hinc decernimus Pastori non licere sine venia Episcopi quamcumque scholam elementarem dimittere seu claudere.' *Conc. Plen.,* III, 1905, decr. 326; see also *Conc. Plen.,* II, 1895, decr. 303.   [30] *Conc. Plen.,* I, 1885, decr. 37, 42 (b).
[31] Report of Inspector of Catholic Schools, Ballarat, 1924. *Advocate,* 8 January 1925, p. 10, c.

should,[32] to thinking of it as an essential part of the parish (*quasi partem essentialem Parochiæ*). The school itself kept the pastor in close contact with his children and with their families and welded a strong link between them and the Church.[33] It shared in, and became an integral part of, the liturgical and social life of the parish. The children grew up in it, returned to it in after-school years as the centre of their youth organizations, their clubs, their societies. In the end they, in their turn, supported it and sent their own children to it.

These advantages were so obvious that the bishops in Australia early adopted a policy of 'schools before churches'; not that the one was more important than the other, but without the school the church would have been severely handicapped in the carrying out of its mission: the one was the complement of the other.[34] Actually, in many dioceses the one edifice served a dual purpose: on week days it was the school, on Sundays it was the church. In some cases it even aspired to do the work of a cathedral! The first concern of Bishop Murphy in Adelaide had been the erection of a 'large and commodious school-house' which was to be used as a temporary place of worship . . . until the Cathedral . . . [could] be erected'.[35] Vaughan, too, putting a temporary roof over St Mary's Cathedral then in process of erection, shelved all building plans and diverted the whole of his cathedral income to the cause of education.[36]

This practice, adopted as an emergency in certain dioceses, was later accepted as general policy. According to the First Plenary Council, the school was to take precedence of the church itself (*ipsa sacra sedes scholae postponatur*), being built without delay (*statim . . . primitus*) and, if necessary, used as a church in the meantime.[37]

In this the Australian bishops deliberately reversed the precedent created by their brother bishops in America. There, it is true, the primary parochial school was given a high priority, but it was definitely *post ecclesiam parochialem* and not *ante*.[38] Where, too, the American Catholics had invested heavily in institutions for secondary and even tertiary education, the Australians had gone the other way round. It was their agreed policy to develop a complete system of elementary parochial

---

[32] The Second Plenary Council of Australia quoted here the educational decrees of the Third Plenary Council of Baltimore, 1884. *Conc. Plen.*, II, 1895, decr. 313.

[33] 'Catholic Education', Information Service, June 1951, p. 1.

[34] This idea had been stated before by the Anglican Bishop Broughton. Debates on education, 1839. Quoted in Rev. F. T. Whitington, *Augustus Short: First Bishop of Adelaide*, p. 104.

[35] *The South Australian Almanack and General Directory*, p. 71.

[36] Catholic Education Board (Sydney), 1883-4. Minute Book (Archives, St Mary's Cathedral, Sydney).

[37] *Conc. Plen.*, I, 1885, decr. 240.

[38] Decree of Third Plenary Council of Baltimore, 1884, quoted in *Conc. Plen.*, II (Aust.), decr. 313.

St. MARY'S COLLEGE, LYNDHURST, GLEBE.

8. ST MARY'S COLLEGE, LYNDHURST, GLEBE, IN THE 1870S

From the original in the Mitchell Library, Sydney

schools first; this done, others might follow. The reasons the bishops had in pursuing this policy were explained by Archbishop Carr in an address he gave in 1916 in connection with a Catholic college then being planned at the University of Melbourne. 'The Catholic Church,' he said, 'like the wise man in the gospel, looked first to the foundation of the house . . . primary education. Next she built the walls of secondary education. It was only when these two were securely provided she thought to crown the edifice with a roof—university education.'[39]

Where the policy of 'schools before churches' had not already been observed, it began, after the promulgation of the Council's decree, to be followed on a much wider scale than before. Subsequent Councils drew attention to it,[40] and bishops alluded to it in their pastorals and addresses.[41] Bishop Gibney, for example, informed the Catholic people of Western Australia that his desire to provide educational facilities for the people of his diocese was so great that he had resolved never to 'allow a Catholic Church to be erected where a school room [was] needed'.[42] Dr Reynolds of Adelaide likewise 'had gloried in the erection of Churches, but he almost regretted that he had been instrumental in the erection of so many. Could he start his episcopate again he would never erect a Church until he had first of all started a school'.[43]

But primary schools were not the only concern of the Church. For the nineteenth century, it is true, the education of the masses involved only a primary education; but, even though this branch became its first concern, secondary education was by no means neglected nor its importance in any way underestimated.

SECONDARY SCHOOLS: BOYS'

The Early Phase

In the development of Catholic secondary schools, both boys' and girls', several distinct phases can be observed. In the case of the boys' schools, for example, four separate periods are discernible: first, the early phase under the first bishops in Australia; second, the later early phase under the new suffragan bishops of the sixties and seventies; third, the phase corresponding with the great influx of religious orders after the seventies; and fourth, the present stage, the beginning of which coincided with the entry of the state into the field of secondary

[39] Address of Archbishop Carr at Warrnambool, Victoria. *Argus*, 6 March 1916, p. 6, f.
[40] Pastoral Letter of the Cardinal Delegate, Fourth Plenary Council, 1895, p. 19.
[41] E.g., in address of Dr O'Reilly, Archbishop of Adelaide, to people of North Adelaide. *Southern Cross*, 3 February 1899, p. 75.
[42] In a speech at Greenough, W.A. Quoted in Reilly, J. T., *Reminiscences of Fifty Years' Residence in Western Australia*, p. 494.   [43] *Adelaide Observer*, 21 July 1888.

education towards the end of the first decade of the present century. This last phase might conveniently be further sub-divided into the pre-World War II period and the post-1945 period which ushered in the 'secondary education for all' phase.

The type of education characteristic of the first period was determined largely by the condition of society at the time. Education was a special need in a new country like Australia. Preoccupied, as the great mass of the population was, with the arduous task of eking out an existence, deprived too of the ordinary comforts and encouragements that an older society would have provided, and leavened with a stock which, whether guiltless of crime or not, had lain under a social ban, the people were in constant danger of losing the power to appreciate the higher things in life. Not only therefore must the leaders of society labour, as Abbot Gregory wrote, 'to produce the results of a sound and liberal education, but . . . also to create amongst [their] people the taste and power to appreciate them'.[44] For this purpose some scheme of higher education was necessary—an education that would transcend the mere bread-and-butter preoccupations of the masses and prepare an *élite* from among whom the offices of Church and state could eventually be filled.[45] In each of the early colonies, therefore, an attempt was made to establish at least one Catholic secondary school.

The first of such schools was St Mary's Seminary in New South Wales. This school Polding established in his own house at Woolloomooloo, Sydney, in 1837, shortly after his arrival in the colony;[46] later on it was removed from Woolloomooloo to the grounds of St Mary's Cathedral. Its first president was the Reverend Charles Lovat, a Stonyhurst man, whom Dr Ullathorne had selected specially for the position.[47] Polding had intended to open the seminary earlier, but the 'almost total absence of pecuniary means', as he described it, and the 'small available force' he could spare to staff it made the whole venture an 'experiment' he had 'some dread to hazard, seeing that there [were] several schools with means of every kind already established'; and failure, he realized, 'would have spread a fatal influence over many years'.[48] With the

[44] In this the Abbot is setting out Polding's aims. Ragguaglio della Missione nolla Nuova Olanda. Printed in Birt, Rev. Norbert, *Benedictine Pioneers in Australia*, vol. 2, p. 173.

[45] Petition of Roman Catholic citizens to Commissioner Bigge, 12 February 1820. Bigge Appendix, vol. 127, p. 3943, B.T., box 21 (ML).

[46] See Mgr. J. McGovern, 'John Bede Polding', *Australasian Catholic Record*, vol. ix, no. 4, p. 199. 'Reminiscences of Old St Mary's Seminary', *Freeman's Journal*, 30 December 1876.

[47] 'I have fitted up,' wrote Polding, 'by means of the Australian funds the Chapel House for a School and Seminary on a small scale. As soon as Mr Lovat comes, whom Mr Ullathorne gives me reason to expect shortly, I shall open the Seminary.' Polding to Heptonstall, 6 June 1836. Printed in Birt, op. cit., vol. 1, p. 306.

[48] Ibid.

coming of Lovat, on the other hand, the new venture was firmly established and, for the better part of twenty years, remained the only official Catholic boys' secondary school in Sydney.

By the fifties, however, Polding saw the need of expansion. In order that wealthy Catholics might be able to provide their sons with an opportunity of sharing in the inheritance of the cultural riches of the Church which was theirs by right, he proposed a more ambitious scheme of higher education, one that would provide Catholics with an institution capable of preparing boys not only for the church but for the university and the civil service as well.[49] It is not unlikely, furthermore, that Polding saw in this project a means of bolstering up and revivifying the morale of his own Benedictine community, since to their care the new college would be confided.[50] Accordingly, a second St Mary's, this time St Mary's College (Plate 8), was opened in 1852.[51]

This new college was established on the site of a former Anglican College of St James[52] on the Lyndhurst estate, a mile or two out of the city. Its first President was the Rt Reverend C. H. Davis, O.S.B., who had come out to Australia to be Bishop of Maitland, but who never occupied his see. A scholar with a record of fine scholastic associations, the 'object of Downside's worship',[53] he appears to have been the very man to give effect to Polding's plans. As well as reorganizing St Mary's Seminary,[54] which still continued as a day-school, he proposed plans for Lyndhurst which, had they been carried into effect, would have made it quite different from an ordinary secondary school. Being himself a useful member of the senate of the newly founded University of Sydney, he attempted to have the college affiliated with that insitution in such a way that young men might study in Lyndhurst and yet take out degrees in the University. Dr Woolley, the Chancellor, and others on the senate of the University, opposed Davis's plan and even invoked the support of the Colonial Secretary, Deas Thomson, in opposition to it.

Woolley's grounds of objection were twofold: in the first place, if such affiliation were granted to Lyndhurst, it could not very well be withheld from other places which, he said, might be 'unfit to prepare candidates for our degree'.[55] Secondly, it would entirely destroy the significance of university teaching; and in support of this argument he quoted the precedent created by Oxford in regard to a similar suggestion

49 Polding's aim is stressed by Marie Forster who has made a special study of Benedictine education in Australia. See 'Lyndhurst and Benedictine Education', pt. 1, *Australasian Catholic Record*, October 1946, p. 261.

50 Ibid.   51 *Ordo Divini Officii Recitandi*, p. 79.

52 *Sydney Morning Herald*, 22 December 1846; Forster, op. cit., p. 263.

53 This is Birt's description of Dr Davis. Forster, op. cit., p. 265.

54 McMahon, Rev. J. J., 'History of Catholic Secondary Education in New South Wales'. Australian Catholic Historical Society Records, Sydney, 1950, p. 2.

55 Letter, Woolley to Deas Thomson, 1 September 1853. Deas Thomson Papers, vol. 3, pp. 471-4 (ML).

from the High Church party in England. Reluctant to regard itself only as a place for granting degrees, Oxford had rejected the High Church proposal on the ground that university education was not merely a matter of acquiring scientific knowledge; it implied something more, something 'derived from the academical life', intangible, and communicated by the '*genius loci*'. Sydney, according to Woolley, did not want to become a second London University.[56]

Notwithstanding this setback, Lyndhurst would appear to have realized most of Polding's hopes. The founding of the University had created a demand for Catholic institutions of the Lyndhurst type as a means of bridging over the gap between elementary and higher education; and the Church itself stood in great need of a learned and cultured Catholic laity which would further its interests and uphold its prestige.[57] Both these objects were achieved. At the University itself no other school could boast of more successful alumni: of the forty-five Catholic graduates by 1874, thirty-five were ex-students of Lyndhurst. In the learned professions, too, Lyndhurst men predominated: by the eighties half of Sydney's Masters and Bachelors of Arts and most of its Doctors of Laws were products of Lyndhurst; and the greater number of these had graduated with honours in classics, mathematics, physics and chemistry.[58]

What Polding achieved in Sydney, others attempted to achieve elsewhere. In Perth, in 1846, Dr Brady established St John's College,[59] having for that purpose, according to the prospectus, 'brought from Europe Professors,[60] whose literary qualifications and experience, it [was]

---

[56] Ibid.   [57] This idea is emphasized by Dr McMahon, op. cit., p. 2.

[58] Forster, Marie, 'Lyndhurst and Benedictine Education', pt. iii. *Australasian Catholic Record*, April 1947, p. 119. All sorts of prizes went to ex-Lyndhurst men with, as Forster says, 'monotonous regularity'. Some of the prizes carried off by them in the seventies were:

The Levy Scholarship	1867	P. Farrell
General Proficiency	1870	W. A. Hynes
,, ,,	1871	*idem*
,, ,,	1872	E. Butler
,, ,,	1873	*idem*
The Cooper Scholarship	1872	W. A. Hynes
	1873	T. Butler
The Barker Scholarship	1873	E. J. Butler
The Deas Thomson Scholarship	1873	E. Butler
	1875	T. Butler
The Lithgow Scholarship	1872	E. Butler
	1872	T. Butler
The Belmore Medal	1874	E. Butler
The Morris Alexander Bursary	1875	E. Raper

[59] See reference to this in letter, Bishop Serra to Henry Wakehurst, Private Secretary to Governor Kennedy, 24 June 1857, no. 1036, p. 5. C.S.O. Records, 1857, encl. v, 380 (WA-A).

[60] One of these, Nicola Caporelli, had an interesting career. It is not known that he had any skill or experience at teaching, but he carried with him, presumably to add to his prestige and importance in the colony, a parchment proclaiming him, under the Seal

hoped, [would] ensure success for the college, and merit, under his [Brady's] auspices, the esteem of a discerning and enlightened public'.[61] The college was open for students of all denominations, provided they could produce testimonials of character and be recommended by some 'respectable person of known standing in the colony'.[62] The first President of the college appears to have been the Very Reverend J. Joostens,[63] who was replaced after the first year by a layman, Farley.[64] But the college[65] had a remarkably short career. After 1847 it is not heard of again.[66]

The following year, 1848, saw the opening of the first Catholic secondary school in Victoria, a few months after Dr Goold's appointment as first Bishop of Melbourne. The institution was known as St Francis's Seminary; and, although it is believed[67] to have been, like its counterpart in Sydney, for both clerical and lay students, Goold himself describes it in his diary simply as a 'Seminary for Ecclesiastical

---

of the Holy See, Pontifical Consul-General in Australia for the Papal States—'with all the ordinary faculties of exercising the Consular jurisdiction and of enjoying all the honours, privileges and emoluments that are attached to the office'. (Translation of official document of his appointment. The document is signed by Cardinal Deacon Riario Sforza, Chamberlain to Pope Gregory XVI, 15 April 1845, Governor's Duplicate Despatches, 1845-6.) Caporelli presented his papers to the Governor, Sir Andrew Clarke, in July 1846. Clarke sent them to Earl Grey. Grey passed them on to the Foreign Affairs Dept., which sent them to Italy for verification. Campbell Scarlett, who received them at Florence, sent them on to Petre at Rome. Giovanni Corboli Bussi assured Petre that they were genuine and prayed that they would be recognized by the 'Regal Britannic Government' (Duplicate translation from Rome, 7 June 1847). Eventually they were returned to Grey, who informed Clarke: 'It appears to me to be a sufficient reason for declining to recognize the appointment of a consul to act for any foreign State in a British Colony that the Consul so appointed would have no consular duties to perform.' Grey to Clarke, 12 February 1847, Duplicate Desp. no. 17, C.O.D., 1847 (WA-A).

Caporelli left the colony in 1848. See Shipping Intelligence, *Inquirer* (Perth), 29 October 1848.

For other details see C. Gamba, 'A Papal Consul-General in Western Australia, 1846', *Australian Quarterly*, December 1949, pp. 101-5.

[61] 'Perth Catholic College', prospectus in *Perth Gazette*, 7 March 1846, p. 2, a.

[62] Ibid.   [63] Blue Book: Colony of Western Australia, 1846, p. 142.

[64] Letter to editor from 'A Friend to Education', *Inquirer*, 20 October 1847, p. 4, a. A certain John O'Reilly, who was giving public lectures on 'Grammar and Logic' every Saturday evening in the college was the Professor of Mathematics and Philosophy on the college staff. *Perth Gazette*, 6 June 1846, p. 1, b.

[65] The actual site of the college is not revealed, but the Prospectus describes it in full colour: 'The site of the College is in the suburbs of Perth, retired from the hustle of the town and sequestred from every distraction; immediately over it is a rising and beautiful hill, which commands a delightful prospect of Perth, the Swan River, and all the variegated picturesque scenery which environs the town; this will serve for recreation ground, and is exceedingly well adapted for invigorating the spirits and preserving the health.' *Perth Gazette*, 7 March 1846, p. 2, a.

[66] The college was still functioning at the end of 1847. W. Dacres Williams, Master of the Colonial Free School, in a letter to the editor of the *Inquirer* (1 December 1847, p. 3), referred contemptuously to the 'Bishop's College' which would 'soon offer the increased desideratum of having a master a-piece for a select number of pupils!'

[67] Corrigan, Br Urban, *The Achievements of Catholic Education in Australia*, p. 21.

students'.[68] Earlier Dr Geoghegan and Father R. Walsh had been interested in a non-denominational venture which, under the name of Port Phillip College,[69] was to have provided secondary education for the colony; but the project never matured. St Francis's itself, under the presidency of Dr Sheil, the future Bishop of Adelaide, eventually grew into St Patrick's College, which, by means of a government grant[70] five years later, was established on Eastern Hill (Plate 9).

The following year, 1854, the Reverend P. Dunne approached the Denominational Schools Board on the matter of establishing a Catholic Grammar School at Geelong.[71] The Board complied, and within a year the school, under the title of St Mary's Superior Boys' Boarding and Day School was in full swing. The time had come, thought Father Dunne, when such schools were essential, particularly since they would act as 'feeders' to the grammar schools and University.[72] Owing to some misunderstanding, however, between Dunne and his Bishop, the school did not survive.

At this time, 1856, the Austrian Jesuits, who had settled in South Australia eight years earlier, opened at Sevenhill the first Jesuit college in Australia—St Aloysius'.[73] Meanwhile, a secondary school had been opened in Hobart. An English priest, Father William Bond, who had spent ten years in Van Diemen's Land as a chaplain to convicts,[74] was requested by Bishop Willson upon the cessation of transportation in 1853 to remain in the island in order to establish a secondary school for boys.[75] Accordingly in 1854, with Father Bond as president, St Mary's Seminary, Hobart, opened its doors.[76] The institution was successful,[77]

[68] Bishop Goold's Diary. Quoted in Moran, Cardinal P. F., *History of the Catholic Church in Australia*, p. 730.

[69] 'Garryowen' (Edmund Finn), *The Chronicles of Early Melbourne*, p. 630. Fathers Geoghegan and Walsh attended several of these meetings and lent the movement their support (*Port Phillip Gazette*, 15 August 1840, p. 2). An outline of the course to be given in the college was drawn up, also the 'fundamental truths' which were agreed upon as forming the basis of the course in Religious Knowledge. It was further announced that a Catholic Bishop of Madras, India, had given his sanction for such a college in that city. *Melbourne Directory* (Kerr's), 1840, p. 186.

[70] An account of this and other grants for similar colleges for other denominations is given in Rankin, D. H., *The History of the Development of Education in Victoria*, p. 210.

[71] Letter, Dunne to Chairman, D.S.B., 27 December 1854. D.S.B. (Vic.), Inward Letters, 1854 (v-A).

[72] Letter, Dunne to Chairman, D.S.B., Geelong, 5 April 1855. This school was in McKillop Street. New premises, apparently, were found later in the year in Gheringhap Street. Letter to Board, 17 October 1855. D.S.B. (Vic.), Inward Letters, 1855 (v-A).

[73] *Jesuit Directory and Year Book*, p. 167.

[74] Enclosure in Despatch no. 257, Denison to Duke of Norfolk, 25 November 1853. Governor's Duplicate Despatches, vol. 79, p. 1109 (T-A).

[75] Kelsh, Rev. Thomas, *Personal Recollections of the Rt Rev. R. W. Willson*, p. 68.

[76] Ibid., p. 148.

[77] Report of Royal Commission on Superior Education, evidence of Inspector J. J. Stutzer, p. 32, *P.P.*(Tas.), 1860, paper 18. In 1858, the school achieved some success in the Newcastle scholarship, and four of its pupils ranked high in the public examinations of 1860. *Mercury* (Hobart), 4 April 1860, p. 3, e.

students coming to it even from the mainland,[78] but when Father Bond returned to Europe in 1860 it collapsed.[79]

The same year the government in the new colony of Queensland passed its Grammar School Act,[80] whereby it became lawful for it to assist, on a half-and-half basis, in the establishment of grammar schools provided, as the Act stated, that a 'sum of not less than £1,000 [should] have been raised by donation or subscription'.[81] But the Act remained a dead letter: no one was found to give it expression until Bishop Quinn arrived.[82] Having brought with him teachers for just such a project,[83] the Bishop set about collecting funds to raise the necessary amount. Within six months he was able to put down as his guarantee the sum of £5,000 —£3,000 for a grammar school in Brisbane,[84] and £2,000 for another at Ipswich[85]—and asked that the Governor might order suitable sites to be made over to him so that he could 'prepare proper plans and specifications'.[86]

Immediately there was an outcry from the Protestant section of the community. The Catholics, according to the *Moreton Bay Courier,* were desirous of receiving additional subscriptions from Protestants, and, in return, promised to employ a certain number of Protestant teachers, being prepared even 'to accept the principles of the national system as the basis of their operations'.[87] Protestants, the correspondent continued, had better bestir themselves or else be prepared to accept their education 'from the liberality of the Catholics'. But the government demurred, obviously unwilling to accept Quinn's offer. Its proposal to reconsider the matter the *Courier* dismissed as a 'shuffling pretext' for further delay. If the government would not honour its promise, then the only alternative was to repeal the Act.[88]

The fiercest opposition to Quinn's plan came from the Nonconformist party through the *Queensland Guardian.* Admitting the 'high and holy mission' on which the Bishop had come to the colony and the 'wide

[78] A fact which necessitated Father Hall's travelling to Victoria to collect debts. Kelsh, op. cit., p. 148.

[79] The main reason for Father Bond's return to England was to assist at the death-bed of one of his parents. *Mercury* (Hobart), 4 April 1860, p. 3, e.

[80] Act, 24 Vic., no. vii.

[81] Ibid., clause 1.

[82] Report of Select Committee on Education on the Board of General Education, evidence of Dean Rigney, p. 57, *P.P.*(Q'ld.), 1861, I, p. 661. See also Report of Royal Commission on Education, written evidence of Dr James Quinn, p. 120, *P.P.*(Q'ld.), 1875, II, p. 83.

[83] Reference to this was made by Ratcliffe Pring, Attorney General, during debates on Sir Samuel Griffith's Bill to abolish the non-vested schools in 1874. *Parl. Deb.* (Q'ld.), 16, 1874, p. 503. See also *Moreton Bay Courier,* 18 July 1861, p. 3.

[84] Letter, Rigney to Col. Sect. (20/61), 22 June 1861 (copy in Archives, Archbishop's palace, 'Wynberg', Brisbane).

[85] Letter, Rigney to Col. Sect. (21/61), 5 July 1861 (copy in Wynberg Archives). See also *Guardian* (Q'ld.), 17 July 1861, p. 3.

[86] Letter, Rigney to Col. Sect. (21/61).

[87] Reported by Ipswich correspondent in *Moreton Bay Courier,* 18 July 1861, p. 3.

[88] Ibid.

principles of his church' which prompted this action of his in regard to the education of youth, the paper took the view that he could not be 'supposed to be acquainted with the views of the legislature in passing the Act'.[89] Those views, according to the *Guardian,* were that 'the education to be given in [the] Grammar Schools should be secular only, and that no ecclesiastical influence should be exerted in their management'. If the Act did not convey this impression, and admittedly it did not, then it was 'clear' (to the *Guardian* at any rate) 'that it require[d] revision'.[90]

But the Act was not revised. Instead, Quinn was informed by the Executive Council[91] that the intention of the Act was to 'establish schools on strictly unsectarian principles, that is to say, schools open to all classes and denominations irrespective of peculiar tenets',[92] to which the Bishop replied that he 'never contemplated to establish any sectarian schools that would not be open to all classes of denominations of Her Majesty's subjects'.[93]

Unperturbed, he went ahead, selected a site for his Brisbane school, and asked that the allotments concerned be reserved for him for this purpose.[94] In the meantime, immediate preparations were put in hand for the opening of the school in temporary quarters;[95] but the government, deterred apparently by the wave of bitter sectarian rancour[96] which

[89] *Guardian* (Q'ld.), 3 July 1861, p. 2, c, d.

[90] Letter, Rigney to editor, *Moreton Bay Courier,* 23 July 1861, p. 2, e; also 29 July 1861, p. 2, e, f. See the *Guardian's* reply, 24 July 1861, p. 2.

[91] Col. Sect., in answer to question from Mr Raff in Leg. Assembly, 17 July 1861, P.P.(Q'ld), 1860, p. 176.

[92] Letter, A. W. Manning, C.S.O., to Rigney, 22 July 1861 (copy in Wynberg Archives).

[93] As a precedent for his argument Rigney instanced St Stephen's 'where children of the various denominations [were] receiving excellent primary education without interference with their religious tenets'. Rigney to Col. Sect., 26 July 1861 (copy in Wynberg Archives).

[94] The allotments he wanted were nos. 243, 244, and 246, situated in the eastern suburbs of north Brisbane. Rigney to Col. Sect., 30 July 1861 (copy in Wynberg Archives).

[95] A notice in the *Moreton Bay Courier* (20 July 1861, p. 2) ran: 'A grammar school under supervision of Dr Quinn, the Catholic Bishop, was temporarily opened in Brisbane Monday last.' Three days later the following letter appeared from Dean Rigney: 'The Grammar School is not yet open, properly speaking. All that has yet been done is merely preliminary. The boys have been carefully examined, and some efforts have been made to assign them their several classes; and their relative attainments, tastes, prospects, and destinations have been the subject of patient and skilful investigation. The house on Wickham Terrace is undergoing some necessary alterations; suitable school furniture, fittings and proper apparatus are nearly ready. Arrangements are in progress for opening classes, after another week or two, in the ancient classics, three modern European languages—French, German, and Italian—mathematics, geography, and natural science. Highly accomplished professors are ready to conduct these classes under the patronage of the Bishop . . . ' (ibid., 23 July 1861, p. 2, e). These professors were most probably laymen. They could not have been the French Assumptionists, as Tissot and his companion sailed with Quinn, the day before, for the north (shipping list, ibid.).

[96] A series of meetings, particularly at Ipswich, ended in unseemly chaos. The Nonconformist bodies grouped themselves, it would seem, so as to prevent the government's

Quinn's move had aroused, eventually shelved the idea of grammar schools on the grounds that its funds were so small 'as to preclude the possibility of affording the rate of assistance to more than one school'; and, since Quinn's was the only school offering at the time, it would absorb all the funds. Thus 'the very object of the grant would be frustrated'.[97]

Nothing more happened until 1864 when, without any government aid, Father Brunn, one of the French Assumptionists whom Quinn had brought out with him, opened a secondary school at Ipswich. But the venture was short-lived.[98]

Three years later, when there was question of establishing a grammar school by another group of interested citizens, Quinn renewed his application for assistance, assuring the government that he was prepared to abide by their interpretation of the Act, and to conduct it, as they insisted, on purely non-sectarian lines.[99] This was not what the Bishop would have desired, but it was the best he could expect. With the privilege, as principal donor, of nominating three of the seven trustees,[1] he believed he would be able to exclude hostile religious teaching and to exercise some control over the appointment of professors.

In going so far the Bishop was obviously making a concession and exposing himself to criticism among his own flock. He went 'to the utmost limit', he said, 'to which it was lawful for [him] to go'. Some felt that he was going beyond it. In any case, it was to no purpose; the government refused to act.[2]

The Bishop's plans actually went much further than those of the government. Besides the grammar school he himself was endeavouring

---

following out the terms of the Grammar School Act and making a grant to the Catholics. Of the committee of fourteen to arrange for a grammar school at Ipswich eight men were elected to represent the Presbyterians, Wesleyans, Independents and Baptists, yet according to one of the Catholic representatives who claimed to quote from previous census returns, 'these four denominations numbered not exactly half the number of Catholics and not above one-third of the members of the Church of England'. The first meeting on 21 July 1861 ran from 7.30 p.m. till after midnight. It was orderly for a time but the last part was 'little else than a scene of tumult'. It was adjourned. (*Moreton Bay Courier*, 22 July 1861, p. 2, f, g; *Guardian*, 21 July 1861, p. 3.) The second meeting 'ended in an uproar'. (*Courier*, 29 August 1861, p. 3, c, d.) The *Guardian* gave a full leader on 'the very deplorable proceedings', 31 August 1861, p. 2.

[97] Letter, Manning to Rigney, C.S.O., 5 August 1861 (copy in Wynberg Archives). In this letter the Colonial Secretary made it clear that the government would not make any grant 'except in cases where different denominations shall co-operate in the establishment of Grammar Schools'.

[98] This fact was told to the writer by the present Archbishop of Brisbane, Dr Duhig.

[99] Letter, Quinn to Col. Sect., 18 October 1867. Report of Royal Commission on Education, 1875. Appendix F, p. 19. P.P.(Q'ld.).

[1] Dr Quinn, himself, made this clear: ' . . . it is not in the power of the donor, even though he should desire, to frustrate the object of the Act, which provides for its own administration by seven trustees, the majority of whom are to be appointed by the Governor in Council.' Letter, Quinn to Col. Sect., 20 November 1867, Report of Royal Commission, 1875, p. 121.

[2] Ibid.

to set up in Brisbane, he envisaged three or four such schools, scattered in different parts of the colony and belonging to other bodies. Such a plan, he believed, would have the

additional advantage of forming the basis of a university, which might be called into existence, whenever the Government thought it desirable, by erecting into a University Board the heads or some of the Professors of such institutions, together with such other men of science and letters outside them . . .

On this principle, he claimed, the best modern universities, such as the London University and the University of Belgium, were formed.[3] Quinn's ideas, however, were too advanced for the young colony and he had to wait until 1875 before he was to see the establishment of his own secondary school. The University he was never to see.

The Second Phase

Whilst Dr Quinn was trying to induce the government to assist him with his grammar school project in Queensland further developments had taken place in the other colonies. Earlier, in the sixties, the Catholic journal in Victoria, the *Advocate,* had been pressing the government to offer some assistance to secondary education. 'With us,' (i.e., Catholics), it said, 'there are no leisured classes, that is synonymous with superior education. And there can be little doubt that the best wisdom of Parliament should be employed on the same question at the earliest opportunity.'[4] Similar views had been expressed even before this in New South Wales. Without a secondary department of instruction, the *Australian* had pointed out, 'the organization of Christian education would be gravely defective'.[5] Then at the end of the sixties, according to some authorities,[6] the question of secondary education was discussed by the bishops assembled in Melbourne for their Provincial Council. Certainly, during the succeeding decade, a new interest in Catholic secondary schools is discernible throughout nearly all the colonies.

In New South Wales three new colleges were opened in quick succession—one at Bathurst, another at Maitland, and a third at Goulburn. Vaughan, at the opening of the last-named college, said that he saw in this new chain of colleges the dawn of another era, the portent of new developments: 'I see in my dreams flourishing domes of learning arising in each of the dioceses of this great continent, and the choicest

---

[3] Letter, Quinn to Col. Sect., 18 October 1867. Report of Royal Commission, 1875. See also *Moreton Bay Courier,* 23 July 1861, p. 2.

[4] *Advocate,* 6 March 1869, p. 9.

[5] *Australian* (Sydney), 31 January 1885.

[6] This is the view taken by Corrigan and McMahon. (Corrigan, op. cit., p. 21; McMahon, op. cit., p. 7.) Neither writer gives his authority for this view, and it is difficult to discover just how they attribute this new interest to the 1869 Council.

specimens of rising genius concentrating from each of them upon the great college of St John' (the Catholic college within the University of Sydney).[7]

Previously, with the exception of Lyndhurst and St Mary's Seminary in Sydney, there had been no intermediate schools between St John's and the primary schools of the colony. Now, said the *Freeman's Journal*, the 'broken link' in the Catholic educational chain was being mended.[8]

The first of these new secondary schools was St Stanislaus', Bathurst. Actually, it had been established by Bishop Matthew Quinn[9] as St Stanislaus' High School early in 1867, two years before the Provincial Council mentioned above.[10] Its first president was Father James McGirr and its principal teacher Mr Michael McGirr, former headmaster of the Catholic denominational school at Bathurst.[11] The High School itself was housed in rooms made available in the denominational school. Later, boarders were taken and domiciled in adjacent cottages; thereupon the name was changed to St Stanislaus' College. Finally, in 1873, a permanent home was found for the whole plant in a new building specially designed for the purpose on the hill just outside Bathurst.[12]

In the year before St Stanislaus' was finally established in its permanent home the Maitland project was launched. Like St Stanislaus', it too began as a high school: the 'Sacred Heart' Catholic High School it was called.[13] From the beginning, however, boarders were received.[14] In 1875 it was given the name, Sacred Heart College, and officially opened as such in October of that year. Its first president was Father M. Matthews; its headmaster was a layman by the name of Canty, who conducted the school with a staff of other lay teachers.[15] In the same year the third of this series of new secondary schools was opened at Goulburn by Bishop Lanigan. The college was dedicated to St Patrick and given as its first president the accomplished scholar and future Bishop, Dr Gallagher.[16]

Similar developments were taking place in the southern colonies. In South Australia Bishop Sheil established in North Adelaide a new secondary school for boys under the title of St Francis Xavier's Seminary,

[7] *Freeman's Journal*, 7 February 1874, p. 10, c.
[8] *Freeman's Journal*, 3 January 1874, p. 8, d.
[9] Dr Quinn made this clear in his address to the people of Orange in September 1867. *Times* (Bathurst), 11 September 1867, p. 2, g.
[10] *Times* (Bathurst), 25 December 1867, p. 2, c. See also Moran, op. cit., p. 626.
[11] Hall, Rev. John, *History of St. Stanislaus' College, Bathurst*. pp. 26, 27.
[12] Ibid., pp. 27-8.
[13] Advertisement in *Freeman's Journal*, 18 October 1873, p. 1, b.
[14] Both Corrigan and McMahon, who seems to be following Corrigan, place the beginning in 1875. This is incorrect: arrangements were made for receiving boarders right from 1873. *Freeman's Journal*, 18 October 1873, p. 1, b.
[15] *Ordo Divini Officii Recitandi*, p. 50. See also McMahon, op. cit., p. 9.
[16] Annals of St Patrick's College, Goulburn, p. 3 (Archives of St Patrick's College, Goulburn).

and appointed as its first president Father Bernard Nevin.[17] This was in 1871. The following year an attempt was made in Perth to revive the Catholic college that Dr Brady had established twenty-five years earlier. The public were 'respectfully informed' that under the patronage of His Lordship, Dr Griver, 'a Boarding School [had] been opened at the Subiaco House'.[18] The president was not named but, since all correspondence was to be addressed to the Reverend Matthew Gibney, it may be presumed that he had charge of it. An elaborate prospectus appeared in the Perth papers,[19] but apart from that nothing further was heard of the college; it apparently died an early death. In the same year St Mary's Seminary in Hobart, which had been closed since Father Bond's departure in 1860, was revived, its new Rector being Father Thomas Kelsh, who had been a pupil there under Father Bond.[20] While it was closed Catholic boys had been attending non-Catholic schools[21] and, indeed, many continued to do so even after it was reopened.[22] But, later in 1872,[23] its standing in the colony was considerably raised by its elevation to the status of 'Superior School',[24] which meant that it could then receive pupils awarded scholarships by the Council of Education.[25] By 1876, however, the doors of St Mary's had once more closed,[26] and were never opened again.

Nearly all the colleges established during this period followed the same pattern: the president was generally a member of the diocesan

[17] *Chaplet and Southern Cross* (S.A.), 30 September 1871, p. 283, a. At its resumption of studies in 1872, the staff consisted of Rev. B. Nevin, Rev. P. Byrne, Mr G. Williams, Mr W. McBride. *Chaplet and Southern Cross*, 22 January 1872.

[18] Announcement in *Perth Gazette and Western Australian Times*, 3 May 1872.

[19] See p. 363.

[20] *Catholic Standard* (Tas.), January 1872, p. 111, e.

[21] Particularly the Hutchins School. Royal Commission on Education, 1860, evidence of Rev. John Buckland, p. 28.

[22] After six months it had only forty students. *Catholic Standard* (Tas.), June 1872, p. 185, b.

[23] This was on 16 August 1872. *Mercury* (Hobart), 29 August 1872, p. 2, b, c. The *Mercury* took exception to this privilege granted to St Mary's: 'We see so many and so grave objections to it alone receiving that distinction' when other longer-established schools had been refused.

[24] Other 'superior' schools were the High School, Hutchins, Church Grammar (Launceston), and Horton College (Ross). Later, the rule allowing that scholarships be tenable only at these schools was expunged and replaced by the following: 'The exhibitions will be tenable at such schools as shall be named by the parent or guardian, and approved by the Council.' *Mercury*, 5 October 1872, p. 2, a.

[25] The Council of Education was established in 1858 by Act of Parliament. P.P.(Tas.), 1858, p. 195; also 'Rules and Regulations of Council of Education' in Third Report of Council of Education, P.P.(Tas.), 1863, paper 10.

Father Hall was a member of the Council until he died in 1867. Thereupon Dr Murphy and the Rev. Father Dunne were elected. Report of Council of Education, p. 4. P.P.(Tas.), 1867, paper no. 16. Besides being a member of the Council, Father Dunne was also a member of several local school boards. *Catholic Standard* (Tas.), January 1883, p. 3, a.

[26] *Walch's Tasmanian Almanac*, 1875, p. 153, reveals the seminary as still in operation. The same authority for 1876 (p. 156) makes no mention of it, from which it may be supposed that it closed at the end of 1875.

clergy, the rest of the staff were generally laymen. Sometimes, however, one or two more priests gave full-time or part-time services to the college. Thus three priests including the president were seconded to St Patrick's College in 1876,[27] and in Bathurst at the same period three had been appointed to St Stanislaus'.[28]

Besides these official Catholic secondary schools there were several others of a semi-official type, proprietary schools whose headmasters were generally the owners. In Sydney, before the arrival of Dr Polding, there were two such 'high-class' Catholic schools;[29] and even as late as 1872 there was still one in the Glebe district where it was possible to secure 'a thorough course in English, French, Latin and Mathematics'.[30]

In Victoria there was a long procession of these 'private' Catholic schools, Lucerne House Collegiate School being perhaps the most famous. Enjoying the patronage of Dr Goold, Lucerne House could boast of an experienced staff of distinguished teachers: W. C. Atchison, the headmaster, was formerly a professor at St Edmund's College, Ware, England; while the second master, James Plunket, an alumnus of St Mary's College, Oscott, had been the mathematics master at Sedgley Park Collegiate School, England.[31] Lucerne House had a some-what longer career than most of the others; starting in the middle fifties,[32] it was still functioning well into the sixties. Leaving Lucerne House about 1864, James Plunket opened Oscott House, Elsternwick, as a 'boarding school for young gentlemen'. This flourished around the end of the decade.[33] About the same time Dr Goold conferred his patronage on a college for Catholic boys in Ballarat. The principal of this college was a Stonyhurst man, J. W. Rogers,[34] who later became Inspector of schools under the Catholic Board of Education in Vaughan's time in Sydney.[35] Four other masters assisted Rogers.[36] Later, in the early seventies, another 'Catholic boarding and day school for young gentle-men' was opened in South Melbourne by Denis O'Donovan, formerly professor in the Collège Stanislaus (University of France) and the Collège des Hautes Études des Carmes, Paris.[37] O'Donovan had earlier

27 *Ordo Divini Officii Recitandi,* 1876, p. 76.   28 Ibid., p. 74.
29 McGuanne, John Percy, 'Early schools of New South Wales', *Journal and Proceedings of the Royal Australian Historical Society,* vol. 2, 1906, pt. iii, pp. 70-1, and vol. 2, 1906-7, pt. iii, pp. 73-87. See also McGuanne, John Percy, 'Early School Days in New South Wales' (read before the Australian Historical Society of New South Wales, 10 October 1906).   30 Advertisement, *Freeman's Journal,* 10 February 1872, p. 1, a.
31 Advertisement, *Herald* (Melbourne), 13 January 1855. See letter from the Rev. L. Sheil (later Bishop) to Chairman, D.S.B., 11 February 1856. D.S.B. (Vic.), Inward Letters, 1856 (v-A).   32 *Herald* (Melbourne), 17 January 1855.
33 *Advocate,* 2 January 1868, p. 1.
34 Advertisement in *Advocate,* 23 January 1869, p. 1.
35 Rogers, Report on Catholic Schools, 1883.
36 *Advocate,* 23 January 1869, p. 1. Later it was proposed to convert this school into a boarding college. See advertisement in *Advocate,* 20 February 1869, p. 15.
37 *Advocate,* 19 April 1873, p. 2, c.

conducted a similar school in Sydney.[38] Towards the end of the century appeared two more of these schools: the Victoria College in East Melbourne, conducted as a co-educational Catholic secondary school by a wholly lay staff under a principal named James McClean;[39] and a much better known school at Benalla, conducted by a certain Thomas McCristal. Later this college was removed to Mentone where it became known as Mentone College.[40]

South Australia and Tasmania also had their private Catholic secondary schools. In the fifties a David Cremen who had come from Sydney with Dr Murphy set up a 'Mathematical and Mercantile Academy' in Adelaide.[41] Late in the sixties Father Woods engaged the services of a layman named Besley, late of St Aloysius, Sevenhill, to conduct 'an upper school and also a commercial school'. The school was advertised as 'entirely guided by Father Woods in the studies, management, etc.', and 'under his supervision'.[42] Also under the direction of Father Woods was a 'Classical and Commercial Academy' conducted by a layman named McLaughlin.[43] Across Bass Strait, too, in the eighties, 'St Patrick's Seminary for Boys' at Launceston was offering Greek, Latin, French and mathematics but 'only in the senior classes'.[44]

The Third Phase

By this time the third stage in the development of Catholic secondary education had been reached. This phase, extending roughly from the eighties to the end of the first decade of the present century, was one of greater activity. Not only did it coincide with the great influx of religious in the eighties,[45] but it was contemporaneous also with the first three Plenary Councils each of which laid down important legislation concerning secondary education. The first of these Councils recommended that the number of secondary schools 'be increased'[46] and exhorted Catholics to 'keep alive [their] zeal in this important section of Christian education'. The Catholic primary school system, it said, would 'remain but half complete as long as its children could find no kindred atmosphere to pass on to when they [left] its protection'.[47] With secondary schools thus 'multiplied . . . [in] every town of reasonable size' parents were to be not only urged to allow their children to use them[48] but even obliged to do so ('gravi obligatione').[49]

[38] Freeman's Journal, 6 July 1867, p. 15, d.
[39] The wife of the principal cared for the small number of boarders. Advertisement in Advocate, 8 January 1898, p. 13, b.   [40] Advocate, 2 January 1904, p. 14, a.
[41] Commercial Directory and Almanac for 1856 (Young's), p. 60.
[42] S.C. and C.H., 20 January 1868, p. 65.   [43] S.C. and C.H., 20 April 1868, p. 124, a.
[44] This was in Launceston. Catholic Standard, January 1885, p. 205, a.
[45] See ch. 7.   [46] Conc. Plen., I, 1885, decr. 246.
[47] Pastoral Letter of First Plenary Council, 1885, p. 33.
[48] Decrees of the Diocesan Synod, Bathurst, 1883, decr. iv.
[49] Conc. Plen., IV, 1937, decr. 632.

A further fillip to the development of Catholic secondary schools came from the various government proposals to establish state grammar schools, as in New South Wales,[50] and to encourage secondary education generally by issuing scholarships and bursaries.

The effect of these developments was apparent from the eighties on, yet even in the seventies a new vitality was observed in New South Wales. In that colony profound changes were taking place. Benedictine education, never extremely popular, was obviously on the wane.[51] Associated, as it was, with Benedictine influence in the wider ecclesiastical life of the time, it was doomed to failure.[52] St Mary's Seminary had ceased to exist and Lyndhurst was already losing favour. Added to this was the fact that the education imparted at Lyndhurst, though of a superior type, was considered too ambitious for the needs of colonial life. Its strong classical bias[53] and its intimate connection with an ecclesiastical seminary[54] were factors which, in the eyes of the new commercial and trading classes, rendered its course of studies quite inappropriate.[55] It became obvious, therefore, as the seventies wore on, that Lyndhurst would not long survive Polding's death.[56] And this is exactly what happened: Polding died in March 1877,[57] and Vaughan closed the college a few months later.[58]

But from the remains of this last Benedictine college arose a host of other schools. Six thousand of the £30,000 realized from the first sales of the Lyndhurst estate was given to the Jesuits by Archbishop Vaughan to enable them to start St Ignatius' College, Riverview, in 1880.[59] The year before, the same Fathers had also opened a secondary school at St Kilda House in Woolloomooloo.[60] Four years before this first Jesuit foundation the Marist Brothers, in response to repeated requests from certain classes in Sydney,[61] had opened a secondary school of their own at St Patrick's, on Church Hill.[62] The school was an

[50] Act, 43 Vic., xxiii, clause 6, v.

[51] Forster, 'Lyndhurst and Benedictine Education', *Australasian Catholic Record*, pt. iii, p. 124.

[52] Ibid., pt. iii, p. 124; pt. iv, p. 205-6. See also *Freeman's Journal*, 26 February 1859; 20 December 1872, p. 8, d.

[53] See ch. 9.

[54] The ecclesiastical students from St Mary's Seminary had been transferred thither in the fifties. Besides being a seminary it also housed Benedictine novices.

[55] See McMahon, op. cit., p. 5.   [56] Forster, op. cit., pt. iii, p. 122.

[57] Moran, op. cit., p. 404.

[58] Forster, op. cit., pt. iv, p. 208.

[59] Ibid., p. 209. See *Jesuit Directory and Year Book*, 1950, p. 185.

[60] Ibid., p. 191. After 20 years (1883-93) in Surry Hills, this original Jesuit foundation, then known as St Aloysius' College, was transferred across the harbour to Milson's Point.

[61] Marist Brothers' Annals, pp. 4-5 (Archives, Provincial House, Mittagong, N.S.W.).

[62] Ibid., p. 11. The original High School, established at Church Hill and subsequently twice removed—in 1883 to St Mary's and in 1910 to Darlinghurst—still remained, at the end of the first half of the present century, as the oldest Catholic boys' secondary school in the archdiocese of Sydney. McMahon, op. cit., p. 10.

immediate success, and five years later the Brothers established a similar
school for boarders at Hunter's Hill.[63]

Meanwhile the bishops in the suffragan dioceses of New South Wales,
finding it increasingly difficult to spare enough priests from the mission
to staff their diocesan colleges, called in the services of the new orders
of priests and Brothers. In this way Sacred Heart College, Maitland,
was taken over by the Patrician Brothers, St Stanislaus', Bathurst, by
the Vincentians in 1889,[64] and St Patrick's, Goulburn, by the Christian
Brothers in 1897.[65] After a few years the Maitland college reverted to
the diocesan clergy under the rectorship of the Reverend P. V. Dwyer.
When the latter was appointed Coadjutor to Dr Murray in 1898, however, it was handed over to the Marist Brothers.[66]

In addition to replacing the diocesan clergy in the older colleges, the
religious began to open schools of their own. Thus the Christian Brothers,
who, on Cardinal Moran's invitation, had returned to Sydney in 1887,
immediately established secondary classes in the school at Balmain.[67]
This was followed by three other secondary schools set up by the Brothers
in rapid succession—St Joseph's, Lewisham, in 1889; St Charles', Waverley, in 1903; and St Patrick's, Strathfield, in 1908.[68] The Patrician
Brothers opened Holy Cross College, Ryde, in 1890;[69] St Patrick's at
East Armidale in 1892; and a high school in Bathurst later in the same
decade.[70] Closed temporarily in 1899, the College at Armidale was reopened as De La Salle College by the De La Salle Brothers in 1906.

All these new secondary schools in New South Wales met a need
which had long been felt. Between the University and the elementary
schools there had been only Lyndhurst (see p. 321); but that institution
was quite beyond the means of the humbler classes. In the sixties and
early seventies, it is true, the country colleges had opened; they helped
to close the gap somewhat,[71] and the Jesuit schools carried on where
Lyndhurst had left off, but the great bulk of the Catholic youth in and
around the metropolitan area had only the Marist Brothers' High School

[63] Marist Brothers' Annals, p. 22.

[64] Hall, Rev. John, History of St Stanislaus' College, Bathurst, p. 96.

[65] Annals of St Patrick's College, Goulburn, p. 4 (College Archives).

[66] McMahon, 'History of Catholic Secondary Education in New South Wales'.
This was in 1898. In 1904, the Brothers closed the boarding school on the argument
that the diocese had not honoured its part of the contract in effecting certain material
improvements. The day boys were transferred to St John's in Maitland itself, where
the Brothers had been conducting a day school. The college, however, had not been able
to compete with the new colleges in Sydney, St Joseph's and St Ignatius.

[67] McMahon, op. cit., p. 12.   [68] A.C.D., 1895, p. 65; 1910, p. 14.

[69] Ibid., 1900, p. 36.

[70] St Patrick's College was built by Bishop Elzear Torreggiani. It was staffed by the
Patrician Brothers from 1892 to 1899 when it was closed temporarily owing to shortage
of staff. Catholic Press, 18 January 1906; 8 February 1906.

[71] 'Our great College of St John's has been a comparative failure from want of
colleges like this [St Stanislaus' College, Bathurst] to prepare boys for matriculation'
(editor), Freeman's Journal, 13 September 1872, p. 8, b, c.

at St Mary's whither it had been transferred in 1883 from Church Hill.[72] Until the new secondary schools began to appear at the turn of the century,[73] this school remained the only middle class secondary school for boys. Those who could not be admitted there had to be content with what the primary schools could offer.[74]

In the other colonies the pattern of development was somewhat similar. Up to the sixties Dr Goold had found great difficulty in inducing religious orders to open schools in Victoria[75] and, to add to his embarrassment, his own diocesan college of St Patrick's in East Melbourne had fallen into insolvency and come close to ruin.[76] It was then that he managed to persuade the Jesuit Fathers to take over in 1865.[77] In the seventies the Fathers pushed ahead with the building of a second college which they opened at Kew in 1878 under the title of St Francis Xavier's.[78] The Christian Brothers, too, who reached the colony in 1868 lost no time in establishing secondary classes at their new place on Victoria Parade.[79] In subsequent years they opened further schools: at St Kilda in 1878,[80] and, in the early 1900s, at North Melbourne and South Melbourne.[81]

Facilities for secondary education were provided also in the country dioceses. The Christian Brothers, having sent a community to staff the primary school at Ballarat in 1876,[82] approached Bishop Moore about opening a boarding college. His Lordship refused, announcing at the same time his intention of establishing a college under an order of priests.[83] His choice fell upon the Holy Ghost Fathers who, at their famous Blackrock College in Dublin, had been achieving brilliant results in the Irish intermediate examinations.[84] In 1889, accordingly, a community of priests arrived and the new Holy Ghost College of Ballarat was opened with great *éclat*, the Bishop obviously intending it to be

---

[72] See note 52, above.

[73] For example, fees for the first of these high schools in Sydney were 6d., 9d., and 1s. This was the year 1875. Marist Brothers' Annals, p. 11.

[74] Letter to the editor from Jos. I. Spruson, jnr. *Freeman's Journal*, 11 January 1873, p. 9, b.

[75] A correspondent of the *Victorian* (13 June 1863), referred to the difficulty of introducing preceptorial orders into Australia: other countries were not willing to part with them.

[76] This failure of St Patrick's was regarded as having brought some discredit on the Church. Dr Goold acted resolutely and roused the clergy and laity to join him in wiping off 'this slight stain' upon the Catholic name. *Victorian*, 15 November 1862, p. 307.

[77] *Jesuit Directory and Year Book*, 1950, p. 227.   [78] Ibid.   [79] A.C.D., 1888, p. 87.

[80] Ibid. St Kilda was presenting pupils for matriculation by the end of the eighties. *Advocate*, 11 January 1890, p. 8, a.   [81] A.C.D., 1910, p. 63.

[82] Annals of St Patrick's College, Ballarat, p. 1 (Archives, St Patrick's College, Ballarat).   [83] Ibid., p. 3.

[84] See statistics of Irish examination results in P.J.H., 'The Intermediate Education System', *Christian Brothers' Educational Record*, 1893, pp. 214, 216, 217, 220:

Year	Best Catholic school	No. of exhibs.	Best Protestant school				No. of exhibs.
1879	Blackrock	11	Royal Acad. Inst. Belfast				10
1880	,,	14	,,	,,	,,	,,	8
1881	,,	30	,,	,,	,,	,,	12
1882	,,	17	,,	,,	,,	,,	7

second to none in the land.[85] The staff did not disappoint him,[86] for within a few months of the opening of the college some pupils were sent up for the University matriculation examinations—an action so gratifying to his Lordship that he encouraged the Fathers 'to look forward to a singularly brilliant future for their rising institute'.[87] But instead of the expected success, disaster followed: the first matriculation candidates failed, sickness thinned the ranks of the little community, and the superior, stunned and humiliated, returned to France.[88] A new president was appointed[89] and the Bishop grew even more prodigal with his encouragement;[90] but the college did not recover and in 1891 was closed. Two years later Dr Moore, not a little mortified at the failure of his scheme, invited the Christian Brothers to take over the college. They did so, but this time on their own terms;[91] what had been Holy Ghost College was then revived as St Patrick's.

Then followed other secondary schools. In 1902 the Christian Brothers opened St Joseph's College, Warrnambool,[92] and in 1893 the Marist Brothers opened colleges at Kilmore[93] and Bendigo.[94] Assumption College, Kilmore, was a secondary school from its inception, but the Bendigo school, although it sent up pupils for the University matriculation quite early in its career, did not organize official secondary classes until after 1900.[95]

In Queensland the struggle to provide secondary education for Catholic boys still continued. Dr Quinn never desisted. Repulsed by the government in 1861 and 1867, he turned elsewhere in the seventies. The Christian Brothers, who, it will be remembered, came to his assistance in 1875, established their school at St Stephen's[96] where, from the very beginning, stress was laid on the fact that it was intended for secondary education.[97] Within two years the Brothers' new college on

85 The boys themselves wore Eton suits for best wear. Annals of St Patrick's College, Ballarat, p. 4.
86 The first president, Father Reffe, C.S.Sp., was a former superior of the Blackrock College, Dublin. Others on the staff were Father Broagh, C.S.Sp., Father Brennan, C.S.Sp., and Father Schmidt, C.S.Sp. Advocate, 20 December 1890, p. 8, b.
87 Address of Dr Moore at First Annual Distribution of Prizes, 1889. Advocate, 4 January 1890, p. 7, c.   88 Annals of St Patrick's College, Ballarat, p. 5.
89 This was Father G. Lee. Advocate, 20 December 1890, p. 8, b.
90 'The College,' he said, 'had been an unqualified success. It was as yet only in its infancy. Institutions of its kind took time to develop. He knew there were a great many difficulties in establishing such a college, but he felt certain that, under the prudent and careful direction of the Reverend President (Father Lee) and the other Fathers, these difficulties would be surmounted.' Advocate, 27 December 1890, p. 8, b.
91 The terms were that (1) the Bishop took on himself all the existing financial liabilities, (2) that the deeds of the property be handed over to the Brothers. Annals of St Patrick's College, Ballarat, p. 7. The Bishop had never handed the deeds over to the Holy Ghost Fathers. Ibid., p. 4.
92 A.C.D., 1910, p. 73.   93 A.C.D., 1900, p. 58.   94 Ibid., p. 70.
95 Classes were then arranged: class vi (govt. merit), sub-matriculation, matriculation, Advocate, 2 January, 1894, p. 15, a.   96 Brisbane Courier, 6 July 1875, p. 3, c.
97 Ibid. See also Annals of Christian Brothers' College, Gregory Terrace, p. 5.

Gregory Terrace[98] was ready and the senior boys from St Stephen's moved in.[99]

But Dr Quinn, in his concern for the education of country boys, had wanted Gregory Terrace to be a boarding college. Hindered by certain scruples,[1] however, as well as by the financial burden involved in equipping a boarding school,[2] the Brothers refused; whereupon the Bishop established St Kilian's College in South Brisbane[3] and appointed the Reverend Dr John Cani[4] as its first president. Associated with Dr Cani on the staff were Father J. B. Breen[5] and, according to one contemporary authority,[6] some Christian Brothers. When Dr Cani was made Bishop of Rockhampton, however, in 1878, St Kilian's was closed and, at the Bishop's request, a few of the senior boarders were squeezed in at Gregory Terrace;[7] but after 1883 all boarders had to be excluded.[8] In 1886 Quinn's successor, Dr Dunne, pressed for a reopening of the boarding school and promised financial assistance for the additions required for the purpose. Eventually, in 1890, the Brothers decided to shift the boarding establishment to the country. Hence arose St Joseph's College, Nudgee, whither all boarders were transferred by 1892.[9]

Besides these two colleges in Brisbane, the Christian Brothers, during this period, opened four others in different parts of the colony: St Mary's, Ipswich, in the 1890s;[10] and, in the 1900s, St Patrick's, Toowoomba; St Mary's, Maryborough, and St Patrick's, Gympie.[11] All took secondary classes as well as primary.

At the other side of the continent the Christian Brothers, with more and more recruits from Ireland, were opening additional colleges. Their college on St George's Terrace, Perth, was opened in 1894,[12] that in Fremantle in 1901, and a third at Kalgoorlie in 1906.[13]

[98] Two ex-pupils from the Brothers' schools in Cork had, in the fifties, bought a plot of ground on Gregory Terrace, which plot they had kept for the purpose of one day establishing a Brothers' school there. 'Foundation and History of St Joseph's College, Nudgee', *Nudgee College Jubilee*, 1941, p. 34.

[99] Annals of Christian Brothers' College, Gregory Terrace, p. 6.

[1] According to the Annals, the Brothers doubted whether they could accept fees. Annals, p. 6. This doubt, however, is hard to reconcile with a decision made earlier, in the time of Ignatius Rice himself. See p. 289.

[2] The Brothers considered themselves not sufficiently backed financially to face the cost of building a college big enough to receive boarders. Annals, p. 6.

[3] In Leichhardt Street, close to the present Christian Brothers' College of St Laurence's.

[4] John Cani, an Italian, born at Bologna, 1836, educated at Roman University at Sapienze where he graduated D.D., and LL.D. He was ordained in 1859 and was parish priest at Warwick until 1868. From 1868 to 1878 he was in Brisbane. Mennell, Phillip, *The Dictionary of Australian Biography*, p. 79.

[5] *McNaught's Directory*, 1879, p. 209.

[6] *Ordo Divini Officii Recitandi*, 1878, p. 48. This is not corroborated by any other authority. No mention is made of it in the Christian Brothers' Annals.

[7] Annals of Christian Brothers' College, Gregory Terrace, p. 6.

[8] This was through staffing and accommodation difficulties. Ibid., p. 9.

[9] Ibid., pp. 10-11.   [10] *A.C.D.*, 1900, p. 92.

[11] *A.C.D.*, 1910, pp. 113-14.   [12] *A.C.D.*, 1895, pp. 129-30.

[13] *A.C.D.*, 1910, pp. 97-8. The school at Kalgoorlie was parochial and, at first, only

In South Australia several changes had taken place. By the middle of 1873 the Jesuit Fathers had taken over St Francis Xavier's Seminary from the diocesan clergy and had changed its name to St Francis Xavier's Collegiate School.[14] It would seem, however, that the school went out of existence early in 1875.[15] Meanwhile the other Jesuit college at Sevenhill continued as the only secondary school for Catholic boys in the colony until the end of the decade when the Christian Brothers had opened their Wakefield Street college in the capital.[16] As a day school this new college would have been of little use to the Catholics scattered over the rural areas of the south-east. For these districts Sevenhill was too far away; something had to be done, therefore, to accommodate their needs.[17] Accordingly, with special dispensation from their constitutions, the Brothers were enabled to convert their Adelaide college into a complete boarding school.[18]

With the more populous south and south-east thus catered for by the college in Adelaide, the middle north by itself was no longer able to support the college at Sevenhill. The college was closed, therefore, in 1886.[19] Before the century was out, however, Adelaide had grown sufficiently large to warrant another boarding school. This was opened by the Marist Brothers at Port Adelaide. Subsequently it was removed to Largs Bay and finally to Glenelg where, under the title of Sacred Heart College, it found its permanent home.[20]

Meanwhile developments had taken place in Tasmania. Since the closing of St Mary's Seminary in the seventies, Hobart had been without any official Catholic secondary school for boys. St Joseph's Catholic school in that city had been endeavouring to supply the need by offering some desultory instruction in the classics in the eighties,[21] but that was not sufficient to keep Catholic boys away from the big non-Catholic schools of Hutchins and Christ's College.[22] Finally, Dr Murphy acquired

---

primary, as was another at Clontarf.

    At this time the Oblates of Mary Immaculate were conducting an industrial school at Leederville. Ibid., p. 97.

    [14] *Irish Harp*, 30 May 1873, p. 7; *Harp and Southern Cross*, 4 September 1874, p. 8.

    [15] Morrison, Rev. R. A., 'The Story of Catholic Education in South Australia', p. 14 (Catholic Church of South Australia Archives, Adelaide).

    [16] Annals of Christian Brothers' College, Adelaide, pp. 3-5 (Archives of Christian Brothers' College, Wakefield Street, Adelaide).

    [17] Ibid., pp. 3, 18.

    [18] Ibid., p. 11. This was the first real boarding school of the Christian Brothers in Australia.

    [19] Ryan, Rev. Wilfrid (S.J.), 'The Story of Catholic Education in South Australia', *Australian Catholic Education Congress*, p. 99.

    [20] *A.C.D.*, 1900, p. 78.

    [21] The principal at the time was a Mr T. Mitchell. *Catholic Standard* (Tas.), May 1885, p. 269, a.

    [22] This was revealed in a speech of Mr J. Roper at a meeting of Catholics in Hobart to consider the establishment of a Catholic college, 1885. *Catholic Standard*, October 1885, p. 343, a.

a large disused building at Carnarvon, the site of the former convict settlement on the Port Arthur peninsula, and called several public meetings of Catholics with a view to establishing a boys' college there.[23] But the project did not come to fruition. The first permanent secondary school for Catholic boys was not established until well into the present century and belongs, therefore, to the last phase of development.

The Fourth Phase

Beginning roughly at the end of the first decade of the present century, this last phase was a period of phenomenal growth, especially the last twenty years. (See Table LI[24] and Fig. 18 which is based on it.) In studying this phase of development it is necessary to bear in mind that many of the earlier schools were ephemeral. Of the half-dozen founded in the early phase only three survived until the seventies—Lyndhurst, Sevenhill, and St Patrick's, Melbourne; within another decade the last alone remained; and of those founded during the second phase of development no more than two—St Stanislaus', Bathurst, and St Patrick's Goulburn—were still open in 1950. Far greater stability characterized those schools established by the religious orders after the seventies: with but two exceptions all were functioning by the middle of the present century.

TABLE LI

Development of Boys' Secondary Schools

Year	Number of schools	Year	Number of schools*
1830	0	1910	33
1850	2	1930	55
1870	4	1950	103
1890	18		

One important factor underlying the development of these secondary schools of the last phase was the rapid development of state secondary education. Before the turn of the century this had remained largely undeveloped. Some colonies, it is true, had at least considered the matter. Tasmania, having set up a Council of Education in 1860, felt obliged to develop secondary schools.[25] Victoria gave some consideration

23 In October 1885. Ibid.

24 This table is compiled from the *A.C.D.*: for the years 1895 to 1900, *passim;* for the earlier period, 1870-90, the *Ordo Divini Officii Recitandi;* for the 1830-70 period, the numbers were compiled from the various sources listed in the notes on pp. 1035-44.

25 The Council of Education advised that the scheme finally adopted should utilize the schools already in existence: 'The question, we think, practically admits of one answer. The efforts that have hitherto been made in this direction are so respectable, and have accomplished so much in spite of surrounding difficulties, that it would be both impolitic and unjust to drive them out of the field by new State Schools, with which they would be unable to compete. The advantage of a symmetrical system, great

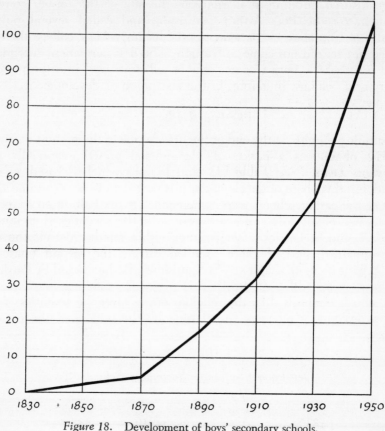

Figure 18.   Development of boys' secondary schools,
irrespective of enrolments

to the matter of providing for 'the best education of those who may fill the highest places of the State' in 1870,[26] but did nothing for another forty years. New South Wales, in 1880, had empowered the government to develop secondary schools,[27] but it was not until another thirty years passed that any wide-scale development occurred. In South Australia, the government was not 'at present' ready in 1881 to 'recommend the establishment of State Grammar Schools';[28] while the High School Acts

though it may be, would be sufficient to compensate for the injury that would be thus inflicted upon the voluntary energy of the people. We fall back, then, upon the alternative of assisting such schools, and those particularly which have the strongest claim to assistance.' Board of Royal Commission on Education, 1860, p. 13, P.P.(Tas.), 1856, V, paper 28.

[26] Board of Education (Vic.), Annual Report, 1870, pp. xvii-xviii. The Board recommended an organized system open to talent from primary school to university.

[27] Act, 43 Vic., no. xxiii, clauses 6, 25, 26. See also Knibbs, G. H., and Turner, J. W., Report of the Commissioners mainly on Secondary Education, 1904, p. 32.

[28] Statement by Mr Parsons, Minister for Education, in reply to question in the House of Assembly, 12 July 1881, P.P.(S.A.), 1881, I, p. 52.

of 1875[29] and 1876[30] in Western Australia had not been taken seriously by anybody.[31]

By 1910, however, most states had made a determined move to establish secondary schools. In that year Victoria introduced a Bill to extend secondary education. Definite progress had already been made in New South Wales[32] when the University Amendment Act and the Bursary Endowment Act came in 1912.[33] These gave an enormous fillip to secondary schools of all types, state and private.[34] Similar development after 1900 in South Australia led to a Bill in 1910,[35] a Royal Commission in 1913 and the High School Act of 1915.[36] By this time, too, Western Australia and Queensland had both launched successful schemes for secondary education, the one in 1910,[37] the other in 1912.[38]

The immediate effect of these developments on Catholic authorities was one of apprehension. Confronted with the Victorian Bill in 1910, Archbishop Carr expressed the hope that it 'would not result in giving to the State the monopoly of the whole work of secondary schools'.[39] But Carr's fears were not realized. Although the potential danger was there, it was in the best interests of the state that it should not become actual.[40] 'We can,' wrote Frank Tate, the Director of State Education, 'work out a scheme for keeping what is best in our system of private schools . . . It is desirable that many types of schools shall be developed amongst us,

---

[29] Act, 39 Vic., no. xiv. Assented to 31 December 1875.

[30] Act, 40 Vic., no. viii.

[31] To one journal the scheme was 'in advance of the present educational requirements of the colony'. *Inquirer and Commercial News*, 15 December 1875, p. 2. The Fremantle paper went further: 'In the name of the struggling community we represent—in the name of common sense—in the name of consistency—we protest against the frittering away of the revenue of the colony in such meaningless and Quixotic schemes . . . we protest against such an unbusiness-like system—such ruinous extravagance.' *Herald* (W.A.), 11 December 1875, p. 2; see also 25 December 1875, p. 3.
Public meetings of protest were held. These drew a 'numerous attendance, not only of Catholics, but also of Protestants . . . '. Supplement to *Record* (W.A.), 23 September 1876, p. 1. Earlier the Catholics had forwarded a petition to Downing Street, 1876, in Despatch no. 17. Lord Carnarvon, Sect. of State, actually asked Her Majesty the Queen to disallow the Act and recommended the Grammar School Act of Queensland as a model. C.S.O. Records, 1876, Ecclesiastical (WA-A). See also *Record* (W.A.), 6 September 1876, p. 3.

[32] Elliott, W. J., *Secondary Education in New South Wales*, p. 3.

[33] Act, 2 Georgii V.

[34] Elliott, op. cit., p. 5.

[35] *Parl. Deb.* (S.A.), 1910, p. 26.

[36] Act, 6 Georgii V, no. 1223, clause 32, a, b.

[37] This was the Modern School. Rankin, D. H., *The History of the Development of Education in Western Australia, 1829-1923*, p. 181.

[38] Duhig, Archbishop James, Notes on Education in Queensland (Wynberg Archives, Queensland).

[39] Address of Archbishop Carr at consecration of new buildings at St Joseph's Primary School, Camberwell, Victoria, 21 August 1910. *Argus*, 22 August 1910, p. 9.

[40] For example, New South Wales had a limited system of secondary education with roughly 8,500 pupils being instructed. In Victoria the figure was relatively higher—6,600 out of a population of 1,258,000. Yet in Victoria this secondary education cost the state practically nothing. All expense was borne by the private schools; but they received very little recognition. *Argus*, 5 September 1910, p. 6.

State-controlled schools, private schools, and Great Public Schools.'[41] Tate's desire was respected in the ensuing Act.

Similar counsels prevailed in the other states and the threat of state monopoly gradually disappeared. Nevertheless, this general Australia-wide multiplication of state secondary schools remained as a new challenge to Catholic secondary schools and a powerful stimulant to further development. By the end of the first decade of the present century there were, as has been shown,[42] between thirty and forty Catholic secondary schools for boys already in existence. Small though this number was, it was quite sufficient for the number of Catholic boys seeking secondary education, for on the whole Catholics had not fully availed themselves of the opportunities offered. Speaking to a Ballarat audience in the year 1916, Dr Mannix asserted that Catholics, according to their proportion in the community, should have possessed at least a quarter of the wealth of Victoria. If they did not, the reason was 'that they had not made as much use of higher education as others'.[43] This factor, his Grace maintained, kept Catholics at the bottom of the social scale.

Still, it cannot be justly claimed that Catholics were indifferent to the value of higher education. They were not; but the deterring factor of poverty was still sufficiently real to make secondary education for most of them altogether out of the question. 'Our people,' wrote a Catholic observer in the nineties, 'have been, and still remain, relatively poor, and in secular matters uneducated. On account of their limited means, they are unable to leave their sons as long at school as do the wealthy Protestants.'[44] The cost of education in many of the Catholic colleges was certainly high,[45] and so, rather than jeopardize their religious training by sending their children elsewhere, Catholic parents preferred to forgo the advantages of a secondary education altogether.

This fact is evidenced in the early leaving age that existed in Catholic schools. In Victoria, for example, about 1900, the number of children in the top three classes of the primary schools never rose above twenty per cent. In the top class itself it was never higher than two per cent. This is illustrated in two representative schools in Table LII.[46]

---

[41] Tate, *Preliminary Report*, 1908, pp. 22, 91.
[42] See ch. 8.
[43] Address on behalf of Newman College appeal, *Argus,* 6 March 1916, p. 6, f.
[44] *Christian Brothers' Educational Record,* 1894, p. 509.
[45] In 1910, for example, at St Joseph's College, Hunter's Hill, N.S.W., the annual 'pension' was thirty-three guineas for higher classes and thirty guineas for the lower (*A.C.D.*, 1910, p. 201). At St Patrick's College, Ballarat, 'board and tuition' per term was ten guineas with a £3 entrance fee for boarders (ibid., p. 204). At the convent of the Sacred Heart, Rose Bay, N.S.W., the 'pension' was forty-five guineas; but lessons in music, drawing and painting were extras (ibid., p. 205).
[46] This table was compiled from Report of Inspector of Catholic Schools, archdiocese of Melbourne, 1900. *Advocate,* 8 December 1900, p. 6, b.

TABLE LII

Early School Leaving Age in Catholic Schools, Victoria, 1900

Class	Pupils in each class	
	School A	School B
Infants under 6	140	100
Infants under 7	40	29
Class I	47	44
Class II	45	22
Class III	44	22
Class IV	21	25
Class V	12	11
Class VI	6	4
	355	257

The loss in social prestige and professional standing which this condition imposed upon Catholics was considerable. It was precisely to counteract such a condition that Polding had planned Lyndhurst, and his suffragans their own diocesan colleges. But the condition persisted and it was one of the things that forced itself upon the notice of Dr Mannix when he came to this country from Ireland in the early part of the present century.[47] Frequently, too, it had been a subject of lament for headmasters of Catholic institutions. 'Many an intelligent lad', it was claimed, had 'to cut short his course and abandon what would be most probably a University career because his parents [could] not support him at a Catholic college, and [would] not through conscientious motives send him where they believe[d] his religious education [would] be neglected'.[48]

It was this impecunious condition among the population generally that was largely responsible for the lack of support given to the first state high schools. In New South Wales, for example, within two years of the passing of the 1880 Act nine grammar schools had been established, but they were never popular, the people as a whole being unprepared for them. Within a few years, therefore, they began to dwindle[49] until in

---

[47] *Argus*, 6 March 1916, p. 6, f.

[48] Report printed in 'Colonial Notes', *Christian Brothers' Educational Record*, 1895, p. 519.

[49] Gollan, Kenneth, *The Organization and Administration of Education in New South Wales*, p. 99. In 1886, both Goulburn schools (i.e., Boys' and Girls') closed; in 1887 Bathurst Boys' and, in 1898, Bathurst Girls', closed. The decline is shown below (ibid., p. 45):

Year	Number of schools	Year	Number of schools
1881	0	1885	8
1882	9	1895	5
1883	6	1890	5
1884	8	1900	4

1900 there were only four left.[50] The same was true of most of the other states: people had to be helped to appreciate the value of secondary education. Above all they had to be helped financially; the obstacle created by their poverty had to be removed. This was done by the scholarship system.

Designed at first to foster the development of state secondary schools and, by direct financial aid, to enable parents to meet the expense entailed in giving their children a few extra years at school, the scholarship system did in fact overlook the needs of those attending non-state secondary schools. Not secondary education as such but state secondary education was its primary objective. For Catholics this constituted a grievance of the first order: where such a policy may have had little bearing on the wealthier non-state institutions it was, the bishops maintained, particularly harmful to Catholic schools, which, in point of fact, stood in greater need of financial assistance than the state schools themselves.

Apart from a few minor variations the pattern was consistent from colony to colony. In Queensland, the scholarships were 'only open to scholars from primary schools' and 'the exhibitions would give free admission to any State grammar school for a period of three years'.[51] Likewise Mr W. C. Windeyer in proposing scholarships for New South Wales in 1878 insisted that they should apply exclusively to pupils in public schools and be tenable only at public high schools.[52] In South Australia the conditions were more liberal: 'boys . . . obtaining scholarships could . . . go to any college, even', as the Minister of Education said, 'the Christian Brothers'!'[53] It is to be noted, on the other hand, that to win a scholarship in the first place a pupil had to attend a state school.[54] Similar conditions were laid down in Western Australia[55] and Victoria.[56]

Under these circumstances the scholarship system threatened the existence of the Catholic secondary schools. For the weaker Catholics,[57]

[50] Knibbs, G. H. and Turner, J. W., Interim Report of the Commissioners on Certain Parts of Primary Education, p. 10; also Knibbs and Turner, Report on Secondary Education, p. 41.

[51] Sir Samuel Griffith, Attorney-General, introducing the 1875 Education Bill. Parl. Deb. (Q'ld.), 1875, 18, p. 533.   [52] P.P.(N.S.W.), 1877-8, I, pp. 135, 189.

[53] Speech at speech night of Christian Brothers' College, Adelaide, 1898. Southern Cross, 20 January 1849, p. 43.   [54] Ibid., Southern Cross, 27 January 1899, p. 58.

[55] The regulation covering these scholarships was: 'Two scholarships of the value of £50 each per annum, tenable for three years, at the High School, Perth, will be annually offered to boys attending the Government and Assisted Schools of the Colony.' Govt. Gazette (W.A.), 27 December 1884, p. 640. These scholarships were later reduced in amount but the number of them was greatly extended. Chief Inspector's Report in Report of Minister of Education, 1896, p. 30. P.P.(W.A.), 1896, I, paper 19.

[56] Advocate, 29 September 1900, p. 12, a.

[57] From Bishop Gallagher's remarks on certain educational proposals of the Labour government. Argus, 16 December 1910, p. 10. See also Bishop Lanigan's pastoral letter, printed in Record (Bathurst), 15 April 1879, p. 180, a.

said Dr Gallagher, the system was a real snare. Others[58] looked upon it as a straight-out 'bribe'[59] calculated, as Dr Carr believed, to attract to state schools 'some of the brightest and cleverest pupils of the Catholic schools'.[60]

To counteract the danger of this subtle threat to its own system the Church launched a campaign for a less exclusivist administration of the scholarship scheme[61] and, at the same time, proposed a scholarship scheme of its own, which the bishops recommended to 'the more wealthy and benevolent members of the faithful'.[62] From them they expected certain 'endowments and bursaries' ('*fundationes et proemia*') which, when properly applied, would not only save Catholic children from state schools, but also help Catholic education as a whole. But the type of Catholics to whom the bishops appealed were not sufficiently interested. The result was that instead of a system of scholarships named after wealthy Catholics, those that did spring up came to be known variously as the 'Bishop's scholarships', the 'Archbishop's scholarships', or the 'Cardinal's scholarships'.[63] In point of fact, even these scholarships had no real foundation, since the bishops themselves had no means of financing them. In most cases the children holding them were simply admitted to the various schools free, the scholarships becoming, in other words, the direct gifts of the orders themselves.[64] In a few instances the different Catholic societies, such as the Catholic Federation, were able to contribute a little to the scholarship funds; but the amount was meagre and, by itself, wholly inadequate.

Meanwhile, despite vigorous opposition from the Protestant denominations,[65] the bishops relaxed none of their efforts to secure what they

[58] Annual Report read at Christian Brothers' College, Nudgee, 6 December 1894. It was very difficult, Br J. G. Hughes pointed out, to retain pupils in Catholic secondary schools. *Brisbane Courier*, 7 December 1894, p. 7, e.
[59] The view of the *Southern Cross*, 20 January 1899, p. 43.
[60] Address at third annual meeting of federal council of the C.Y.M.S. *Advocate*, 29 December 1894, p. 15, d.
[61] *Conc. Plen.*, I, decr. 247: 'Muneris nostri esse ducimus reclamare contra eam publicae pecuniae juventuti liberalius instituendae ab aerario assignatae distributionem quae fiat in favorem exclusivum scholarum acatholicarum.' This campaign was continued in subsequent Councils; see *Conc. Plen.*, II, decr. 315; III, decr. 342.
[62] *Conc. Plen.*, I, decr. 247.
[63] Cf. special scholarships instituted by Archbishop Carr. *Advocate*, 29 December 1894, p. 15, d. By 1915, twelve such scholarships were being offered in Melbourne. Report of Inspector of Catholic Schools, archdiocese of Melbourne, 1915. *Advocate*, 11 December 1915, p. 27, c.
[64] *Catholic Primary Schools' Report*, archdiocese of Sydney, 1913, p. 3. The beginnings of these scholarships date to a scholarship offered for two years by the Jesuit College of St Aloysius when it was at Surry Hills. This was in response to an appeal by Inspector J. W. Rogers, Inspector of Schools in the archdiocese. *Express* (Sydney), 29 September 1883, p. 5.
[65] This opposition was particularly strong in Queensland. The Methodist Conferences of 1900 and 1910, for example, saw in the scholarship scheme nothing but a 'violation of the undenominational principles of the educational system of this State'. Minutes of Annual Conference (Wesleyan Methodist), 1901, p. 60.
Numerous petitions against this extension of scholarships were lodged in the Leg.

considered an equitable[66] share in the state scholarships. Not only was the 'injustice' kept fresh before the minds of their own people,[67] but it was repeatedly thrust upon the notice of the various governments concerned.

The campaign was conducted in all states, but in none more vigorously than in Victoria. There, in 1900, a deputation consisting of Archbishop Carr and two of his suffragans, Bishop Moore of Ballarat and Bishop Reville of Sandhurst, waited upon the Minister of Education with the request 'that the recently created State school scholarships should be thrown open for competition to the pupils of private schools'.[68] Similar requests continued to be made throughout the early years of the century, but all to no purpose, for at the end of the first decade, the Archbishop was still making deputations.[69]

Early in the second decade, however, a change occurred. A slight concession was made[70] and the campaign given fresh impetus by the arrival of Dr Mannix.[71] But just at that time the extension of the scholarship scheme to encourage enrolment in the new state high schools appeared as a further threat to Catholic schools. This brought the Catholic Federation into the matter.[72] In 1914 a deputation from this body waited on the Minister for Education. Confronting him with the full text of the Catholic case, they protested: first, that since the scholarships were financed by funds obtained by 'equal taxation from all citizens alike', they should be 'equally distributed among the children of all citizens alike'; secondly, since Catholics could not, 'for conscientious reasons', make use of the scholarships in state schools, they should be allowed 'the right of selecting the scholastic establishments' in which they preferred to take out the scholarships, 'without distinction' as to

---

Assembly; for example, from Albion Baptist Church, 17 December 1900, *P.P.*(Q'ld.), 1900, i. p. 561; others: 27 November 1900, ibid., p. 448; 18 December 1900, ibid., p. 567; 19 December 1900, ibid., p. 575; 20 December 1900, ibid., p. 585.

[66] It was in these terms that the Catholics made their demands: they wanted a 'more equitable distribution' of the scholarships. *Age* (Brisbane), 24 December 1892, p. 2, a.

[67] It was the reiterated theme of platform and speech night addresses. E.g., Christian Brothers' College, Nudgee, speech night, 6 December 1894, *Brisbane Courier*, 7 December 1894, p. 7, e.

[68] *Advocate*, 29 September 1900, p. 12, a.

[69] *Austral Light*, July 1910, pp. 614 ff.

[70] Until then forty general scholarships and twenty exhibitions were open to state school pupils only, with a few agricultural and mining scholarships open to non-state pupils thrown in. In 1911, after persistent requests from Dr Carr and 'after some demur' ten scholarships and five exhibitions were added for competition among non-state schools. 'The Education Campaign', *Austral Light*, 1 September 1913, p. 790, b.

[71] 'I can hardly believe,' said Dr Mannix, 'that for the sake of these puny bursaries an effort will be made to tempt the cleverest Catholic children to go over to the State schools.' Address to parishioners of St Monica's, Essendon. *Argus*, 6 October 1913, p. 6.

[72] Inspired by the New South Wales Bursary Act, the Catholic Federation became active. They asked the Director of Education, Frank Tate, 'that both [the departmental and the extra-departmental schools] should be placed in the same position by extending to the latter the privileges relating to scholarships, instruction in cookery, and provision for medical inspection'. *Argus*, 24 June 1913, p. 9, d.

whether such institutions were directly under the control of the Education Department or not.[73]

In the meantime some of the other governments had modified their schemes so as to make more equitable provision for pupils in non-state schools—Queensland in 1900[74] and again in 1913,[75] and New South Wales in 1912[76]—whereupon Victoria quickly came into line. Tasmania did likewise in 1915.[77] As a result of these amendments new life was infused into Catholic education. The schools, both secondary[78] and primary,[79] availed themselves to the full of the opportunities offered.[80]

By this time, too, other factors had begun to operate. The improved social condition of Catholics following upon the industrial movement and legislation providing endowments and services of various kinds were not without their effect: they removed the threat of poverty and opened the door of opportunity. In addition, the Irish, who predominated among Catholics and who were very conscious of their lower social position as labourers,[81] saw in education a means of improving their lot and securing for their children an entry to the coveted 'white-collar' positions and the higher social rank that went with them. Besides, the Irish liked art and music and had a traditional respect for 'the larnin'' itself. The raising of the school-leaving age and the general movement towards

[73] Meeting of the Victorian Council of the Australian Catholic Federation. *Argus*, 16 February 1914, p. 7.

[74] By motion in Assembly 28/10, P.P.(Q'ld.), 1899, I, p. 283; and by executive minute to the resolution, P.P.(Q'ld.), 1900, II, p. 139. Cf. Wyeth, E. R., 'History of Education in the Moreton Bay District of New South Wales and in Queensland'. Unpublished M.Ed. thesis, University of Melbourne, vol. iii, p. 55.

[75] The number of scholarships available after 1900 was only thirty-six. *Govt. Gazette* (Q'ld.), 1 September 1900, vol. ii, p. 511. In 1913, it was announced: 'A scholarship will be awarded to each candidate who gains not less than fifty per cent of the total number of marks.' *Govt. Gazette* (Q'ld.), 1913, vol. ii, p. 390.   [76] Act, 2 Georgii V.

[77] See Reeves, Clifford, *A History of Tasmanian Education*, p. 108. For earlier history of the scholarship system in Tasmania see P.P.(Tas.), 1856, p. 24; letter, Board of Education to J. Roper, 16 May 1860, Board of Education Correspondence, 1860 volume, p. 177; *Report of Council of Education*, 1863, Appendix IV; *Rules and Regulations of Council of Education*, regs. 27032, *Report of Council of Education*, 1863, p. 11, P.P.(Tas.), 1863, X, paper 4.

[78] Father Maurice O'Reilly, C.M., President of St Stanislaus' College, Bathurst, became the first Catholic representative on the Bursary Board. (*Freeman's Journal*, 19 December 1912, p. 11, a.) St Stanislaus' itself claims to have been the first Catholic secondary school to apply for inspection and registration under the Board (*Echoes from St. Stanislaus*, vol. 8, no. ix, p. 3). Other Catholic secondary schools followed immediately: Marist Brothers' High School, Darlinghurst (*Freeman's Journal*, 19 December 1912, p. 13, b); St Ursula's College, Armidale (ibid., p. 15, c); Mercy College, Goulburn (ibid., p. 19, a); De La Salle College, Armidale (ibid., p. 23, d); Riverview (ibid., p. 8, d); St Patrick's College, Goulburn (ibid., p. 9, a).

[79] For example, in 1915 twenty scholarships were available for registered schools. The Catholic schools secured thirteen of them. Report of Catholic schools in the archdiocese of Sydney, 1915. *Advocate*, 11 December 1899.

[80] For instance, special scholarship schools were established. Annual Report of Inspector of Catholic Schools, 1930. *Advocate*, 11 December 1930, p. 18, a. See also account of special central school for senior secondary classes. 'Some Notable Incidents in Australia'. *Christian Brothers' Educational Record*, 1919, p. 30. 'Catholic Education', Information Service, p. 2.   [burn.

[81] Pointed out to writer by His Grace, Archbishop Eris O'Brien, of Canberra and Goul-

education for all helped also to bring about a great expansion of Catholic secondary education.

But this expansion was attended with a host of new problems, one of the most pressing being that of accommodation. During the latter part of the nineteenth century and the first twenty or thiry years of the present, Catholic secondary education had been the preserve of the religious orders. In the seventies and eighties the parochial authorities had been hard pressed enough in providing adequate primary education without bothering about secondary; that was left to the orders, who built their own colleges and then were compelled to charge fees sufficiently high to pay for them. The ecclesiastical authorities, glad to see the orders undertaking these heavy financial responsibilities, made no attempt to interfere, with the result that the Catholic secondary school system developed haphazardly. The relatively high fees, furthermore, tended to make it exclusive; and, although suited to the educational needs of the earlier period, it proved inadequate to meet the new demands that were beginning to be made on it. Given a vast new secondary school population, unable for the most part to pay the higher college fees and depending largely on scholarships and other forms of government assistance, it became obvious that the older system could not be expanded indefinitely.

There was but one alternative. The responsibility had to fall back on the parish. As in the past the parish or diocese had made itself responsible for primary education, so now, towards the middle of the present century, it began to make itself responsible for secondary education as well. Occasionally the parish and an order would combine, and a school would be built on a joint basis.[82] But that was not common. Up to 1950 nothing prescriptive on these matters had appeared in the legislation of the Church,[83] although the origins of the movement are to be found as far back as the time of Dr Matthew Quinn.[84]

Thus twentieth century development of Catholic secondary education was characterized by the emergence of this new parochial, or in some cases inter-parochial, system of secondary schools, growing up alongside, and hardly to be distinguished from, the older schools. Both were staffed by religious of the same orders, and offered identical courses of study.

Such factors help to explain the steep rise in the secondary schools over this last phase of development. The greatest growth occurred in the populous eastern states (see Table LIII);[85] and it is here also that the greatest differentiation of types is to be observed.

82 For instance, schools of the De La Salle Brothers (East Hills Line, Sydney) and Marist Brothers (Bunbury, W.A.).
83 *Conc. Plen.*, IV, 1937, decr. 632. The responsibility is still left to the family.
84 Quinn, Bishop Matthew, Pastoral Letter to the Clergy and Laity of the Diocese, p. 6.   85 Table compiled from *A.C.D.*, 1910, 1920, 1930, 1940, and 1951, *passim*.

TABLE LIII

New Catholic Secondary Schools in Fourth Phase of Development

State	Number of schools
New South Wales	45
Victoria	17
Queensland	15
South Australia	4
Western Australia	7
Tasmania	3
	91

All these schools were conducted by the religious orders. Of the ninety-one opened during this last period eighty-six[86] were in the hands of the teaching Brothers;[87] the remaining five were conducted by religious orders of priests: the Missionaries of the Sacred Heart at Downlands in Toowoomba and at Chevalier in Burradoo, New South Wales; the Augustinians at Villanova, Brisbane; and the Jesuits at St Louis', Perth and St Ignatius', Adelaide.[88] The last five schools, furthermore, were owned by the orders themselves, whereas the general movement of the whole period was in the opposite direction; that is to say, in the direction of the parochial or semi-parochial secondary school, where the whole plant remained the property of the parish authorities and where the religious worked for a minimum salary. In this way school fees were kept much lower than in the other schools and within reach of the working man's income. Three out of every four schools established in New South Wales during this period and one out of every two in South Australia were of this type. The trend was unmistakable, but whether it was a passing phase following the depression era of the thirties or a permanent trend is, at this stage, difficult to say. It is obvious that the diocesan authorities, who are faced with the problem of financing a rapidly expanding primary system, will not place any obstacles in the way of orders willing to undertake the responsibility of opening secondary schools, even though it entails the sacrifice of a certain amount of diocesan control. Signs of this were already evident by 1950.

[86] Not including schools listed as 'post-primary'; that is the De La Salle Brothers' schools at Surry Hills and Haberfield and the Patrician Brothers' schools at Redfern and Forest Lodge.

[87] That is the Irish Christian Brothers, the Marist Brothers, the De La Salle Brothers, and the Brothers of St John of God. The Brothers of St John the Baptist, founded in South Australia by Monsignor Healey, conducted the parochial school at Thebarton and an institution at Brooklyn Park. They were later replaced by the Marist Brothers (at Thebarton) and the Salesian Fathers (at Brooklyn Park).

[88] A.C.D., 1951.

SECONDARY SCHOOLS: GIRLS'

The development of Catholic secondary schools for girls was no less complex than was the development of the boys' schools. Similar forces operated, with the result that more or less comparable phases of development are to be observed. The growth-curve (see Fig. 19)[89] for the girls' schools reveals three clearly defined stages of development: the first stage, from the fifties to the early seventies; the second stage, from the seventies to about the end of the first decade of the present century; and then the third and last stage.

The schools belonging to the first phase (see Table LIV)[90] were, in

TABLE LIV

Development of Girls' Secondary Schools

State	1850	1870	1890	1910	1930	1950
New South Wales	—	5	44	96	97	139
Victoria	—	2	15	53	58	73
South Australia	—	1	4	15	20	37
Western Australia	1	2	3	22	23	29
Queensland	—	4	16	22	23	36
Tasmania	—	1	3	4	5	7
Totals	1	15	85	212	226	321

the main, select schools for the upper classes, catering for an exclusive coterie—the daughters of the well-to-do and the newly accepted squatter classes. Those developing during the second phase were still select schools, but they extended their clientele to embrace the increasing middle classes. The third phase saw many of the earlier schools still in existence, but adapting themselves to changing conditions. It witnessed also, especially with the development of secondary education for all classes, a vast new growth of schools, springing up alongside the older institutions, challenging them, if not in social esteem, at least in numbers, and opening their doors to all regardless of rank or station. Thus, from a mere fifteen or so schools at the end of the first phase the number had increased to over 200 by the end of the second phase. By the middle of the present century it had reached 321.

The First Phase

The first phase extended, as has been shown, to about the end of the 1860s or the early seventies. It began with the Sisters of Mercy who, three years[91] after their arrival in Perth in 1846, opened a 'school for the

[89] Based on Table LIV.
[90] Table compiled from *Ordo Divini Officii Recitandi*, 1876, pp. 67-78; A.C.D., 1888, *passim;* 1890, 1910, 1930, and 1950.
[91] On 3 September 1849. Recollections of Mother Ursula Frayne, p. 43 (Archives, Convent of Mercy, Victoria Square, Perth).

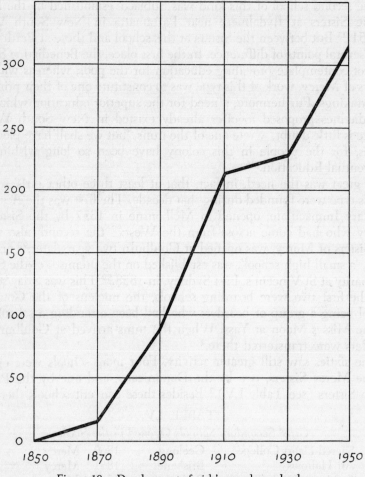

Figure 19. Development of girls' secondary schools,
irrespective of enrolments

children of the gentry'.[92] The school was not essentially a secondary school even though it probably retained girls for more advanced studies; the conspicuous feature about it was that it was 'distinct from the poor school',[93] and was established, not in response to a demand for secondary education for Catholic girls—there was no such demand at the time—but in an endeavour simply, as the first Superior said, 'to lighten the burden on the mission'[94] by earning extra money.

[92] Letter, Frayne to Archbishop of Dublin, 25 September 1852. Quoted in Moran, op. cit., p. 567.
[93] Ibid., and Blue Book: Colony of Western Australia, 1846, p. 4.
[94] Letter, Frayne to Archbishop of Dublin, 25 September 1852. The Free School, which was established earlier, was, financially, entirely the responsibility of the mission. Moran, op. cit., p. 567.

The second school of this kind was Subiaco, established by the Benedictine Sisters at Rydalmere near Parramatta in New South Wales in 1851.[95] But between the Sisters at this school and those at Perth there were several points of difference. In the first place, the Benedictine Sisters did not contemplate providing education for the poor; whereas with the Sisters of Mercy, work of this type was to constitute one of their principal undertakings. Furthermore, a need for the superior education which the Benedictines proposed to offer already existed in New South Wales: 'There is little doubt,' wrote one of the nuns, 'but we shall have plenty of chicks, for the people in this colony have been so long wishing for Conventual Education.'[96]

So great was the need, in fact, that at least three other girls' schools of this type were founded during that decade. The first was the Academy of Mary Immaculate, opened in Melbourne in 1857 by the Sisters of Mercy who had come across from the West;[97] the second, also under the Sisters of Mercy, was opened at Goulburn two years later;[98] and the third, 'a small high school', was established on the premises of the Sisters of Charity at St Vincent's, East Sydney, in 1858.[99] This was a day school, but the first two were boarding schools, the nucleus of the Goulburn school being a group of boarders who had been attending a school kept by the Misses Moon at Yass. When the nuns arrived at Goulburn the boarders were transferred there.[1]

The sixties saw still greater activity. Four more schools were opened by the Mercy Sisters, two by the Dominicans, and one by the Presentation Sisters (see Table LV).[2] Besides these convent schools there had

TABLE LV

Girls' Secondary Schools Opened in the Sixties

Sacred Heart College	Geelong	1860	Mercy
All Hallows	Brisbane	1861	Mercy
St Mary's High School	Bathurst	1867	Mercy
St Mary's Priory	Maitland	1867	Dominican
St Mary's College	Hobart	1867	Presentation
Convent of Mercy	Albury	1868	Mercy
Franklin St Priory	Adelaide	1868	Dominican

[95] The community was installed 2 February 1849; the school was opened 25 March 1851. *Subiaco*, Rydalmere, p. 1.

[96] Letter, from Dame Magdalen le Clerc to Dr Barber, then President of the English Benedictines. Quoted in Birt, op. cit., vol. 2, p. 164.   [97] *Mercy Centenary Record*, p. 17.

[98] *Brief History of the Goulburn Foundation of the Sisters of Mercy*, p. 2.

[99] On 1 May 1858. Wilson, Sister Dunstan, 'The Sisters of Charity in Australia', Australian Catholic Historical Society Records, p. 12.

[1] *Brief History of the Goulburn Foundation of the Sisters of Mercy*, p. 2.

[2] Ignatius, Sister M., 'The Sisters of Mercy in Victoria', Sacred Heart College, Geelong, pp. 1-2 (Archives, Convent of Mercy, Geelong); *Ordo Divini Officii Recitandi*, 1876, p. 72; *Times* (Bathurst), 25 December 1867, p. 2, c; *Brief History of the Goulburn Foundation of the Sisters of Mercy*, p. 3; *Ordo Divini Officii Recitandi*, 1876, p. 74; *Advocate*, 13 February 1869, p. 1; *Catholic Standard* (Tas.), June 1868, p. 112, b.

grown up, flourished for a while and then disappeared again, a whole host of private schools for Catholic girls. These young ladies' seminaries, as most of them were called, appeared in all the eastern colonies, Queensland,[3] New South Wales,[4] Victoria,[5] South Australia,[6] and Tasmania,[7] and they did, for a time, serve a useful purpose. But they are beyond the scope of the present work.

The dozen convent schools that appeared during this first phase of development were more or less homogeneous in character, their pupils being, as has been shown, children of the gentry, the grown-up daughters[8] of the wealthier classes who, up to that period, had relied for their education on governesses in their own homes.[9] Furthermore, as many of the nuns of the early communities were Irish or English ladies of birth, culture and refinement[10] it followed that the first pupils found themselves enjoying a school life that was to afford them an entrance into all that was highest and most cultured in colonial society of the time. It was a superior home-training that these young ladies received and, as befitted their station, those at Sacred Heart College, Geelong, for example, dressed for dinner each evening.[11]

The Second Phase

But in the second phase circumstances changed. In the post-gold-rush economy of the seventies the ex-digger challenged the squatter's right to control the land and a new middle class of small traders arose in the cities and large country towns.[12] The new Education Acts, furthermore, had rendered a reorganization of the Catholic primary school system imperative. The Sisters, as has been pointed out, were henceforth called upon to take charge of the parochial schools and to fill the places left vacant by lay teachers who, now that government support was withdrawn, had to seek employment elsewhere. In this way the lower and middle classes came to make heavier demands on the personnel of the teaching Sisters.

[3] For example, schools of a Miss Davis (Warwick) and Mrs Dowsdel. Advertisements in *Brisbane Courier*, 5 July 1875.

[4] For example, day school under a Miss Tray. *Australasian Chronicle,* 6 February 1841, p. 3.

[5] For example, Preston House, Catholic Seminary, *Melbourne Directory,* 1857; see also 'Ladies Seminary Conducted by Mrs McDonnald', advertisement in *Herald* (Melbourne), 22 January 1951; the Misses Ecck's in Melbourne, letter, Bleasdale to Chairman, 31 January 1859, D.S.B., Inward Letters, 1859; *Victorian,* 16 August 1862, p. iii; *Advocate,* 23 March 1872, p. 18, 26 April 1873, p. 2, c.

[6] *Irish Harp and Farmers' Herald,* May 1870.

[7] Kelsh, *Personal Recollections of the Rt Rev. R. W. Willson,* p. 6.

[8] For example, at All Hallows' in Brisbane in the sixties the ages of these senior girls ranged from nineteen to twenty-three. Register of All Hallows' Convent School, for years 1863-6 particularly (Archives, All Hallows', Brisbane).

[9] Ignatius, op. cit., sections on Sacred Heart College, Geelong.

[10] *Brief History of the Goulburn Foundation of the Sisters of Mercy,* p. 3.

[11] Ignatius, op. cit., p. 1.

[12] For example, doctors, publicans, blacksmiths, coachbuilders, etc. See Register of All Hallows' Convent School, years 1863-6, *passim* (Archives, All Hallows', Brisbane).

The 'young lady', therefore, gradually disappeared from the convent classrooms and the child took her place.[13] The schools themselves began to pay less attention to the elegancies and accomplishments demanded in polite society, and more to the important task of training girls to earn a living.

In this phase secondary schools multiplied rapidly, spreading out from the cities into the smaller country towns. In the first decade more schools were opened than had been opened over the whole earlier period. They were established mainly by the Mercy and the Presentation Sisters (see Table LVI).[14]

TABLE LVI

Girls' Secondary Schools Opened in Seventies

School	Place	Date of opening	Order
Monte St Angelo	Sydney	1873	Mercy
Presentation Convent	Windsor (Vic.)	1873	Presentation
St Anne's	Warrnambool	1874	Mercy
Sacred Heart	Wagga	1874	Presentation
St Catherine's	Singleton	1875	Mercy
St Joseph's	Kilmore	1875	Mercy
Mary's Mount	Ballarat	1875	Loreto
Convent of Mercy	Yass	1876	Mercy
St Mary's	Bendigo	1876	Mercy
Good Samaritan	Sydney (Pitt St)	1879	Good Samaritan

Over the two following decades the development of this type of girls' secondary school was so rapid that enumeration of new openings would be tedious. Practically every new convent that was opened developed its own little high school with its handful of boarders drawn from the neighbouring countryside.[15] By the end of the eighties the number had reached eighty-five, more than half of them being in New South Wales (see Table LIV). By 1900 it was 153, almost double that of a decade earlier.

One striking feature of the convent schools during these years was

13 Ignatius, op. cit., pp. 1-2.
14 *Ordo Divini Officii Recitandi*, 1876, p. 76; A.C.D., 1888, pp. 87, 94; O'Connor, J. G., *A Brief History of the Sacred Heart Presentation Convent, Wagga*, p. 8; *Ordo Divini Officii Recitandi*, 1876; *Mercy Centenary Record*, p. 73; Yeo, Mary E. J., 'The Early Days of Yass' (collection of a series of articles appearing in *Yass Evening Tribune*, 1920 (ML); A.C.D., 1920, p. 113; Clare, Sr M., 'The Story of the Institute of the Good Samaritans'. Australian Catholic Historical Society Records, p. 23.
15 In the diocese of Goulburn, however, Bishop Lanigan was for a time opposed to the idea of nuns' boarding schools. He 'did not approve of girls being continually mixed up with the religious as that would prevent the nuns from carrying out the mode of life to which they were vowed in all its integrity'. He considered the result would be 'harmful to both pupils and teachers'. This was in special reference to the proposed boarding school at Wagga. Annals of Presentation Convent, pp. 18, 21 (Archives of Presentation, Mt Erin Convent, Wagga).

the large number of Protestant girls attending them. In 1852 the children attending the Sisters of Mercy select school in Perth were 'all Protestants'.[16] In New South Wales convent schools in the eastern part of the colony reported a high percentage of Protestant girls,[17] while one convent school hidden in the far west, at Wentworth, had more Protestants enrolled than Catholics.[18] In Victoria, as late as 1900, one in every eight or nine girls in the Catholic secondary schools was a Protestant.[19] In Queensland the proportion was far higher. At one stage in the sixties, for example, between two and three out of every five girls at All Hallows' were Protestants.[20]

To this practice of Protestant girls attending Catholic schools Protestant leaders were generally strongly opposed.[21] At the time, however, there was very little choice. Even when state high schools and grammar schools were opened in the present century many Protestants, objecting to the secular nature of the education offered therein,[22] sent their daughters to the convent high schools 'in order', they said, 'that they might receive the moral education which [they] considered necessary'.[23] They apparently felt no mistrust of the nuns, who in fact displayed far greater zeal than anyone else in seeing that Protestant children performed their own religious duties and attended their own services.[24]

The Catholic authorities, on their part, held no strong objections to the presence of these Protestant girls. For one thing many of the convents depended, in no small degree, on the financial support of Protestants. In the Melbourne archdiocese, about the 1900s, the school fees paid by Protestants would have amounted to approximately twelve per cent of the total; in Brisbane, a little before this time, to between forty and fifty per cent;[25] and in Perth, in the early days particu-

16 *Recollections of Mother Ursula Frayne*, p. 4. See also letter, Mother Ursula Frayne to Archbishop of Dublin, 25 September 1852. Quoted in Moran, op. cit., p. 567.

17 For example, at the Dominican School, Maitland. O'Hanlon, Sr Assumpta *Dominican Pioneers in New South Wales*.

18 Ignatius, op. cit., section on Wentworth, pp. 4, 6.

19 The figures were: number of schools: 20, number of girls: 1,748, number of Protestants: 226. Report of Inspector of Catholic Schools, *Advocate*, 8 December 1900, p. 7, a.

20 These ratios are computed from the school register. Register of All Hallows', years 1863-66, *passim* (Archives, All Hallows', Brisbane). See also *Sketch of the Life and Labours of the Rt Rev. Dr O'Quinn, First Bishop of Brisbane*, p. 26.

21 Address of Anglican Coadjutor Bishop of Brisbane at Anglican Diocesan Synod, 1896. *Brisbane Courier*, 5 June 1896, p. 6, d. See also speech delivered by a speaker at the Presbyterian Assembly, N.S.W., 1879. *Freeman's Journal*, 22 November 1879, p. 17.

22 'The brutality of secularism', as the Anglican Coadjutor Bishop of Brisbane called it. *Brisbane Courier*, 5 June 1896, p. 6, d.

23 Stated by the Rev. G. Pringle at the Brisbane Diocesan Synod, 1896. The speaker admitted that the church [the Anglican Church in Brisbane] derived more attendants from the convent school than from either of the grammar schools. Unless the Church of England took hold of its children and educated them in religious matters, it would lose hold of them altogether. *Brisbane Courier*, 5 June 1896, p. 6, d.　　　24 Ibid.

25 In other ways besides paying school fees Protestants helped Catholics. Bishop Quinn of Brisbane was quick to appreciate this. See *Sketch of the Life and Labours of the Rt Rev. Dr O'Quinn, First Bishop of Brisbane*, p. 27.

larly, to almost a hundred per cent.[26] From the viewpoint of religion, there was no great impediment, the girls admitted being from highly respected Protestant families and thoroughly Christian. In fact some Catholic schools not infrequently advertised that they were 'open to pupils of any denomination'.[27] It was only later in the present century that the practice of accepting non-Catholic children was discouraged: at first it was simply the problem of accommodation, but later, especially when the better Protestant stock disappeared from Catholic schools, it also became a matter of safeguarding the religious spirit.[28]

The presence of these Protestant girls in Catholic schools illustrates a significant phase in the development of secondary education in this country. For a span of over fifty years, embracing the latter part of the nineteenth century and the early part of the present, the convent high schools constituted practically the only organized system of secondary education for girls that Australia possessed. The state system, properly speaking, was a product of the present era, taking its beginning, as was shown in the case of the boys' schools, from the second decade of this century.

The Third Phase

By that time, 1910, there were over two hundred Catholic secondary schools for girls scattered throughout the Commonwealth. Of these, ninety-six were in New South Wales, fifty-three in Victoria, fifteen in South Australia, twenty-two in each of Western Australia and Queensland, and four in Tasmania.[29] By 1920, however, the number had fallen. The decline was no more than six or seven per cent and was not so marked in some states as it was in others,[30] still, it was significant, and coincided with an important event in the development of secondary education. This was the passing of the various Bursary and Registration Acts in several of the eastern states and the consequent reorganization of secondary school education which these Acts entailed.

The convent high schools during the first two phases of their development in Australia were not, as has been suggested, secondary schools in the modern acceptation of the term. They were, properly speaking, 'superior' or 'select'[31] schools and, notwithstanding the fact that many of them did offer advanced secondary work, the distinction between them

[26] Letter, Mother Ursula Frayne to Archbishop of Dublin, 25 September 1852. Quoted in Moran, op. cit., p. 567.
[27] For example, 'Rosebank' Good Samaritan Convent, Five-Dock, N.S.W. A.C.D., 1900, op. cit., p. 173.
[28] Report of Third National Catholic Conference of Directors and Inspectors, 1944, p. 7.
[29] See Table LIV.
[30] In 1910, for example, the figure was 212 (see Table LIV); in 1920 it was 195. Computed from A.C.D., 1920.
[31] See A.C.D., 1888, pp. 74-92, passim.

and the parochial schools, as with many of the boys' schools, was social rather than scholastic.[32] The idea of secondary education as a stage following upon elementary education was, in these schools, virtually unknown.[33]

Gradually, however, this concept of high school education began to give way and, although vestiges of it are still to be found, secondary education in the convent schools, even before the turn of the century, began to assume many of the features that are characteristic of it at the present day. The turning point of this evolutionary process came with the Education Acts mentioned above. They conferred a definite form and shape on the developments that had already taken place and set the pattern and standards along which secondary schools were later to be organized. Accordingly the Registration of Teachers and Schools Act of Victoria in 1905 not only required that all schools[34] and teachers[35] be registered, but also stipulated certain definite standards in the organization of the school[36] and in the training of the teachers.[37] A similar Act[38] in Tasmania did the same for that state in 1906. Likewise, in New South Wales, the Bursary Endowment Act of 1912 empowered the Board which it established to draw up a set of regulations[39] touching on such matters as the organization and equipment of the school, the method and range of instruction, the efficiency of the teaching staff, and the general conduct of the school as a whole.[40]

Compliance with these regulations was essential for a school if it hoped to maintain status in the eyes of the public. In this way the Act had a 'toning-up' effect on Catholic secondary schools generally, inducing them to review their position and 'put their houses in order'.[41] Efficiency was greatly increased,[42] but only at a price—new and heavy demands upon already depleted staffs and financial resources. As a result, not only were new schools slow to open but several of the older schools compelled to surrender all pretention to secondary status and to

[32] For example, the Good Samaritan Sisters at Maitland, before the arrival of the Dominicans, catered only for the poor. It was in this strain that Dr Murray wrote in inviting the Dominican nuns from Ireland: 'The schools conducted by the nuns here are intended for the poorer or rather I should say, for the humbler class of people, this professed object debars the children of the rich from attending their schools . . . ' Letter, Murray to Dominicans of Kingstown, Ireland, 20 November 1866. Quoted in O'Hanlon, op. cit., p. 49. See also A.C.D., 1895, p. 141.

[33] The same attitude existed in England throughout the whole of the nineteenth century. See G. A. N. Lowndes, The Silent Social Revolution, p. 50.

[34] Act, 5 Edwardii VII, no. 2013, clause 5 (1).

[35] Ibid., clause 7 (2).   [36] Ibid., clause 15 (1).   [37] Ibid., clauses 2, 6, 16.

[38] Act, 6 Edwardii VII, no. xv.   [39] Act, 2 Georgii V, clause 11 (1a).

[40] Regulations providing generally for the Registration of Schools under sub-clauses (a) and (b) of Clause I of Section II of the Bursary Endowment Act, regs. 4, 7, 8.

[41] Borgia, Rev. Brother (F.M.S.), Annual Report at Marist Brothers' High School, Darlinghurst, Sydney. Freeman's Journal, 19 December 1912, p. 13, a.

[42] Little, Rev. Father J. (S.J.), Prefect of Studies at St Ignatius' College, Riverview, N.S.W., Annual Report, 1912. Freeman's Journal, 19 December 1912, p. 8, d.

revert to the elementary level. After a short respite, however, the curve took another upward turn (see Fig. 19).

But other influences were also at work, and the convent high school pattern that emerged from the nineteenth century began to be still further modified by factors which became real only as the present century developed. During the earlier period, for example, the high school and the parochial school had, in the vast majority of cases, grown up side by side;[43] the same religious community, generally speaking, was responsible for both schools. The quality of teaching in each case, therefore, may be presumed to have been identical; yet, in the one case the pupils paid relatively high fees,[44] in the other, virtually nothing.[45] Carried over into the present century, this practice became a distinct obstacle to the efficient organizing and general husbanding of Catholic educational resources. It meant, in the first place, an unnecessary duplication of staffs—one staff to teach the classes in the parochial school and another to teach the parallel grades in the superior school; and, in the second, the perpetuation of a social distinction that, in the present century, was no longer real and certainly no longer acceptable.[46]

Accordingly there began a movement which, in effect, was both social and educational. The one parochial school, henceforth, was to provide primary education for all classes, middle and lower, and the convent high, or erstwhile superior school, assuming a new role, was to relinquish its pretensions to exclusiveness and open its doors to secondary students of all types, both rich and poor.[47] But the movement was extremely slow and lagged far behind social developments in other directions, so much so that the bishops in some cases felt obliged to press the issue. Bishop O'Farrell of Bathurst, for example, then Bishop Fox of Wilcannia-Forbes, and, later still, Dr Guilford Young, Auxiliary of Canberra and Goulburn, stepped in and directed that the conversion to the new system be made without further delay.[48] In other dioceses direct action of

[43] See A.C.D., 1880, passim.

[44] For example, the annual pension at Sacred Heart Convent, Rose Bay, in 1900 was forty-five guineas excluding extras. A.C.D., 1900, p. 171. The 'middle class' schools charged fees of about half that amount; for example, the Mercy schools in Queensland, at the end of the eighties were charging, weekly—Bundaberg 8s. 6d., Dalby 10s., Gympie 10s., Helidon 10s., Ipswich 12s., Maryborough 12s., Roma 10s., Stanthorpe 8s. 6d., Toowoomba 12s., Warwick 12s., Nudgee 10s. A.C.D., 1888, p. 115.

[45] Of the order of 6d. or 1s. a week, if they could afford it. If they could not, they were admitted gratuitously. See A.C.D., 1895, p. ix.

[46] Report of The Fifth National Catholic Education Conference of Directors and Inspectors of Schools, p. 2 (Archives, Catholic Education Office, Melbourne).

[47] This practice is being generally adopted in the newer parishes, especially in the dioceses of New South Wales, e.g., Ashbury, N.S.W.

[48] In the Bathurst diocese this movement began under Bishop O'Farrell. It was carried into the Wilcannia-Forbes diocese by Bishop Fox. This information was made available to the writer by Bishop Fox himself, in a letter 26 June 1952. Dr Guilford Young began to put this scheme into operation in the Catholic schools of Yass, New South Wales, in 1951.

this nature was not always possible, with the result that even as late as 1951 the National Conference of Directors and Inspectors of Catholic schools, while commending the improvement in this matter over the few preceding years, were forced to admit that the position at the half-century mark still left 'much to be desired'.[49]

A related feature in the development of girls' secondary schools in this third phase was the gradual assumption by the parish of the responsibility for secondary education and the consequent pushing up of the parochial school into the secondary level. This movement had not been so complete as the corresponding development in the boys' schools,[50] but it was already more widespread; with the result that, by 1950, the new system of parochial high schools was already challenging, at least in numbers, the older system of convent secondary schools. In the archdiocese of Sydney, for example, in that year, thirty-eight (more than half) of the seventy-odd girls' secondary schools were of the intermediate parochial type. Further down the scale and not included in the above figures was another type of parochial school just emerging—the post-primary; of this type there were fifty-five.[51] In the archdiocese of Adelaide, to take but one further example, nine of the twenty-eight schools included under secondary were of the older type and offering a full secondary course; the rest were parochial schools with junior secondary departments attached.[52]

As a result of these developments the total number of Catholic girls' secondary schools had, after a momentary lull in the early part of this third phase, vastly increased. Omitting the large number of schools in Sydney labelled 'post-primary' but including the rest, the total for the whole of Australia, at the end of the half-century, stood at 321 (see Table LIV).

---

[49] *Report of the Fifth National Catholic Education Conference of Directors and Inspectors of Schools,* p. 2.

One remaining difficulty was the parent. It was contended that if a parent was able and willing to pay more for the education of a child he was entitled to the extra advantages—smaller classes, more select companions, and so on—that were to be found in the higher-feed schools.   [50] See p. 340.

[51] *A.C.D.*, 1951, pp. 156-7.   [52] Ibid., p. 313.

9

The Curriculum: Profane Subjects

THE PRIMARY CURRICULUM
Improving Methods and Courses of Study

EDUCATIONALLY, the elementary parochial schools of the earlier nineteenth century had been at such a low ebb that the Church's motives in retaining these schools had been more than once called in question. Since, it was argued, the motive could hardly have been education, then it must have been something ulterior. 'It appears,' wrote one observer, 'that Irish priestcraft is a well-drilled and thoroughly organized society, having for its object collective power rather than independent culture.'[1] Whatever evidence there may have been for criticism of this type, Dr Carr, who answered this particular charge, was able to point to the improvements that had already been effected in Melbourne since his arrival and to cite in support of his case the observations made by state school inspectors on certain Catholic school exhibits at the Melbourne Education Exhibition. The exhibits, they said, gave evidence of 'excellent methods' in use in the schools. 'In some of the appliances . . . they were notably in advance of the State-supported institutions.'[2]

But that was in 1890 and Dr Carr's refutation did not deny that defects had existed earlier. In the eighties, the programme had been both meagre and inadequately taught. Speaking of the education given in state schools in New South Wales just after 1900, Professor Anderson of the Sydney University said that it was narrow and bookish,[3] concentrating on rote memory and neglecting the other mental faculties of the child.[4] The same criticism could have been aptly applied to the Catholic schools of a little earlier.[5]

Reading, according to the Inspector of Catholic schools in the Mait-

---

[1] This criticism came from an *Argus* correspondent who took the name of 'Pedagogue'. *Advocate*, 6 June 1891, p. 11, d.   [2] Ibid.
[3] Anderson, Francis, *The Public School System of New South Wales*, p. 3.
[4] Ibid., p. 8.
[5] 'The mental faculties,' wrote the Inspector of Catholic schools for the Goulburn diocese, 'are not educated . . . Any system of education which ignores thinking, and consequently neglects to develop the faculties, must lead to failure.' Report of Inspector of Catholic schools, Father Carr, Goulburn, 1883. *Record* (Bathurst), 7 February 1884, p. 65, b.

land diocese, was largely mechanical, the children paying no attention to the meaning of the words they repeated.[6] In the Sydney schools, it was 'generally well taught', according to Inspector J. Rogers of the archdiocese, but there was often a 'want of precision' and, in a number of cases, 'great carelessness about the letter "h" '.[7] In spelling, oral methods prevailed—with not too successful results. Since it was a subject to be 'learned by the eye rather than the ear', Rogers recommended the practice of transcription rather than dictation.[8] Arithmetic, observed the Maitland Inspector, was 'well taught in many of the schools', but was restricted to the purely mechanical aspects, little exercise being given in problems that 'require[d] a little thinking'.[9] In Catholic schools, the subject was badly taught. The real weaknesses, it is true, lay 'chiefly to the lower classes' but they involved fundamentals and were 'attributed partly . . . to the tables being neglected in the first instance and forgotten in the second'.[10] History, on the other hand, was 'taught well . . . as a memory subject' but its scope was inadequate. Rogers therefore advocated the addition of topics from both Irish and Australian history.[11] Later, in Victoria, in order to eliminate this unintelligent emphasis on memory work, it was suggested that history, natural science and freehand drawing be made subservient to the teaching of geography.[12] This, it was found, gradually changed the 'mechanical drudgery of committing to memory long catalogues of names and places into a most interesting and attractive educational exercise'.[13]

No one was more acutely aware of this need for improvement in the Catholic primary schools than Archbishop Carr of Melbourne. Accordingly in 1890 he initiated a wide programme of reform which had, within a few years, not only raised 'the status of primary education in the diocese'[14] but, in the words of the *Advocate* report, brought this fact forcibly to the 'recognition of Catholic parents'.[15]

The Archbishop's plea had been for a more realistic approach to teaching. 'Teach the children about things,' he said, 'not themes; exercise their senses before making demands on their intelligence.' As a result, technical aids began to make their appearance; better control and organization followed.[16] Newer methods of teaching which tended 'to develop the perceptive and intellectual faculties' replaced the older pro-

6 Dwyer, Rev. P. V., *Report on the Primary Schools*, Maitland diocese, 1884, p. 6.

7 Rogers, J. W., Report on Catholic Schools, archdiocese of Sydney, 1883 (Archives, St Mary's Cathedral, Sydney).

8 Ibid.   9 Dwyer, op. cit., p. 6.   10 Rogers, op. cit.   11 Ibid.

12 Report of Inspector of Catholic Schools, archdiocese of Melbourne, 1895. *Advocate*, 14 December 1895, p. 10, b.   13 Ibid.

14 Editorial comments on the 1890 Report. *Advocate*, 13 December 1890, p. 12.

15 Archbishop Carr, commenting on Report on Schools in the archdiocese of Melbourne, 1890. *Advocate*, 13 December 1890, p. 12.

16 Report of Inspector of Catholic Schools, Melbourne, 1894. *Advocate*, 8 December 1894, p. 8, b.

cesses 'of inordinately overloading the memory with hard and ill-digested facts'. Teachers were reported to have learnt from experience 'that the old plan of inordinately cultivating the memory [was] not only defective as an educational process but that it [was] frequently injurious to its own purpose'.[17] Further evidence of the effectiveness of Carr's work[18] is found in the fact that many of the best schools were already 'furnished with complete sets of object-lesson charts and kindergarten appliances'.[19] These object-lessons, long since outmoded, but then the very acme of respectability in teaching method, indicate an obvious readiness on the part of the Catholic school authorities to move with the times. The change brought about by these innovations was so pronounced that within five years the Reverend W. Ganly, Inspector of Catholic schools, was claiming that 'there is scarcely a new idea which has gained the approval of progressive educationists that does not find practical expression in our schools'.[20]

'In secular subjects,' he reported, 'great improvement [had] been made in the whole work of the programme.'[21] In arithmetic, the tests administered were, 'as a rule, accurately solved, and according to the shortest methods'. Grammar was 'well taught', a fact which was 'manifest from the readiness with which pupils parsed and analysed the most complicated passages'.[22] Compositions, 'from a syntactical point of view . . . were . . . generally faultless'. Geography, 'hitherto . . . treated in so many schools as the Cinderella of the programme' was then 'receiving proper attention'. 'The old and self-condemned system of loading the learner's memory with names of places [was] gradually giving way to the more reasonable method of historical and topical association.' The teaching of science and history, too, had been 'greatly facilitated' owing to the adoption of certain measures that had been suggested earlier by the Inspector.[23] Similar improvements had been reported in other places.[24]

[17] Report on the Catholic Primary Schools of the Archdiocese of Melbourne, 1893. Advocate, 16 December 1893, p. 7, b.
[18] The schools generally, after 'careful and exhaustive examination', showed a satisfactory position: 1st class: 51 schools   3rd class: 11 schools
                                                    2nd class: 32   „   4th class: 4   „
(Report on Primary Schools, Melbourne, by Rev. W. Ganly, 1893. Advocate, 16 December 1893, p. 7, b.)
[19] Report of Inspector of Catholic Schools, Melbourne, 1894.   [20] Ibid.
[21] Report on Primary Schools, Melbourne, 1893, p. 7, c.
[22] Ibid. See also Report on Catholic Primary Schools, Sydney, 1915, p. 276.
[23] Report on Primary Schools, Melbourne, 1893, p. 7, c.
[24] In the diocese of Maitland, for example, it is possible to trace the improvement over the eighties by the percentages awarded at the annual inspections, as in the following table (from Dwyer, op. cit., 1886, p. 5):

Year	Below standard	Up to, and above standard
	Percentage	
1883	32	68
1887	6	94

By this time too the course of studies was considerably more enriched than it had been in the decade before. In Queensland, for example, the subjects of instruction in 1895 were 'Reading, Writing, Drawing, Arithmetic, English, Grammar, Geography, History, Elementary Mechanics, Object Lessons, Drill and Gymnastics, Vocal Music, and (in the case of girls) Sewing and Needlework'.[25] In addition to these subjects the Victorian schools, from 1900, were offering elementary science and domestic economy with 'Cookery in the principal Convent Schools'.[26] The New South Wales schools had gone further and were offering, besides the subjects listed above, geometry, Irish history, typing, shorthand and book-keeping.[27]

After 1900, too, such subjects as art, crafts, music, and physical education began to receive greater attention. In Melbourne, various forms of handicraft were offered for boys in the principal city schools—sloid, wood-carving, stencilling and the like.[28] From the early eighties the tonic sol-fa system of music was being urged in New South Wales as 'well suited for primary schools';[29] while in Victoria, in the nineties, the 'provision in the programme for the development of the musical and artistic faculties of Catholic children [was] bearing abundant fruit'.[30] Physical education existed in the girls' schools in the form of 'extension and calisthenic exercises',[31] and in the boys' schools as military drill.

This form of exercise, 'so beneficial to boys and', according to Inspector Rogers, 'necessary for future contingencies', had almost died out in the Sydney Catholic schools conducted by lay teachers—a fact regarded by the Inspector as a 'positive misfortune'.[32] Apart from the mere physical exercise that such drill afforded, the provision of elementary military training in Catholic schools offered other important advantages. It was attended with political and social implications that could not be overlooked.[33] Teachers of boys' schools therefore were bade 'recollect that military drill [was] on the programme'.[34] In Victoria, it was done, and done well. Company and battalion drill, said the Inspector's report, were

[25] H. B. O'H., 'State Education in Queensland', *Christian Brothers' Educational Record*, 1895, p. 196.

[26] Report of Inspector of Catholic Schools, archdiocese of Melbourne, 1900. *Advocate*. 8 December 1900, p. 6, b.

[27] *Report on Catholic Primary Schools*, Sydney, 1913, pp. 7-9.

[28] Report of Inspector of Catholic Schools, archdiocese of Melbourne, 1915. *Advocate*, 11 December 1915, p. 27, c.

[29] Report of Inspector of Catholic Schools, archdiocese of Sydney, 1883, p. 4 (St Mary's Cathedral Archives). The Inspector counselled Saturday classes where teachers could receive training in singing and music.

[30] Report of Inspector of Catholic Schools, archdiocese of Melbourne, 1893. *Advocate*, 16 December 1893, p. 7, c. 'A good theoretical knowledge,' the Report continued, 'either of the Tonic sol-fa or of the common notation is now shown in the majority of the city and suburban, and in a few of the country schools.' See also Reports for 1894 and 1896 in the *Advocate*, 8 December 1894, p. 8, c; 12 December 1896, p. 7, d.

[31] Report of Inspector of Catholic Schools, archdiocese of Melbourne, 1893.

[32] Rogers, op. cit.   [33] Ibid., p. 4.   [34] Ibid.

practised 'with an amount of popularity approaching enthusiasm'; and cadet corps, established at the principal Melbourne schools, performed 'their manœuvres in most efficient and reassuring style'.[35]

Adopting the State School Standards

This general improvement in the instruction given in parochial schools was reassuring, both to parents and to ecclesiastical authorities. But reasons were brought forward for pushing it still further. Among these was one that could not be overlooked—the competition from state schools.[36]

The force of that argument had long been recognized. If Catholic schools were to attract pupils they would be obliged to offer them all that the state schools had to offer.[37] Bishop Polding had been very much aware of this fact and had laid it down that Catholic schools must not only 'rival the public schools', but 'successfully rival them'.[38] Vaughan had recognized the same need[39] and his Catholic Board of Education was gratified to observe that the schools of the Sisters of St Joseph, newly come to the archdiocese, were 'holding their own against . . . public schools in the neighbourhood'.[40] Eventually, in 1883, the Inspector of Catholic schools in Sydney recommended that 'the standard of proficiency in [Catholic] schools be assimilated, as far as [might] be found advisable, to that adopted in the revised form by the Government'.[41]

No official pronouncement on the subject came from the First Plenary Council held two years later,[42] there being some aversion apparently to linking standards in Catholic schools with those of the state. In the meantime the need for some standardization became imperative. Accordingly, in 1890, three Bishops—Dr Carr of Melbourne, Dr Doyle of Lismore and Dr Higgins, the Auxiliary Bishop of Sydney—were appointed by the Australian Hierarchy to draw up a standard of proficiency (*normam*) for use in the Catholic schools of Australia.[43] What form this standard took, how practical it was, and how widely it was used, are now difficult to discover. The Sydney Diocesan Synod of 1891, however, directed that it be 'strictly followed' in the schools of the archdiocese;[44] while in the archdiocese of Melbourne, two years later, it

35 Report of Inspector of Catholic Schools, archdiocese of Melbourne, 1893.
36 Archbishop Carr, commenting on Report on schools in archdiocese of Melbourne, 1890. *Advocate*, 13 December 1890, p. 12.
37 Catholic Education Board (Sydney), Minute Book, p. 7, c.
38 Letter, Polding to Clergy, St Mary's, 27 August 1867, on co-operating with the Council of Public Education. *Sydney Morning Herald*, 24 November 1869, p. 5.
39 Vaughan, Roger B., *Pastoral Letter to the Clergy and Laity of the Archdiocese of Sydney*, 1879, p. 11.
40 Catholic Education Board (Sydney), Minute Book, p. 48.
41 Rogers, op. cit., p. 2.
42 Although there was no direct reference in the decrees themselves, there was a slight reference in the pastoral that was issued by the Council.
43 *Decrees of Diocesan Synod*, Sydney, 1891, decr. xvi.
44 Ibid. decr. viii.

was reported that 'the ideal of excellence' which it proposed to 'both pupils and teachers' alike had 'infused fresh vigour into [the] schools'.[45] But extending this uniform standard throughout the whole of Australia was another question: however desirable it may have appeared in theory, it proved difficult and premature in practice. The scheme was dropped therefore, and the schools reverted to the practice of following the state-school standards. This seems to have been the intention of the Second Plenary Council, for in the *Acta et Decreta* of that Council are included significant extracts from the education decrees of The Third Council of Baltimore.[46] The American bishops had been instructed by Rome in 1875 that the standards in Catholic schools were on no account to be lower (*haud inferiores*) than those in the public schools, and that in teaching and discipline (*institutione et disciplina*) Catholic schools were to be the equals of those of the state.[47] This instruction the Baltimore Council had implemented by decreeing that Catholic schools should be advanced 'to the highest degree of perfection (*ad altiorem perfectionis gradum*)'.[48]

In another sense, this high standard was already presupposed in Australian ecclesiastical law. Under this law Catholic parents were required, under severe penalties, to send their children to Catholic schools; but, in doing so, explained Bishop Dwyer of Maitland, they should not be thereby asked to jeopardize their children's prospects.[49] Catholic schools therefore were to be maintained at a high standard of efficiency.

The same motive was already stressed in the constitutions of many of the religious orders. Mother Mary of the Cross had realized the importance of this and stressed it from the outset.[50] The *Customs and Directory of the Sisters of Mercy* had likewise laid down that the schools of the Sisters should be in no way inferior to those conducted by the state, but 'should rather be superior in every way, for the greater glory of God'.[51] Similar motives, just as specifically stated, were set before the members of other orders.[52]

[45] Report on Primary Schools, archdiocese of Melbourne, 1893. *Advocate*, 16 December 1893, p. 7, d.
[46] *Conc. Plen.*, II, decr. 313.
[47] Instructio de scholis publicis ad Episcopos U.S., 24 November 1875, printed in Smith, S. B., *Elements of Ecclesiastical Law*, vol. 1, Appendix III, p. 545.
[48] *Conc. Plen.*, II, decr. 313, p. 106.
[49] Dwyer, Bishop P. V., *What Steps may be taken to advance the Interests of our Religious Primary and Higher Schools?* p. 8.
[50] McKillop, Mother Mary, *Statement in Rome*, p. 7 (Archives, St Joseph's Convent, Mount Street, North Sydney).
[51] *Customs and Directory of the Sisters of Mercy*, 1865, p. 13.
[52] For example, *Constitutions of the Institute of the Blessed Virgin Mary for Houses dependent on the Mother House, Rathfarnham*, ch. XLX, art. 218. See also *Rule of St. Augustine and the Constitutions of the Congregation of the Dominican Sisters of New South Wales*, 1941, pt. 1, ch. 24, art. 214.

In short, there was general agreement on the point that the standards in Catholic schools should be in no way inferior to those of the state schools. Only the official approval of the Hierarchy was needed. This came in 1905. Hopeful of what the new Commonwealth would bring, the bishops assembled at the Third Plenary Council decreed that, until a uniform national system was established for the whole of Australia, a thing which was most desirable (*valde exoptandum*), Catholic schools in each state were to conform, as far as possible, to the standard laid down for the public schools of that state.[53]

But Archbishop Carr had already anticipated this decision of the Council. After several unsuccessful attempts he had abandoned the idea of drawing up a course of studies of his own, and, in August of that year, formally announced that Catholic schools of the archdiocese should adopt not only the state course of studies, but also its 'Method of Inspection and Examination'.[54] It proved to be a timely move. According to the inspectors' report for that year, the decision was welcomed 'with great satisfaction by all'.[55] The example was followed in other dioceses,[56] and by the middle of the present century the state course of studies, with exceptions in a few dioceses, was being followed in all phases of school work, primary, secondary, and technical. In one or two places—Victoria, for example—the Catholic schools were following a separate history syllabus which had been approved by the state.[57] But this applied only in the primary schools; the secondary courses need to be studied separately.

THE SECONDARY CURRICULUM: BOYS'

The Classics

The type of education given in the Catholic secondary schools that grew up over the hundred years between 1850 and 1950 was determined largely by the social condition and needs of the Catholic body; to satisfy these needs was its chief function. 'The school,' said Cardinal Moran, 'should promote the interests of those whom it educates, and should correspond to the requirements of the social progress in which we live.'[58] This principle, it will be seen, was observed, more or less closely, throughout the whole century. In developing Lyndhurst, for example, Polding

[53] *Conc. Plen.*, III, decr. 339.
[54] Report on Primary Schools, archdiocese of Melbourne (Nicholas J. Cooke, Inspector), 1905. *Advocate*, 9 December 1905, p. 13, a.
[55] Ibid.
[56] For example, in Ballarat. Report of Inspector of Schools, diocese of Ballarat, 1924. *Advocate*, 8 January 1925, p. 10, c.
[57] 'Catholic Education', Information Service, Education Department, Victoria, June 1951, p. 1.
[58] Moran, Cardinal P. F., 'The Aims of the Catholic Church in Australia at the beginning of the Twentieth Century', *Austral Light*, 1 October 1905, p. 698.

had in mind the education of Catholics of the upper classes: he wished to give them a training that would fit them to take their place among the leaders of society in all walks of life, professional, political, and ecclesiastical; and for such, at the time, the hall-mark of distinction was a sound classical education, capped, if possible, by the qualification of a university degree.

The provision of this type of training was to be Lyndhurst's primary function. But there was a serious difficulty. A Catholic aristocracy—monied, landed, or intellectual—such as Polding's plans presupposed did not exist in New South Wales in sufficient numbers to support a college of this type. Polding was not unaware of the fact, but his great aim was to lift the Church socially, and to raise Catholics from the status of an under-privileged minority in a penal colony to be the equals of their non-Catholic fellow colonists. In that broad scheme the Lyndhurst of his dreams would naturally play a major role. But circumstances compelled the Archbishop to modify his plans; and, in order to arrest the decline in enrolments at the college and make provision for the sons of the new merchant class for whom the purely classical education was too unreal, he was obliged to extend the curriculum so as to include some preparation for commercial occupations.

Still further modifications were made in the schools of the newer orders. Without entirely losing sight of the classical tradition of the Great Public Schools of England that had come down through Lyndhurst, these new schools, particularly those of the teaching Brothers, evolved a course of studies of their own[59] which has continued to form the basis of secondary education in boys' schools down to the present day.

Subsequent modifications occurred from time to time: one was the inclusion of science, another the introduction of the public examination system. Examinations, set by the Universities or Public Boards, and carrying, as they did, entrance to all the learned professions, to commerce, and to the public service, were readily accepted and in a very short time enjoyed a wide vogue. Not only did they gratify the social aspirations of the middle-classes, but they gave assurance and proof that the Catholic schools were, in this respect at least, not inferior to others. Nevertheless the curriculum was still what might be called, by present-day standards, bookish and heavily academic. Subsequent differentiation into technical and agricultural types, for example, was much slower in Catholic schools than it was in state schools,[60] though this tardiness is to be ascribed more to economic reasons than to any great reluctance to accept the principles

[59] The prototypes of these developments had already appeared in Europe. Battersby, Rev. W. J., *De La Salle, a Pioneer of Modern Education*, ch. 11.
[60] Report of Fifth National Catholic Education Conference of Directors and Inspectors of Schools, Hobart, 1951, p. 2 (Archives, Catholic Education Office, Melbourne).

upon which such changes were based. The religious orders of teaching Brothers showed no great opposition to these changes, as becomes obvious from a perusal of courses of study in their schools. On the other hand, the orders of priests showed some alarm at the growing tendency, in academic secondary schools, to forsake the humanities and concentrate on the sciences and mathematics. Up to the mid-century mark, however, no effort of theirs had been able to arrest it.[61]

A strong classical tradition, as has been suggested, characterized the early secondary schools. Even where the classics did not monopolize the curriculum[62] they predominated, sharing the field with a nondescript assortment of subjects which were supposed to impart to education a 'mercantile character',[63] and which, though never really acceptable to the authorities, had been admitted as a concession to the new merchant class. Questioned before the New South Wales Select Committee on Education in 1854, for example, Father McEncroe described both Lynd- hurst and St Mary's Seminary as 'grammar schools',[64] the subjects taught being Greek and Latin classics and mathematics.[65] The classics also figured prominently among the early studies at St Stanislaus', Bath-

---

[61] Direct evidence of this concentration was revealed in a survey carried out by the Vocational Guidance Section of the State Department of Labour and Industry and Social Welfare, Parramatta Branch. The survey covered 500 students who, drawn from all types of schools, passed their leaving certificate examination in 1950. The results show that the concentration on maths and science in Catholic schools is relatively much heavier than it is for the state schools, and within Catholic schools themselves, much heavier than it is for the humanities.

Percentage who passed L.C. and took the particular subject from:

Subject	State schools	Catholic schools	Private schools
Chemistry	29.9	72.1	45.8
Physics	23.3	49.7	34.4
Maths I and II	36.3	54.8	41.0
General maths	54.5	31.6	37.7
Modern history	62.0	54.9	57.3
French	61.2	46.4	50.9
Latin	9.2	32.9	11.4
Economics	34.5	6.4	19.6
Geography	48.3	25.1	50.9

Table compiled from Report in files of Parramatta Vocational Guidance Office, N.S.W.

The fear of such a trend was expressed half a century earlier by the Headmaster of Wesley College, Melbourne. *Report of Royal Commission on Technical Education* (Vic.), 1899-1901, evidence of Thomas Palmer, q. 11857. See also *Our Studies* (Chris- tian Brothers, Strathfield), October 1930, vol. 2, no. 2, p. 27, a.

[62] The horarium at Lyndhurst in its first days is given by Forster: Latin, 8 hours; Greek, 5¼ hours; writing, 2½ hours; geography, 3¼ hours; mathematics, 9 hours; French, 4 hours; elocution, 2 hours; history, 5 hours; Christian doctrine, 4-5 hours; singing, 2½ hours. Forster, op. cit., pt. ii, p. 26.

[63] See course of studies in advertisement for St Mary's Seminary and St Mary's College, Lyndhurst, *Catholic Almanac and Directory for Divine Service in the Arch- diocese of Sydney and the Diocese of Maitland*, pp. 95-6.

[64] Report of Select Committee on Education (N.S.W.), 1854, p. 24, qq. 4, 8. P.P.(N.S.W.), 1854, II.

[65] Ibid., q. 3.

urst, St Patrick's, Goulburn,[66] and Sacred Heart College, Maitland.[67] The curriculum at St Stanislaus' in its first year included Latin, Greek, French, mathematics, geography and 'mental calculations';[68] a decade later it was the same except that mathematics had been specified as arithmetic, algebra and geometry, and three extra subjects were included —history, English language, and composition.[69]

One of the great strongholds of the classical tradition was St Patrick's, Goulburn, its president, Dr Gallagher, being estimated by Professor Badham of the Sydney University 'as the best classical man in the whole colony'.[70] No similar reputation became attached to the contemporary Catholic colleges in the colonies; yet, in St Aloysius' at Sevenhill,[71] St Francis Xavier's in Adelaide (both under the diocesan clergy[72] as well as under the Jesuits),[73] St Mary's Seminary in Hobart,[74] the short-lived St John's in Perth,[75] and in the prospectuses of the other still-born Catholic college in that city in 1872,[76] the classical emphasis was strong.

The same tradition lingered in a few of the later schools. Dr James Quinn, for instance, secured the services of a layman to teach Greek in the Christian Brothers' first college in Queensland,[77] while it continued to be taught at St Patrick's, Goulburn, long after the Brothers had taken charge. Under the influence, moreover, of University matriculation requirements, it was taught with great success[78] in the Christian Brothers' Colleges of Adelaide and Perth.[79]

But it was in the Jesuit colleges that the classical tradition found its strongest support. Riverview in Sydney[80] and Xavier in Melbourne held to it firmly, from the lowest class to the highest.[81] In the late eighties

---

[66] *Freeman's Journal*, 10 January 1874.   [67] Ibid.

[68] Account of public examinations at Catholic schools, December 1867. *Times* (Bathurst), 25 December 1867, p. 2, c.

[69] See prize list, 1879. *Record* (Bathurst), 1 January 1880, p. 11, a, b. Whether English was accidentally omitted from the earlier account, or whether it was not taught as a separate subject is not clear. From an undated document, however, which announced that 'no pains would be spared in imparting a thorough sound Classical, Mathematical and English education' it seems likely that it was taught during the presidency of the first president, the Rev. J. J. McGirr. Hall, *History of St Stanislaus' College, Bathurst*, p. 27.

[70] Dr Badham referred to Gallagher as 'the Irish priest up at Goulburn'. Newspaper cutting, undated (Archives, Presentation Convent, Wagga).

[71] *Chaplet and Southern Cross*, April 1871.

[72] *Chaplet and Southern Cross*, 22 January 1872.   [73] *Irish Harp*, 30 May 1873, p. 7.

[74] *Catholic Herald* (Tas.), December 1872, p. 85, a, b.

[75] Prospectus in *Perth Gazette*, 7 March 1847, p. 2, a.

[76] Prospectus in *Perth Gazette*, 3 May 1872.

[77] Annals of Christian Brothers' College, Gregory Terrace, Brisbane, p. 5.

[78] By a Brother Ambrose Fitzgerald whose pupils won first place in Greek for five years in succession. Brother Fitzgerald had taught earlier at St Patrick's, Goulburn. See obituary notice, *Evening Post* (Goulburn), 4 April 1934.

[79] Perth, at that time, took the Adelaide University examinations.

[80] The prospectus for 1887 stipulated Greek (grammar, composition, authors) and Latin (grammar, composition, authors). *St. Ignatius' Prospectus*, 1887, pp. 12-13.

[81] Hughes, Rev. Father (S.J.), Prefect of Studies, Xavier College, Melbourne, Annual Report, 1889. *Advocate*, 21 December 1889, p. 8, b.

Xavier had an honours class in which boys spent a year after they had passed the formal matriculation examination, the course consisting entirely of classics, mathematics, history, English, French, and Christian doctrine.[82] Notwithstanding this already liberal dose of Greek and Latin, the Prefect of Studies felt impelled to raise his voice against what appeared to him to be a neglect of the classics. 'The unchanging nature both of the end aimed at in every system of education, as well as the means employed to attain that end' constituted, he thought, sufficient reason to justify a necessary repetition in the routine of college life and a certain conservative reluctance to admit subjects which he would regard as innovations and questionable departures.[83]

The retention of the classics was stoutly defended: they moulded character;[84] they contained unsurpassed treasures of graceful poetry and deep philosophy; they were perfect examples of logical and accurate use of language; and, above all other subjects, they produced the trained and disciplined mind.[85]

These views, expressed in evidence before the Clarendon Commission on Public Schools in England, represented the case for the classics when Lyndhurst was at the height of its career in Sydney, and when such men as the Quinns, Lanigan, Gallagher, and the first band of Irish Jesuits were preparing to leave their homeland for the Australian mission. All found ready acceptance in Australia. But the last, namely, that a study of the classics exerted a disciplinary effect on the mind, persisted well into the present century. Evidence of this is found in the statements of prominent teachers at the Fink Commission in Melbourne in 1900. 'We press on Greek', said George E. Blanch, Headmaster of the Melbourne Church of England Grammar School, particularly 'as a disciplinary subject'.[86] Alexander Morrison, the Principal of Scotch College, 'felt strongly the necessity of there being something above the present State School education . . . they [the pupils] do not get sufficient mental exercise to train their minds properly'.[87] Particularly in the Jesuit colleges was this idea of a 'well developed intellect'[88] kept before pupils (and parents) as the goal of the course of studies, whether classical, mathematical or scientific. The curriculum was laid down and 'the general order of studies [could] not be interfered with'; no student 'under ordinary circumstances' would be allowed to 'limit his application to certain

[82] 'I observe in general,' said the Prefect of Studies, 'that those who, after matriculation, join our college honour class get through the course of arts with flying colours.' Ibid., p. 8, a.   [83] Ibid., p. 8, c.
[84] Report of Public Schools Committee (England, Clarendon Commission), 1864, p. 28. Quoted in Kandel, I. L., History of Secondary Education, p. 325.   [85] Ibid.
[86] Final Report of Royal Commission on Technical Education (Vic.), 1899-1901, evidence of George E. Blanch, Headmaster, Melbourne Church of England Grammar School, q. 11889.
[87] Ibid. Evidence of Alexander Morrison, Principal of Scotch College, Melbourne, q. 11822.   [88] St. Ignatius' Prospectus, Sydney, 1887, p. 7.

easier subjects'. Such a course, the Jesuit Superiors deemed, 'would be a grave injury to the boy's educational progress'.[89]

Commercial Subjects

But the day of the classics was done. Although it could be shown that Latin at least never really disappeared from Catholic schools, the full classical tradition was out of step with the utilitarian spirit that permeated the second half of the nineteenth century. To the average Australian of the seventies and eighties such studies failed to meet the needs of the colonial lad. One observer wrote:

Here in New South Wales we move among a class essentially commercial . . . The battle of life is to be fought on a mercantile ground, not in the unpaying lists of a classical arena: consequently the muse must . . . yield at once, and retire before the day book and the ledger . . . Under the outward pressure of circumstance, the Latin grammar may be a very respectable book, but it must enter the field against 'double entry': the Ethics of Aristotle are all very well, but will hardly become current at the Corn Exchange.[90]

And it was the Corn Exchange and the Wool Exchange that mattered: their claims could not be ignored.

The Superiors of Lyndhurst and other Catholic colleges understood this well. Already, on paper at least, they had given assurance that full provision for a commercial education would be made.[91] Thus, the prospectus of St Mary's Seminary, Sydney, announced in the fifties that 'the education imparted [was] principally of a mercantile character', but that 'the rudiments of a good classical education [were] given when required'.[92] It then listed the subjects taught: 'Mathematics, Classics, French and English'.[93] St John's College in Perth proposed even in the forties to include courses that had a direct bearing on commercial pursuits—orthography, penmanship, arithmetic, book-keeping, and the theory and practice of land-surveying;[94] while the Catholic college that Dr Griver proposed to establish in the early seventies labelled one whole section of its curriculum 'Commerce', and included thereunder 'Book-keeping—single and double entry; Arithmetic—Mental and Practical; Forms of Notes and Bills'.[95]

[89] Ibid.
[90] 'Quilibet' in the *Australian Free Religious Press*, vol. 1, 7 February 1870, no. 1, p. 51.
[91] One reason that made this essential was that other schools were offering these subjects and so attracting boys to them.
For example, the course at Dr Lang's Australian College included a 'mercantile department for writing, arithmetic and book-keeping'. See Johnstone, S. M., *The History of the King's School, Parramatta*, p. 38.
[92] *Catholic Almanac and Directory for Divine Service in the Archdiocese of Sydney*, p. 105.   [93] Ibid., p. 106.
[94] Prospectus in *Perth Gazette*, 7 August, 7 March 1847, p. 2, a.
[95] Prospectus in *Perth Gazette and Western Australian Times*, 3 May 1872.

From its beginning St Stanislaus', Bathurst, besides affording pupils the ordinary classical education, was to aim also at 'fitting them for commercial pursuits'.[96] Dr Quinn had stressed the point himself;[97] nevertheless, only in the middle school was book-keeping or anything else that might constitute a direct preparation for a commercial career included.[98] When the Vincentians took over the college at the close of the eighties, however, not only was book-keeping included in the general course but shorthand and Spanish were offered as well.[99]

The other colleges of the time—St Mary's, Hobart,[1] St Patrick's, Goulburn,[2] Sacred Heart, Maitland, St. Aloysius', Sevenhill[3] and St Francis Xavier's, Adelaide—all offered some form of commercial education. Some offered navigation[4] and land surveying.[5] In the Jesuit colleges the commercial branch was admitted, but only with reluctance. The apparent readiness of St Francis Xavier's, which advertised that 'particular attention' would be given to the commercial branches 'when parents or guardians desire[d] it',[6] would have been looked upon as a concession to utilitarianism by the colleges of the Irish Jesuits in the eastern colonies. At Xavier, Melbourne, at the close of the eighties, book-keeping was offered, but in the lowest class only;[7] at Riverview, in Sydney, the planners of the course announced that they bore in mind the boy who might wish to 'apply himself to mercantile pursuits',[8] but nothing in direct preparation for this was included in the general studies; book-keeping and phonography (Pitman's) were extras.[9]

At Lyndhurst commercial studies had been excluded altogether—at first; later they were admitted grudgingly. This attitude of the Benedictine Superiors to the popular demands for a more utilitarian type of education—their defiance first and later their capitulation—throws a strong light on Polding's educational aims. For the first ten years of the existence of the college Polding insisted on a curriculum in the full classical tradition.[10] Confronted, however, by the mounting prejudice

96 Hall, *History of St Stanislaus' College, Bathurst*, p. 27.
97 Quinn, Bishop Matthew, *Pastoral Letter to the Clergy and Laity of the Diocese*, 1882, p. 4.
98 See prize list, St Stanislaus' College, 1879, *Record*, 1 January 1880, p. 11.
99 *Echoes from St Stanislaus'*, vol. 1, December 1889.
1 *Half-Yearly Report of St Mary's Seminary*, June 1874, p. 31.
2 *Freeman's Journal*, 10 January 1874, p. 1, b.
3 *Catholic Almanac and Directory of Divine Service in the Archdiocese of Sydney*, 1862, p. 82.
4 At St Mary's, Hobart. *Catholic Standard* (Tas.), January 1872, p. 112, c.
5 At Sacred Heart, Maitland. *Freeman's Journal*, 10 January 1874, p. 1, b.
6 Advertisement in *Harp and Southern Cross*, 4 September 1874, p. 8.
7 Report of the Prefect of Studies, Xavier College, Melbourne, 1889. *Advocate*, 21 December 1889, p. 8, b.
8 *St. Ignatius' Prospectus*, Sydney 1887, p. 7.   9 Ibid., pp. 12-13.
10 Forster, 'Lyndhurst and Benedictine Education', *Australasian Catholic Record*, pt. ii, p. 27. This view and those which follow are those of Marie Forster. Her researches on Benedictine education are deep, her interpretations just, her conclusions reliable and acceptable.

against an exclusively classical education and a falling enrolment in the college itself, he was compelled to give way. A new prospectus,[11] issued in March 1861, announced that henceforth the details of each pupil's course were to be 'decided by the intentions, and so far as was practicable, by the wishes of the parents'. The Principal was to be informed of the occupation planned for each pupil and the approximate number of years he would be left at the college; then, for those who proposed 'early to engage in commercial pursuits', a 'good English education' was to be designed, 'complete and thorough in its scope'.[12] That was the first concession; five years later other and more thorough-going ones were made. In 1866 'a modern department' was created in which special attention was to be paid to such matters as official correspondence, book-keeping, banking, bills, stocks, funds and the like.[13]

But all these additions were concessions made against Polding's better judgment.[14] The great need of the Church in New South Wales, he felt, was for better-educated Catholics. A few short years spent at college in pursuit of commercial qualifications would be no substitute for that deep and solid training which was the only safeguard against the sophistries of the time, and the 'best worldly defence against the false spirit which cultivate[d] Liberalism in place of Christian Charity'.[15] Against the new spirit that was abroad a sound education, which to the Benedictine Superiors meant a classical one, was the only bulwark.

But the classics were now faced with another rival. Commerce, an intruder at first, had succeeded eventually in having its claims recognized.[16] Now it was science.

Science

Science made its way into the curriculum of Catholic schools in Australia in two ways: first, by virtue of a sort of academic recognition of the importance of scientific thinking; secondly, in deference to the demands for trained and skilled artisans who might apply the content of science to industry. Both movements owed much to the influence of Spencer[17] and Thomas Huxley;[18] but the second was largely Continental in origin and, although the need for it was stressed in Australia over the last part of the nineteenth century, the great impetus towards its realiza-

11 Ibid.   12 Ibid., from *Prospectus*, Lyndhurst College.   13 Ibid.

14 Ibid.: 'It may be inferred,' writes Forster, 'that these modifications were sanctioned but reluctantly.'

15 Address by Father Norbert Quirk, O.S.B., *Freeman's Journal*, 21 December 1867; also Forster, p. 28.

16 See *Final Report of Royal Commission on Technical Education* (Vic.), 1899-1901, evidence of George E. Blanch, Headmaster, Melbourne Church of England Grammar School, q. 11904.

17 Particularly in his work *Education: Intellectual, Moral and Physical*. This was published first in 1859.

18 Cf. Huxley's *Science and Education* (Cubberley, Ellwood P., *The History of Education*, p. 778).

tion came from the two big commissions on education early in the present century, the Knibbs and Turner Commission in New South Wales[19] and that of Theodore Fink in Victoria.[20]

The earlier of these movements might be considered first. The Clarendon Commission in England in the sixties had given partial recognition to the claims of science by conceding a small place for 'a branch of natural science'.[21] In the same spirit Lyndhurst had, from the middle fifties, included natural philosophy;[22] and in anticipation, as it were, of Herbert Spencer's *Education*,[23] introduced elementary physiology.[24] Later it added a sort of elementary chemistry.[25] Science was not offered in the early days of St Stanislaus', Bathurst, but it appeared as natural philosophy and chemistry on the first curriculum issued under the Vincentians.[26] Natural philosophy also figured on the early curriculum of Sacred Heart College, Maitland, but it was absent from St Patrick's, Goulburn.[27]

Science of this type was also offered in the early Catholic secondary schools of the other colonies. At Sevenhill, for example, beside the classical and commercial education, 'due attention' was to be 'paid to Natural Sciences'.[28] St John's College in Perth was to teach natural philosophy, chemistry, and the use of globes';[29] whereas the curriculum of its successor thirty years later, except for a bare reference to 'the use of globes' under the general heading of English, made no allusion whatsoever to science.[30] The revived St Mary's Seminary in Hobart purported to prepare pupils for the Associate of Arts Degree[31] which listed among its subjects the elementary principles of hydrostatics and mechanics and the elements of chemistry, zoology, botany, and geology.[32] Xavier in Melbourne, in the late eighties, was offering physics in the three classes leading to matriculation but not in its honours course;[33] Riverview, Xavier's counterpart in Sydney, gave an ordinary course of science con-

[19] George Handly Knibbs and John William Turner were commissioned to 'proceed to Europe and America for the purpose of inquiring into existing methods of instruction in connection with primary, secondary, technical, and other branches of education and of recommending for adoption whatever improvements you may consider might with advantage be introduced into the State of New South Wales'. Letter of Appointment, Lt.-Governor F. M. Darby to Commissioners.
[20] *Final Report of Royal Commission on Technical Education* (Vic.), 1899-1901.
[21] *Report of Public Schools Commission* (Clarendon), p. 53.
[22] *Catholic Almanac and Directory*, 1855, p. 105.　　　[23] See note 1, above.
[24] *Catholic Almanac and Directory*, 1855, p. 105.
[25] Forster, op. cit., pt. ii, p. 26. For achievements of Lyndhurst men in science at the University, see pt. iii, p. 119.　[26] *Echoes from St Stanislaus'*, vol. 1, no. 1, December 1889
[27] *Freeman's Journal*, 10 January 1874, p. 1, b.
[28] *Catholic Almanac and Directory*, 1862, p. 82.
[29] Prospectus in *Perth Gazette*, 7 March 1846, p. 2, a.
[30] Advertisement in *Perth Gazette and Western Australian Times*, 3 May 1872.
[31] *Half-Yearly Report of St. Mary's Seminary*, June 1874, p. 31.
[32] Regulations for A.A. Degree, reg. 4. *Report of Council of Education*, 1863, P.P.(Tas.), 1863, X, p. 10.
[33] Report of Prefect of Studies. *Advocate*, 21 December, 1889, p. 8, b.

sisting of heat, light, sound and electricity, and offered geology, physiology, chemistry and botany as extras.[34] Holy Ghost College, Ballarat, provided a science course labelled natural philosophy.[35]

With one or two possible exceptions, none of these courses in science appears to have gone further than the recommendations of the Clarendon Commission. The subject still continued to play only a minor role in the curriculum,[36] but in the community at large it was destined to win wider support. Thirty years before the Knibbs and Turner Commission, the importance of science in industry had been put forward as an argument for increasing the time allotted to it in school. 'The manifest destiny of all the colonies . . .', argued a contemporary correspondent to the press, was 'clearly to be commercial, agricultural, manufacturing and industrial to an extraordinary degree, and consequently the cultivation of the physical sciences must come to the front'.[37] Fear of trade competition, too, from Continental countries such as Germany, awakened a new interest in the application of science to industry.[38] In addition, the gradual disintegration of the old apprenticeship system[39] and the onset of an economic depression in the nineties had both pointed to technical education as perhaps the best means of effecting a remedy and safeguarding the future.

It was from this new interest in technical education that science received its strongest support. The chief hope for the development of technical education in the secondary schools lay, it was thought, 'in the extension of the science work'.[40] The time had come, said the protagonists, when it was necessary for the secondary schools to 'extend the practical side of their work as distinct from the cultural side', for it was 'unlikely that the exaggerated tendency towards the learned professions [would] be maintained'. This became one of the strongest recommendations of the Fink Commission: not only should more attention

---

34 St. Ignatius' Prospectus, Sydney, 1887, p. 13.
35 Account of distribution of prizes. Advocate, 20 December 1890, p. 8, b.
36 Knibbs and Turner, Report on Secondary Education, 1904, p. 17.
37 Letter, to editor, Australian Free Religious Press, vol. 1, 4 April 1870, p. 85.
38 Knibbs and Turner, op. cit., p. 85. This point was stressed over and over again in the reports of Knibbs and Turner, and in both the evidence and report of the Fink (Technical Education) Commission in Victoria. See Knibbs and Turner, Interim Report on (Primary) Education, p. 9, also ch. 1, secs. 5, 10, 12, 14, 15; Report on Agricultural, Commercial, Industrial, and other forms of Technical Education (N.S.W.), 1905, p. 41. For references in the Fink Commission, see Final Report of the Royal Commission on Technical Education (Vic.), 1899-1901, pp. 17, 26, 252; also evidence of J. W. Fleming, Mayor of Brunswick, on the pottery industry, q. 8382; evidence of Alexander Wales on trade with other colonies, q. 8389; evidence of George Dupree on leather industry, q. 9819; on study of economic geography, evidence of Alexander Morrison, q. 11809. Technical Education was also being urged by the various Chambers of Manufactures; for example, in South Australia, Adelaide Observer 31 March 1883, p. 25, d.
39 Final Report of the Royal Commission on Technical Education (Vic.), 1899-1901, evidence of George Dupree, Sect., Tanners and Curriers' Society, q. 9821.
40 Ibid., evidence of George E. Blanch, Headmaster, Melbourne Church of England Grammar School, q. 1185.

be paid to the development of 'a scientific and modern side of secondary schools', but the idea itself should receive more encouragement from the state. Immediate action was regarded as 'essential'.[41] The action suggested was: first, the making of grants 'for the equipment and maintenance of laboratories'[42] and, secondly, the raising of the matriculation requirements in science.

This latter stimulus, it was agreed, should come from outside the schools—from the University, for instance, or from some examining body. Victorian teachers had already displayed a willingness to teach science, if the University would examine in it;[43] and the Irish Christian Brothers, who, by that time, had secondary schools in all states save Tasmania, were clamouring for it.[44]

In New South Wales, actually, the teaching of science in the Catholic secondary schools had anticipated the recommendations of the Knibbs-Turner Report. In fact, to imply, as some did, that the secondary schools of that state had seriously neglected science teaching would have been, according to the Commission, 'somewhat misleading'.[45] In the first place, only two state secondary schools for boys existed at the time as against the half dozen corresponding Catholic schools; then, in the second place, a comparison of the amount of science taught in representative types of schools reveals a significantly heavier concentration on science in the Catholic schools (see Table LVII).[46] Sydney Boys' High School is taken as a representative state high school, Riverview as a representative Catholic school taught by priests and St Joseph's as a representative school taught by Brothers. In addition to the differences revealed in this table, the well-equipped laboratories at St Joseph's,[47] the Riverview observatory that enjoyed already a world-wide repute, and the Röntgen or X-ray experiments at St Stanislaus' College during the nineties[48] as well as its long run of physics exhibitions in the junior and senior public examinations[49] would appear to have put the Catholic secondary schools a considerable distance ahead[50] in the teaching of science.[51]

[41] Ibid. (Final Report), p. 256.   [42] Ibid., p. 260.
[43] Ibid. Evidence of George E. Blanch, q. 11885.
[44] Christian Brothers' Educational Record, 1898, pp. iv, ix. They recommended a reduction in the amount of poetry and history in order to make more room for science. The Record early in the 1900s carried articles on the teaching of science, Christian Brothers' Educational Record, 1901, pp. 594, 598 ff.
[45] Knibbs and Turner, Report on Secondary Education, 1904, p. 44.
[46] Ibid., p. 42, course of studies at Sydney Boys' High School, 1903. Science appears to have been omitted altogether in lower forms; ibid., p. 35, course of studies at St Ignatius', Riverview, 1903; ibid., p. 34, course of studies of St Joseph's College, Hunter's Hill, 1903. Here, natural science was taken in junior forms. In upper forms, chemistry and geology were alternatives.   [47] Ibid., p. 34.
[48] Hall, History of St Stanislaus' College, Bathurst, p. 110.   [49] Ibid., p. 102.
[50] The evidence of Thomas Palmer (Headmaster of Wesley) before the Final Commission reveals the position of science teaching generally in Victoria. Science, he said, had been taught in state schools since 1883, but 'the amount . . . that is taught is worthless, and not worth setting an examination paper for. Further, in 1900, the number of

TABLE LVII

Science in Three Representative Schools, New South Wales, 1903

School	Branch				Hours per week	
	Physics	Chem.	Geol.	Nat. sci.	Upper school	Lower school
Sydney Boys'	Yes	—	—	—	2	—
Riverview	Yes	Yes	—	—	1½	1
St Joseph's	Yes	Yes	Yes	Yes	6	2

Whether this ready admission of science into the curriculum of Catholic secondary schools was the result of a broadening of the concept of liberal education[52] or whether it was to be attributed to pressure from below—from the demand of the middle and lower classes for an education that was more vocational or technical—is at first a difficult question. Some light is shed on it by a consideration of what might be called the public examination era in Catholic schools, for here the two influences converge.

Public Examinations

Examinations held an important place in the Catholic secondary schools right from the start. The chief function of Lyndhurst, in Polding's eyes, was the preparation of students for the university, the church and the civil service.[53] Just how successful the college was in the first of these tasks has been shown from the university careers of some of its alumni.[54] Besides the matriculation examination, however, Lyndhurst had created for itself a formidable internal examination system of its own.[55] At St Stanislaus', the university examinations began to be taken seriously from 1876,[56] but one student at least had matriculated in the sixties even while the college still bore the unpretentious title of High School. From their foundation, both St Patrick's, Goulburn,[57] and

students who sat for the matriculation exam was 1,300; of these 124 took Physics, fewer took Chemistry; while eighty per cent of this 124 came from only three different schools'. *Final Report of Royal Commission on Technical Education* (Vic.), 1889-1901, evidence of Thomas Palmer, qq. 11863, 11854.

51 The science taught generally connoted physics and chemistry only. Very little biological science was done. Ibid., q. 11865.

52 Knibbs and Turner, *Report on Secondary Education*, 1904, p. 43.

53 Forster, 'Lyndhurst and Benedictine Education', *Australasian Catholic Record*, pt. ii, p. 28.   54 See p. 314, and Forster, op. cit., pt. iii, p. 119.

55 No master examined his own pupils. Senior classes were examined (written) by the leading scholars of the day—Dr Woolley (Chancellor of the University), Professor Pell (of Maths), Dr Forrest, Rector of St John's, and others. Forster, op. cit., pt. ii, p. 32.

56 *Echoes from St Stanislaus'*, p. 41. An early prospectus of St Stanislaus' College (p. 27) announced that the 'System will aim principally at preparing students for the University and fitting them for commercial pursuits'.

57 *Freeman's Journal*, 1 February 1874, p. 1, b. St Patrick's, Goulburn, claims to have been the first Catholic institution in New South Wales to have presented pupils for the public examinations. That was in 1874, when five out of six passed the senior University examination. Its success encouraged others to present pupils for these examinations. Annals of St Patrick's College, Goulburn, op. cit., p. 3.

Sacred Heart, Maitland,[58] prepared boys for the university; so too did the Jesuit colleges.[59] Even in those colonies where no universities existed at the time, the schools found means of taking public examinations.

Queensland and Western Australia were cases in point. In both these colonies Catholic secondary schools were established years before the universities. In the meantime, therefore, pupils were obliged to take the examinations set by the universities in the neighbouring colonies: in Queensland they took the Sydney examinations, in Western Australia those of Adelaide. In this way the Christian Brothers' College in Perth was responsible for introducing the Adelaide University examinations into Western Australia, thereby giving a strong impetus to secondary education in that colony.[60] In Queensland, Dr Quinn had insisted from the very beginning that his secondary schools take the university examinations. 'There [was] one thing in connection with the Christian Brothers' School', he pointed out on the opening day in 1875, which he particularly wanted known: namely 'that their curriculum comprise[d] the 'University Matriculation course'.[61] He had himself already approached the University of London and sought permission for Queensland students not only to matriculate from the colony but to pursue their studies from there as well. This part of his plan did not eventuate but, beginning from 1879, both the Christian Brothers' College and St Kilian's sent pupils for the Sydney University junior and senior examinations.[62] The lead once given, others followed. By the eighties practically all the Catholic secondary schools were engaged in preparation for university, or public, examinations.[63]

In this a significant evolutionary process is to be observed. The major Catholic secondary schools, erected in the episcopal cities, were doing

[58] Freeman's Journal, 1 February 1874, p. 1, b.
[59] St Ignatius' Prospectus, 1887.
[60] Battye, J. S. (ed.), The Cyclopaedia of Western Australia, vol. ii, p. 77. Annals of Christian Brothers' College, pp. 2, 3, 9, 28, 29 (Archives of Christian Brothers' College, St George's Terrace, Perth). For exhibitions and scholarships gained see, for example, Report of Board of Education (W.A.), 1904, p. 31. P.P.(W.A.), 1905, II, paper 11.
[61] Dr Quinn's address at opening of Christian Brothers' school in the old church in Elizabeth Street, Brisbane, 1875. Brisbane Courier, 6 July 1875, p. 3, c.
[62] Report of University of Sydney, 1879, pp. 12-13. P.P.(N.S.W.), 1879-80, p. 463; also Annals of Christian Brothers' College, Gregory Terrace, Brisbane, p. 10.
[63] For example, in the 1879 senior examinations those presenting successful candidates were: St Stanislaus', Bathurst, 6; Sacred Heart, Maitland, 1; St Patrick's, Goulburn, 2; St Kilian's, Brisbane, 2. Record (Bathurst), 1 January 1880, p. 19. For the junior examinations: St Patrick's, Goulburn, 5; St Mary's, Ipswich (Q'ld.), 7; St Stanislaus', Bathurst, 2; Sacred Heart, Maitland, 6; St Kilian's, Brisbane, 2. Record (Bathurst), 1 January 1880, pp. 18-19.
For later results in the eighties see Record (Bathurst), 15 January 1881, p. 40; ibid., 15 May 1881; Express (Sydney), 3 November 1883, p. 4; ibid., 29 December 1883, p. 5. Record (Bathurst), 2 January 1884, p. 78; ibid., 18 December 1884, pp. 560-1.
In Victoria see Advocate, 11 January 1890, p. 8, a; ibid., 8 December 1900, p. 7, a.
In Adelaide, Annals of the Christian Brothers' College, Perth, pp. 13, 17, 19.

for their respective dioceses what Lyndhurst was doing for Sydney, namely, preparing their pupils for the university or for the church. But alongside these, as has been shown, there arose another type of Catholic school intended primarily to provide a superior, or secondary, education for the middle classes. These schools may not have found university examinations necessary nor even helpful, yet within a short time they were completely absorbed into the university system, taking distinction in the examinations as their sole criterion of success.

Illustrations of this phenomenon abound. As indicated, the first secondary school opened by the Marist Brothers in Sydney was established at the request of those who found Lyndhurst too far out of the city and considered its curriculum irrelevant to their needs, and who in any case would have found the tuition fees well above their means.[64] Unlike the type of secondary education then traditional in the colony, the curriculum of this school was evolved from that of the primary school— religious instruction, penmanship, mathematics, globes, English history, English composition, book-keeping, drawing, and music[65]—subjects which had a direct, practical value in the mercantile occupations the pupils were later to follow. To these subjects French and—for obvious reasons in a Catholic school—Latin were added.[66] Then within a few years, pupils from the school were being presented for the public examinations along with pupils from the older schools.[67]

A similar evolution is observed in other schools of this type.[68] When, for example, the Christian Brothers returned to Sydney and settled at Balmain, their school began to retain its pupils after the elementary grades and, by expanding its curriculum a little, was in a short time taking the junior and senior examinations.[69] Likewise, the Brothers'

[64] The fees at the first high school of the Marist Brothers in Sydney were 6d., 9d., and 1s. per week. Marist Brothers' Annals, pp. 4-5, 11.

[65] Ibid., p.11. For course of studies at Christian Brothers' College in Perth, in the nineties, see Record (W.A.), 22 March 1894, p. 2. At St Joseph's College, Nudgee, Queensland, it was stated that 'whilst university tests are an excellent standard by which to judge the efficiency of a school, the Brothers regarded the training of boys for commercial pursuits and for trade as of quite as much importance . . . ' Annual Report, 1892, Age (Brisbane), 24 December 1892, p. 2, b.

The type of pupil enrolling precluded anything but a sober, utilitarian course of studies. For example, in South Australia: 'For many years after the opening of the boarding part of the college, the boarders were largely made up of farmers' sons from the bush, who had grown almost to manhood without any tincture of religion or education. The object of such in coming to our college was to receive the elements of an English education, and to prepare for the Sacraments.' 'Education in South Australia', Christian Brothers' Educational Record, 1898, p. 6.

[66] French was regarded as possessing distinct commercial value. The fact that it was the native tongue of many of the first Brothers in the colony has no bearing on its introduction into the course of studies. Latin, the official language of the Church, was included, not only for its cultural and disciplinary value, but also because many boys from this school would eventually go into the priesthood.

[67] See lists of schools in the Record (Bathurst), January 1884, pp. 7-8.

[68] For example, Marist Brothers' School, Bendigo. Advocate, 2 June 1904, p. 15, a.

[69] See p. 326.

primary school at Ballarat was holding on to its pupils and presenting them for the Melbourne University matriculation even before the Holy Ghost College was established in that city.[70]

Such examples illustrate the fact that the line of demarcation between primary and secondary education in the Brothers' schools was always obscure.[71] The real object of the teachers was to give the pupils as good an education as possible in the time available, irrespective of whether it was labelled primary or secondary. In fact, any distinction that might have existed was, as in the case of many of the girls' schools, one of social rather than academic status. These 'superior' or 'private' schools drew their pupils from the better-off classes of society and so were able to retain them longer at school. In this way they were able to develop the higher studies. Such was the origin of schools like the Christian Brothers' College on Victoria Parade in Melbourne,[72] the Brothers' High School at Lewisham in New South Wales,[73] and most of the other Brothers' secondary schools. It was this type of school, evolving out of the elementary school and providing a middle-class education for people of the middle and even working-class means, that became the normal Catholic secondary school of later times. The older, official secondary schools continued, but they were greatly outnumbered.[74]

This middle-class type of secondary school, however, was not wholly original. The teaching orders had brought the idea with them from Europe where schools of this type had been founded by De La Salle over a century earlier.[75] Similar schools had been later established by the Marist Brothers in France and by the Christian Brothers in Ireland.[76]

[70] Annals of St Patrick's College, Ballarat, p. 3.

[71] Report of Inspector of Catholic Schools, archdiocese of Melbourne, 1893, Advocate, 16 December 1893; Report of 1896, 12 December 1896, p. 7, d. See arrangement of classes in many Catholic schools in Victoria, Advocate, 2 January 1904, pp. 14, c, 15, a.
For Western Australia, Chief Inspector's Report in Report of Minister of Education, 1895, p. 26. P.P.(W.A.), 1896, I, paper 19.
See also Final Report of Royal Commission on Technical Education (Vic.), 1899-1901, evidence of Thomas Palmer, Headmaster of Wesley, q. 11864.

[72] See, in this connection, the 'private' or high school established by the Marist Brothers in Sydney in 1875 as compared with the parochial school established there in 1872. A similar distinction was made between St Francis' school where the Christian Brothers first taught in Melbourne and the school they established on Victoria Parade in 1871. J.B.L. and J.P.O'M., 'A Short Sketch of the Christian Brothers' Institute, Australia'. Christian Brothers' Educational Record, 1892, p. 101.   [73] A.C.D., 1895, p. 71.

[74] It is sometimes stated that the Catholic secondary schools in Australia stemmed from the Great Public Schools of England. G. V. Portus, Free, Compulsory and Secular—a Critical Estimate of Australian Education. Studies and Reports, no. XI. This generalization, in view of the statements made in the text, is more wrong than right.

[75] See Margaret O'Leary, Education with a Tradition, p. 28. Another French authority claims that 'Il (De La Salle) a fondé des pensionnats de l'enseignement moyen qui inaugurèrent l'enseignement secondaire. Par ce genre d'institutions, il a assuré à la bourgeoisie une formation scientifique de plus en plus indispensable par suite des progrès de l'industrie'. Herment, Jules, Les idées pédagogiques de Saint Jean Baptiste de la Salle, p. 14.

[76] Originally the work of the Irish Christian Brothers lay primarily in the elementary schools. Circumstances, however, compelled them to develop middle-class schools. Christian Brothers' Educational Record, 1898.

Both orders, therefore, found it a simple matter to adapt the idea to Australian conditions.

To this type of secondary school, especially in the way it developed in Australia, the public examination system was a distinct advantage. In the first place, it supplied a recognized test of the efficiency of the school, thereby raising it considerably in public estimation.[77] In the second place, the examinations gratified parental aspirations in an age in which parents not only laid great store on examination results, but as has been suggested, also desired for the children the honour and character attached to a profession or position in the public service.[78] The Irish Christian Brothers, moreover, who had seen the advantages[79] of the intermediate system in Ireland, were quick to seize the opportunities offered by the examination system in Australia,[80] and the bishops gave them every encouragement.[81] Lastly, the public examinations had the effect not only of co-ordinating,[82] and creating a uniform standard among Catholic secondary schools,[83] but of forging a useful link between the Catholic system and the non-Catholic system.

[77] 'Is the Intermediate a success in our schools?' *Christian Brothers' Educational Record*, 1889, p. 165.

[78] This desire of parents, according to the *Christian Brothers' Educational Record* (1894, p. 508), 'seems to have helped in causing the establishment in New South Wales and South Australia of two examinations called respectively the Junior and the Senior'.

[79] See P.J.H., 'The Intermediate Examination System', *Christian Brothers' Educational Record*, 1893, p. 247. Further, 'Is the Intermediate a Success in our Schools?' *The Christian Brothers' Educational Record*, 1889, p. 166.
The Holy Ghost Fathers, too, launched upon public examinations in the same year of their establishment at Ballarat. *Argus*, 20 December 1890, p. 8, b.

[80] 'University Examinations' (Australasia), *Christian Brothers' Educational Record*, 1898, p. 14. 'We are anxious that our senior pupils should distinguish themselves by their secular knowledge at Intermediate and University examinations.' J.J.B., 'Educating versus Teaching', *Christian Brothers' Educational Record*, 1895, p. 188.

[81] The Irish Hierarchy, in 1869, had demanded a system of intermediate education. 'The Intermediate Education System'. *The Christian Brothers' Educational Record*, 1893, pp. 213-49.
It was a system after this style that the Australian bishops desired. To the bishops assembled at the First Plenary Council in 1885 'visum est perutile ut systema Intermediae, ut aiunt, educationis, saltem ex ea parte quae respicit examen et proemia, institutum a Gubernio Britannico et cum felicissimo successu in Hibernia vigens in has colonias a respectivis Guberniis introducatur'. *Conc. Plen.*, I, 1885, decr. 248; II, 1895, decr. 316; III, 1905, decr. 343.

[82] It was a lack of co-ordination that struck the Commissioners, Knibbs and Turner, as one of the chief defects of the New South Wales system. Knibbs and Turner, *Report on Secondary Education*, 1904, p. 357. 'Our present undirected educational drift is hopelessly inconsistent with the attainment of a high degree of excellence.' Ibid., p. 5. See also the *Interim Report*, p. 469; and Gollan, *The Organization and Administration of Education in New South Wales*, p. 5.

[83] Many Catholic secondary schools began, immediately on the passing of the Bursary Act, to reorganize their classes. See Annals of St Patrick's College, Goulburn, p. 30; Annual Report of St Joseph's College, Hunter's Hill, *Freeman's Journal*, 18 December 1913, p. 13, a; St Stanislaus', Bathurst, *Freeman's Journal*, 19 December 1912, p. 11, a; Marist Brothers' High School, Darlinghurst, *Freeman's Journal*, 19 December 1912, p. 13, b; St Ursula's, Armidale, ibid., p. 15, a; Our Lady of Mercy College, Goulburn, ibid., p. 19, a; De La Salle College, Armidale, ibid., p. 23, d; St Ignatius', Riverview, ibid., p. 8, d, etc.

But the system as a whole was not an unmixed blessing. In one sense it tended to retard progress. A Catholic school that had any pretentions at all to the name of secondary school was obliged to send its pupils for the public examinations. In this way the somewhat narrow, academic curriculum imposed by the examination syllabuses came to be accepted in the Catholic schools as the only recognized form of secondary education. The school, moreover, that was successful in imparting this type of education accumulated a social, economic, and educational status that far exceeded its real importance. Scarcely any other concept of secondary education existed: for people to think of secondary education in terms of anything but leaving certificate or matriculation examinations was just as difficult as it was a century earlier to think of it in terms of anything but a thorough training in the classics.

But the disintegration of that concept was inevitable.[84] It had, in fact, been going on in Australia since the beginning of the present century.[85] An attempt had been made by the Catholic Teachers' Association of New South Wales in 1911 to modify the existing system by introducing in its place a type of accrediting system in conjunction with the University of Sydney,[86] but the project was not followed up. Nothing more was done until the twenties; the chief obstacle apparently was lack of funds. Technical courses had been suggested as the alternative to the academic courses prescribed for the public examinations, but the religious, who, through their vow of poverty and the careful husbanding of resources had been able to build their secondary schools, could not face up to the expense of equipping the more costly technical schools.[87]

Gradually, however, the example of the state system[88] and a deepening awareness of the inadequacy and lack of diversity in the Catholic system[89] made some modification of the older system necessary. Added to this was the need for skilled Catholic artisans[90] and the realization

[84] *Year Book of Education,* pp. xviii-xix.

[85] Cf. the recommendations of the Knibbs and Turner and the Fink Commissions.

[86] Catholic Educational Conference of New South Wales, 17-20 January 1911; *Statement, Resolutions, Proceedings,* p. 46.

[87] Aloysius, Brother, 'St John Baptist de La Salle and his Institute in Australia', *Australian Catholic Historical Society Records,* April 1951, p. 14. Catholics, said Archbishop Mannix in 1925, 'were sorry they had not been able to follow in the footsteps of the State authorities much sooner in regard to technical instruction . . .' Address at opening of Catholic Technical School, South Melbourne. *Advocate,* 8 March 1925, p. 8, d.

[88] As evidenced in the High School Act of South Australia, 1915. Act, 6 Georgii V, no. 1223, d. 33(1).

[89] Brother A. B. Hanley, 'Catholic Technical Schools of Australia'. *Australian Catholic Education Congress,* p. 315. See also: *Advocate* (8 March 1925, p. 8, b), address of Mr T. M. Burke, prominent Catholic layman, at opening of South Melbourne Catholic Technical School; address of Archbishop Mannix, p. 8, a; *Report of Fifth National Catholic Education Conference of Directors and Inspectors of Schools,* 1951, p. 2 (Archives, Catholic Education Office, Melbourne).

[90] As a result of this need, said Archbishop Mannix, 'Australia was living a sort of lopsided economic life'. Address, *Advocate,* 8 March 1925, p. 8, d.

9. ST PATRICK'S COLLEGE, MELBOURNE, IN THE 1860s

By courtesy of the Jesuit Fathers, Melbourne

that, if secondary education were to expand so as to absorb the vastly increased secondary school population that had resulted from the raising of the school leaving age, it would have to do so by means of a type other than the academic: secondary education for all implied not only more facilities for education, but above all more variety.[91]

As a result, technical schools began to be added to the Catholic secondary system.[92] The first was in 1925. In that year the Christian Brothers[93] added a technical department to their old school at Balmain. Within ten years similar departments were added to their schools at Rozelle, Strathfield, and Paddington.[94] Beginning in 1939, the Marist Brothers undertook similar work: they added a technical department to their High School in Newcastle and later converted their city schools, St Patrick's and St Benedict's, in Sydney, into technical schools.[95] Later still, in the middle of the century, they switched their school at North Sydney from an academic to a technical curriculum.

Similar developments in Victoria also date from the year 1925, when the Christian Brothers added a technical branch to their school in South Melbourne.[96] Under the impetus from the new Apprenticeship Commission in that state, this school was brought up to the standard required for junior technical registration[97] and a second centre was developed at the Christian Brothers' school, Abbotsford.[98]

Subsequently technical schools were established in other places:[99] in Goulburn,[1] Ballarat,[2] and Perth[3] by the Christian Brothers; and in Bendigo and Adelaide by the Marist Brothers.[4] In nearly all cases the schools were owned by the diocesan authorities and staffed by the Brothers.

Agricultural schools constituted the next development. In the 1930s the Marist Fathers introduced agricultural subjects into the new college

[91] Address of Brother Hickey, Provincial of the Christian Brothers, at opening of Catholic Technical School, South Melbourne. *Advocate*, 8 March 1925, p. 8, b. See also *Report of the Consultative Committee on the Education of the Adolescent*, pp. xix, 173.

[92] As early as 1894 woodwork, as a type of extra-curricular activity, had been introduced at St Stanislaus' College, Bathurst. But it did not survive as a subject. Hall, *History of St Stanislaus' College, Bathurst*, p. 104.

[93] The Irish Christian Brothers entering upon the Australian mission in the early part of this century enjoyed a keener sense of the importance of technical work. They had, for example, been painfully aware of the thousands of Irish immigrants coming to Australia and America—young men and women who were unskilled and tradeless. 'A few Notes and Observations on Mental Instruction', *Christian Brothers' Educational Record*, 1895, pp. 171-5.   [94] Hanley, op. cit., p. 310.   [95] *A.C.D.*, 1951, p. 146.

[96] *Advocate*, 8 March 1925, p. 8, a.   [97] Cf. Hanley, op. cit., p. 309.

[98] Ibid., p. 310. This was in 1930. Both the Abbotsford and South Melbourne schools are owned by the diocesan authorities but staffed by the Christian Brothers.

[99] In Queensland the question of technical education was approached differently. In that state technical subjects may be taken as part of the ordinary public examinations.

[1] Annals of St Patrick's College, Goulburn, p. 98.

[2] Annals of St Patrick's College, Ballarat, p. 71.

[3] *A.C.D.*, 1951, p. 334.   [4] Ibid., pp. 294, 313.

at Woodlawn on the north coast of New South Wales and the Marist Brothers converted their boarding schools at Campbelltown in New South Wales and Mt Gambier in South Australia into complete agricultural colleges.[5] In the same decade Bishop McGuire of Townsville established the first Catholic agricultural college in Queensland at Abergowrie, near Ingham, and invited the Christian Brothers to staff it.[6] Later, at Cygnet in Tasmania, the Christian Brothers developed a small agricultural project along the lines of the Tasmanian Area School.[7]

These developments were significant, but they left the main problem —that of catering for the huge numbers concerned—more or less untouched. Technical schools, moreover, created new problems for the Church: for the religious orders the problem of providing the specially trained teaching personnel, and for the dioceses the problem of meeting the huge financial outlay required for plant and equipment. New Catholic schools, it is true, continued to be opened, but the majority were of the academic type; the development of the non-academic and technical types did not keep pace with the needs. The result was that by the middle of the present century the lack of diversity in the Catholic secondary system was still perhaps its most conspicuous weakness.[8]

THE SECONDARY CURRICULUM: GIRLS'

'Accomplishments and Amiability'

The curriculum laid down for the Benedictine School for Young Ladies, Subiaco, in the early fifties was typical of the 'culture and accomplishments' curriculum of the nineteenth century. The 1854 course offered 'Christian doctrine, English, French, and Italian; Penmanship, Arithmetic, Epistolary Correspondence, Needlework of every description, Drawing, Dancing, and Music'.[9] Twenty years later, with the exception of a few additions, the course had scarcely changed. History, geography, and 'the use of the globes' had been added, and the needlework was described as 'plain and ornamental'. That, apparently, constituted the ordinary programme; Italian, German, Spanish and Latin, painting, and 'Finishing lessons in Singing and Drawing' were available, but only as 'extras'.[10] After a further thirty years the basic curriculum was still substantially the same, except that all extras save the 'elements of Latin' had either been discarded or incorporated into the ordinary syllabus.[11]

The course of studies in the other girls' schools was much the same

[5] A.C.D., 1940, pp. 137, 280. [6] Ibid., p. 342. [7] A.C.D., 1951, p. 302.

[8] Report of Fifth National Catholic Education Conference of Directors and Inspectors of Schools, 1951, p. 2. The conference put forward the suggestion that extra personnel could be released for wider secondary courses by restricting the teaching Brothers to secondary classes only. [9] Advertisement in Catholic Almanac and Directory, 1854, p. 96.

[10] Advertisement in Ordo Divini Officii Recitandi, 1876.

[11] A.C.D., 1910, p. 209.

as that offered at Subiaco. Certain features, however, stand out. Nearly all the schools offered what they termed 'an English education'.[12] This included, it would seem, such things as grammar, history, geography, astronomy, the use of the globes, writing and arithmetic[13] and served, apparently, as a core around which other subjects were grouped.

The foreign languages—French, Spanish, Italian, and German—were listed generally as extras;[14] of these most schools offered at least two, sometimes more. Latin appears to have been less frequently taught.[15]

Needlework was an essential subject throughout all the convent schools.[16] It was designated generally as 'plain and fancy'.[17] Quite frequently other handicrafts were associated with it—leather and alum work,[18] making wax and paper flowers, and wax modelling.[19] Also associated with these accomplishments were various types of landscape and figure drawing, oil and water-colour painting, lustrian and china painting, and illuminating.[20] To these were added the accomplishments of music, instrumental and vocal,[21] and dancing.[22]

[12] For example, All Hallows', Brisbane (A.C.D., 1880, p. 115); St Mary's College, Hobart (Catholic Standard (Tas.), January 1878, p. 12, a, b); Academy of Mary Immaculate, Melbourne (Victorian, 16 August 1862, p. 111); Sisters of Mercy Boarding and Day School, Perth (Record (W.A.), 6 July 1876, p. 2); Dominican Priory, Maitland (A.C.D., 1888, p. vii); Convents of the Sacred Heart in Sydney and Melbourne (A.C.D., 1895, p. vii); Mary's Mount, Ballarat (A.C.D., 1888, p. xl); Brigidine Convent, Beechworth (A.C.D., 1888, p. xvi).

[13] For some reason or other arithmetic was in some schools announced as being given 'special attention'. (A.C.D., 1888, p. xiii.) Sutherland, Report on Loreto Abbey, Mary's Mount, Ballarat. Advocate, 7 January 1905, p. 16, d. See also advertisement, Southern Cross and Catholic Herald, January 1869, p. 252.

[14] Cf. Dominican Convent, Adelaide (Southern Cross and Catholic Herald, January 1869, p. 252); Academy of Immaculate Conception, Melbourne (Victorian, 16 August 1862, p. 111); St Mary's, Hobart (Catholic Standard (Tas.), January 1878, p. 12, a, b); Dominican Priory, Maitland (A.C.D., 1888, p. vii); St Brigid's, Coonamble, N.S.W. (ibid., p. xiii); Mt St Joseph's, Beechworth (ibid., p. xvii); St Ann's, Warrnambool, Vic. (ibid., p. xv).

[15] It was taught at Sacred Heart Convent, Rose Bay, N.S.W., and at Sacré Coeur, Malvern, Vic. (A.C.D., 1895, p. vii); and at St Joseph's, Beechworth, Vic. (A.C.D., 1888, p. xiii).

[16] At Dominican Convent, Adelaide (Southern Cross and Catholic Herald, January 1869, p. 252); at Academy of Immaculate Conception, Fitzroy, Melbourne (advertisement, Victorian, 16 August 1862, p. iii); at the Dominican Priory, Maitland (A.C.D., 1888, p. xiii); at Sacred Heart, Rose Bay, and Sacré Coeur, Malvern (A.C.D., 1895, p. vii); at Mount St Joseph's, Beechworth (A.C.D., 1888, p. xvi); at Good Samaritan Convent, Richmond, N.S.W. (ibid., p. xvi).

[17] For example, at St Mary's College, Hobart (advertisement, Catholic Standard (Tas.), January 1868, p. 112, b); and at St Ann's, Warrnambool (A.C.D., 1888, p. xv).

[18] At Convent of Mercy, Goulburn (A.C.D., 1888, p. xii); at St Ann's, Warrnambool (ibid., p. xv).

[19] See prospectus of Sisters of Mercy First Class Boarding School, Perth. Record (W.A.), 6 July 1876, p. 2.   [20] St Ann's, Warrnambool, A.C.D., 1888, p. xv.

[21] See prospectus for St Vincent's College, Sydney, 1895 (A.C.D., 1895, p. viii). This was provided in all convents—piano, violin, singing, theory of music; and, in some cases, the harp, mandoline, and guitar (advertisement for All Hallows', Age, 16 December 1899, p. 24).

[22] St Ann's, Warrnambool (A.C.D., 1888, p. xv). To this calisthenics was generally added. Sacred Heart Convent, Rose Bay, N.S.W. (A.C.D., 1900, p. 171).

Less bookish and considerably less academic than that of the present century, this curriculum permitted, furthermore, a different organization of pupils. The typical organization of the twentieth century—in classes according to educational achievement—was only dimly fore-shadowed in the organization that existed in the earlier period of the nineteenth century. In the sixties and seventies conventional classification on the lines of current practice was rendered well-nigh impossible. The problem then was one of accommodating in the one school the small country child with no previous schooling and the 'young lady' who had enrolled merely for a 'finishing off'.

The classification adopted at Mary's Mount, Ballarat, serves as an illustration. This institution, a typical convent school of the superior type, was arranged in three divisions: junior, senior, then first school. The junior school catered for the under twelves and the senior the twelve-to-sixteens, sub-dividing them further into five groups or classes. The first school took care of the young ladies who were 'supposed to have passed through the classes of the senior school',[23] but in practice it took in others as well. In fact it came to be known as the 'Young Ladies' division, and the girls were free to spend the time perfecting them-selves in 'various accomplishments which [would] tend to render them agreeable members of their home circle and of society in general'.[24] Later, when girls who had been longer at school came up from the better organized classes below, this 'Young Ladies' division became the culture class. In it, grammar was replaced by logic, and a study of the world's history and representative authors pursued with the purpose of 'awakening philosophic inquiry' and clarifying 'literary ideas'.[25]

As an impetus to studies Mary's Mount had adopted a practice used in some of the better boys' schools. In the nineties, it annually secured the services of outside examiners from the University of Melbourne.[26] Besides providing extra stimulus to class work these contacts with the University enabled the Sisters to keep abreast of educational develop-ments outside the convent.[27] For the pupils themselves there were still other incentives—the winning, and wearing, for example, as marks of special distinction, of academic gowns of traditional design. These gowns,

[23] Institute of the Blessed Virgin Mary, Loreto Convent, Mary's Mount, Ballarat. *A Retrospect, Programme of Concert and Prize List*, pp. 6-8.

[24] Ibid., p. 8.

[25] Mary's Mount, *Annual Magazine*, 1901, p. 20.

[26] In the early years of the present century these inspectors were Mr Irving, and Mr Sutherland. *Advocate*, 7 January 1905; *Annual Magazine*, 1901.

[27] The school policy was stated: 'Although . . . preparation for matriculation is not the all absorbing work, the need was early recognized of outside examinations. It is difficult for the teacher to divest herself completely of individual sympathy in reviewing examination work . . . Outside examination possesses in addition other advantages; it gives an impetus to class work and keeps the teacher in touch with new methods.' Ibid.

of 'the blue of wild hyacinth',[28] were awarded at impressive graduation ceremonies, after the stipulated academic standard had been reached.[29]

But, with the gradual passing of the 'Young Lady' and the advent of the present century, only a few of the very select schools could offer this type of educational luxury.[30] Even these were eventually constrained to conform to the general pattern. Those that did not passed out of existence.[31]

New demands were being made. The leaving and intermediate (or in Queensland the senior and junior) certificates had come into their own and, as was the case with the boys' schools, good examination results were now regarded as the hallmark of success. For women, moreover, it was the age of careers, and young ladies entering the professions and semi-professional occupations needed such qualifications. Lastly, as has been already implied, recognition under the various Bursary or Registration Acts came to be looked upon as necessary for survival. Practically speaking, it was the only guarantee of educational efficiency that was socially acceptable.

All this involved a great deal of reorganization. Gradually the older curriculum gave way to something new, and many of the so-called accomplishments, particularly music and needlework, that had for so long been characteristic of the training given in convent schools, suffered a virtual eclipse. The tendency was still further accentuated by the somewhat rigid and restricting matriculation prerequisites of the various university faculties. Henceforth there was less time for non-essentials. Many of them persisted, nevertheless, even though relegated to a sort of extra-curricular status, with the result that the convent school reputation for music,[32] art,[33] and other typically female subjects was never seriously challenged. But the all-round 'English education' of earlier times, robbed now of its unifying quality, gradually disintegrated into the typical secondary school subjects of the early part of the present century.

[28] This was the colour worn by pupils in the German schools of the Institute in the days of Mary Ward, the foundress. The colour is still preserved in many of the present-day Loreto schools. Ibid., p. 20.

[29] A high value was set on this distinction: 'To secure the honour of wearing these robes candidates must obtain (1) Honours in the History and Literature taught in the Culture class, (2) a good pass in French or German, (3) a pass in logic or a mathematical subject or in Harmony, (4) must write a good essay. To win a higher distinction and add to the graduate robes a symbolic stripe, the candidate must present herself for a second examination and obtain (a) Honours in German or a pass in Latin, (b) a pass in Geometry or Algebra and Physics.' Ibid., p. 20.

[30] See suggestions for an Arts degree taken out in a convent. Bella Guérin, *Loreto Eucalyptus Blossoms*, p. 8; *A Retrospect, Programme of Concert and Prize List*, p. 10.

[31] For example, the Benedictine Convent School of Subiaco, New South Wales.

[32] See pp. 297-8.

[33] At Loreto in Ballarat, for example, the art syllabus was that of the Kensington (England) School of Art, several of the nuns having received their own training in that institution. Mary's Mount, *Annual Magazine* (Ballarat), 1901, p. 25. For art exhibitions held at All Hallows', Brisbane, see *Brisbane Courier*, 10 December 1895, p. 6, g.

Influence of the Public Examinations

The first signs of disintegration in the older curriculum appeared in the seventies. From then on the movement gathered force. In most schools it was supported and encouraged, in a few it met with a long-drawn-out and obstinate resistance.

As early as 1879 the convent high schools in Queensland were presenting girls for the public examinations conducted by the University of Sydney.[34] Later, All Hallows' (Plate 10) prepared girls not only for the Sydney matriculation but for that of Melbourne as well.[35] By the eighties the schools in the other colonies had also entered on this type of examination work—seven of them in New South Wales,[36] and the bigger ones in Victoria.[37] In some cases the prospectus announced unequivocally that 'the course of instruction [would] include all the subjects required for Young Ladies by the Matriculation, Senior and Junior University examinations';[38] in others, it would proudly enumerate the school's examination results and hold them up 'as a proof of the success of the system adopted by the Sisters of . . .'[39]

The public demand for examination results from girls' schools was already strong. The day of mere accomplishments was over, and the schools themselves, sensitive to the prevailing mood of the community at large, were anxious to refute the charges of unreality and aloofness that had been levelled against them.[40] 'It has been said over and over again,' wrote the editor of the Freeman's Journal in 1884, 'that nothing was taught in our convent schools but drawing, needlework and music, but such a state of things, if it ever existed, may be safely considered to have passed away forever, and a new and brighter era opened.'[41]

To this increasing popular demand for examination results, however, there was a noticeable resistance, not only from inside certain convents,

[34] Report of University of Sydney, 1879, pp. 12-13. P.P.(N.S.W.), 1879-80, p. 463.
[35] Advertisement in Age (Brisbane), 16 December 1899, p. 24.
[36] Freeman's Journal, 6 December 1884, p. 14, c. Foremost among these was St Vincent's College, Pott's Point, Sydney, conducted by the Sisters of Charity. Success of the Sydney college was noted in the Annals of other convents of the order; see Annals of St Joseph's Convent, Hobart. An advertisement, in 1888, draws further attention to this success in examinations: 'In 1885, the college obtained in the Junior University Examinations first place of all Ladies' Schools and Colleges in New South Wales and Queensland. In 1887 one young lady matriculated, two passed the Senior Examination and sixteen passed the Junior.' A.C.D., 1888, p. viii.
[37] See matriculation results for 1889. Advocate, 11 January 1890, p. 8, a.
[38] A.C.D., 1895, pp. viii, xiv. For example, Mount St Joseph, F.C.J., Convent Vaucluse, Richmond, Victoria (A.C.D., 1888, p. x). St Ann's, Warrnambool, announced: 'Parents wishing their children prepared for matriculation or Civil Service Examinations, will require to have their names entered the beginning of the first term.' (Ibid., p. xv.)
Also, 'Star of the Sea' Convent, Elsternwick, Vic.: 'Over sixty had passed the matriculation by 1910.' (A.C.D., 1910, p. 209.)
[39] A.C.D., 1880, p. viii.
[40] Teresa Magner, 'The Education of Our Girls', Austral Light, 1 July 1903, p. 485, a.
Bella Guérin, 'Higher Education for Women', Loreto Eucalyptus Blossoms, 1886, p. 7.
[41] Freeman's Journal, 6 December 1884, p. 14, c.

but from the outside as well. The examination system, it was argued, tended to denude the curriculum of too much that was essential in the education of girls, making it narrow and restricted. The 'mental education' of girls, it was said, was falling 'a long way below what it ought to be. The first aim of the school seem[ed] to be in the pursuing of some examination at the end of the year'. The blame for all this was laid at the feet of the parents. 'The fact,' wrote the same critics, 'that teaching often degenerates into mere cram is not so often the fault of the teachers, as the fault of the parents, who demand that their Katie or Mary should be pushed on.'[42]

The resistance from within the convents was restricted to certain orders—the Benedictines[43] and the religious of the Sacred Heart mainly,[44] and, to a less extent, the Loreto Sisters; but as none of these orders catered for a very wide clientele, their total influence in the community was small. Nevertheless the arguments advanced by the Loreto Sisters were not without point: it was not so much the public examinations that they deplored, but what had to be jettisoned in order to make room for them.

At Mary's Mount in Victoria, the Sisters 'formed . . . a matriculation class' for those who, 'at the desire of their parents', undertook to 'study for the University examinations'. But the Sisters themselves were 'by no means desirous that the class should be a large one'. Their aim, they said, was 'to *educate* the pupils, by forming their tastes, strengthening their judgment, and encouraging the habit of serious reading'. All this, they believed, would be 'impossible', if the children were obliged 'to keep exclusively, or at too early an age, to the text books prescribed for public examinations'. If a girl had 'no other education than what she [had] obtained by the mere study of text books, she [was] not likely to have acquired a taste for intellectual pursuits'.[45] On the other hand, the Sisters did not regard the public examinations as entirely incompatible with their work. 'Although matriculation is not the work of the school,' said the *Loreto Annual*, 'Mary's Mount has a creditable roll of matriculation students.'[46]

Thirty years before this Dr James Quinn in Queensland had been giving the strongest possible support to the idea of public examinations. If for no other reason than that of refuting the misstatement that only music and painting were taught in the convent schools,[47] the Bishop

[42] Teresa Magner, op. cit., p. 485.
[43] No mention of examinations, for example, is made on the prospectuses and advertisements. See *A.C.D.*, 1910, op. cit., p. 205.
[44] Ibid., p. 209.
[45] Loreto Abbey, Ballarat, *A Retrospect, Programme of Concert and Prize List,* 1885, pp. 9-10.
[46] Mary's Mount, *Annual Magazine,* 1901, p. 18.
[47] See *Catholic Leader* (Brisbane), 10 December 1931, p. 13.

had been urging the Sisters of Mercy to present their pupils for the university examinations at the very first opportunity. The convent schools, he realized, depended for their existence on public support; they must, therefore, consider the public demand.

To find a way of meeting this demand and at the same time satisfying their own higher concept of education was a problem Quinn and the other bishops left to the nuns themselves. And in this the Sisters were, apparently, not wholly unsuccessful; for Cardinal Moran, having critically observed the nuns' efforts over a period of ten years, came to the conclusion that 'in no part of the world' was there to be found 'a more useful or a higher and more ennobling teaching carried on than in [the] convent schools'.[48] Archbishop Carr was also impressed by the success with which the religious orders of women had been able to adapt the curriculum to the changing needs of society and at the same time save all that was essential and precious in the older education. 'It would be interesting,' he said, 'to trace the progress of the movement for the higher education of women from the time when it contained only two elements, namely, "accomplishments and amiability", to the present day when it embraced practically all the elements which were found in the higher education of men'.[49]

Since Carr's day, however, the pendulum has swung back. With the gradual broadening of the intermediate and leaving certificate courses and the post-war tendency to abolish faculty prerequisites at the university, the older accomplishments, especially music and needlework which, in the interval, had lost favour, began to be revived and reinstated as integral parts of the ordinary curriculum.

[48] *Advocate*, 28 July 1894, p. 8, b.
[49] Address at inauguration of Catholic Training College, 1906. *Age* (Melbourne), 6 August 1906, p. 6, a.

IO

The Curriculum: Religious Education

DOCUMENTS AFFECTING RELIGIOUS EDUCATION

THE DEVELOPMENT in secular instruction outlined in the preceding chapter was accompanied by a corresponding development in religious instruction. Here, as in the case of the profane curriculum, the influence of secular pedagogy was not without its effect, but, as might be expected, the main influence came from forces operating within the Church.

These forces from within the Church had a twofold origin: the legislation of the Church itself and the traditions and practices of the teaching orders. Ecclesiastical legislation up to 1880 has been dealt with in an earlier part of this work. Post-1880 legislation has been cited here and there in the two preceding chapters but the documents themselves now need to be considered in their historical setting.

Those coming immediately after 1880 were the *Acta et Decreta* of the first three Plenary Councils. These in their turn were contemporaneous with the great encyclicals of Leo XIII. None of these Councils added any new principle to what had been laid down before, all important decisions affecting Catholic education in Australia having been made during the pontificate of Pope Pius IX. But of all that Pontiff's encyclicals[1] and pronouncements[2] the only ones quoted by the Australian bishops were the 'Quam Non Sine' (14 July 1864) and the 'Syllabus Errorum'.[3] For the rest, the bishops appear to have relied on the sound basic theology and philosophy of men like Geoghegan and Polding, and the decisions of their brother bishops in Ireland. To a certain extent, as has been shown, the Australian bishops were also influenced by the American bishops in the early Baltimore Councils.[4] For the most part,

---

[1] 'Nostris et Nobiscum' (8 December 1849), 'Singulari Quidem' (17 March 1856), 'Cum Nuper' (20 January 1858), 'Maximae Quidem' (18 August 1864), and the two letters, 'Quo Graviora' (8 July 1862) and 'Quam Non Sine' (14 July 1864).

[2] For example, 'Quibus Luctuosissimis' (5 September 1851), 'Maxima Quidem' (9 June 1862), 'Inconsistoriali' (1 November 1850), 'Multis Gravibusque' (17 December 1860), and 'Nunquam Certe' (22 June 1868).

[3] *Joint Pastoral* of Archbishop and Bishops of New South Wales, 1879, pp. 8-9; *Decrees on Education adopted by the Archbishop and Bishops assembled in Provincial Council*, at Melbourne, 1869, no. 7.

[4] Especially the First Plenary Council (1852), Second Plenary Council (1866), Third Plenary Council (1884). See also Conway, Rev. James (S.J.), 'Catholic Education in

however, it would appear that they were obliged to dispense with precedent and, working from first principles, solve their own problems as they came to them.[5]

The decisions made on these occasions were confirmed by the First Plenary Council which took place in Sydney in 1885, one year after the arrival in the colony of Cardinal Moran and, therefore, before[6] the appearance of the better known encyclicals of Leo XIII.[7] The *Acta et Decreta* of this Council under three sections—De Educatione Primaria seu Elementaria,[8] De Scholis Intermediis,[9] and De Educatione Universitaria[10]—codified all that had issued from earlier synods and from the statements of bishops in their pastorals. In so doing they laid down the legislation that was to guide the future development of Catholic education in Australia. The Second[11] and Third[12] Plenary Councils in 1895 and 1905 respectively, with the addition of a word here and there, but without any substantial alteration, repeated the decrees of the First Council. The synodal decrees of the various dioceses—Sydney,[13] Melbourne,[14] Goulburn,[15] Bathurst,[16] and the rest—did little more than interpret the decrees of the Plenary Council and adapt them more effectively to the exigencies of local needs.

After World War I further developments took place. The first was the codification of canon law by Cardinal Gasparri, in which momentous undertaking the compilers brought together and systematically arranged,

---

the United States'. Proceedings of *Second Australasian Catholic Congress*, Melbourne, 1905. It is known that Vaughan came into the possession of a copy of the Baltimore decrees in 1873; see Concilii Plenarii Baltimorensis II, *Acta et Decreta*, 1868. An autographed copy of these *Acta* is to be found in Vaughan's 'Ex libris' at St Patrick's College, Manly, N.S.W.

[5] The principles on which these problems were solved were founded 'on the one hand, on the dictates of right reason, and on the other, on the teaching of our Lord Jesus Christ'. This statement was made in an important address by Bishop P. Moran, of Dunedin, on the education question at the First Plenary Council, in Sydney, 1885. *Advocate*, 5 December 1885, p. 9, a.

[6] Leo XIII's influence on educational development in Australia, actually, was slight. See Lenten Pastorals of Dr Reville of Bendigo, p. 15, a, and of Dr Corbett, p. 16, a, b. *Advocate*, 27 February 1904.

[7] For instance, 'Inscrutabili' (21 April 1878), 'Nobilissima' (8 February 1884), 'Quod Multum' (22 August 1886), 'Sapientiae' (10 January 1890), 'Militantis Ecclesiae' (1 August 1897), 'Affari Vos' (8 December 1897), and in letters, 'Officio Sanctissimo' (22 December 1892), 'Quae Coniunctim' (23 May 1892), and 'Litteras a Vobis' (2 July 1894).   [8] *Conc. Plen.*, I, 1885, decr. 231-45.

[9] Ibid., decr. 246-8.   [10] Ibid., decr. 249-51.

[11] *Conc. Plen.*, II, 1895, decr. 202-321.   [12] *Conc. Plen.*, III, 1905, decr. 315-48.

[13] *Decrees of the Diocesan Synod of Sydney*, 1891, decr. vi-ix.

[14] Decrees on Education adopted by the Archbishop and Bishops assembled in Provincial Council at Melbourne, in April 1869, printed in *Acta et Decreta secundi concilii provincialis Australiensis*, 1869. Reprinted by *Advocate*, 1891. See also *Acta et Decreta primae synodi diocesanae Melbournensis*, 1875; *Acta et Decreta secundae synodi diocesanae Melbournensis*, 1885; *Acta et Decreta tertiae synodi diocesanae Melbournensis*, 1887; *Acta et Decreta synodi provincialis Melbournensis*, 1907.

[15] *Statuta Synodalia pro Diocesi Goulburnensi*, 1888.

[16] Decrees of Diocesan Synod, Bathurst, 1883. *Catholic Monthly*, February 1883, p. 18.

among other things, all the Church's legislation on education.[17] Next, in point of time, appeared the encyclical, 'Divini Illius Magistri', of Pius XI in 1929; then, the 'Official Pronouncement of the Australian Hierarchy on Education', made public by Archbishop M. Sheehan at the time of the Adelaide Education Congress of 1936.[18] Lastly, in 1937, appeared the decrees of the Fourth Plenary Council.[19] Preserving the tripartite division of the decrees of the earlier Councils but named somewhat differently—De Scholis Elementaribus,[20] De Scholis Mediis et Collegiis,[21] and De Universitatibus[22]—these decrees were completely re-edited and presented in a way that was more in conformity with the requirements of the new code of canon law. At the close of the first half of the present century they still remained the last word on ecclesiastical law in so far as it concerned Catholic education in Australia.[23]

The 'Divini Illius Magistri' referred to above is significant in another way. Published in English under the title of *The Christian Education of Youth*,[24] this encyclical became the authoritative statement on Catholic education, not only in Australia but throughout the world.

The document itself was timely. Pius IX had been engrossed with what he considered the pretensions of a false liberalism. Leo XIII had been concerned with the important social problems touching on education, redefining, for example, the respective educational rights of the parents, the Church, and the state. A generation later Pius XI was confronted with a different problem. Half a century of state education that was in many countries thoroughly secular—*de facto,* if not *de jure*—had almost succeeded in cutting education and social life adrift from their Christian moorings, with the result that the world was facing a new paganism, harder even and more materialistic than that of the pre-Christian era. To expect, furthermore, that Catholic schools, whilst remaining in that world, should be unaffected by this neo-pagan atmosphere was to expect too much. To draw attention to this fact therefore, to point out the dangers and to re-establish the true Christian basis of education, Pius XI gave the world his new encyclical letter.

PARENTS AND TEACHERS

The first point to which the Pontiff drew attention was the modern

---

17 *Cod. Iur. Can.* (ed. Petro Card. Gasparri), p. 400.

18 Sheehan, Archbishop Michael, 'The Official Pronouncement of the Catholic Hierarchy of Australia on the Education Congress', *Australasian Catholic Record,* January 1937, pp. 11-18.

19 *Conc. Plen.,* IV, Australiae et Novae Zealandiae, 1937.

20 *Conc. Plen.,* IV, decr. 598-631.

21 Ibid., decr. 632-44.   22 Ibid., decr. 645-52.

23 A summary of these decrees was given in *Christian Education in a Democratic Community.* Social Justice Statement, 1949. Published with the Authority of the Archbishops and Bishops of the Catholic Church in Australia.

24 See the American edition published in 1929.

tendency to relax parental discipline.[25] The parents, he stressed, were the first teachers, and education would be efficacious in proportion to their teaching and example.[26]

Taken up instantly by the Australian bishops, this point was emphasized in their 'Official Pronouncement' of 1935[27] and the Fourth Plenary Council of 1937.[28] A glance backwards, however, reveals that the same thing was implied in their earliest pronouncements of the nineteenth century,[29] and not only in the statements of the Hierarchy,[30] but in those of the laity[31] and teachers as well.[32] 'As a means . . . of realizing the highest aims of the Catholic Church,' said the bishops in 1905, 'there is nothing of more value and efficacy than the influence of home life.' 'The home is the child's first school, its mother is its first teacher.'[33]

It was for this reason, obviously, that the bishops showed so much concern for the higher education of girls.[34] 'The education of youth,' said Dr Sheil in welcoming the Dominican nuns to Adelaide, 'could not be overrated; but when considered in relation to the female portion of the community it assumed a most solemn and sacred aspect . . . for on the proper education of our females depends the spiritual and temporal welfare of the family and, by consequent necessity, that of society.'[35] Thus it was that the two Quinns, Murray of Maitland, Brady of Perth, and Torreggiani of Armidale, had all either brought orders of nuns with them when they came to Australia or made arrangements for them to follow immediately.[36]

Half a century later Pius XI was even more forthright and, echoing

---

[25] Pius XI, 'Divini Illius Magistri', 1929, p. 74.

[26] Ibid., p. 73.

[27] Sheehan, 'Official Pronouncement of the Catholic Hierarchy in Australia on the Education Question'. *Australasian Catholic Record,* January 1937, p. 11.

[28] *Conc. Plen.,* IV, decr. 598, 599. 'Parentes . . . primas orationes edoceant, et in praecipuis fidei doctrinis erudiant, eisque exemplo sint in adimplendis religionis officiis.' Ibid., decr. 600.

[29] All were based, apparently, on St Thomas, II-II, q. 111, a. 1; and suppl., St Thomas, III, q. 41, a. 1.

[30] See diocese of Bathurst, *Synodal Decrees on Education,* decr. 11. Printed in *Record,* 16 January 1883, p. 38.

'Moneantur parentes de gravissima obligatione quae adstringuntur suos filios in iis omnibus quae fidem et mores spectant sedule instruere.' *Synodus Diocesana Maitlandensis,* 1888, de Educatione, 2.

Conc. Plen., IV, 1937, decr. 600; I, 1885, decr. 231; II, 1895, decr. 232; III, 1905, decr. 235.

[31] Catholic petition to Leg. Council against the Education Bill of 1844. P.P.(N.S.W.), 1844, II, p. 67.

[32] McKillop, Mother Mary. *Statement in Rome.* See ch. 10.

[33] Pastoral Letter of the Cardinal Delegate, Plenary Council, 1905. *Austral Light,* October 1905, p. 718.

[34] *Conc. Plen.,* I, 1885, decr. 92.

[35] Address of Bishop Sheil in response to a welcome back to Australia in December 1868. *Southern Cross,* 20 December 1868, pp. 241, e, 242, a, b, c.

[36] See Quinn's 1871 Report to Propaganda. Quoted in *Sketch of the Life and Labours of the Rt Rev. Dr O'Quinn, First Bishop of Brisbane,* p. 27. See also *Pastoral Letter of the Archbishops and Bishops of Australasia in Plenary Council Assembled,* 1885, p. 34.

a page from Herbert Spencer,[37] lamented that many parents, though equipped for other offices, received little or no preparation for discharging the fundamental duty and obligation of educating their children. Pastors were therefore to warn parents of their grave obligation not in a 'merely theoretical and general way but with a practical and specific application to their various responsibilities concerning the religious, moral and civil training of their children'.[38] This directive was taken up in Australia after World War II, not in the schools but in the various Catholic youth organizations, by the establishment of the Cana and Pre-Cana conferences. Named after the Marriage Feast of Cana and conducted generally by panels of instructors consisting of priests, Catholic medical men and other lay men and women, these conferences proved immensely popular and, by the end of the forties, according to a report of the Hierarchy to Rome, were 'producing good fruit'.[39]

After the family came the school, with a corresponding shift of emphasis from the parent to the teacher. 'Perfect schools', for Pius XI, were 'the result not so much of good methods as of good teachers'.[40] The same principle had been enunciated earlier by Leo XIII, who had insisted that, for this office, 'only the best and worthiest (optimi ac probatissimi)' be chosen.[41] By then, however, the Church in Australia had already committed itself to a system of schools staffed by religious, and irrespective of whether that decision had been prompted by motives of expedience, or of straight-out preference for religious, or of both, it was subsequently confirmed many times and finally, in 1937, incorporated into ecclesiastical law. Each school, said the Fourth Plenary Council, was to be given 'as a general rule to some religious family'.[42]

The use of the term 'family' at this time was especially significant. The conflict of aims and purposes that had been inevitable in the secular way of life was, by the 1920s, only too obvious. The disintegrating effect it had upon society as a whole was becoming evident in the schools themselves.[43] To arrest this tendency ingenious attempts had been made to develop a keener appreciation of the educative influence of the corporate life of the school, regarding it not merely as a place of learning but as a social unit or society in which the older and younger members,

[37] Education: Intellectual, Moral, and Physical, ch. 1.
[38] Pius XI, 'Divini Illius Magistri', 1929, p. 74.
[39] Beovich, 'Catholic Education and Catechetics in Australia'.
[40] 'Divini Illius Magistri', 1929, p. 80.
[41] Leo XIII to German bishops in commemoration of Blessed Peter Canisius. 'Militantis Ecclesiae', 1 August 1897. Acta, vol. xvii, p. 246.
[42] 'Quaelibet schola tradatur, ut plurimum, alicui familiae religiosae . . . ' Conc. Plen., IV, decr. 607. It is coincidental that the report of the above committee and the Acta et Decreta of the Fourth Plenary Council appeared at the same time.
[43] See Board of Education. Curriculum and Examinations in Secondary Schools. Report of the Committee of the Secondary School Examinations Council appointed by the President of the Board of Education, 1941 (the Norwood Report).

the teachers and taught, shared a common life.[44] It was precisely this corporate life that the bishops wished to preserve in handing the school over to a *'familia religiosa'*.[45] The community life of the one would be the guarantee, so to speak, of the corporate life of the other, and through the union of the religious community with the living Church[46] there would come down to the child the immense spiritual vitality of the Church itself.[47]

In this view of education a great deal depended on the religious community. It was not that religious were essential. For Pius XI it sufficed that the teachers be 'good teachers'; but given the non-Catholic environment of Australia and the consequent greater need for a positively Catholic environment in the Catholic school, the bishops had consistently preferred religious. The selection of religious in the first place, then their years of preparation[48] and regular periods for the renewal of spirit,[49] conferred on them, it was generally believed, a special stamp. Vaughan himself, it will be recalled, had frequently grown eloquent on the matter and rejoiced at the effect this religious personality of the teacher would have on the mind of the child.[50] Even in the junior classes, observed Archbishop Sheehan in later times, the pupils were being 'steadily influenced' by it. That personality, according to the Archbishop, drew its force, not only from the supernatural unselfishness of the Sister's or Brother's life, but [also] from the natural virtues practised from a supernatural motive'.[51]

In addition, the religious had contracted certain professional obligations. Principal among these was scholarship. Important as holiness of life was, it was not regarded as a substitute for learning. The Church's view on this matter was that, ordinarily speaking, the scholar

[44] Board of Education, *Report of the Consultative Committee on Secondary Education,* with special reference to Grammar Schools and Technical High Schools (the Spens Report), pp. 146-7.

[45] See note 42, above.

[46] See *Rule of St. Augustine and the Constitutions of the Dominican Sisters of New South Wales,* pt. i, ch. 24, art. 215.

[47] *Règlements des Ursulines de Paris,* art. 268. Quoted by Marie de St Jean Martin, O.S.U., *Ursuline Method of Education,* p. x. Religious teachers, furthermore, shared in the apostolic ministry of the Church; see, for example, *Common Rules of the Institute of the Marist Brothers of the Schools,* pt. ii, ch. ix, art. 214; pt. iii, ch. viii, art. 398; *Pastoral Letter of Cardinal Delegate,* Plenary Council, 1905, p. 711.

See also Acts, xvii. 28: ' . . . it is in Him that we live, and move, and have our being'; again, St Paul in 1 Cor. iii. 6-7. See also *Customs and Directory of the Sisters of Mercy,* 1865, p. 13; *Constitutions of the Institute of the Blessed Virgin Mary,* ch. xviii, art. 210.

[48] See *Common Rules of the Institute of the Marist Brothers of the Schools,* pt. ii, art. 273.

[49] *Règles Communes des Frères des Écoles Chrétiennes,* ch. xxix; and *Common Rules of the Institute of the Marist Brothers of the Schools,* pt. i, ch. xi, art. 100, 108.

[50] See Address at Wagga Convent, 1876. O'Connor, J. G., *A Brief History of the Sacred Heart Presentation Convent, Wagga,* p. 66.

[51] Address to Catholic Teachers in Sydney, 1928. Catholic Education Association, *Teachers' Conference,* 1928, p. 8.

who was a saint would have a decided advantage over the saint who was not a scholar.[52]

Thus study and the acquisition of knowledge became a conscientious duty for members of the teaching orders.[53] They were, as the constitutions of one order put it, 'to aim at acquiring every attainment useful in their profession' and to 'obtain those professional qualifications' necessary for the success of their mission.[54] And what applied to the teachers of the secular branches applied with equal force to the teachers of religion.[55] According to the Fourth Plenary Council, these were to be 'teachers distinguished for their competence'.[56]

RELIGIOUS INSTRUCTION
The Syllabus of Religious Instruction

This competence in the teaching of religion was the principal justification for the separate existence of religious teachers. In the constitutions of the various teaching orders it was set down as their 'principal care'.[57] Reports from the early schools, moreover, bore witness to the impression that was inevitably created in the minds of the pupils. To them religious instruction seemed everywhere 'first in dignity and importance'.[58] The same emphasis was noted in eccelesiastical directives. Those of the present century[59] no less than those of the nineteenth[60] continued to put the teaching of religion as the unequivocal centre of Catholic education.

Ecclesiastical surveillance sought to maintain the emphasis. After the 1900s, when the bulk of lay teachers in Catholic schools had been

---

[52] *Exhortations on the Rules of the Institute of the Blessed Virgin Mary*, 1910, II, p. 413. [53] Ibid., p. 415.
[54] *Common Rule of the Institute of the Marist Brothers of the Schools*, pt. i, art. 270.
[55] See *Common Rule of the Institute of the Marist Brothers of the Schools*, pt. ii, ch. vi, art. 185; Report of First National Catholic Education Conference, 1936 (reprinted in *Report of Third National Conference*, 1944); *Christian Brothers' Educational Record*, 1887, p. 1; 1894, p. 512; 1895, pp. 113, 127, 134, 171.
[56] *Conc. Plen.*, IV, 1937, decr. 648. See also *Rule of St Augustine and the Constitutions of the Dominican Sisters of New South Wales*, art. 216.
[57] *Les Constitutions des Ursulines*, ch. vi, art. 1; I.B.V.M., *Usual Customs and Observances*, p. 95; *Guide des Écoles*, ch. 1. According to the 1932 edition of this work, 'L'enseignement de la religion et la pratique de la vie chrétienne constituent *le but primordial* que s'est proposé le Champagnat en fondant la Congrégation'; *Règles Communes des Frères des Écoles Chrétiennes*, ch. vii, art. 5. See also *Management of Christian Schools*, p. 30.
[58] Goulter, M. C., *Schoolday Memories*, p. 25. See also Report of Prefect of Studies, Xavier College, Melbourne, 1889 (*Advocate*, 21 December 1889, p. 8, a); and advertisement for St Patrick's College, Ballarat (*A.C.D.*, 1895, p. vi).
[59] See *Cod. Iur. Can.*, can. 1329; *Conc. Plen.*, III, 1905, p. 136; Beovich, Archbishop M., 'Religious Education: its Place in the Catholic Schools', *Australian Catholic Education Congress*, 1936, p. 317.
[60] See Leo XIII to Hungarian bishops, 28 May 1896. *Acta*, pp. 132-42; Pius IX, 'Gravissimos inter', ad Gregor. Archiep. Mor. et Frising, 11 December 1862. Quoted in *Conc. Plen.*, I, 1885, decr. 234. See also *Cod. Iur. Can.*, p. 402, for references to 19th century documents.

replaced by religious, less anxiety was felt about religious instruction. It was natural, perhaps, for pastors to look upon it as being in safe hands. But the Church was not able thus to shelve so important a responsibility. She therefore retained for herself the right and duty of inspection, a precaution that was made all the more necessary by the tendency on the part of some orders to arrogate to themselves certain immunities from, and independence of, ecclesiastical control. On the authority, then, of canon law, which subjected the religious education of children in all schools whatsoever (*in scholis quibuslibet*) to the 'authority and inspection of the Church',[61] the Fourth Plenary Council laid down definite regulations. A syllabus of religious instruction, 'carefully drawn up and printed' with the approbation of the bishop, was to be 'accurately' followed in the religious instruction classes.[62] On it, furthermore, all pupils were to 'stand an examination once a year',[63] the examination being set by the diocesan examiner who was in every case to be a priest.[64] This applied not only to the parochial elementary schools: even in the secondary schools all pupils were to undergo a 'written and oral examination in the matter set for religious instruction', the oral examination being presided over by the diocesan examiner or another priest or religious appointed by the bishop.[65]

Procedure roughly similar to this had been adopted in Australia from earlier times but special recommendations from Rome on the matter in 1930 called for a general tightening-up. Addressed primarily to the major superiors of religious congregations, the document in question carried a list of regulations concerning the training and examination of prospective religious teachers; at the same time it stressed the need for a careful organization of the whole programme of religious teaching.[66]

The result is seen in the Hierarchy's 1949 report to Rome on the subject of catechetics. Each diocese[67] was described as having its carefully drawn-up syllabus of Christian doctrine, based generally on the catechism but including 'prayers, doctrinal and devotional instructions, Bible History and Church History stories, and, in the higher grades,

[61] *Cod. Iur. Can.*, can. 1381 (1): 'auctoritati et inspectioni Ecclesiae'.

[62] *Conc. Plen.*, IV, 1937, decr. 616: 'diligenter et accurate conficiatur et cum approbatione Ordinarii typis mondetur. Juxta syllabum ita ordinatum institutio religiosa adamussim tradatur.'

[63] Ibid., decr. 617. English from the translation in *Decrees of the Fourth Plenary Council which concern Religious and Catholic Schools.*   [64] Ibid., decr. 618.

[65] Ibid., decr. 639. English from approved translation.

[66] Sacra Congregatio de Religiosis, *Instructio ad supremos moderatores et moderatrices religiosarum laicarum familiarum de obligatione subditos in doctrina christiana rite imbuendi. Acta Apostolicae Sedis,* 28 January 1930, p. 28.

[67] See, for example, Catholic Schools of Victoria, *Syllabus of Religious Instruction,* 1950; *Syllabus of Religious Instruction for Primary and Secondary Schools in the Archdiocese of Brisbane and in the Dioceses of Cairns, Rockhampton and Townsville, 1949; Syllabus,* archdiocese of Adelaide, 1946.

10.　ALL HALLOWS' CONVENT, BRISBANE
The first building, 1863, and a later building, 1881

By courtesy of the Sisters of Mercy, Brisbane

apologetics, the New Testament, Church History and Christian social principles'.[68] The teacher was to present doctrinal truths dogmatically and by appropriate methods, but at the same time he was to centre his instruction in, and have it revolve around, the personality of Jesus Christ, thus making it 'Christo-centric'[69] and expressive of a way of life.[70]

Compared with the courses of instruction in use during the nineteenth century, those of the later period were considerably enriched. Whereas the older courses tended to restrict themselves to the catechism text, the newer ones embraced more extensive work on liturgy, sacred scripture, church history, and the rest.[71] But development had been slow. The First Plenary Council went only so far as to state that parents and teachers were to teach the children 'the truths necessary to be known';[72] some of the pedagogical works of the religious orders went further and gave more specific details of the work to be treated;[73] but the turning point would appear to have been the 'Acerbo nimis' of Pius X. In this encyclical, besides directing that the basis of any course or text for school use was to be the catechism of the Council of Trent, the Pope gave instructions on the way in which syllabuses of religious instruction were to be drawn up.[74]

The same year the Third Plenary Council of Australia appointed an episcopal committee to draw up a syllabus of Christian doctrine. The committee consisted of the same three bishops—the Archbishop of Melbourne and the Bishops of Lismore and Ballarat—who, it will be recalled, had been appointed to draw up a uniform course of secular studies in 1890 (see ch. 9). This syllabus, like the other, was to be in the form of a 'standard of proficiency' and was to be used 'in all the Australian dioceses'.[75] The uniformity at which it aimed was apparently desirable but, for many reasons, most difficult to achieve. Ten years earlier the Second Plenary Council had decreed that 'the same Catechism' should be used in all the Australian dioceses;[76] the Third Council repeated the injunction,[77] and the Fourth Council, as late as 1937, was still repeating it, extending the scope this time to the New Zealand dioceses as well.[78] By the end of the thirties still

[68] Beovich, 'Catholic Education and Catechetics in Australia', p. 4.
[69] Catholic Schools of Victoria, Syllabus of Religious Instruction, 1950, p. 3.
[70] 'I am the way, the truth, and the life.' John xiv. 6.
[71] See Syllabus, archdiocese of Adelaide, 1946, p. 10.
[72] 'Veritates scitu necessarias.' Conc. Plen., I, 1885, decr. 236.
[73] See, for example, Guide des Écoles, 1853, pt. ii, sec. iv. 'Des principales choses qu'un frère doit apprendre à ses enfants'.
[74] Pius X, ep. encycl., 'Acerbo nimis', 1905, printed in Conc. Plen., III, 1905, p. 142.
[75] Conc. Plen., III, 1905, decr. 329. Author's translation.
[76] 'Decernunt Patres ut idem Catechismus in omnibus Diocesibus Australiensibus tradatur.' Conc. Plen., II, 1895, decr. 232.   [77] Conc. Plen., III, 1905, decr. 252.
[78] 'Idem Catechismus in omnibus diocesibus Australiae et Novae Zealandiae tradatur.' Conc. Plen., IV, 1937, decr. 616.

nothing had been done, whereupon the Second National Catholic Education Conference ventured its 'opinion . . . that a uniform syllabus in Christian Doctrine throughout Australia was desirable'. A start should be made, added the Conference, by 'a minimum syllabus in Prayers, Catechism, Bible History and Liturgy'.[79] Then World War II intervened and the idea was shelved once more. In 1949, however, the province of Victoria, consisting of the archdiocese of Melbourne and the suffragan dioceses of Sandhurst, Ballarat, and Sale, produced a common syllabus. This came into operation in January 1950.[80]

Throughout this development the Church had insisted on full instruction in dogma and revealed truth in all classes, from the elementary school to the university,[81] thereby putting herself at variance with many of the prevailing educational philosophies: with the pedagogy of naturalism, which, deriving from Rousseau and Spencer, was opposed to authority and especially the positive teaching of the Church concerning man—his origin, nature and destiny;[82] with the ultra-experimentalists who considered that 'the ultimate source, authority, and criterion for all belief and conduct [were] to be found in ordinary human experience';[83] and with the pragmatism[84] of Dewey who, rejecting revelation, believed that 'Faith in the divine author' with its 'inherited ideas of body and soul' had become 'impossible for the cultivated mind of the Western World', and who advocated scepticism as the 'mask and even the pose of the educated mind'.[85] Instead of the need for determining all truths experimentally and for the continual reconstruction of experience, as Dewey and the progressives advocated, the Church maintained that in the Catholic theory many things were already fixed.[86]

Despite the gulf that separated the Catholic philosophy from that of the progressives there were, nevertheless, numerous ways in which the latter exerted an influence on Catholic practice in Australia, especially in the matter of techniques. This becomes apparent from a study of the methods of teaching religion adopted over the last half-century.

[79] Report of Second National Catholic Education Conference, 1939, p. 4.
[80] Catholic schools of Victoria, Syllabus of Religious Instruction, 1950, p. 2. In the province of Queensland, four out of five dioceses had adopted a uniform syllabus in 1949. Syllabus of Religious Instruction for Primary and Secondary Schools, 1949.
[81] Conc. Plen., II, 1895, p. 108; Conc. Plen., IV, 1937, decr. 635, 637, 649, 650; Cod. Iur. Can., can. 1373. See also Catholic Educational Conference of New South Wales, January 17-20, 1911. Statement, Resolutions and Proceedings, p. 5.
[82] Pius XI, 'Divini Illius Magistri', 1929, p. 69. See also Rev. Francis de Hovre, Le Catholicisme: ses Pédagogues, sa Pédagogie, p. 417.
[83] Childs, John L., Education and the Philosophy of Experimentalism, p. 61.
[84] Dewey, John, Reconstruction in Philosophy, pp. 156-7.
[85] Dewey, J., 'What I Believe', Forum, March 1930. Quoted in McGucken, Rev. W., The Catholic Way in Education, p. 22.
[86] See Rev. Francis de Hovre, op. cit., p. 406. See also Pius XI, Divini Illius Magistri, 1929, p. 70.

Methods of Teaching Religion

This development in methods had kept pace with the gradual enriching of the syllabuses of religious instruction, and was in fact part of the same movement. It had come, too, as a reaction against the over-emphasis on memorization associated with the catechetical method of the earlier period.

The catechisms in use in the old denominational schools have been dealt with.[87] Gradually they were replaced. First came the catechism of Father Deharbe, reprinted in South Australia by Dr Reynolds in 1882.[88] Then in 1886, in response to a decree[89] of the First Plenary Council, the first general catechism for the whole of Australia appeared.[90] From that time on the 'penny' catechism, as it was known, became the basic, and in many cases, the only text in religious knowledge. Actually the text was not original, but an adaptation of that issued by the National Council of Ireland in 1875.[91]

Despite the universal popularity of this catechism,[92] it suffered from many defects. From the early part of this century criticism of it became general. One objection was that it was too 'technical', full of 'professionally worded definitions' such as theologians only would use[93] and therefore not suitable for children. Actually the same thing had been said of the earlier catechism used in Sydney in 1883: the matter, it was admitted, was 'excellent', but it needed breaking down for young minds'.[94] Another objection was that in so far as the catechism definition tended to emphasize knowledge that rested on a purely notional basis rather than on a basis of experience 'lived out by the child' himself, it was unpsychological. By its very nature, too, the catechism tended to make abstract those things which children could see only in the concrete.[95] Further, whereas nothing was spared on the production of other text books, the 'cheapest possible dress suffice[d]' for the catechism. Its appeal for children was thereby destroyed.[96]

Others were opposed to the question and answer form,[97] believing

---

[87] See pp. 114-16.
[88] *Deharbe's Catechism of the Catholic Religion* (for use in the schools of the Diocese of Adelaide). This edition bears the 'imprimatur' of Dr Reynolds.
[89] *Conc. Plen.*, I, 1885, decr. 182.
[90] The catechism approved by the Plenary Council of Australasia. (An edition was printed in Sydney by Finn Brothers in 1891; but the third, in 1902, was again printed by Gill in Ireland.)
[91] *Conc. Plen.*, I, 1885, decr. 182.
[92] 'The staple diet for all digestions.' De Sales, Mother M., 'Teaching of Religion in Primary Schools', *Australian Catholic Education Congress*, p. 421.
[93] Sheehan, Archbishop M., *A Child's Book of Religion*, p. vii.
[94] Rogers, Report on Catholic Schools, 1883, p. 3. This sentence was struck out on the original galley proofs.
[95] O'Brien, Rev. A. E., 'Uniformity of Method in the Teaching of Christian Doctrine', *Austral Light*, March 1911, p. 239.   [96] Ibid., in *Austral Light*, April 1911, p. 323.
[97] This was the so-called 'logical' approach. De Sales, op. cit., p. 421.

that children found it 'dry and unpalatable'.[98] If that form had to be retained, would it not appear more reasonable, they asked, to reverse the roles and have the teacher answering and the pupils themselves putting the questions.[99]

A final objection to the catechism was that it called for excessive memorizing.[1] Inspectors complained of 'insufficient . . . explanations' and too much 'mechanical answering', of children 'even in advanced classes' not understanding 'the answers they repeated from memory'.[2] It was all very well, they said, for children to 'know the words of the Catechism'; but it was better for them both to 'know and understand them'.[3] Examples of this 'parrot-like repetition', as Archbishop Beovich of Adelaide designated it, were widely reported in the early decades of this century[4] and were still to be found even as late as the thirties, though in a 'minority'.[5]

Further criticism of this *memoriter* approach to the teaching of religion closely resembled that of William Wilkins fifty years earlier. It was quite futile, it said, to 'store the minds [of children] with the essence of moral principles in a few general laws and rules' and then to hope that 'some time later their significance might dawn upon them'.[6] 'Too much reliance [was] placed on the mere memorizing of doctrinal formulæ, and too little intelligent effort expended in rendering the saving truths of Religion functional in the minds and hearts of the pupils.'[7] According to this criticism, it was 'a fundamental principle of pedagogy that all educational activities [should] orientate with the child's capacity. Memory work in any subject of the curriculum was not sufficient, but more especially [was] this true with regard to the subject of Religion'. Religion, it was claimed, must act upon what was 'deepest in [the child's] conscious life'; it must 'control and sanctify' it.[8]

Criticism of this sort seemed to imply that it was not the catechism that was at fault but the way it was used. 'For the past twenty-five years,' wrote a priest-inspector of Catholic schools in Perth, 'we have listened to the lamentations of Catechetical Jeremiahs . . . who glared and growled at the Catechism text as a thing unholy.'[9] Countless suggestions had been

[98] O'Brien, Rev. A. E., 'The Practical Aim of Religious Teaching', *Australasian Catholic Record*, April 1926, p. 126.

[99] The views of Brother Hanrahan, former Provincial of the Christian Brothers. Hanrahan, Brother M. B., 'The Teaching of Catechism', *Australasian Catholic Record*, January 1925, p. 39.

[1] See De Sales, op. cit., p. 424.   [2] Rogers, op. cit., p. 3.

[3] Dwyer, *Report on the Primary Schools*, Maitland diocese, 1884, p. 6.

[4] Report on Primary Schools, Melbourne, 1900. *Advocate*, 8 December 1900, p. 6, c.

[5] Beovich, 'Religious Education: its Place in Catholic Schools', *Australian Catholic Education Congress*, p. 319.

[6] O'Brien, 'Uniformity of Method in the Teaching of Christian Doctrine', *Austral Light*, March 1911, p. 238.   [7] Ibid., p. 236.   [8] Ibid, p. 241.

[9] McMahon, 'Irish Renaissance in Christian Doctrine', *Australasian Catholic Record*, July 1929, p. 224.

made about bringing out an ideal catechism, dropping its theological terminology and recasting it in language intelligible to children—a task which was eventually undertaken by a group of priests under the direction of Dr Beovich.[10] But this new catechism, vast improvement though it was on the old,[11] did not remove all the difficulties. It did, however, bring home the fact that something more than an improved text-book was required. Thoroughgoing reform, it was realized, depended more on the training of teachers than, as the critic cited above had warned, 'transforming the Catechism text into a manual of baby-talk'.[12]

A further part of the remedy, according to this same critic, was to be sought in removing the discrepancy that so noticeably existed between the methods used in the teaching of religion and those used in the teaching of secular subjects.[13] Secular pedagogical reform, particularly in the field of methodology, had already been accepted and successfully exploited in Catholic schools for the teaching of the secular branches. Why not adopt these methods, therefore, where they were compatible, in the teaching of religion? This was the substance of the argument used by those who advocated reform.[14] The time had come, they maintained, to 'break away from the traditional way of instructing the young in their religion . . . and . . . to take up again in the classroom something of the idea that informed the old miracle plays, and with all possible reverence press into the service of Religion every appliance that has helped to simplify and make pleasant our secular teaching'.[15]

Once mooted, the idea quickly caught on. The educational journals of the various teaching orders encouraged it[16] and individual religious, trained in the secular institutes of education attached to the universities, began to make the necessary adaptations. By the end of the thirties results were already apparent. The 'desire . . . to bring the teaching of religion into harmony with the accepted principles of modern pedagogy', observed one critic, was already 'ardent' and widespread.[17]

[10] This was at the direction of the bishops and resulted, presumably, from the discussions of the Fourth Plenary Council. The catechism which resulted bore the inscription 'Issued with episcopal authority on the occasion of the Fourth Plenary Council, 1937', and was published by the Australian Catholic Truth Society in 1938.

[11] The catechism was used in Victoria, South Australia, parts of Tasmania, and one or two dioceses of New South Wales. Sydney and the remaining dioceses of New South Wales retained the old catechism—but not, so far as it can be ascertained, for any pedagogical or theological reasons.   [12] See Hanrahan, op. cit., pp. 23-4.

[13] Ibid. Here the critic is basing his remarks on the 1923 'Motu Proprio' of Pius XI. He insists that 'the knowledge of religion in all schools, from Primary to University, as a matter of principle, keep pace with that of secular subjects'.

[14] Pius X, 'Acerbo nimis', printed in Conc. Plen., III, 1905, p. 140.

[15] From Report of Rev. James Nolan, Superintendent of Parish schools, 1907, quoted by A. E. O'Brien, 'Uniformity of Method in the Teaching of Christian Doctrine', Austral Light, March 1911, p. 235.

[16] J.J.B., 'Educating vs. Teaching', Christian Brothers' Educational Record, 1895, p. 188.

[17] O'Brien, Rev. A. E., 'The Practical Aim of Religious Teaching', Australasian Catholic Record, April 1929, p. 130.

One indication was the number of new text-books on religion. In addition to the new catechism mentioned above there were books on the Mass—one for primary and one for secondary classes—by Dr J. T. McMahon;[18] books on the liturgy by the same author[19] and by the Reverend P. J. Lynch of Tasmania;[20] an entirely fresh presentation of doctrine by Archbishop Sheehan in the two volumes of *A Child's Book of Religion;* and different approaches again in a *Companion to the Catechism* by Dr Beovich, and *Christian Doctrine Notes* by the Very Reverend P. Carey. In addition to these were several overseas texts, notably the Sower Series[21] by Father Drinkwater, which were intended mainly as teachers' texts to accompany the ordinary catechism. Earlier the Catholic Readers written by Dr Thomas Shields and published by the Catholic University of Washington had been strongly advocated[22] but, owing to their high cost, they had not been widely used. Later in the 1940s the Second National Catholic Education Conference made a move to improve the format of the ordinary catechism, retaining however the official text.[23]

Perhaps the most remarkable and widely used of the above books were those of Dr Sheehan. Besides *The Child's Book* referred to above the Archbishop also produced *Religion by Letter;* this was intended mainly for correspondence work, and was obtainable either in leaflet or in book form. The former, however, remained the more important contribution; a great deal of research had gone into its preparation. After experiment, the continuous prose form in which the lessons in the book were first written was dropped in favour of the dialogue form, with this difference that it was the child who asked the question[24] and the teacher who supplied the answer, thus creating for the child, as one reviewer of the work said, 'the pedagogic moment'.[25] Besides the dialogue of the lessons the book also contained prayers and devotional exercises at the end of each lesson;[26] for, as the author said in his preface, the aim of the book

---

[18] *Pray the Mass*, pts. i and ii (7th edition), 1951.
[19] *Liturgy for the Classroom.*   [20] Lynch, Rev. P. J., *A Liturgical Catechism.*
[21] Drinkwater, Rev. F. H., *Teaching the Catechism.*   [22] Hanrahan, op. cit., pp. 125-6.
[23] The Conference suggested that the cover, paper, painting and pictures should be of 'excellent quality' and that the price should still be kept at 3d. per copy. Each Diocesan Inspector, furthermore, was invited to make suggestions with a view to revising and simplifying the text. *Report of Second National Catholic Education Conference,* 1939, p. 8.
[24] Sheehan, *A Child's Book of Religion,* pp. v, vi. The book was acclaimed by critics such as Fr O'Brien and Dr McMahon. *Australasian Catholic Record,* April 1926, p. 128; April 1935, pp. 180-6. Sheehan was not an innovator in this twist that he gave to the questions. Father Julian E. T. Woods had actually published a little booklet for children in the 1870s which was no less ingeniously worded than Sheehan's book. See Woods, Rev. Julian E. T., *A Guide to Confession and First Communion,* p. 3. Cf. Sheehan, op cit., pt. ii, pp. 17, 80.
[25] But, McMahon observes, the 'secular manner' is avoided. McMahon, 'Archbishop Sheehan's Book of Religion—A Short Commentary', *Australasian Catholic Record,* April 1935, pp. 180-6.
[26] See Sheehan, *A Child's Book of Religion,* pp. 18, 70, 86, 121.

was 'not only to teach children their religion, but also to teach them to be religious'.[27]

After the appearance of Dr Sheehan's book in 1934 other innovations followed. The so-called 'Catholic Evidence' method was developed by Sister M. Anselm O'Brien of the Dominican order and used widely in the secondary classes of the Dominican schools. As the name implies, it was simply an adaptation to school purposes of the kind of preparation given to members of the Catholic Evidence Guild. In practice it was found to arouse great interest among the pupils, with the result that the study of religion was completely revivified.[28] Another technique introduced about this time was the 'case' method which had been developed by the Vincentians in England. By the end of the thirties, it was being extensively used in the schools of New South Wales.[29] In addition to these were the various activity methods recommended by the new syllabuses of religious instruction—projects, for groups as well as for individuals, dramatization, sketching, handwork, and the like.[30] The catechism, no longer the exclusive text or lesson, came to receive less than a quarter of the attention formerly devoted to it.[31]

Many of the ideas underlying these departures in method appear at first to have been borrowed directly from the secular pedagogy of the time. The idea, for instance, of stressing the importance of self-activity in the learning process strongly suggests the progressives, to whom the important thing in the learning process was not the truth but the 'activity which the mind under[went] in responding to what [was] presented from without'.[32]

A second, closely related, idea stressed the importance of the social setting in which the activity or learning occurred. The mere pursuit of school studies—catechism, Bible history, or any of the secular branches—had, in the eyes of the progressives, no more than 'a technical worth'. Only if they were 'acquired under conditions where their social significance was realized', would they be in a position to 'feed moral interest and develop moral insight'.[33] A third idea, largely a synthesis of the other two, stressed the shift in emphasis from the subject matter to the child, from the logical approach to the psychological.

These ideas found expression in the writings of Dewey and his

27 Ibid., p. iii.
28 Anselm, Sister M. (O.P.), *Catholic Evidence Guild in Secondary Schools*, p. 4.
29 Especially in schools of the Marist Brothers. The innovation was due largely to the efforts of the Rev. Br Andrew, F.M.S., who was Provincial Superior during the greater part of the 1930s and 40s. The text used was an Australian edition of the American work, *The Catholic Faith*.
30 *Syllabus of Religious Instruction for Primary and Secondary Schools in the Archdiocese of Brisbane*, etc., 1949, pp. 19-20. See also *Refresher School in Christian Doctrine*, pp. 5-20.
31 See Catholic Schools of Victoria, *Syllabus of Religious Instruction*, pp. 12-24.
32 Dewey, J., *The Child and the Curriculum*.
33 Dewey, J., *Democracy and Education*, pp. 413-14.

followers in America and men like Durkheim[34] in Europe. By the 1930s they had found wide acceptance also in England[35] and Australia.[36] In great part, moreover, but not necessarily in all their implications, they had been adopted by the leading Catholic educationists in Germany[37] and Ireland[38] where they had given rise to a veritable renaissance in catechetical instruction. On the other hand, their acceptance by Catholics was not universal. They appeared differently to different people: to some as too radical a departure from accepted Catholic practice and too dangerous a leaning towards pedagogic naturalism;[39] to others, as a timely return to the traditional ideas of the Church.

The activity principle, for example, found full support in the Church's view (based on St Thomas Aquinas)[40] that the primary cause in the learning process was not the teacher, helpful and very important though he might be, but the internal vital activity of the pupil himself.[41] The teacher was no more than an instrument.[42]

The second idea—that the learning process began in the day-to-day social experience of the child—was seen to be no more than a restatement of the traditional Catholic view that it was really the community that educated. To Pius XI, in his 1929 encyclical, education was 'essentially a social and not a mere individual activity'.[43] To the Australian bishops, in their concern to have the child reared in a Catholic atmosphere, this fact had been obvious all along.[44] Polding in fact was able to find no better way of describing education than to call it 'a thing of life'.[45] In the Catholic sense, then, no less than in Dewey's, society was educative: life was its own pedagogy.

[34] See de Hovre, op. cit., p. 417.

[35] Board of Education, *Report of the Consultative Committee on the Primary School* (Hadow Report), 1931, p. 93.

[36] *Final Report of Royal Commission on Technical Education* (Vic.), 1887-1901, evidence of Frank Tate, qq. 1272, 1276. See also G. S. Browne, *The Case for Curriculum Revision.*

[37] McMahon, Rev. J. T., *Some Methods of Teaching Religion*, p. 2.

[38] McMahon, 'The Irish Renaissance in Christian Doctrine', *Australasian Catholic Record*, July 1929, p. 225. See also *Christian Brothers' Educational Record*, 1887, p. 8; 1888, p. 54.

[39] For an account of this from a slightly different angle see J. S. Brubacher, *A History of the Problems of Education*, p. 351.

[40] *De Veritate*, q. xi, De Magistro, a. 2 ('Utrum aliquis possit sui ipsius magister esse'). [41] Ibid., art. i.

[42] For example, the Dominican Rule informs the teacher that she is 'to stimulate the child's God given intelligence, to aid her to acquire and assimilate knowledge; she is, therefore, definitely a co-adjutor, and relatively subordinate to the pupil'. *Rule of St Augustine and the Constitutions of the Congregation of the Dominican Sisters of New South Wales*, pt. i, ch. 24, art. 211. See also Jacques Maritain, *Education at the Cross Roads*, p. 32.

[43] 'Educandi munus non singulorum hominum, sed necessario societatis est.' Pius XI, 'Divini Illius Magistri', 1929, p. 52.

[44] See address of Dr Gallagher at the blessing of the foundation stone of a new school at Gundagai, N.S.W., in 1898. *Gundagai Times*, 1 November 1898.

[45] Polding, Pastoral on Education, 1859. Quoted in Bishop P. B. Geoghegan's *Pastoral Letter to the Clergy and Laity of the Diocese on the Education of Catholic Children*, p. 8.

The third idea—the psychological approach to the child regardless of the logic of the subject matter—likewise appears to be not so much a borrowing from the modern secular pedagogy as a return to early practice within the Church. The Munich, or so-called psychological method, developed by the catechists of south Germany, is a case in point. While obviously indebted to Herbart and others of his time and later, the method itself has been claimed to be little more than a modern rendering of the principles of catechizing laid down by St Augustine in his *De Catechizandis Rudibus*.[46]

These claims apart, however, it must be admitted that the impact of secular pedagogy on the methods of teaching religion was both profound and salutary. In Australia, however, the impact was indirect rather than direct, and other factors cannot be overlooked.

Catholic Writers on Methods of Teaching Religion

Foremost among these were the directives from Rome. In 1878 Leo XIII stressed the need for apt and solid methods of study.[47] In 1905 Pius X's 'Acerbo nimis', besides giving specific directions on the subject matter of religious instruction, called for an all-round improvement in method as well.[48] In 1910 the decree, *Quam singulari,* by lowering the age for admitting children to their first Holy Communion, further stimulated the search for suitable methods of instructing the young in what they required for the reception of the Sacrament.[49] Five years later Benedict XV renewed the efforts already made to consolidate the teaching of religion.[50] In 1923, Pius XI, in his 'Motu Proprio', called for still further improvement, and set up a special office in connection with the Sacred Congregation of the Council, which was to serve as an 'instrument to urge obedience to its laws regarding the Christian instruction of the people throughout the world'.[51]

The impact of these directives from Rome as well as the development in catechetical instruction in Western Europe and America began to be felt most strongly in Australia from the 1920s onwards, chiefly through the group of educational writers who flourished at that period.

Earliest among these was the Reverend A. E. O'Brien of Bathurst. From 1911, Father O'Brien had been inveighing against what he

---

46 McMahon, *Some Methods of Teaching Religion.*
47 Ep. encycl., 'Inscrutabili', 24 April 1878.
48 See *Conc. Plen.,* III, 1905, pp. 131-44.
49 S. Congregatio de Sacramentis, 'Decretum de aetate admittendorum ad primam communionem eucharisticam' (Ad primam Confessionem et ad primam Communionem necessaria non est plena et perfecta doctrinae christianae cognitio. Puer tamen postea debebit integrum catechismum pro modo suae intelligentiae gradatim addiscere). *Acta Apostolicae Sedis,* 1910, p. 582.
50 See Sharp, Rev. John K., *Aims and Methods in Teaching Religion,* p. 30.
51 Pius XI, Motu Proprio on 'The teaching of Christian Doctrine, throughout the world', 29 June 1923. *Australasian Catholic Record,* January 1925, pp. 5-6.

imagined to be defects in the catechetical instruction of the time.[52] His early articles, appearing in the *Austral Light* and strongly influenced by similar contemporary work in the United States,[53] were mainly negative in their criticism. Those of the later period, published in the *Australasian Catholic Record,* were much more constructive. By this time, too, he had also come under the influence of the German catechetical writers from whom he had learnt much. For example, he no longer conceived the teacher's function as that of 'building the structure of knowledge in the child's mind' but rather of 'minister[ing] to the process of development'. As he put it, the centre of interest in school 'had shifted from the static to the dynamic'.[54]

But O'Brien was not a mere relayer of German and American ideas. Prepared to accept and advocate much of what the advanced secular educational writers of the day had to say, he was nevertheless one of those who held strongly to the view that, in adopting these principles, Catholics were doing no more than returning to the traditional practice of the Church. These principles, he maintained, underlay - Christ's method of teaching; they were 'structural in the organic teaching of the Church' and 'embodied in her liturgy and her sacramental system'.[55]

Other seminal writers in Australia in the 1920s and 1930s were Archbishop Michael Sheehan (referred to above), Brother Hanrahan of the Christian Brothers, the Reverend T. J. O'Connor, all of Sydney, and the Reverend Dr J. T. McMahon of Perth. Directly connected with the revival in catechetics in Ireland, Sheehan continued his interests in that field when he came to Australia in 1922 as coadjutor in Sydney. Associated with him in the experimental stages of the preparation of his *Child's Book of Religion* were the first two mentioned above, O'Connor and Hanrahan, who, as Inspector of Schools in the archdiocese and Provincial of the Christian Brothers respectively, aided in the propagation of the new ideas. In addition, the latter published articles on the matter in the *Australasian Catholic Record.*[56] Dr McMahon, who, as Inspector of Schools in the archdiocese of Perth, had gained valuable experience in devising schemes for the religious instruction of children of the outback, expounded his ideas in various ecclesiastical journals[57] and even

[52] O'Brien, A. E., 'Uniformity of Method in the Teaching of Christian Doctrine', *Austral Light,* March 1911, pp. 233-44.

[53] See Report of Rev. Thomas Devlin, Superintendent of Parish Schools, Pittsburg, U.S.A., quoted by O'Brien, op. cit.

[54] O'Brien, A. E., 'The Practical Aim of Religious Teaching', *Australasian Catholic Record,* April 1929, p. 127.

[55] O'Brien, 'Uniformity of Method in the Teaching of Christian Doctrine', *Austral Light,* March 1911, p. 242.

[56] Hanrahan, Br M. B., 'The Teaching of Catechism', *Australasian Catholic Record.* Six articles appeared under this title between April 1924 and July 1925.

[57] McMahon, Rev. J. T., 'A Liturgical Programme for schools', *Australasian Catholic Record,* October 1931, pp. 297-304.

by means of school texts themselves.[58] Other ideas, the result mainly of his post-graduate studies in catechetical methods abroad,[59] he made available in his doctoral thesis, *Some Methods of Teaching Religion,* which he published in 1928.

In the meantime, the teaching orders had not remained inactive. A certain readiness to adopt these new methods had been in evidence all along.[60] Catholic teachers, in fact, strongly resented the imputation that they were opposed to the more recently advocated ideas on teaching simply on account of their non-Catholic origin. 'Provided the essentials of Christian education are secured,' they said, 'the Church welcomes whatever the sciences may contribute towards rendering the work of the school more efficient.'[61] Besides this, the teaching manuals of some of the orders themselves remained fully sensitive to the developments that were going on about them.[62] The training colleges also played an important role. Through the use of modern text-books[63] and under professors trained in the secular universities yet 'steeped in the Catholic tradition',[64] most of what was useful in modern developments was assimilated and adapted to the teaching of religion.[65]

But the teaching of religion as such, regarded simply as a body of revealed truth to be delivered, was not the only purpose of the Catholic school. Knowledge, even of holy things, was not its ultimate goal. That goal, according to the 1950 *Syllabus of Religious Instruction* for Victoria, was for teachers to form the image of Christ in the children entrusted to them. Formation, in other words, was as important as information.

[58] These two texts, *Pray the Mass I* for primary and *Pray the Mass II* for post-primary, were recommended by the Second National Conference, in 1939. *Report of Second National Catholic Education Conference,* 1939, p. 4.

[59] The ground covered was: pt. i, dealing with methods of teaching religion: the Munich method, the Yorke method, the 'Sower' scheme, the Catechetical method, the Shields method; pt. ii, dealing with the project method: projects in doctrine, projects in Sacred Scripture, the Mass, the method in detail.

[60] Marist Brothers, *Calendrier Religieux,* 1952, p. 101. See also *Constitutions of the Institute of the Blessed Virgin Mary for the Houses dependent on the General Mother House, Rathfarnham,* 1938, xix, art. 220.

[61] Catholic Education Association, *Teachers' Conference,* 1911, pp. 13-15. At the Third National Conference, for example, in 1944, it was decided that 'the potentialities of the radio for imparting religious instruction have not been sufficiently exploited'. 'Greater success,' it was thought, 'might be attained by improving technique in presenting programmes.' *Report of Third National Education Conference,* 1944, p. 6.

[62] *The Teacher's Guide or Principles of Education for the use of the Marist Brothers of the Schools,* p. 63. The method advocated here is in striking contrast to the more deductive approach, with the emphasis on memory, of the original edition of the *Guide.* See *Guide des Écoles,* 1852, pt. ii, ch. 11.

[63] See John K. Sharp, *Aims and Methods in Teaching Religion.* Baierl, Joseph J., Bandas, Rudolph G., and Collins, Joseph, *Religious Instruction and Education.* Bandas, Rudolph G., *Catechetics in the New Testament.*

[64] Beovich, 'Catholic Education and Catechetics in Australia', 1949, p. 6.

[65] McKenna, K. C., 'Progressivism and the Roman Catholic Schools' (unpublished B.Ed. thesis, University of Melbourne, 1951, pp. 76-93).

MORAL AND RELIGIOUS FORMATION

Formation of this type tended to be overlooked in some of the state school systems that developed in Australia. In the New South Wales system it was noticeably absent.[66] The development of 'human character', said the report of the Knibbs and Turner Commission, constituted 'the fundamental purpose in education'; the cultivation of the body and mind were merely 'ancillary and secondary thereto'.[67]

Dealing with the same problem, but employing an entirely different terminology, Pius XII was to say the same thing half a century later.[68] To him orthodox Catholic practice embraced a threefold formation: First, an education to discipline—guarding the child against his own weakness, encouraging watchfulness and penance; second, an education to truthfulness—arming the child with a genuine concept of liberty and developing in him a Christian outlook, mentality or judgment; and third, an education to prayer—training him in the use of the various supernatural aids with which religion provided him.[69] In these three ways most of the pedagogical devices used by the Church in carrying out the ends of moral education are to be observed. Taking them in order, the question of discipline might be considered first.

Discipline and Supervision

On this matter of discipline no less than in others Catholic schools were exposed to the influences of common school practice around them, but on this particular point, perhaps more than on others, Catholic pedagogy found itself at variance with the naturalistic tendencies of secular pedagogy. The Australian bishops had branded as 'pernicious . . . the attitude of those who assert that moral formation should be given according to the false principles of naturalism and materialism'.[70] Pius XI, in his 1929 encyclical, had been more specific and singled out the particular areas where Catholic practice found itself most in danger of being imperfectly understood: in matters such as surveillance and correction, liberty and self-government in the school, sex-instruction and co-education, and so on.[71]

In its approach to the question of surveillance and restraint the Church, it appears, worked on two principles: first, that the effects of original sin—'weakness of the will and disorderly inclinations'—still survived in human nature; second, that these disorderly inclinations were

---

[66] Designated by the Knibbs and Turner Commission as 'one of the most serious defects' of the whole system. Knibbs and Turner, *Interim Report of the Commissioners on Certain Parts of Primary Education*, p. 25.
[67] Ibid., p. 14.
[68] Pius XII on the education of conscience. *Advocate*, 10 April 1952, p. 5, b.
[69] Ibid., p. 5, d.   [70] *Conc. Plen*, IV, decr. 601.
[71] Pius XI, 'Divini Illius Magistri', 1929, p. 69.

to be curbed and held in control, since it was better to prevent evil than to let it go unchecked.[72] On that account, said Pius XI, 'extended and careful vigilance was necessary';[73] no amount of purely intellectual training would suffice. On this point, the bishops responsible for founding the present system of Catholic education in the nineteenth century had been unanimous;[74] similar unanimity was also to be found in the manuals of pedagogy of the orders themselves.[75] The use of this preventive discipline was enjoined on all: the pupils were never, under normal circumstances, to be left without supervision.[76]

In practice this close supervision appeared in no way irksome to the pupils, being tempered by certain wise prescriptions of rule,[77] but its effect was immediately discernible[78] and made the new schools of the religious in the 1860s and 1870s stand out sharply from those of the lay teachers.

Despite this seemingly close supervision,[79] the manuals of the various orders all stressed the importance of respect for the personality of the child[80] and of the necessity of approaching him as an individual.[81] This did not mean that the teacher was to approve of the child's every whim. 'Understanding youth', said Pius XII, did 'not mean approving of every idea, taste, or caprice presented to youth'; it meant rather 'the discovery and approval of that in which youth is right, and the search for the cause of errors'.[82] And, if errors did exist, the cause was to be found not in any supposed obsoleteness of the moral code of the Ten Command-

[72] Ibid.   [73] Ibid., p. 81. See also *Conc. Plen.*, I, 1885, decr. 236.
[74] See remarks of Dr Matthew Quinn. Address at prize distribution at the Certified Denominational School, Bathurst, 16 December 1867. *Bathurst Times,* 25 December 1867, p. 2, d.
[75] *Les Constitutions des Ursulines,* I, ch. vi, p. 7; *St Ignatius' Prospectus,* p. 6.
[76] I.B.V.M., *Usual Customs and Observances,* pp. 96, 98. See also *Common Rules of the Institute of the Marist Brothers of the Schools,* pt. iii, ch. v, arts. 350, 354-6; *Guide des Écoles,* 1923, ch. x; *Règles Communes des Frères des Écoles Chrétiennes,* ch. vii, art. 3.
[77] See *Common Rules of the Institute of the Marist Brothers of the Schools,* pt. iii, ch. iv, art. 342.
[78] Reports of Inspector Reilly on Catholic Schools, 1866, Report on Balmain Nuns' School, April 1866. (ML). Many Protestants were attracted by this very fact. See Rogers, Report on Catholic Schools, 1883, p. 2. In some cases, the proportion of Protestants was as high as 20 per cent.
[79] For example, carefully worded regulations concerning conduct were laid down. These extended even to directions as to the modesty of girls' frocks. See direction of Sacred Congregation of Council, Rome, 12 January 1930, in *Australasian Catholic Record,* July 1930, p. 198; and *Conc. Plen.,* IV, 1937, decr. 296.
[80] *Rule of St Augustine and the Constitutions of the Congregation of the Dominican Sisters of New South Wales,* pt. 1, ch. 24, art. 211. See also *Common Rules of the Institute of the Marist Brothers of the Schools,* pt. iii, ch. iv, art. 338.
[81] Cf. *Constitutions of the Institute of the Blessed Virgin Mary,* ch. xviii, art. 213. See also *Common Rules of the Institute of the Marist Brothers of the Schools,* pt. ii, ch. xiii, art. 275; *Les Constitutions des Ursulines de Paris,* pt. i, ch. iv, art. 2; 'Pour attendre son but, l'education doit s'adapter à la nature de l'enfant,' *Guide des Écoles,* 1923, p. 10; *Constitutions of the Institute of the Blessed Virgin Mary,* ch. xix, art. 219.
[82] Allocution to International Congress of Teaching Nuns, 1951, at Rome. *Catholic Weekly,* 4 October 1951, p. 2, c.

ments but, as Pius XI had already pointed out, in the nature of the child.[83] To claim to 'emancipate' the child, therefore, by liberating him from this code was to 'make him the slave of his own blind pride and of his disorderly affection'.[84]

To the duty of supervision was added the much more difficult task of correction, which was treated with correspondingly greater detail in the manuals. This detailed treatment, though it seemed to put Catholic practice more out of touch with modern tendencies, clearly indicated the attitude of the Church. Corporal punishment had been in use almost everywhere until the nineteenth century, but for the teaching orders it was wholly proscribed.[85] In its place other forms of punishment were recommended.[86] The mere interdiction of corporal punishment,[87] however, was not sufficient to stamp it out entirely, nor was it found that the entire suppression of it was always in the best interests of either the school or the pupil. Admitting this fact and yet at the same time maintaining its opposition on principle, the Third National Catholic Education Conference tolerated it, but 'only as a last resort' and 'for some grave transgression—never for mere failure in answering questions'.[88]

In the earlier period, this punishment for failure in answering had constituted a grave abuse, practically the sole and universal motive for learning being the threat of corporal punishment. In the schools of the religious, on the other hand, a more positive incentive was substituted—emulation.[89] The principle itself found application in numerous ways: 'card' days or 'marks' days,[90] terminal or yearly competitions,[91] diocesan exhibitions, scholarships, and prizes,[92] eisteddfods,[93] and the like.

[83] Pius XI, 'Divini Illius Magistri', p. 70.　　[84] Ibid.

[85] See Règles Communes des Frères des Écoles Chrétiennes, p. 95.

[86] Management of the Christian Schools, pt. ii, ch. ii. Guide des Écoles, pt. ii, ch. xii. Common Rules of the Institute of the Marist Brothers of the Schools, pt. iii, ch. vi, art. 366, 375, 378, 381.

[87] It was forbidden, for example, in the archdiocese of Sydney. In the archdiocese of Adelaide a distinction was made: corporal punishment was 'never' to 'be administered to girls'. In the case of boys its administration was to be 'limited as much as possible'. Archdiocese of Adelaide, Syllabus, 1946, p. 38.

[88] Report of Third National Catholic Education Conference, 1944, p. 7.

[89] For this they were criticized by the Port Royalists, by Rousseau, and by Kant. See Sister Marie de Saint Jean Martin, Ursuline Method of Education, p. 312.

The rivalry the Jesuits strove to arouse, with their senior students at any rate, was not the noisy rivalry of small boys. The rivalry they intended was one devoid of ill-will. Farrell, Rev. Alan P., The Jesuit Code of Liberal Education, pp. 81, 277-9, 290.

See also O'Leary, M., Catholic Church and Education, p. 63; Management of Christian Schools, p. 123; Guide des Écoles, 1923, pp. 120-6.

[90] 'Merit' day, for example, was established at St Stanislaus' College, Bathurst, in 1895. Hall, History of St Stanislaus' College, Bathurst, p. 104. For the practice in Loreto schools see I.B.V.M., Usual Customs and Directory, pp. 100-1. See also St Ignatius' Prospectus, p. 7.

[91] For example, in the Marist and Christian Brothers' Schools. In some instances, different groups of nuns joined in these competitions. The Sisters of Charity, for example, in New South Wales did the same examinations as the Marist Brothers.

[92] These were organized in practically every diocese.

[93] These became popular among the schools of the Christian and Marist Brothers, particularly in Sydney and Melbourne. The work embraced singing and speechcraft.

A further relaxation of the more coercive discipline of earlier times came from the impact of the secular pedagogy with its ideas of free discipline, self-government, and the like. But here Rome felt obliged to interpose: Catholics were to reject those systems which appealed to a 'pretended self-government and unrestrained freedom on the part of the child', and which diminished or even suppressed 'the teacher's authority and action', attributing to the child 'an exclusive primacy of initiative, and an activity independent of any higher law, natural or divine'.[94] If, on the other hand, any of these new terms—self-government, for instance —were used to denote the necessity of 'a generally more active co-operation on the part of the pupil in his own education', if the intention was to 'banish from education despotism and violence, which . . . just punishment [was] not', then the Church would wholeheartedly support them.[95]

But such warnings seemed unnecessary in Australia. If teachers erred, it was on the side of excessive control rather than of excessive freedom —a fact attested by the efforts of over forty years to inject a greater measure of pupil responsibility into the Catholic system. The defects of too close a supervision and too rigid a control were obvious. As early as 1911 the Catholic Education Conference in New South Wales adopted a resolution proposed by Father Maurice O'Reilly, then President of St Stanislaus' College, Bathurst, that 'some attempt should be made by the last year of the college course to brace the moral fibre by accustoming the senior pupils to the exercise of liberty and self-control'. The resolution referred especially to girls' schools where, it was considered, the training was 'to a large extent continental'. It was unwise, Father O'Reilly believed, to treat girls 'like exotics'.[96] With a similar end in view—the development of self-responsibility—the first and second National Catholic Education Conferences urged that measures should be adopted to avoid regimentation, particularly in the approach to the Sacraments.[97] The Third National Conference went further and recommended that 'it should be the aim of the school to provide an atmosphere not too unlike that of adult life and to stress self-discipline rather than compulsion'.[98]

Response to this movement, however, was slow. The orders were not unsympathetic, but either through blind attachment to a diehard tradition or a healthy respect for the accumulated wisdom of long experience they were disinclined to give up practices that had already proved reliable. The religious of the Sacred Heart, for instance, still con-

[94] Pius XI, 'Divini Illius Magistri', p. 69.
[95] Ibid., p. 70.
[96] Catholic Education Association, Teachers' Conference, 1911, p. 47.
[97] Report of First National Catholic Education Conference, 1936.
[98] Report of Third National Catholic Education Conference, 1944, p. 7.

tinued to place great store on discipline and obedience, criticism and correction, as well as on vigilance—'not the nervous vigilance, unquiet and anxious, which arouses to mischief the sporting instinct of children and stings the rebellious to revolt', but the calmer, unobtrusive and more intelligent vigilance.[99] The Dominicans followed similar rules.[1] Some of the male teaching orders were even more sceptical. 'With all allowance for the newer ideas', said the 1931 English edition of the Marist Brothers' *Guide des Écoles,* there still remained, especially in the boarding schools, a problem to be faced, which 'excessive supervision at least recognized squarely and met not unsuccessfully'.[2] The problem, it considered, could be quite well met under the old system of supervision provided that the teacher, realizing that such supervision would cease after the pupils' school days were over, exercised his control in such a way as to render the transition to the later stage as smooth as possible.[3]

Nowhere, however, was the cautious approach of Catholic pedagogy to the more modern tendencies in moral education better illustrated than in its attitude to sex instruction. On this matter the Church appeared to be guided by two principles: first, that adequate instruction in matters pertaining to sex was not only lawful but desirable and necessary; second, that such instruction, being insufficient in itself, required to be supplemented by a positive, systematic training in purity.

These two principles remained unchanged, though the manner of applying the first varied a little with the circumstances. When, in 1916, the Minister for Public Instruction in Victoria was approached by a deputation to have instruction in sex-physiology introduced into the schools, he refused. Archbishop Carr expressed himself as 'entirely in accord' with him. Such an innovation, he believed, 'would be most dangerous and demoralizing'.[4] The Archbishop did not deny that such knowledge should be imparted to children, but claimed that it 'should be given individually, not collectively, by natural and religious guardians, not by school teachers'. Besides this, he said, Catholic children enjoyed 'special advantages . . . in the high ideal of purity always held aloft in the Catholic Church, in the observance of modesty . . . in the power of prayer in time of temptation, but above all in the tribunal of penance'.[5] Carr saw in this 'idea' of sex instruction 'imported from America' the influence of the naturalist and experimentalist philosophies. So too did Pius XI twelve

---

[99] Stuart, Janet Erskine, *The Education of Catholic Girls,* pp. 43-4.

[1] *Rule of St Augustine and the Constitutions of the Congregation of the Dominican Sisters of New South Wales,* pt. i, ch. 24, art. 221.

[2] This note is missing from the French editions both of 1923 and 1932. It is found only in the English edition of 1931. *The Teachers' Guide or Principles of Education,* p. 128.

[3] Ibid., p. 129.

[4] *Argus,* 17 July 1916, p. 9, b.

[5] Ibid.

years later. Far too common, he thought, was the error of those who 'with dangerous assurance', falsely imagined that they could forearm youth against the dangers of sensuality by 'means purely natural', such as a 'foolhardy initiation and precautionary instruction for all indiscriminately, even in public'. Such instruction as was necessary was to be given by those who held 'from God the commission to teach and who [had] the grace of state'.[6]

Two years later, in 1931, these views were reaffirmed by the Sacred Congregation of the Holy Office. Asked 'whether the method called sexual instruction or even sexual initiation could be approved', the Congregation returned a definite 'No', refusing to give any approbation whatsoever to these new methods even though they had been advocated in some cases by Catholics themselves.[7] To these rulings the Fourth Plenary Council in 1937 added its own, branding as pernicious and 'altogether to be reprobated (*omnino vitandæ*)' the opinions of those who held that they could, by purely natural means and 'without any help from religion and piety, arm adolescents against the incentive of pleasure and lust'; and as 'utterly false' the pretension of those who, by putting youth in dangerous occasions, imagined that they would thereby 'accustom their minds to such things and, as it were, harden them against the dangers of puberty'.[8]

These decrees became the norm for practice in Australian Catholic schools. At the Second National Catholic Education Conference in 1939 it was agreed that 'sex instruction should never be given in class', but 'privately and individually by the teacher', if—as generally happened—the parents had already failed in their duty. The 'most effective place' for such instruction, the Conference believed, was the confessional.[9]

Early in the 1940s, however, the Archbishop of Melbourne went a step further. Believing that the parents generally did fail in this duty and realizing that the confessional presented other difficulties, Dr Mannix decided that the task of instruction would have to fall back upon the school. Thenceforth 'all pupils in Catholic schools [were to] receive sex instruction before leaving school' and, to facilitate individual interviews, 'general class instruction might be given'.[10] The responsibility for

6 Pius XI, 'Divini Illius Magistri', p. 71.

7 Decree of the Sacred Congregation of the Holy Office on sex instruction, 21 March 1931. 'Esteem, desire and love of the angelic virtue,' read the decree, 'must be instilled into their young minds and hearts. They must be fully alive to the necessity of constant prayer, assiduous frequentation of the Sacraments of Penance and the Holy Eucharist, and directed to foster a filial devotion to the Blessed Virgin as Mother of Holy Purity, to whose protection young people must entirely commit themselves.' Decree translated in *Australasian Catholic Record*, July 1931, pp. 190-1.

8 *Conc. Plen.*, IV, 1937, decr. 602.

9 *Report of Second National Catholic Education Conference*, 1939, p. 4.

10 Circular to Melbourne Schools and Religious Houses from the Director of Catholic Education, 3 May 1944 (copy in files of Catholic Education Office, Melbourne).

having this carried out was left entirely in the hands of the principal or head teacher, but the actual giving of the instruction could be delegated to others, preferably to senior religious on the staff.[11] To ensure, furthermore, that the religious themselves were properly informed, a special course of lectures, at which the Archbishop presided, outlined both the methods and the matter to be used in the classroom.[12]

This reserve and caution which the Church displayed in regard to sex education was also to be observed in its attitude towards co-education. Following upon the custom established under the old Denominational Boards, the Church, where possible, established separate schools for boys and girls. With the coming of the religious orders the practice was continued; and, even in the present century, despite the increasing popularity of co-education and the many advantages it offered, the Church held out for separate schools for the sexes. 'A large amount of moral injury' was done, it believed, by 'mixing boys and girls together in large schools'.[13] For much the same reason Knibbs and Turner refrained from recommending any changes in the system of separate schools that had already become the established custom in New South Wales.[14] They admitted that co-education found favour in America; and, on 'grounds of economy and convenience', Turner would support the idea here, but on no other.[15]

On the belief that the scheme was founded on misconceptions concerning the nature of the sexes and therefore not acceptable to Catholics, Pius XI denounced it as 'false and harmful'. According to the Pontiff, it was founded largely upon 'naturalism' and a 'deplorable confusion of ideas' that mistook a 'levelling promiscuity and equality for the legitimate association of the sexes'. Since nature had fashioned the two sexes different 'in organism, in temperament, [and] in abilities', there was nothing to suggest that there ought to be promiscuity, 'much less equality', in their training.[16] Above all was it to be avoided at the adolescent period.[17] Accordingly mixed schools for boys and girls (*utriusque sexus adolescentes*) were condemned by the Fourth Plenary Council, unless, in the opinion of the bishop, special circumstances advised differently.[18]

---

[11] Ibid. In some instances, the circular continued, 'It may be possible for the Principals or Head Teachers to satisfy themselves that the parents are undertaking the duty of giving instruction. If it is clear that this is so, no further action is necessary'.

[12] Circular to Provincial Superiors of all the male teaching orders in the archdiocese, 6 November 1943 (copy in files of Catholic Education Office, Melbourne). A similar notice was addressed to the Superiors of the female religious orders.

[13] *Royal Commission on Education* (Tas.), 1883, evidence of Rev. T. Kelsh, q. 4.

[14] Knibbs and Turner, *Interim Report of the Commissioners on certain Parts of Primary Education*, p. 95.   [15] Ibid., p. 92.

[16] 'Fallax atque infensa.' Pius XI, 'Divini Illius Magistri', p. 72. English translation by American Paulist Press.   [17] Ibid., pp. 72-3.

[18] *Conc. Plen.*, IV, 1937, decr. 621.

In legislating thus, however, it does not appear that the bishops wished to impose a complete segregation of the sexes during adolescence; that, apparently, would have been equally unnatural. Some dioceses, therefore, began to encourage legitimate association. In 1944 the Third National Catholic Education Conference recommended that 'schools should arrange mixed social functions under adequate supervision', the purpose being 'to train senior pupils in sensible deportment'.[19] The 'adequate supervision' mentioned here, moreover, implied far more than mere supervision or vigilance in the narrower sense. In practice it developed into a positive attempt to sublimate and Christianize an important part of normal social intercourse. But this introduces the second aspect of Catholic formation referred to above—the development of a Christian mentality.

The Christian Mentality

Tenison Woods had written into the Rule of the Sisters of Saint Joseph that the institute was 'for the Catholic education of poor children'[20] and not just simply 'for the education of poor Catholics'. The distinction is significant. Not only the schools of the Sisters of Saint Joseph, but all Catholic schools were supposed to give the type of education here envisaged by Tenison Woods. In practice, however, the distinction was in constant danger of being overlooked. Drawing attention to this fact twenty years later, the Diocesan Synod of Sydney pointed out that a cross on the gable and a Catholic name on the gate were not sufficient to make a place a Catholic school: Catholic schools, it decreed, were 'to be truly religious in spirit and discipline, no less than in their name and material ornamentation'.[21] The mere fact, wrote Pius XI, 'that a school gives some religious instruction (often extremely stinted), does not bring it into accord with the rights of the Church . . . or make it a fit place for Catholic pupils'.[22] It had to be Catholic, as the Fourth Plenary Council decreed, 'not only in name, but in reality'.[23]

That had been the goal in establishing a separate Catholic system, but subsequent events revealed the difficulties that lay in the way of its practical achievement. To build schools and staff them with religious was not always sufficient. Surrounded, as they were, by the far more numerous schools of a vigorous and progressive state system and following the same courses of study and methods, Catholic schools were constantly in danger of slipping from their ideal. Acutely aware of the fact, succes-

19 *Report of Third National Catholic Education Conference*, 1944, p. 7.
20 *Rules for the Institute of St Joseph for the Catholic Education of our Children.*
21 *Decrees of Diocesan Synod*, Sydney, 1891, decr. 11. See also Mother Evangelist, 'The Use of Secular Subjects as a Medium of Religious Formation', *Australasian Catholic Education Congress*, p. 471.
22 'Divini Illius Magistri', p. 77.
23 'Non solum in nomine sed ipsa re.' *Conc. Plen.*, IV, 1937, decr. 634.

sive Popes had indicated precautions to be taken. Pius IX, for instance, had spoken of the necessity of having all branches of learning 'expand in closest alliance with religion',[24] and Leo XIII of 'every discipline' being 'thoroughly permeated and ruled by religion'.[25] Thirty years later, Pius XI felt obliged to restate the principle in still more specific terms. 'All the teaching,' he said, 'the whole organization of the school . . . its teachers, syllabus and text books in every branch [were to] be regulated by the Christian spirit.'[26]

Efforts had been made before the turn of the century to do something about the text-books. The First Plenary Council (1885), considering it a matter of utmost importance that books should be free from all error against faith and morals,[27] had directed that a series of texts be brought out 'especially adapted to Australian schools'.[28] No books were forthcoming, however, and at the Synodal Conference in Sydney in 1890 the three bishops who had already been requested to draw up a standard of proficiency for the Catholic schools were further requested to plan an 'Australian series of Catholic school books'.[29] Still nothing was done, whereupon the Second Plenary Council directed the same three bishops to enter into communication with the Catholic publishing house of Benziger Brothers in America concerning a series of text-books for Australia.[30] By the end of the nineties these books had arrived and were being widely disseminated.[31] In the meantime schools had fallen back on a Burns Oates series from England and the Christian Brothers' books from Ireland. Neither of these series, however, had been satisfactory, both having been written for northern hemisphere conditions.[32]

After the 1900s further developments took place. The Marist Brothers, Christian Brothers and the De La Salle Brothers began to produce books of their own; but these were mainly of a technical nature—art,[33] elementary mathematics,[34] grammar, and so on. In those subjects where Catholic text-books were most needed and where they might conceivably have

[24] Quoted in Evangelist, Mother M., 'The Use of Secular Subjects as a Medium of Religious Formation', *Australian Catholic Education Congress*, p. 471.
[25] Ep. encycl., 'Militantis Ecclesiae', 1 August 1897. *Acta*, vol. xvii, pp. 255-6.
[26] 'Divini Illius Magistri', p. 77.
[27] 'Immunes sint ab omni errore . . .' *Conc. Plen.*, I, decr. 243.
[28] Ibid., decr. 244.
[29] *Decrees of Diocesan Synod*, Sydney, 1891, decr. 1891.
[30] *Conc. Plen.*, II, decr. 312.
[31] *Advocate*, 18 February 1899, p. 16, a.
[32] Apart from the fact that they were predominantly Irish in their setting, particularly in history and geography, they were strongly nationalistic in their outlook and to that extent anti-British. For this reason they were attacked and submitted to a piecemeal dissection by the Protestant paper, *Queensland Evangelical Standard*, 7 October-18 November 1875.
[33] For example, Morgan, J. A. and Price, A., *Architecture for Intermediate Students*.
[34] For example, *Arithmetic for Secondary Schools*, the Christian Brothers, 1929. See also the Marist Brothers' *Arithmetic for Fourth Class*. Others in these series include English, science, and history notes.

made their greatest contribution to Catholic education—in the social studies, literature, and the like—none or very few were forthcoming.[35] Victoria, it is true, produced what was claimed to be a satisfactory series of history readers for the elementary and middle grades,[36] a panel of Catholic teachers in New South Wales produced an acceptable history text for junior secondary classes,[37] and books on social principles appeared.[38] Victoria and New South Wales also developed a school paper or magazine for the elementary grades,[39] but the mere fact that such papers were Catholic in tone and character was no excuse for their being inferior in other respects to the corresponding papers issued by the state.[40]

On the whole, the results, after fifty years' effort, were disappointing. Cost of production and lack of co-ordination between the various dioceses and the different states appeared to have crippled every attempt.[41] Meanwhile, although the absolute need for Catholic text-books in Australia might have grown somewhat less urgent, the desirability of having them was in no way diminished.[42]

Another difficulty was the public examination system. Welcome by most, this system of examinations came to be regarded by some as a 'mortal tyranny' that was doing 'incalculable harm' to Catholic education.[43] Participation in the system was contingent upon the acceptance of

35 'Probably,' wrote one critic in 1911, 'we shall have to wait some time before we have satisfactory history text-books in connection with the lesser University examinations, and the responsibility for this rests, we think to some extent, on Catholic shoulders.' 'News and Notes', *Austral Light*, March 1911, p. 245, a.
   In 1932, the Christian Brothers published a *History of Australia and New Zealand for Catholic Schools*.
36 Catholic History Readers. Six books made up the series: pt. i, *The Kings of the Earth*; pt. ii, *The Speaking Word*; pt. iii, *The Victory of the Cross*; pt. iv, *The Story of the Middle Ages*; pt. v, *The Changing World*; pt. vi, *The Modern World*.
37 Mother McCay (ed.), *Early and Mediaeval History*.
38 Maher, F. K., *An Introduction to Social Principles*.
39 The Victorian paper, the *Children's World*, was issued at three different levels for primary school children. The New South Wales paper was the *Catholic School Paper*, approved by the bishops of New South Wales for use in the Catholic schools.
40 This would appear to be one of the chief reasons for the fact that many schools, particularly in New South Wales, preferred the state school paper. In Victoria, where Catholic schools were under some pressure to use the *Children's World*, it is not uncommon to find the state paper being used as well. See also Beovich, Archbishop M., 'Religious Education: its place in the Catholic Schools', *Catholic Education Congress*, 1936, p. 322.
   The Third National Catholic Education Conference recommended the appointment of a standing committee for the purpose of producing better Catholic texts in the future. *Report of Third National Catholic Education Conference*, 1944.
41 *Report of Third National Catholic Education Conference*, 1944, p. 4.
42 Cf. Council of Trent, sess. v, ch. 1; Ep. encycl. 'Nostris et Nobiscum', 8 December 1849; Allocut., 'In Consistoriali', 1 November 1850; 'Syllabus Errorum', 1864, prop. 45. See also Const., 'Romanos Pontifices', 8 May 1881; Ep. encycl., 'Constanti Hungarorum', 2 September 1893; S.C. de Prop. Fide, instr. (ad Archiep. Hiberniae), 7 May 1860, n. i; instr., 25 May 1868; instr. (ad Vic. Ap. Sin.), 18 December 1883, n. xi, 5, 6; *Cod. Iur. Can.*, can. 1381.
43 Frewin, Mother Frances, 'Some Fundamental Principles in the Training of Religious Teachers', *Australian Catholic Education Congress*, 1936, p. 437.

the various departmental syllabuses,[44] thus bringing Catholic schools, to a degree, under the direction of the state[45]—not that this was bad in itself but, as was pointed out by the Knibbs and Turner Commission earlier, it involved the Catholic schools in a system from which escape, even if they desired it, would have been very difficult.[46]

In the meantime, a likely way out of the difficulty did arise in Victoria. This was the 'Class A' accrediting system developed by the University of Melbourne through the Schools' Board.[47] This system of internal examination provided a suitable alternative for schools dissatisfied with the prescribed syllabus or desirous of escaping the coercion of external examinations. Catholic schools, however, did not appear interested and for over twenty years little was done[48] until, in 1944, the Third National Catholic Education Conference seized upon the idea that an 'accrediting system offer[ed] Catholic schools a valuable opportunity of informing the whole curriculum with a Catholic spirit'.[49] The Victorian scheme seemed to offer the necessary guarantees, but the schools still appeared reluctant to embark upon it, notwithstanding the encouragement and even gentle pressure that was brought to bear by the Catholic education authorities.[50] The schools, though aware of the advantages offered by the system, were deterred by other factors. The result was that by the middle of the century only a handful of Catholic schools—all girls' save one—had accepted the scheme.[51]

A similar accrediting scheme was proposed in Tasmania in 1938, and Archbishop Simonds, believing that the Catholic schools 'would gain more by joining [it] than by standing apart', wanted them to fall in with the proposal.[52] The schools would have done so, had not an unexpected

[44] Address of Rev. Brother Boniface, Holy Cross College, Ryde, N.S.W. *Freeman's Journal*, 11 December 1913, p. 48.

[45] This was the view of Professor MacCallum, expressed at Riverview speech night, 1913. *Freeman's Journal*, 11 December 1913, p. 36.

[46] Knibbs and Turner, *Report of the Commissioners, mainly on Secondary Education*, p. 52.

[47] Beginning from the 1917 period.

[48] There were certain inconveniences in the system. Sydney University, for example, refused to extend matriculation rights to Victorian students who passed the Leaving Certificate by internal examination. One Catholic school, St Kevin's College, entered the system, but later withdrew. The main objection of the Christian Brothers was summed up in the following words: 'While there is some uncertainty about the benefits derived by boys there can be no doubt that it imposes an altogether too severe burden on the staff.' This burden, it is understood, referred to extra corrections and the keeping of records. *Our Studies* (Christian Brothers, Strathfield), October 1929, p. 32, a.

[49] *Report of Third National Catholic Education Conference*, 1944, p. 13, c.

[50] That is, by Archbishop Mannix and the Rev. D. Conquest, Director of Catholic Education. Miss Julia Flynn, retired Chief Inspector of the Department of Education, devoted the last years of her life to visiting and assisting Catholic schools in an attempt to have them enter the Class 'A' system.

[51] Actually seven girls' schools. *Handbook of Public and Matriculation Examinations*, University of Melbourne, 1948, p. 10.

[52] Letter, Archbishop Simonds to Mother Anthony of Presentation Convent, Launceston, 20 April 1938 (Archives, Presentation Convent, Launceston, Tasmania).

last-minute move on the part of the Tasmanian Schools Board compelled the Archbishop, 'with keen disappointment', to withdraw.[53]

Notwithstanding these two set-backs, the accrediting system, in the eyes of some, still offered Catholic schools what up to then appeared the best means of integrating their studies according to Catholic aims and ideals, keeping them at the same time closely parallel to the state system.[54] It was to be a real integration with something distinctly Catholic and not merely an exclusion of error. As the Reverend A. E. O'Brien said, echoing Leo XIII, 'more than negation [was] required; something positive [was] needed'.[55]

But studies apart, there still remained another way in which the child could be influenced and orientated towards a more Christian mentality. This was by the sodalities and other similar associations. The sodalities, in the hands of the Church,[56] were really special training grounds within the general training of the school; they aimed at cultivating higher ideals and stressed the obligation of self-improvement and of using one's influence for good, thereby turning to account the latent capacities of leadership, stimulating them and directing them to the common good.[57] Essentially, the sodalities were for a small nucleus, an élite;[58] they were to act as cells exercising an influence for good upon the larger organism. So effective were they that at times the tone of the school as a whole was judged by the standard of the sodalities.[59]

In origin they dated back to the Jesuit schools of the last part of the sixteenth century,[60] but the idea, spreading to the Ursulines[61] and others, subsequently became quite general. In Australia the sodalities in Catholic schools go back to the coming of the religious. The first Children of Mary sodality, for example, was established in the Benedictine Convent, Subiaco, near Sydney, in the first year of the school's existence, 1851.[62] The same sodality was established in All Hallows', Brisbane, in 1865, four years after the foundation of the school.[63]

[53] Letter, Archbishop Simonds to Hon. A. G. Ogilvie, Premier, 10 March 1939 (copy in Archives, Presentation Convent, Launceston).
[54] Report of Third National Catholic Education Conference, 1944, p. 13. Contemporaneously the same matter was being seriously considered by the Catholic schools in England. Battersby, Rev. W. J., 'Educational Work of the Religious Orders of Women', The English Catholics (ed. Rt Rev. G. A. Beck), pp. 337-64.
[55] O'Brien, 'Uniformity of Method in the Teaching of Christian Doctrine', Austral Light, March 1911, p. 325.
[56] Pius XI, 'Divini Illius Magistri', p. 75.
[57] See Stuart, Janet Erskine, The Education of Catholic Girls, p. 78.
[58] Guide des Écoles (1932 edition), p. 94.
[59] I.B.V.M., Usual Customs and Observances, p. 95.
[60] Brodrick, Rev. James (S.J.), The Progress of the Jesuits, 1556-1579, p. 277.
[61] Règlements des Ursulines (1895 edition), Appendix. See Farrell, The Jesuit Code of Liberal Education, pp. 246-357.
[62] McMahon, Rev. J. J. (M.S.C.), 'The History of Catholic Education in New South Wales', p. 3. Australian Catholic Historical Society Records, 1950.
[63] The Arches of the Years (All Hallows' Convent School Magazine), 1933.

Similarly, the Jesuits' school, St Ignatius,[64] the Vincentians',[65] the Dominicans',[66] the Loretos',[67] and so on, within a short time after each school was opened, formed a sodality. The First Plenary Council, in 1885, and the three that followed it, all decreed that sodalities should be established in schools.[68] The Fourth Council even specified the names of the sodalities to be used.[69] Earlier, in the Loreto schools for example, there were three junior sodalities[70] through which a child normally graduated before achieving the distinction of being admitted to the senior group.[71]

Related to the sodalities and resembling them in so far as they also aimed at developing the tone and morale of the pupils and diffusing a thoroughly Christian spirit throughout the school, were the various pious associations, such as the Apostleship of Prayer and the Sacred Heart Association or League, both of which were operating in the schools of the religious well before the turn of the century.[72] More recently established associations were those of the Confraternity of the Divine Child and the missionary association of the Holy Childhood which was specially recommended by the Fourth Plenary Council.[73] These associations differed from the sodalities in that, whereas the latter were restricted in membership, the former embraced practically everybody.

A further elaboration of the sodality idea belonging particularly to the present century was the Young Catholic Students' Movement, or simply Y.C.S. Organized as one of the 'specialized' movements,[74] it formed but one part of what was regarded by the Church as 'a great Crusade'[75]—Catholic Action, the avowed aim of which was 'to penetrate and transform the pagan environment by means of missionary activities'.[76] On the principle, therefore, that environment could either form or deform individuals, it became the particular objective of Y.C.S. 'to change and christianize the environment of school boys and school girls'.[77] Added to that were the secondary objectives: forming pupils for post-school

---

[64] St Ignatius' Prospectus, 1887, p. 6.
[65] Established at St Stanislaus', Bathurst, 1892, p. 101.
[66] At Maitland by 1882. O'Hanlon, Sr Assumpta (O.P.), Dominican Pioneers in New South Wales, p. 64.   [67] I.B.V.M., A Retrospect, p. 12.
[68] Conc. Plen., I, 1885, decr. 93; II, 1885, decr. 96; III, 1903, decr. 3. Decrees of the Diocesan Synod, decr. 13; Conc. Plen., IV, 1937, decr. 622.
[69] Ibid., decr. 308.
[70] The Sodality of the Divine Infant for the little ones, of St Joseph for the 3rd division, and the Holy Angels for the 2nd division. I.B.V.M., Usual Customs and Observances, p. 95.
[71] Promotion to the senior sodality was by no means automatic. See St Ignatius' Prospectus, 1887, p. 6; I.B.V.M., A Retrospect, p. 12.
[72] The Sacred Heart Association, for example, was functioning at St Ignatius' by 1886 (see Prospectus, 1887, p. 6), and at St Stanislaus', Bathurst, by 1899 (Hall, History of St Stanislaus' College, Bathurst, pp. 104, 106).
[73] Conc. Plen., IV, 1937, decr. 30.
[74] Young Catholic Students' Movement, Handbook, p. 91.
[75] Ibid., p. 5.   [76] Ibid., p. 91.   [77] Ibid., p. 11.

Catholic Action and helping them to prepare themselves properly for life in the world.[78] In a way these secondary objectives were just as important as the first. The Australian bishops believed with Leo XIII that, if the ills of society were going to be cured, then they could be cured in no other way than 'by a return to Christian life and Christian institutions'.[79] Only by being good Catholics[80] the bishops argued, could Catholics be good citizens.[81] In the regeneration of society, therefore, these same Catholic citizens were to play a special part.[82]

For the achievement of this end, the christianizing of the environment, the methods and organization of the Y.C.S. were most appropriately adapted. The techniques used—Gospel discussion, 'contact and influence', leaders, sub-leaders, teams, activity groups and general meetings—differed only in minor details from those employed in other movements of Catholic Action. The school was divided into groups according to individual interests and tastes, and a leader chosen in each group. The leaders—six to ten, according to the size of the school—were then taken and trained, not so much to be leaders, for they were that already, but to lead in the right direction. It was upon the leaders' group that the whole movement depended: through the 'review of influence' and the 'enquiry', two specialized techniques for gauging the climate of opinion throughout the environment, the influence of the leaders could be spread throughout the entire school. As with the older sodality prefects, a group of good leaders was often known to change the whole spirit and tone of a school.[83]

The activity groups, as the name implied, were groups dedicated generally to some activity—propaganda, poster work, literature, missions, handcrafts, drama, social studies, music, film discussions, debating, rural life, and the rest. Each group usually met once a fortnight and was

[78] Ibid., p. 12.   [79] Pastoral Letter of Cardinal Delegate, 1905, p. 708.
[80] Report of Royal Commission on Education (Vic.), 1884, pp. 148-9.
[81] The Rules of the two large teaching orders, the Marist Brothers and the Brothers de La Salle, make it an obligation on the part of the Brothers to inculcate in their pupils submission to the state and ecclesiastical authorities. See Common Rules of the Institute of the Marist Brothers of the Schools, pt. ii, ch. 7, art. 199. The Guide des Écoles sets out five ways of achieving this: pp. 11-12; and pt. i, ch. 8, 'Education Sociale'.
See also the Dominican constitutions on developing a 'sympathy with national traditions'. Rule of St Augustine and the Constitutions of the Dominican Sisters of New South Wales, pt. i, ch. 24, art. 214.
[82] See I.B.V.M., Usual Customs and Observances, p. 108.
Leo XIII's encyclical, 'Sapientiae Christianae' (1890), stressed the Catholic's obligations to his own country and demonstrated how conflict between loyalties to Church and state could arise only through misunderstanding of the true principles. Acta, vol. x, pp. 13-14.
Vaughan also held very pronounced views on this matter. See Pastoral Letter to the Clergy and Laity of the Archdiocese of Sydney, 24 August 1879, p. 10.
Lastly, Pius XII, when still Cardinal Eugene Pacelli, stressed the same matter of true civic loyalty in his letter to Archbishop Killian of Adelaide on the occasion of the Education Congress there in 1936. Australian Catholic Education Congress, 1936, p. 32.
[83] Y.C.S. Handbook, p. 18.

responsible for further disseminating the views generated in the leaders' group by a process of penetration of influence within its own environment.[84]

The whole movement was co-ordinated and organized on a national basis with its permanent national secretary who was attached to the National Catholic Secretariat in Melbourne.[85] Presiding over the central body was a member of the Hierarchy[86] who, as 'Episcopal Chairman' of the movement, was responsible for co-ordinating its activities with those of the other Catholic Action movements and with the policy of the Hierarchy in general.[87] The national organization was carried through and completed by a full set of publications: the Handbook, wherein the whole scheme was outlined;[88] the annual Programme, carrying a suggested plan for the whole year;[89] the Leaders' Bulletin, with pointers and suggestions for the meetings of the leaders' groups;[90] the In Manibus Tuis, or bulletin for the religious assistants, that is, the nuns, Brothers, or priests in charge of the individual school movements;[91] and lastly, the rank and file magazine known as the Rising Tide.[92]

The Young Catholic Students' Movement was a comparatively late development in Catholic education, dating in its final form only from 1942, when the Episcopal Committee authorized it 'to exist in primary and secondary schools'.[93] Nevertheless, the decision to enter upon the work of Catholic Action in general had stood since the Fourth Plenary Council in 1937.[94] At that time, however, no plans for its organization had been worked out, the bishops being content to ordain that 'during the year special instructions [should] be given in which the meaning of Catholic Action [should] be clearly set forth and the students [should] be taught the necessity of such action and the practical means of co-operating with the clergy in the salvation of souls'.[95] The direction of the First National Catholic Education Conference that 'encouragement be given to the establishing of school groups of Catholic Action' by organizing the older societies—Campion, St Vincent de Paul, and so on in schools and colleges,[96] was superseded when the new organization was established in 1942. This new scheme was fully endorsed by the Third National Conference in 1944.[97]

---

[84] Ibid., pp. 18-19.　　　　　　　　　　[85] Ibid., p. 1.
[86] From its inception it was Archbishop M. Beovich, of Adelaide.
[87] Y.C.S. Handbook, p. 5.　　　　　　　[88] Ibid., title page.
[89] See Y.C.S. Programme—1951.　　[90] See Y.C.S. Leaders' Bulletin, no. 5, July 1949.
[91] See Y.C.S. In Manibus Tuis, bulletin for Religious Assistants of the Young Christian Students' Movement, no. 3, December 1948.
[92] Y.C.S. Handbook, p. 86.　　　　　　[93] Ibid., p. 92.
[94] Conc. Plen., IV, 1937, decr. 89.　　[95] Ibid., decr. 643.
[96] Report of First National Catholic Education Conference, 1936.
[97] Report of Third National Catholic Education Conference, 1944, p. 4. Some of the teaching orders were directed by their superiors to take up the work of Catholic Action. See Common Rules of the Institute of the Marist Brothers of the Schools, 1947 edition, pt. ii, ch. 9, art. 230.

The organization finally assumed by this Y.C.S. Movement was largely Australian. The initial call to Catholic Action, it is true, came from Rome; but the details of organization were to be worked out by the countries themselves. The Australian scheme adopted many of those principles and methods that had proved effective under the Jocist[98] movement in Belgium and France. In addition, the Y.C.S. training methods and the technique of the 'enquiry'—collecting facts, examining them, sifting them, and extracting accurate conclusions from them[99]— illustrate the scientific method of thinking advocated by the experimentalists.

Useful and powerful, however, as these youth movements and sodalities were, none could touch the individual so intimately as those other elements in the environment of Catholic schools—the Church's liturgical and sacramental life. This was the third aspect of the threefold formation spoken of above, the education to prayer and the role of grace.

An Education to Prayer

By the sacramental life is generally meant the life of grace that flows through the Church and is communicated to men through the sacraments. The sacraments, in other words, constitute the ordinary channels of grace; but according to the Church's teaching,[1] man can by his own acts lay hold of this grace and apply it to his own soul. To induce him to do so would appear to be the immediate objective of every other element in the Church's educational programme.[2] 'To co-operate with divine grace in forming the true and perfect Christian' was, according to Pius XI in 1929, 'the proper and immediate end of Christian education'.[3]

It was this predication of Catholic education on the supernatural that distinguished it ultimately from all other forms of education. Even those outside the Church who failed to appreciate the full significance of the distinction were, nevertheless, fully aware of its existence. Sir Henry Parkes, for example, in introducing the 1880 Bill in New South Wales, could not see why its proposals were not well received by his Catholic fellow citizens. 'Surely,' he argued, 'the Catholic Religion, with all its sacraments, does not depend upon some particular form being taught.'[4] Parkes spoke in this way because he would have just learnt from the Joint Pastoral sent him by Vaughan that, in the Catholic view, part of the moral force by which Christianity acted upon mankind

98 That is the 'Jeunes Ouvriers Chrétiens' movement.
99 See Brubacher, p. 352, for the use of this technique in America. See also McKenna, p. 91.
1 St Thomas, *Contra Gentes* (English translation), III, c. 150, art. 7.
2 *Guide des Écoles*, 1923, pp. 76-80.
3 Pius XI, 'Divini Illius Magistri', p. 83.
4 *Parl. Deb.* (N.S.W.), 1879, 1, p. 274.

was exerted through 'the efficacy of the sacraments', 'through super-natural grace',[5] and that 'these graces and influences of Christianity [were] operating 'throughout the whole period' of education.[6]

Related to these 'influences' and in some respects a part of them, were the influences of the liturgical life of the Church. By means of the liturgy all the elements of a religious atmosphere, material as well as spiritual, were deliberately brought to bear on the impressionable mind of youth—and on the minds of adults[7] also, for in this matter they seemed to remain no less impressionable—a fact which Polding had known and used to good effect in his early days in the colony.[8]

In view of this it is not surprising that the religious,[9] with every encouragement from the bishops, strove to incorporate in the educational environment of their schools as much as they could of this liturgical atmosphere of the Church, making full use of all that the ritual offered—liturgical symbols[10] and chants,[11] solemn masses,[12] the services of Holy Week and Easter, processions, ceremonies of confirmation, and the like. It is not inconceivable that the deliberate, calculated attack on the senses made by these ceremonies left an indelible impression. For a child from the outback, certainly, where religion was shorn of almost everything that could render it impressive and where Mass was said perhaps once a year in a front room of a farm house, even the simplest liturgical ceremony in the school chapel had, it seemed, an atmosphere of magnificence about it.[13]

In addition to these, numerous quasi-liturgical devotions were also pressed into service—the solemnizing of first communion,[14] the ceremony of assigning honourable charges,[15] the pageant of the months, and

---

[5] *Pastoral Letter of the Archbishop and Bishops exercising Jurisdiction in New South Wales*, 1879, p. 6.   [6] Ibid., p. 7.

[7] *Australasian Chronicle*, 20 December 1839, p. 1. See also McGovern, 'John Bede Polding', *Australasian Catholic Record*, January 1936, p. 15. See Dr Gregory's Report to Rome on the Mission of New Holland. Quoted in Birt, op. cit., pp. 172-3; also the account of Dr Brady's functions in Perth, *Inquirer*, 14 January 1846, p. 2, b, c.

[8] Ullathorne, Archbishop W. B., *From Cabin Boy to Archbishop* (Autobiography). According to one of Polding's later biographers, it was like a return to the days of the miracle plays: 'when the Ritual provided a special rite, he used it to the full; when there was none ordered he invented one'. McGovern, op. cit.

[9] Cf. the enthusiasm for liturgical ceremonies displayed by the Blessed Marcellin Champagnat, founder of the Marist Brothers. John Baptist, Rev. Brother, *Life of Marcellin-Joseph-Benedict Champagnat*, pp. 348-50.

[10] *Synodus Diocesana Maitlandensis*, 1888, decr. 7.

[11] *Conc. Plen.*, IV, 1937, decr. 554.

[12] Ibid., decr. 309. See also advertisement in *Catholic Almanac*, 1854, p. 95; and *Common Rules of the Institute of the Marist Brothers of the Schools*, pt. i, ch. 3.

[13] Goulter, M. C., *Schoolday Memories*, p. 4.

[14] The first communion ceremonies which became such a feature in the lives of Catholic children took their ceremonial form from the practices followed at the famous Ursuline Convent of the Rue St Jacques, Paris. O'Leary, *Education with a Tradition*, p. 67.

[15] The 'honourable charges' ceremony occurred at the beginning of the school year: 'the veriest trinkets were handed with elaborate ceremonial, to the elder girls—a tiny model of a priest's biretta, a doll's role of music, tied up with blue ribbon, a miniature

so on. These ceremonies, wanting it seems, the dignity of full liturgical status, were on that account no less powerful in their appeal to youth,[16] as the following account shows.

Written with obvious enthusiasm, it describes one aspect of the month of May devotions and the 'practices' by means of which the nuns sought to strengthen the self-control and determination of their pupils. 'On the last day of April,' the account runs, 'the school was assembled, on tip-toe with expectation, to hear the special virtue which it was to practise during the month of May.' Each class would be represented before a statue of the Blessed Virgin by a lamp which was lit or extinguished according as the class had succeeded or failed. And, explains the author, each class stood or fell together; the defection of one was the disgrace of all.[17]

The simplicity and even childishness of such devices did not detract, apparently, from their effectiveness. 'I scarcely think,' wrote this chronicler, 'that for any of us girls the future will hold a moment as solemn as that when in the bygone Mays of our schooldays, the lamp of our class was lit or extinguished in the midst of a breathless hush, and with the eyes of the whole great household that made up our world focused upon it.'[18]

Spectacular practices of this type might naturally be expected to remain vivid in the memory, but there were others, less spectacular perhaps and, in the eyes of the child, even humdrum—assistance at Mass, the morning oblation, morning and evening prayers, the Rosary, devotion to the Blessed Eucharist, devotion to the Virgin Mary, the presence of God, meditation,[19] and the like.[20] Prescribed in the manuals of all the orders,[21] training in the use of these practices was regarded as 'of the utmost importance',[22] being necessary 'for the preservation

---

cricket bat . . . And yet looking back to those mere symbols, the "new girl" would pronounce them honestly worth their weight in gold—remembering the joys they brought with them, and the habits of initiative and forethought, and the power to shoulder responsibility that they carried in their train. For the tiny biretta symbolized the privilege of daily entry into the Convent sacristy, as the recognized assistant of the nun sacristan. And to realize all that is implied in this, one must believe—or at the least make some attempt to realize—the Catholic doctrine of the bodily Presence of the historical Christ on the altars. For a child who came from the recesses of the country, and whose life was to be spent in remote districts far from churches, it was like being in her girlhood, Maid of Honour at Court, a precious and fragrant memory, to be cherished for the remainder of her years . . . ' Goulter, op. cit., p. 8.

[16] For example, solemn benedictions and special devotions. See Annals of St Patrick's College, Goulburn, p. 82 (Archives of St Patrick's College, Goulburn).

[17] Goulter, op. cit., p. 28.   [18] Ibid., p. 29.

[19] For example, see I.B.V.M., *Usual Customs and Observances*, pp. 96, 104.

[20] Beovich, 'Religious Education: Its Place in the Catholic Schools', *Australian Catholic Education Congress*, p. 318.

[21] For example, see 'Religious Instruction', *Christian Brothers' Educational Record*, 1906, p. 92. See also I.B.V.M., *Usual Customs and Observances*, art. 104; and *Management of the Christian Schools*, p. 115.

[22] *Guide des Écoles*, 1923, p. 76: 'C'est le but final de l'éducation.'

and enlargement of [the child's] spiritual life'.[23] It is interesting to note that the further school texts on religion departed from the spirit of the nineteenth century with its dogmatic preoccupations, the more they began to emphasize this devotional and practical aspect of religion. This movement in Australia is particularly noticeable from the nineteen-thirties onward.[24]

It came to be widely held also that this devotional life of the school should be integrated as closely as possible with the liturgical and sacramental life of the parish so that habits acquired in school would carry over directly into adult life. Where they did not, post-scholastic institutions were established to help them.[25] It was also arranged that a child in a given sodality or pious association in school would find himself automatically in the corresponding parish organization upon leaving school.[26] Likewise the devotional practices acquired at school were to be carried on in after-school days. The result was that this strong supernatural element in the Church's educational battery, once set in motion by the first sacramental grace of baptism, continued through school days to adult age, becoming in effect continuous with life itself.

In this way did the Church propose to solve the problem of continuous education[27] and, by thus maintaining contact with the individual throughout life, bring to fruition the process begun in school—the development of what Pius XI described as 'the true and finished man of character'.[28]

---

[23] Rule of St Augustine and the Constitutions of the Congregation of Dominican Sisters of New South Wales, pt. i, art. 212.

[24] Particularly in the new approach advocated by Archbishop Sheehan of Sydney and Dr McMahon of Perth.

[25] See Guide des Écoles, 1923, pp. 83-6. See also, O'Doherty, Rev. J. P. (O.P.), 'The Need for Catholic Adult Education', Australian Catholic Education Congress, 1936, p. 169; I.B.V.M., Usual Customs and Observances, p. 94; Annals of St Patrick's College, Goulburn, p. 60.

Dr Beovich, in his 1949 report to Rome, gave a list of the various adult education organizations existing within the Church in Australia. 'Catholic Education and Catechetics in Australia', p. 5.

[26] Catholic Education Association, Teachers' Conference, 1911, pp. 15-17.

[27] O'Doherty, op. cit., p. 165. This writer stated with a new emphasis the admitted fact that a child was not fully educated when he left school.

[28] 'Homo germana animi firmitate insignis.' Pius XI, 'Divini Illius Magistri', p. 83.

II

Reorganization and Reaction

IMPROVING THE SYSTEM

A New Outlook

THE CATHOLIC schools described in the preceding chapters were the schools Vaughan had in mind when he assured his opponents that he would solve the school question 'in a way that [would] astonish them'. With the main outlines of that 'way' sketched in, we may now take up the account where we left it—at Vaughan's departure from the colony in 1883. The date itself is not significant, but the decade is, the 1880s representing one of the major turning points in the whole story.

By then the pioneering work had been done and the pioneers themselves nearly all gone. The personnel of the Hierarchy was almost completely changed. In New South Wales Vaughan had been succeeded by Archbishop (later Cardinal) Moran and the suffragans, Matthew Quinn and Lanigan, by Bishops Byrne and Gallagher. In South Australia the place of Geoghegan and Sheil had been filled by Dr Reynolds. Dr Dunne had followed James Quinn in Brisbane and Archbishop Carr had succeeded Goold in Melbourne. In some colonies, too, the Hierarchy had been further strengthened by the establishment of additional sees. All this meant new ideas and a new approach.

This is very noticeable in the attitude of men like Moran and Carr. No sooner had Moran set foot in New South Wales than he wound up the Board that had been left by Vaughan[1] and announced that it was 'his intention to make *other* arrangements for the schools of the Archdiocese'.[2] In Melbourne Archbishop Carr, saying less but going further, introduced many practical reforms which did much to strengthen the position of Catholic schools in Victoria. Where Moran and Carr left off, others carried on: notably Dr Mannix in Melbourne, Dr Beovich first in Melbourne and later in Adelaide, Dr Duhig in a different way in Brisbane, and Dr Prendiville and Monsignor McMahon in Perth.

That these new prelates would see the situation differently was only to be expected. They were less individualistic than their predecessors and

[1] On 13 December 1884. No entries appear in the minute book after that date. Catholic Education Board, Minute Book, p. 67 (Archives, St Mary's Cathedral, Sydney).
[2] *Freeman's Journal*, 11 October 1884, p. 15, c.

far more conventional. Besides, the situation itself had changed. Some difference in approach was therefore inevitable. But did this mean a change of viewpoint on the part of the Hierarchy as a whole?

To that question the answer is both yes and no. In so far as the principles laid down by these later bishops in the four great Plenary Councils between 1885[3] and 1937[4] and in their Official Pronouncement of 1935[5] are substantially the same as those laid down by Polding and the early bishops, the answer is no. But in so far as the attitude of these later bishops towards educational developments, particularly developments outside the Church, differs markedly from that of the earlier members of the Hierarchy, the answer is yes: there was considerable change.

The change is most evident in their attitude towards liberalism. The early bishops had for the most part all been appointees of Pope Pius IX (1846-78) whose policy in regard to liberalism, courageous though it may have been, was nevertheless negative and purely defensive. This policy was faithfully reflected in the utterances of men like Goold and Vaughan. But such a policy ill-befitted the times—a fact which even Pius himself came to realize before he died[6] and which he acknowledged by hinting that the line of action pursued by his successor would need to be greatly modified. The long struggle against liberalism had proved unavailing. Every attempt on the part of the Church to destroy it had ended in failure. It had come to stay. Realizing this, the new Pope, Leo XIII, had determined to lead the Church out of the frustrating cul-de-sac into which his predecessor's policy had led it. He would show Catholics how to live in a liberal world without sacrificing any of their Christian principles[7]. This he did, not only by his famous encyclical letters, but also by the policy he outlined and the men he appointed to implement it.

Foremost among the latter in Australia were Cardinal Moran and Archbishop Carr. Both were Irish, but both were alert to the needs of their new country and were strongly influenced by the thinking of Leo XIII. On that account, it is against Rome's changing attitudes towards liberalism that their policies are to be viewed—not only their policies in regard to the reorganization and expansion of the Catholic school system itself, but also their policies on political and educational development in the community at large. For it was from this wide movement outside the Church that much of the reorganization within the Catholic system originated. Had the Catholic leaders adopted a negative

[3] See *Conc. Plen.*, I, 1885.   [4] See *Conc. Plen.*, IV, 1937.
[5] Sheehan, Archbishop Michael, 'The Official Pronouncement of the Catholic Hierarchy of Australia on the Education Congress', *Australasian Catholic Record*, January 1937, pp. 11-18.
[6] Hughes, Philip, *A Popular History of the Catholic Church*, p. 255.   [7] Ibid., p. 256.

attitude towards this movement, as well they might have, the subsequent history of Catholic education might have been vastly different.

As it was, they were among its strongest supporters. Frequently, it will be remembered, they had stressed the necessity of maintaining in Catholic schools academic standards equal to those of the state schools and, when the education commissions[8] already referred to were proposed early in the century, both Moran and Carr warmly supported them.[9] Likewise in regard to the reforms of the remarkably progressive Directors of Education of that time—Peter Board in New South Wales, Frank Tate in Victoria, and Cyril Jackson in Western Australia—Catholic schools, thanks to the new lead that had been given them, were able to profit from all that was afoot.

Thus a new era had dawned for Catholic schools. The suspicion and hostility that had characterized the dealings between Catholic and state educational authorities in the eighteen-sixties and seventies[10] had completely disappeared, giving place to a new spirit of mutual respect and co-operation, a spirit which succeeding decades served only to consolidate and extend.[11]

But other difficulties remained. The schools inherited by the new bishops of the eighteen-eighties were, it is true, already giving some grounds for assurance;[12] and the religious education being imparted in them was anticipating, by a long way, some of the important recommendations later to be made in Pius XI's *Divini Illius Magistri*. Yet the system as a whole was not without serious defects. Having grown too fast, it lacked proportion: in very few of the dioceses had the school work itself been organized on a diocesan plan. The schools continued to be more or less under the control of the Hierarchy, but whatever organization existed was due not to diocesan direction but to the religious orders operating in their own groups of schools.[13]

The whole system thus remained inchoate and amorphous. The

[8] For example: in Victoria, the Theodore Fink Commission (*Final Report of Royal Commission on Technical Education*, 1889-1901): in New South Wales, the Knibbs and Turner Commission. G. H. Knibbs and J. W. Turner were appointed Commissioners in 1902. Turner had been Headmaster of Fort Street Model School and Principal of the Teachers' Training College, Knibbs a lecturer at the University of Sydney. They left Australia in April 1902 and returned in the December of the following year. The report on Primary Education was submitted on 3 December 1903; that on Secondary Education on 6 October 1904; the third, on Technical Education, on 19 December 1904.

[9] *Freeman's Journal*, 25 January 1905.

[10] This was particularly noticeable after the Synod of 1869 and the Vatican Council of 1870.

[11] See *Report of Second National Conference of Directors and Inspectors of Schools*, p. 5. This conference recommended that Catholic Schools should give approval to 'any proposal that would benefit sound education'.

[12] Dwyer, Rev. P. V., *Report on Primary Schools*, Maitland, 1883, p. 4. See also Pastoral Letter, Third Plenary Council. *Austral Light*, 1905, p. 705.

[13] 'Catholic Education', Information Service, Education Department, Victoria, June 1951, p. 1.

pioneering work had been done, the foundations laid, but there still remained the task of fashioning the edifice into something that was more efficient, more serviceable and more in keeping with the needs of society at the time.[14] To Moran, coming new to the country, this was immediately evident; hence the dramatic suddenness with which, shortly after his arrival, he swept away Vaughan's Educational Board and assumed all its responsibility and functions himself. To others it was not so evident, as is seen from the pointed, almost startled comment of the *Freeman's Journal* that apparently it was 'his Grace's desire to put things on a better footing and to effect many necessary improvements'.[15] Some of these improvements have already been noted, especially those concerning the curriculum and the development of different types of secondary schools (chs. 7 and 9). Others are equally noteworthy, particularly those dealing with the important questions of method,[16] organization,[17] teacher-training, finance, and inspection.

Inspection

Inspection of a sort had always been imposed upon Catholic schools. Pastors had been obliged since the First Provincial Council, in 1844, to see to the erection of schools in their districts and to visit them 'often' so that they might be in a position to 'give counsel to the teachers and instruction to the scholars'.[18] Similar obligations continued to be imposed by the various diocesan synods—of Bathurst,[19] Maitland,[20] Sydney,[21] Melbourne,[22] and the rest—right down through the nineteenth century. Not only were the pastors to supervise carefully (*magno zelo et industria*) the teaching of religion,[23] but they were also to assure themselves that the ordinary literary studies were being given all necessary attention, providing for that purpose only the most suitable teachers (*idoneos magistros*).[24] Even with the later development of systematic inspection by recognized inspectors this obligation on the part of the pastor was to remain, being 'very strongly (*vehementer*)' enjoined by the Fourth Plenary Council in 1937.[25]

[14] Hall, Rev. John, *History of St Stanislaus' College, Bathurst*, p. 61.
[15] *Freeman's Journal*, 11 October 1884, p. 15, c.
[16] Cf., Report of Mr Sutherland (from University of Melbourne) on Loreto Abbey, Ballarat, 1904. *Advocate*, 7 January 1905, p. 16, d.
[17] Dwyer, *Report on the Primary Schools*, Maitland diocese, 1883, p. 5.
[18] 'Consilia magistris, monita scholaribus tradat.' *Acta et Decreta concilii primi provinciae Australiensis*, decr. 1. [19] *Decrees of the Diocesan Synod, Bathurst*, 1883, decr. 1.
[20] *Statuta Synodi Diocesanae Maitlandensis*, 1888.
[21] See *Decrees of the Diocesan Synod of Sydney*, 1891.
[22] *Acta et Decreta* Synodi Provincialis Melbournensis Iae, 1907, decr. 96, 'De Scholis Catholicis'; *Acta et Decreta* secundae synodi diocesanae Melbournensis, die decimanona maii, 1885, decr. 14, 'De Pastorali visitatione et cura scholarum'.
[23] *Statuta Synodi Diocesanae Maitlandensis*, 1888.
[24] *Acta et Decreta* synodi provincialis Melbournensis, 1907.
[25] *Conc. Plen.*, IV, 1937, decr. 610. The English translations here are from *Decrees of the Fourth Plenary Council which concern Religious and Catholic Schools*, published at St Vincent's Boys' Home, Westmead, by the authority of the Archbishop of Sydney.

The object of all this care bestowed upon the schools was evidently to make them more efficient as agents of education.[26] Efficiency had been the theme of many of Leo XIII's letters on education, especially those to the bishops of Scotland and Hungary. To the former the Pontiff had pointed out that, in the matter of efficiency, Catholic schools were to be 'second to none (*nulla in re concedant ceteris*)'.[27] To the latter he had drawn attention to the necessity of appointing a diocesan inspector for each diocese.[28]

This precaution, however, had already been taken in Australia. Inspection of Catholic schools had survived from the earlier period when the schools had been subject to the control of the various Denominational Boards. The conditions, moreover, under which the schools operated after their withdrawal from the government system made inspection all the more imperative.[29] Regular inspection was set up again in most of the dioceses immediately after the break with the state.[30] In Sydney, a layman, J. W. Rogers, was appointed inspector,[31] but in other dioceses priests were appointed: the Reverend P. V. (later Bishop) Dwyer in Maitland[32] and the Reverend R. J. Carr in Goulburn.[33] In Melbourne nothing was done between the 1872 Act and 1886 when, shortly after Dr. Carr's arrival, the Reverend Dr Gräber was appointed.[34] After Gräber came two more priests, Father Ganly (1891)[35] and Father John (later Bishop) McCarthy in 1899.[36] Thereafter, on the initiative of the latter, laymen were appointed,[37] and this example was followed in some of the suffragan dioceses.[38]

---

[26] *Decrees of the Diocesan Synod*, Bathurst, 1883, decr. 1.

[27] Leo XIII, ep. encyc. 'Caritatis Studium', ad Archiepiscopos et Episcopos Scotiae, *Acta*, vol. xviii, p. 112.

[28] Leo XIII, ep. encyc., 'Constanti Hungarorum', ad Episcopos Hungariae. *Acta*, vol. xiii, p. 275.   [29] *Advocate*, 17 June 1876, p. 7, b.

[30] Catholic Education Board (Sydney), Minute Book, session of 7 October 1882, p. 3. Some objection, it was thought, might be forthcoming from the religious orders. Br John, however, the Provincial of the Marist Brothers, assured Vaughan that the Brothers would welcome such an inspection. See also *Record* (Bathurst), 15 July 1880, p. 327, a.

[31] This decision was reached only after 'long and careful discussion'. Catholic Education Board, Minute Book, 11 July, p. 34. See also Report on Schools, 1884, *Freeman's Journal*, 11 October 1884, p. 15, d.

[32] *Express*, 6 September 1884. See also *Pastoral Letter of Bishop Murray*, 5 October 1884; *Record*, 16 October 1884; *Reports on Primary Schools*, Maitland, 1883-7.

[33] Education Report of Half Year, 30 June 1883, Diocese of Goulburn (*Record*, 15 September 1883, p. 419); report of Rev. R. J. Carr (*Record*, 1 May 1883, p. 205). See also *Freeman's Journal*, 22 November 1884, p. 15, a; *A.C.D.*, 1888, p. 77.

[34] See *Advocate*, 16 December 1893, p. 7, a.

[35] *Acta et Decreta* tertiae synodi diocesanae Melbournensis, die decimasexta Novembris 1887, decr. 13, 'De inspectione Scholarum'.

[36] *Advocate*, 1 August 1891.

[37] Report on Primary Schools, Melbourne, 1903. *Advocate*, 5 December 1903, p. 13, c. The first layman inspector was Nicholas J. Cooke. He was succeeded by Charles X. O'Driscoll.

[38] For example, Mr James Conlon was appointed inspector in Ballarat diocese in 1924. Inspector's Report, 1924. *Advocate*, 8 January 1925, p. 10, b, c.

By the nineties inspection had become a matter of national importance. Supervision and inspection by the local pastor were satisfactory but, as Bishop Dwyer pointed out, they were not sufficient. Inspection had to be more than parochial; it had to be diocesan as well.[39] In 1895, accordingly, the Second Plenary Council decreed that, in order to promote the efficiency of all schools a priest was to be appointed inspector and examiner in each diocese;[40] and this regulation, with the addition that the inspector should submit an annual report to the bishop,[41] was later incorporated in the decrees of the Fourth Plenary Council.

But the bishops were not satisfied merely with appointing inspectors of their own. They desired that the Catholic schools be also inspected by the state, and over many years made repeated attempts to bring this about. In Queensland government aid to Catholic schools and, therefore, government inspection were to continue for a further five years after the passing of the Act in 1875. As the end of this five-year term drew near Bishop Quinn approached the Minister of Education, the Hon. A. H. Palmer, with the request that government inspection, as a favour, might be continued. His request was granted,[42] the Minister going so far as to submit to the Bishop all his inspectors' reports on Catholic schools.[43] The result, from the point of view of the Catholic schools, was highly gratifying: the inspectors gave every help and satisfaction. 'Without a single exception', wrote Dr Quinn, the inspectors were spoken of by Catholic teachers, 'especially by [the] nuns . . ., in terms of praise and thankfulness'.[44]

The other bishops followed Quinn's lead. Lanigan of Goulburn[45] and Dwyer of Maitland[46] began requesting government inspection immediately after the last government subsidies were withdrawn in 1883. A type of government inspection was already imposed in South Australia[47] and Western Australia[48] under the Acts of 1878 and 1895, but it was merely a formality and Catholics wanted something more thorough

[39] Dwyer, Rev. P. V., *What steps may be taken to advance the interests of our religious primary and higher schools?* 1901, p. 6.

[40] *Conc. Plen.*, II, 1895, decr. 311.

[41] 'Annuam in scriptis relationem.' *Conc. Plen.*, IV, 1937, decr. 618.

[42] Letter, Quinn to Palmer, Minister for Public Instruction, 31 December 1880. *Brisbane Courier*, 6 January 1881, p. 3, f, g. Reports on Catholic schools are found, for example, in the Report of the Secretary for Public Instruction, 1899. P.P.(Q'ld.), Journals of Leg. Council, 1900, II, p. 423.

[43] A.B.O'H., 'State of Education in Queensland', *Christian Brothers' Educational Record*, 1895, p. 195.

[44] Letter, Quinn to Palmer, Sect., Dept. of Public Instruction, 23 March 1881. *Australian*, 26 March 1881, p. 15, b.

[45] Undated newspaper cuttings (Archives, Presentation Convent, Wagga).

[46] See Pastoral Letter of Dr Murray (Maitland), 5 October 1884. *Record* (Bathurst), 16 October 1884, p. 473.

[47] Act, 41 and 42 Vic., no. 122, 1878.

[48] Report of Minister for Education, 1895, p. 34. P.P.(W.A.), 1896, vol. 1. See also, 'Catholic Education in Australia', *The Christian Brothers' Educational Record*, 1889, p. 188.

and exacting. Similar requests for inspection had been made in Tasmania but with little success. Accordingly, when the Teachers' and Schools' Registration Bill came before parliament in 1906, Dr Delany approached the Minister for Education with a request to have a clause introduced to provide 'that all primary schools other than State schools should be regularly inspected by the Inspectors of State schools'.[49] Upon the Minister's reply that 'public opinion was not in favour of compulsory inspection of private schools', Delany modified his first request and begged that the Minister would undertake the inspection of Catholic schools separately and independently of the Act. The request was granted.[50]

In Victoria similar inspection had been sought for some years. In 1900 a deputation consisting of Archbishop Carr, Bishop Moore of Ballarat, and Bishop Reville of Sandhurst, waited on the Minister of Education with the request that 'the Department should provide inspection for Roman Catholic schools'. They were not only 'willing', they said, 'but anxious' that the state undertake that responsibility.[51] The request was granted in the Registration Act of 1905, but the inspection was left to one inspector. It was not handed over to the district inspectors until 1913.[52]

But the request for government inspection had not been unanimous. Some of the religious orders of women, for instance, were opposed to it on principle;[53] others had objected that, if a denomination had been able to provide capable teachers and a satisfactory course of studies, as the Catholics had done, it could surely provide its own inspectors. And was this not already being done? Official state inspection, moreover, might involve a change in books and methods of tuition.[54]

But the bishops thought differently. Apart from the obvious scholastic advantages, inspection by outside authority would be, as the Victorian bishops said, 'an advantage . . . because it would show the world that they [Catholics] were doing in the matter of secular education what was being done in the State schools'.[55] This appeared to be the general

49 In deference to the Bishop's request, the Minister tried to have provision for state inspection of 'sub-primary and primary' schools inserted in clause vii of the Registration Bill. His proposal was rejected by 15 to 6. *P.P.*(Tas.), 1906, I, p. 140.

50 *Monitor* (Launceston), 31 August 1906, p. 5, d.

51 *Advocate*, 29 September 1900, p. 12, a.

52 *Argus*, 2 April 1913, p. 5, f.

53 The Presentation Sisters, for example, had queried this point before leaving Ireland. In answer to their apprehensions Father Corbett of St Kilda had assured them 'that the schools shall by no means be subject to government or other secular inspection or control'. Letter, Corbett to Superioress of Presentation Convent, Limerick, 17 June 1873 (copy in Archives, Presentation Convent, Windsor).

On this account, also, the Sisters of Charity in Tasmania were averse to any inspection save that of the bishops. Report of Inspector of Schools (Thos. Arnold), 30 May 1853 (T-A).

54 Undated newspaper cutting (Archives, Presentation Convent, Wagga).

55 *Advocate*, 29 September 1900, p. 12, a.

view.[56] It would 'give . . . the public', said Dr Quinn in Brisbane, 'an opportunity of judging the merits of our schools'.[57] When, through such inspection, Catholic schools were recognized to be just as efficient as those of the state, they would, so Catholics believed, have a better claim to equal recognition and, therefore, an equitable share in the government grant.[58]

Teachers and Teacher-training

The provision of adequate inspection was not the only thing that exercised the minds of the Catholic educational authorities, nor was it the most important thing. Of far greater importance was the training of religious teachers. This was one of the Church's most pressing needs, and it continued to be felt until well into the present century.

The position of Catholic teachers in the period immediately following the Education Acts of the seventies and eighties was precarious. For this the bishops themselves were largely responsible. In their frantic efforts to secure adequate staffs in the schools they were opening, their demands upon the orders for extra personnel were frequently importunate. Some of the blame, on the other hand, must rest with the orders themselves: newly arrived in the country, unfamiliar with its educational requirements yet ambitious to take root quickly and spread, they tended to overreach themselves. The combined result was that, in their efforts to make the numbers go round, the teaching power of the religious themselves was drastically impaired.[59] In a number of cases, individual religious who were not even intended for teaching were pressed into service and, as Inspector Rogers in Sydney put it, 'though labouring under a disadvantage as regards previous training',[60] were obliged to take up the chalk. Moreover, the changes from the old denominational system had in some colonies come about with such dramatic suddenness that the authorities, faced with the task of training a large band of teachers in a relatively short space of time, were tempted to curtail the training period and send young teachers into the classroom without any adequate test of their competence.[61]

This policy may have saved the Catholic schools from extinction, but its effect upon the teaching imparted in them was ruinous. 'Some of the methods employed,' wrote one inspector, 'are, in a number of schools,

[56] See Pastoral Letter of Dr Murray, 5 October 1884. Record, 16 October 1884, p. 473.
[57] In an official communication addressed to the Col. Sect. in Queensland. Catholic Standard (Tas.), May 1881, p. 68, a.
[58] Freeman's Journal, 9 April 1905. This idea was put forward by Cardinal Moran in an address before a conference of state teachers and in the presence of Governor Rawson in 1905.
[59] Corrigan, Br Urban, The Achievements of Catholic Education in Australia, p. 12.
[60] Rogers, Report on Catholic Schools, 1883, p. 2.
[61] Ibid.

inferior owing to the want of training on the part of the teachers . . .' 'I think,' said another in reference to a particular boys' school, 'that the money spent on the . . . teachers is simply thrown away.'[62] 'Justice to the cause of Catholic Education,' said a third, 'obliges me to say that the [poor] condition of many of these schools is due to a want of systematic teaching. The erroneous idea that anyone who possesses knowledge of a subject has also the faculty of imparting it seems still to find a congenial home in certain minds.'[63] The teachers were all 'competent enough', reported Father Carr of Goulburn, 'hence the results; they all impart information enough, but they do not impart it to advantage. They instruct rather than educate'. As a result, he found pupils 'sufficiently instructed . . . but lacking the mental culture that should [have] corresponded with such instruction'.[64] This, according to Father Ganly of Melbourne was 'the *fons et origo* of the weak point of the Catholic system'.[65]

This general deficiency in pedagogical science revealed itself also in the faulty organization of the schools themselves. Head teachers, for example, confined themselves too exclusively to the top classes; infant classes were handed over to less experienced teachers; and too many written lessons—writing, dictation, arithmetic—followed one another consecutively.[66]

Much of this criticism, it is true, was levelled at the lay teachers who, through lack of professional competence, had not been able to follow their more able brethren over to the higher-salaried posts in the state system. But a great deal of it applied to the religious and to state school teachers as well. The latter, according to Professor Francis Anderson of Sydney, still persisted with their 'short and easy mechanical ways of teaching'. Such ways, he said, 'fail[ed] to fulfil the purposes for which they [were] devised'—the proper mental and moral development of children's minds[67]—and gave rise instead to an education that was 'narrow . . . exclusive . . . and too bookish'.[68]

This inadequate training of teachers, the Professor thought, was 'the greatest defect in our system'[69] and, according to the Knibbs and Turner Commission, 'the most fundamental step in reform'.[70] This was said in 1902; yet, notwithstanding the gravity of the situation, it was

---

[62] Rogers, Report on Catholic Schools, 1884.
[63] Report on Primary Schools, Melbourne, 1893. *Advocate*, 16 December 1893, p. 7, c.
[64] Final Report of Inspector of Schools, Father Carr, Goulburn, 1883. *Record* (Bathurst), 7 February 1884, p. 65.
[65] Report on Primary Schools, Melbourne, 1896. *Advocate*, 12 December 1896, p. 8.
[66] Rogers, Report on Catholic Schools, 1883, p. 2.
[67] Anderson, Francis, *Tendencies of Modern Education with some Proposals of Reform*, p. 9. [68] Ibid., p. 8. [69] Ibid., p. 22.
[70] *Interim Report . . . on Primary Education*, pp. 38, 50, 53. See also Summary of Recommendations for training teachers, pp. 58-9.

to take the Catholic system between another forty and fifty years to bring its teacher-training programme into full operation. This fact was revealed in the report to Rome, made by Dr Beovich on behalf of the Australian Hierarchy in 1949: 'It can be said what was not so twenty years ago—that every teacher now entering a Catholic school is a trained teacher.'[71]

This frank avowal of the lack of training in Catholic teachers emphasizes a certain priority of values in the mind of the Church. When it was a question of fully trained and equipped teachers or an adequate number of Catholic schools to meet the needs of the growing Catholic population, the Church chose the latter. In doing so it may appear that it slighted or overlooked the importance of teacher-training. That conclusion, however, is hard to reconcile with other facts.

Evidence of the Church's appreciation of the importance of teacher-training abounds. Dr Matthew Quinn of Bathurst had considered 'training schools to procure good teachers' one of the essentials to any efficient system of education.[72] Vaughan's Inspector of Schools had wanted the Departmental examinations for teachers in New South Wales thrown open for teachers in Catholic schools,[73] while Cardinal Moran considered the 'admirable suggestions for the training of teachers' in the Knibbs and Turner Report 'the most delicate and, at the same time, the most important' of all their suggestions.[74]

Further evidence of this sort is found in the support given by the bishops to the Bills requiring the registration of teachers in the three states that introduced them—Tasmania, Victoria[75] and South Australia[76] —and in the decrees of the Plenary Councils. The First Council imposed on each bishop the responsibility of seeing that nuns were given training in 'the art of teaching'.[77] For this purpose a common training college, it was thought, would best meet the needs; but when that proved impracticable, the Third Council suggested the establishment of provincial or even diocesan colleges.[78] This suggestion also failed, whereupon the Fourth Council threw the responsibility back on the orders themselves: institutions 'for the proper training of the religious' were to be erected by each order separately or by several orders combined.[79] Finally, in 1951, the National Catholic Education Conference recommended that the period of teacher training in Catholic institutions be extended at least

[71] Beovich, 'Catholic Education and Catechetics in Australia'.
[72] Record, 15 July 1880, p. 327, a.   [73] Rogers, op. cit., p. 2.
[74] Freeman's Journal, 9 April 1905, p. 18, a, b.
[75] This fact was communicated to the writer by Dr McCarthy who was formerly secretary to Dr Carr. See also Monitor (Launceston), 31 August 1906, p. 5, d.
[76] Letter, Beovich to Jeffries, Minister for Education, South Australia, 20 August 1941 (copy in Archives, Catholic Education Office, Adelaide).
[77] Conc. Plen., I, 1885, decr. 97; II, 1895, decr. 100; III, 1905, decr. 115.
[78] Conc. Plen., III, 1905, decr. 340.
[79] 'Ad religiosos apte instituendos.' Conc. Plen., IV, 1937, decr. 283.

by an extra year, adding in support of their own recommendation the words of Pius XII to the First International Congress of Teaching Sisters: 'See to it, therefore, that they [the teachers] are very well trained, and that their education corresponds in quality and academic degrees with that demanded by the State.'[80]

This idea of giving religious a training equivalent to that received by teachers within the state system had been a principle of the Church all along, but the building-up of an adequate training system was to be the work of many decades. Roughly speaking, three phases of development can be discerned: the pre-training college phase, then the multiplication of the training colleges themselves, and, thirdly, the development of the extra-mural agencies of professional preparation—associations, conferences, refresher courses, and the like.

In the first phase the usual method of training was the apprenticeship, or pupil-teacher type. It was this method that was followed by most of the orders, and by some more successfully than by others. 'The efforts made by the Marist Brothers to train young teachers for their own schools' reported Inspector Rogers in 1883, 'are deserving of all praise, as also are those of several of the convents to train lay pupil-teachers.'[81] Besides this practice of observing the methods of the best teachers, pupil-teachers were urged to make use of the existing manuals on teaching, Gladman's, Morrison's and Landon's being suggested as the most useful.[82] This practice of suggesting manuals for the use of teachers was also followed in other dioceses, notably in Maitland[83] and Melbourne,[84] where it was reported to have exercised a 'most beneficial influence'.

The second phase, that of the training college system, was a development of the twentieth century. However, the origins can be traced farther back. These early training colleges generally began as pupil-teacher centres. From 1864, for example, lay pupil-teachers from the parochial schools under the care of the Sisters of Mercy in Geelong, Victoria, would assemble at the main convent on Saturdays to discuss the best methods and details of class management. The scope of this work was gradually extended until, in 1881, the centre developed into a residential training college for those studying to qualify as teachers in Catholic schools. Under the title of St Aloysius' Teachers' Training College, it

---

[80] The Congress at which this address was given was held in 1951. *Report of Fifth National Catholic Education Conference*, 1951 (Archives, Catholic Education Office, Melbourne).
[81] Rogers, op. cit., p. 2.   [82] Ibid.
[83] Dwyer, *Report on Primary Schools*, Maitland diocese, 1885, p. 4. The manual recommended was Dr Joyce's *School Management and Practical Hints on Infant School Work*.
[84] Report on Primary Schools, Melbourne, 1896. *Advocate*, 12 December 1896, p. 7, c.

trained not only the lay teachers for Catholic schools, but also the religious themselves.[85]

Similar institutions were developed at Ballarat in Victoria and at Nudgee in Queensland. Under the direction of Sister Mary Hilda Benson, a graduate of the Convent Training College at Notre Dame in Liverpool, England,[86] the Ballarat establishment grew from a pupil-teacher centre in 1877 to a residential training college,[87] offering a 'five years' course of studies and practical work'.[88] Known as the Dawson Street Loreto Training College, it accepted girls as 'pupil-teachers' at the age of fourteen or as 'students' at the age of seventeen.[89] Besides preparing students for the matriculation examinations,[90] the college offered a 'thorough grounding . . . in the theory and practice of education'.[91] The Queensland venture, less ambitious but serving a similar purpose, was established by the Sisters of Mercy at Nudgee before the end of the sixties.[92]

At the turn of the century a fresh impetus was given to the training college idea in New South Wales by the report of the Knibbs and Turner Commission, which condemned the pupil-teacher system, discerning in it 'an inevitable and distinctly recognizable tendency to deterioration'.[93] In its place it recommended the European system of training colleges. As a result, the Marist Brothers, within a few years, dropped the well tried scheme of pupil-teacher training which for years had operated at old St Mary's, and concentrated instead on a training school providing a full course of secondary studies preparatory to the undertaking of any professional or practical training. The Christian Brothers did likewise. But for the various orders of nuns, Cardinal Moran planned a more elaborate scheme.

His proposal was to establish a central college[94] in which nuns from the different establishments round Sydney could, by attending lectures given by specially chosen lecturers, thereby fulfil the attendance regulations and secure the necessary qualifications for admission to the examinations in the Sydney University. Moran made this proposal about mid-1910 and the University, which at first favoured the idea, appointed a

[85] Ignatius, Sr M., 'The Sisters of Mercy in Victoria, Geelong', p. 7 (Archives, Convent of Mercy, Geelong).

[86] See 'The Sisters of the Institute of the Blessed Virgin Mary', I.B.V.M., Loreto Jubilee Magazine, 1925, p. 10.

[87] Ibid., p. 11. See also I.B.V.M., A Retrospect, Programme of Concert and Prize List, 1885, p. 14.   [88] Loreto Jubilee Magazine, 1925, p. 10.

[89] Loreto Abbey, Ballarat, Prospectus (undated), p. 1 (Archives, Loreto Abbey, Ballarat).

[90] Ibid., p. 2. See also Report on Loreto Abbey, Ballarat, 1889. Advocate, 21 December 1889, p. 9, d.   [91] Loreto Abbey, Ballarat, Annual Magazine, 1901, p. 47.

[92] Report to Propaganda in Sketch of Life and Labours of the Rt Rev. Dr O'Quinn, First Bishop of Brisbane, p. 26.   [93] Interim Report on Primary Education, p. 17.

[94] This was to be in conjunction with the Convent of the Sacred Heart at Kincoppal, Elizabeth Bay, Sydney.

special committee to work out details.[95] These were accepted by the Cardinal but rejected by the senate—after several months' delay.[96] Thwarted in this direction, Moran persisted with his idea of a University Hall and announced his intention of having it affiliated with the London University. This, he thought, would provide the added advantages of enabling nuns in outlying centres—such as Newcastle and Broken Hill —to participate.[97] But that scheme also failed to mature, and the individual orders were left to develop their own training colleges.

In the meantime the Registration of Teachers and Schools Acts in Victoria and Tasmania had rendered training colleges imperative. Even before this legislation, however, Archbishop Carr had determined on the establishment of a college which, he hoped, would not only 'impart the highest training to intending teachers' but 'serve as an intellectual centre for all their schools and colleges'.[98] Accordingly, the Loreto Sisters, on the invitation of the bishops of Victoria, transferred their Dawson Street institution in Ballarat to Albert Park, Melbourne, where in 1906 it became known as the Central Catholic Training College.[99] The new college was intended for two classes of students: first, those preparing for teaching either as members of some religious institute or as lay teachers; secondly, those who desired to pursue a university course 'in the easiest and most helpful circumstances'.[1]

This one college, however, could not adequately meet the needs of the increasing numbers of several different congregations; nor was the idea of a common training school for religious popular among the orders themselves. Theoretically, it was supposed to confer certain advantages, such as a broadening of outlook, a conserving of specialized manpower, and the like; but for many reasons it was not practicable.[2] The truth of this was further borne out in the failure of a later attempt at a common training college by Monsignor J. T. McMahon of Perth.[3]

Instead, then, of a common college for all orders, Dr Carr began to urge the amalgamation of various groups within the orders themselves.[4] Rome agreed to the proposal and eventually most of the independent groups of the Sisters of Mercy amalgamated under one Mother-

---

[95] Freeman's Journal, 29 December 1910, p. 16, a.
[96] The majority against being 11 to 7. The minority included, among others, the Chancellor (Sir Norman McLaurin), Sir Samuel Griffith, Mr Justice O'Connor, Professor MacCallum and Professor Anderson Stuart.
[97] Freeman's Journal, 29 December 1910, p. 16, a, b.
[98] In address at inauguration of Catholic Training College, Albert Park, Vic., 1906. Advocate, 5 August 1906, p. 6, a.
[99] Age, 6 August 1906, p. 6, a; Loreto Jubilee Magazine, 1925, p. 17.
[1] Age, 6 August 1906, p. 6, a.
[2] This was the view expressed by Dr P. V. Dwyer, in What steps may be taken to advance the interests of our religious primary and higher schools? 1901, p. 4.
[3] This fact was communicated to the writer by Dr McMahon himself.
[4] Annals of Presentation (Mt Erin) Convent, Wagga, p. 1 (Archives, Presentation Convent, Wagga).

General, their combined strength then enabling them to establish their own central training school at Ascot Vale, Melbourne.[5] Their example was followed shortly after by the two independent groups of Presentation Sisters who, amalgamating, established their training college at Elsternwick. With these two institutions well established, the Albert Park College under the Loreto Sisters was shifted back in 1924 to its original home at Dawson Street, Ballarat.[6]

About this time, too, further developments began to take place in New South Wales. Desirous of doing for this state what the Registration of Teachers Act had done for Victoria, the bishops, under the inspiration of Archbishop Sheehan,[7] established a Board of Registration for Catholic training colleges.[8] This, it was hoped, would not only guarantee certain minimum standards in teaching but also stimulate the orders to develop their own training centres.[9] A similar scheme was launched in South Australia by Archbishop Beovich after the failure of the Teachers' Registration Bill in 1941.[10] Neither scheme, it is true, was really instrumental in giving rise to new training colleges, but each helped to co-ordinate and standardize the work of those already in existence (see Table LVIII).[11]

TABLE LVIII

Training Colleges for Religious, 1950

State	Total	No. registered under Council of Public Education of Victoria
New South Wales	7	7
Victoria	3	3
Queensland	3	—
South Australia	2	—

By this time, however, the need for standardization, in New South Wales at all events, lessened, owing to the extension into that state of the Victorian registration scheme. Orders working in Victoria found that

[5] The group established at Ballarat, however, remained independent.
[6] *Loreto Jubilee Magazine,* 1925, p. 17.
[7] See Catholic Education Association, *Teachers' Conference,* 1928, pp. 5-6.
[8] Actually, the Board took its origin at a special meeting in St Mary's at the end of 1927. The functions of the Board were: to inspect the training colleges of the various orders and congregations; to register those that were efficient; to assist by advice and direction those that might not be up to the required standard; and to issue certificates to those teachers who had satisfactorily completed the course of training prescribed by the Board. (Catholic Education Association, *Teachers' Conference,* 1928.)
[9] Board of Registration, *Regulations for the Training and Registration of Catholic Primary Teachers, New South Wales,* p. 1.
[10] Letter, Fr Russell (Director of Catholic Education) to Mr N. M. Gratton, Headmaster of Scotch College, Adelaide, 30 November 1948 (copy in Archives, Catholic Education Office, Adelaide). In fact, as this letter insinuates, once the Catholic scheme was launched, the Archbishop was very much less interested in the government proposal.
[11] A.C.D., 1951, p. 455.

they were able to obtain registration for their training colleges even though they were situated in New South Wales. By the mid-1900s the major orders operating in Victoria had their training colleges registered[12] under the Council of Public Education in Victoria,[13] irrespective of whether they were in New South Wales or Victoria.

With the Victorian Council of Public Education acting as a strong binding force, additional agencies of co-ordination seemed superfluous.[14] Besides, the orders themselves found other ways of stimulating professional interest within their ranks. Principal among these were the various teacher organizations which flourished from time to time. Some, it seems, served a useful purpose, but most enjoyed careers marked by alternating periods of activity and quiescence, depending on the enthusiasm of the current executive officers. The Catholic Education Association of New South Wales, for example, which existed for many years and became a very useful and vital organization in the twenties and thirties, had as one of its chief aims 'to encourage the spirit of co-operation and mutual helpfulness among Catholic educators'.[15] By the forties, however, this association had lapsed. Resuscitated after World War II as the Catholic Secondary Schools Association of New South Wales,[16] equipped with a new constitution[17] and enjoying the added prestige of a member of the Hierarchy, Dr Eris O'Brien, as president, this new association was designed to take up where the older one had left off. But the spirit of the older association did not survive.

Conferences of another type were arranged from time to time within the orders themselves.[18] Some of the orders of Brothers and nuns, for example, adopted the practice of organizing vacation schools in methods of teaching and other allied subjects.[19] These schools, repeated yearly, did much to keep the members of the orders conversant with developments in technique and procedure. In more recent times vacation schools of wider scope and embracing members of all teaching orders were organized in Victoria. The first of these, the 1950 Refresher School

[12] *Report of the Council of Public Education* (Vic.), 1948, p. 12.
[13] This was the body set up to register non-departmental schools and teachers. According to section 83 of the Education Act of 1928, it is composed of officers representing various interests: four representing the Education Department, four representing the registered schools, three the University of Melbourne, three technical schools, one education in music, and five representing industrial interests. *Report of the Council of Public Education*, 1949.
[14] It was proposed to appoint a panel of priests, not to prescribe a course of studies, but to draw up a list of suitable texts. The names suggested were the Rev. Drs. McMahon and Beovich, and the Rev. Fathers Thompson and Lynch. *Report of Second National Catholic Education Conference*, 1939, p. 4.
[15] Catholic Education Association, *Teachers' Conference*, 1927, p. 7.
[16] Catholic Secondary Schools' Association of New South Wales, *Constitution*, 1947.
[17] Ibid., articles 1-11.
[18] Beovich, 'Catholic Education and Catechetics', p. 6.
[19] For example, the summer schools organized by the northern province of the Marist Brothers. *Bulletin of Studies*, Mittagong, N.S.W., 1952, pp. 4-7.

in Christian Doctrine,[20] was attended by over 700 religious from all parts of the state.[21]

Forerunners of this type of in-service training date right back to the beginning of the century. In 1896, for example, Mother Gonzaga Barry, I.B.V.M., brought out from England a Miss Barbara Bell, for the purpose of instructing the Loreto Sisters in new methods of teaching.[22] Miss Bell, a graduate of the Secondary Teachers' Training College, Cambridge, was intended primarily to instruct the novices at Mary's Mount, Ballarat. Gradually, however, her services were extended to Sisters in the other Loreto houses.[23] In 1899, Dr Delany of Hobart invited Miss Bell to Tasmania where she spent some time in each of the principal convent schools of the island, giving lectures and demonstrations as well as advising the Sisters on the organizing of the schools. Then, at the invitation of Archbishop Carr, Miss Bell spent the following four years in the archdiocese of Melbourne: 1901 with the Mercy Sisters at Geelong, 1902 and part of 1903 in their convents at Fitzroy, North Melbourne, Brunswick, Kyneton, Lilydale, Mansfield and South Melbourne; the remainder of 1903 was given to the Presentation Sisters at Elsternwick, Windsor and Daylesford, and part of 1904 was spent with the Faithful Companions of Jesus in their three convents in Victoria. Then, after an absence in New Zealand, she was invited back to Melbourne by Dr Carr to become Mistress of Method at the Training College he had established in Albert Park, and while there was chosen to act as one of the board of six examiners of the Teachers' Registration Committee under the 1905 Act.[24] During the years 1901 and 1902, a sister, Miss Margaret Bell, on the invitation of Bishop Gallagher of Goulburn, conducted a similar course in the convents of that diocese at Wagga, Albury, Goulburn itself, Yass, and other places.[25]

Besides these attempts to develop a professional outlook and to promote intercourse between Catholic teachers themselves there was to be observed, particularly from the 1930s, a marked increase in professional contacts between religious teachers and those in state and other non-Catholic schools. This *rapprochement* was effected mainly through contacts made by members of religious orders serving on School and Examination Boards,[26] and on the Australian Broadcasting Commission

[20] Circular letter to Catholic Schools in Victoria, October 1949, from Director of Catholic Education, Melbourne, para. 4 (copy in files of Catholic Education Office, Melbourne).

[21] *Refresher School in Christian Doctrine*, January 1950, p. 3.

[22] This information was supplied to the author by Miss Bell herself who, at the time of writing, was a religious of the Sacred Heart, Auckland, New Zealand (letter dated 17 June 1952).

[23] *Loreto Jubilee Magazine*, 1925, p. 13.

[24] All these facts were supplied to the author by Mother M. Bell herself.

[25] *Annals of Presentation Convent*, Wagga, p. 42.

[26] For example, in Victoria, religious act as examiners in such departmental examina-

Education Committees,[27] also by participating in university vacation schools[28] and other professional associations such as the Science Teachers' Association in Brisbane and Sydney, and the Great Public Schools' Headmasters' Association.[29] Without such intercourse religious teachers would have incurred the risk of isolation and a corresponding narrowness of outlook.

Recent Organization

This development in professional status among religious teachers was accompanied by a corresponding development in the organization and control of Catholic education as a whole. In the system itself three distinct units emerged—the parish, the religious teaching community, and the diocese. The relationships between the parish and the school were clear, as has already been shown, even before the Provincial Council of 1844, but the organization within the other two units became more complex as the number of schools increased.

Among the first schools established by the religious there was little co-ordination. Set up by different groups, often in isolated parts of the country, they remained unrelated, developing at the same time a strong sense of independence. In some cases, it is true, a certain degree of organization carried over from the old School Boards, but in most instances the religious had had no connection whatsoever with them. With the passing of the Boards, any cohesion there had been was swept away. Certain communities enjoyed a fair amount of local autonomy, being largely independent of the parochial authorities, if not in theory at least in practice. This state of affairs, moreover, had been tolerated and allowed to develop unchecked. The earliest efforts of the Hierarchy had been directed towards the all-important matter of getting schools established. Compared with that, details of organization had been relatively unimportant.

By the close of the first half of this century, however, the pattern of organization from one diocese to the next had become more or less uniform. In each case the bishop exercised his authority and his duty of supervision through his own inspectors. Superimposed on this was a wider provincial organization operating under a Director of Catholic Education in each capital city.[30] But this had been a very gradual development.

tions as Proficiency. They are members of the various Standing Committees of the University Schools' Board. Similar contacts exist in the other states.

[27] For example, see A.B.C., *Broadcasts to Schools* (Primary), Victorian Branch, 1950, pp. 44, 84.

[28] For example, those arranged conjointly by the Schools' Board and the University in Victoria; and those in music arranged at the University of Sydney.

[29] In Sydney, for example, two Catholic schools represented on this association were St Joseph's College, Hunter's Hill, and St Ignatius' College, Riverview.

[30] Beovich, 'Catholic Education and Catechetics in Australia', p. 3.

The earlier forms of organization had lapsed. The committees such as that in South Australia under Tenison Woods and in Victoria under Dr Bleasdale had all either lapsed or been swept away by the Education Acts of the seventies and eighties. Others had arisen to take their place under the new régime, but had failed to survive. Within two years of the passing of the 1880 Act in New South Wales, for instance, Vaughan had set up his Catholic School Board consisting of himself, his Vicar-General, four priests of the archdiocese and Brother John, the Provincial of the Marist Brothers.[31] This Board drew up an elaborate schedule relating to all details of school organization: books, apparatus, registers, the training of teachers, examination and classification, local committees, inspectors of schools, school routine, discipline and methods of teaching.[32] But it was destined for a short career and within two years of its first meeting the secretary, at the bidding of the new Metropolitan, Dr Moran, wrote 'finis' to the last entry in the Minute Book.[33]

Similar boards which struggled on through the eighties were also set up in Maitland[34] and Goulburn.[35] The proposal to form one in Bathurst had been accepted by Dr Quinn but the board itself did not materialize.[36]

In Sydney nothing had replaced the board established by Vaughan. Except for a so-called Catholic Council of Education which enjoyed an insignificant existence, Cardinal Moran dispensed with such committees. A few months before he died, however, in 1911, an attempt was made to appoint a Central Committee with representatives not only from each parish but from each of the suffragan dioceses as well.[37] By then, however, circumstances had changed: the gradual handing over of schools to religious communities falling under direct diocesan or strong central control had greatly reduced the need for such committees and boards. Then came World War I and all attempts at closer co-ordination were deferred.

Nothing more was done until 1936. By that time the need for closer co-ordination was considered long overdue. Accordingly, at a conference of diocesan inspectors of schools assembled in Adelaide for the Catholic Education Congress of that year, it was recommended that a 'Director of Catholic Education . . . be appointed . . . in the capital city of each

---

[31] The four priests were: Very Rev. Deans O'Brien and Leonard, Rev. Fr Huge, and Rev. P. J. McMahon. The date of first meeting was 28 September 1882. Catholic Education Board, Minute Book, p. 1.
[32] Galley proofs of regulations in Catholic Education Board Minute Book.
[33] Ibid., p. 66.
[34] The six were: Very Rev. P. Hand (V.G.), Revs. P. T. Corcoran, T. Nealon, P. Meagher, T. Darcy, M. Foran. Express, 7 October 1882, p. 3.
[35] Record (Bathurst,) 15 September, p. 419.
[36] Ibid., 15 July 1880, p. 327, a.
[37] Catholic Education Conference of New South Wales, Statement, Resolutions, and Proceedings, p. 21.

Province'.[38] The functions of this director, who was to be a priest, were to

treat on behalf of the Archbishop and Bishops of the Province with the Minister of Education, the State Department of Public Instruction, the Faculty of Education at the University, and other public bodies (such as the Australian Council of Educational Research) on matters affecting educational policy and curricula.

The director, moreover, through his contact with the diocesan inspectors, was to keep each diocese informed of educational happenings in the capital city. In his own archdiocese the director was to be the delegate of the Archbishop, responsible for co-ordinating the various parts of the Catholic school system and exercising a general supervision over the various types of schools—primary, central, technical, commercial and secondary.[39]

The Victorian province, however, had anticipated this recommendation. Archbishop Mannix had, in 1932,[40] already established a Catholic Education Office with a director to discharge functions similar to those outlined above.[41] From the outset the arrangement had given satisfaction and the advantages were obvious, particularly those arising out of the director's role as liaison officer between the state Education Department and the Catholic system. The result was that the Fifth National Catholic Education Conference[42] further endorsed the principle and recommended it anew to the bishops in those provinces where it had not been completely adopted.

Within each diocese the organization and delegation of authority aimed at was really a microcosm of that recommended for the province as a whole. The bishops were asked 'to delegate to the Diocesan Inspector such authority as [would] enable him to act as the Bishop's representative in all matters concerning education', and specifically in such matters as school buildings, staffs, qualifications of teachers, and results of examinations.[43] The following year, 1937, the Fourth Plenary Council further decreed that under the authority of the bishop, a school committee should be set up, whose duty it would be to 'consider and arrange (*perpendere et disponere*)' all that concerned the diocesan schools.[44]

These recommendations on diocesan and provincial organization did

---

[38] *Report of First National Catholic Education Conference*, Adelaide, 1936. Reprinted in *Report of Third National Catholic Education Conference*, 1944.
[39] Ibid.
[40] *Advocate*, 13 May 1948, p. 41, b.
[41] 'Catholic Education', Information Service, Victoria, June 1951.
[42] Report of Fifth National Catholic Education Conference, 1951, p. 2.
[43] *Report of First National Catholic Education Conference*, 1936.
[44] *Conc. Plen.*, IV, 1937, decr. 619. *Report of First Catholic Education Conference*, 1936, p. 6.

not necessarily mean anything new. In some cases they were merely giving definite expression to practices already in existence; in others they would have cut right across the prevailing practices.[45] The fact that they had been made did not mean that they received Australia-wide acceptance, much less immediate implementation. Nevertheless, they had been approved by the Hierarchy,[46] and with that approval the pattern of future diocesan organization was more or less complete (see Fig. 20).

For purposes of inter-provincial organization and unity of action the First National Conference also recommended that thenceforward national conferences of directors and diocesan inspectors be held triennially.[47] To cap this the Hierarchy appointed a standing committee of bishops whose special office it was to discuss and prepare recommendations for the general body of the Hierarchy.[48]

One of the principal architects in this scheme of reorganization carried out in the administrative sections of Catholic education between the thirties and 1950 was the Reverend Dr Matthew Beovich. As first Director of Catholic Education in Melbourne under Archbishop Mannix, it was he who proposed the details of this organization to the Adelaide Congress of 1936, and later as Archbishop of Adelaide set up the complete organization in that province. It was natural also that he should have become one of the chief figures on the bishops' Standing Committee on Education and been chosen to draw up the Hierarchy's report on Catholic education made to Rome in 1949.[49]

Before leaving this question of organization it is necessary to draw attention to the organization within the religious communities themselves. As has been indicated these communities, replete with their internal organization, their hierarchy of authority and system of visita-

[45] A.C.D., 1951. In Sydney, pp. 123-5, the title 'Director' was withheld, although it was assumed on certificates issued by the Catholic Registration Board. It was also withheld in Brisbane (p. 350), and in Perth (p. 324).

[46] Report of Second National Catholic Education Conference, 1939, p. 6.

[47] Ibid., p. 6. Representatives at First Conference were:
N.S.W.—Very Rev. J. Thompson (Sydney), Revs. J. McCusker (Goulburn), P. Carey (Lismore), E. Murphy (Bathurst), J. Healy (Armidale), W. Brennan (Wilcannia-Forbes), E. Jordan (Maitland), and M. Lane (Wagga).
Q'ld.—Rev. P. Walsh (Rockhampton).
S.A.—Rev. Frs Tierney and Russell (Adelaide).
W.A.—Revs. J. McMahon (Perth), J. McKay (Geraldton).
Vic.—Revs. M. Beovich and D. Conquest (Melbourne), and Fr Ronan (Sandhurst).
In addition to the triennial conference, it was decided, at the Second Conference, that Directors of Education and Diocesan Inspectors of each province meet annually in their own states (Report of Second National Catholic Conference, p. 3). The same Conference recommended the publication of a Catholic Education Quarterly; it suggested also that Father Carey of Lismore be the editor and that he be assisted by Fathers Pierce and Thompson (ibid., p. 5).

[48] Beovich, 'Catholic Education and Catechetics in Australia', p. 4.

[49] Ibid. The appointment of a 'Director' was made at the suggestion of Dr Beovich, at that time Inspector of Christian Doctrine.

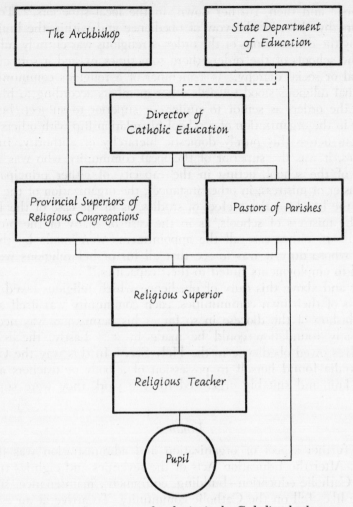

Figure 20. Organization of authority in the Catholic school system

tion,[50] rendered much of the older diocesan organization obsolete; at the same time they introduced a new vitality into Catholic education as a whole.

Supreme authority in an order was, in the case of a papal congregation, vested in a superior-general;[51] in the case of a diocesan congregation, in the bishop.[52] A delegated authority was vested in the provincial

[50] For example, *Constitutions of the Institute of the Marist Brothers of the Schools,* pt. ii, chs. 6, 7. See also *Règles Communes des Frères des Écoles Chrétiennes,* ch. 11.

[51] For example, *Constitutions of the Marist Brothers of the Schools,* pt. ii, ch. 11, art. 142. See also *Règles Communes des Frères des Écoles Chrétiennes,* ch. 12.

[52] For example, the Sisters of St Joseph.

superiors[53] and then, further down, in the local superiors.[54] To these superiors, by virtue of the vow of obedience and within the limits laid down by the constitutions of the order, a religious was entirely subject.[55]

In the schools of the orders there sometimes existed a sort of jurisdictional or social diarchy. As a member of a religious community the individual religious stood towards other members according to his place within the order—as senior to junior, or superior to subject; but as a teacher in the organization of a school his relationship with others might easily cut across this purely domestic hierarchy of authority. In some instances, it was the superior of the local community who was also in charge of the school, acting in the capacity of either principal,[56] or headmaster or mistress; in other instances, the organization of the school was in the hands of the prefect of studies, as in the case of the Jesuits, or of the mistress of schools, as in the case of many of the orders of women.[57] In either case all the appointments were made by the provincial whose duty it was to see that all his or her religious were appointed to employments suited to their capacities.[58]

Over and above this duty of obedience which religious owed to the superiors of their own communities, each community was itself subject to the bishop of the diocese in so far as his permission was necessary before any foundation could be made in it.[59] Lastly, the religious themselves owed obedience to the Holy See.[60] In this way the Church in Australia found herself in possession of a body of teachers already closely knit and suitably organized for the work they were supposed to do.

Finance

One further aspect of organization and administration was that of finance. After the Education Acts of the seventies and eighties the full cost of Catholic education—building, equipment, maintenance, staffing, and the like—fell on the Catholic community. To arrive at an estimate of the actual cost would be extremely difficult as few adequate surveys have been made. It is necessary therefore to rely on figures which are little more than estimates. Unsatisfactory for the purpose as these figures

[53] For example, *Constitutions of the Marist Brothers of the Schools*, pt. ii, ch. 4, art. 180.
[54] Ibid., pt. ii, ch. 7, art. 186.   [55] Ibid., pt. i, ch. 11, art. 54.
[56] In the parochial school it was, technically, the parish priest who was the principal. In Victoria, for legal purposes, he became the 'proprietor' of the school.
[57] *Constitutions of the Institute of the Blessed Virgin Mary*, pt. ii, ch. 11, art. 458.
[58] For example, *Common Rules of the Institute of the Marist Brothers of the Schools*, ch. 4, art. 45.
[59] For example, *Constitutions of the Marist Brothers of the Schools*, pt. ii, ch. 7, art. 93.
[60] *Rule of St Augustine and the Constitutions of Dominican Sisters of New South Wales*, 1941, pt. i, ch. 24, art. 208.

must be, they nevertheless give some idea of the extent of the costs involved.

In an official report to Rome in 1949 the total cost of Catholic education to that date was put down as 'a sum exceeding £100,000,000'.[61] But that must be considered a very general estimate. In the archdiocese of Melbourne, for example, at the beginning of the nineties the annual expenditure on primary schools alone was over £12,000;[62] by the end of the century it was almost double this figure.[63] But that was half a century ago when the value of money was different and when Melbourne had less than 20,000 children in its Catholic primary schools compared with the 36,000 it had in 1950.[64] Without allowing for interest and the cost of building and maintaining community houses the annual upkeep of the parochial primary schools for the whole of Australia in 1935 was estimated at £522,000; or for 171,000 pupils, a cost of £3 1s. 2d. per head.[65] In addition to the parochial schools there were the secondary schools which, because of the smaller number of pupils,[66] could be conducted only at a far greater cost per child.[67]

Added to this was the cost of maintaining the training establishments of the religious orders. In 1935 the various orders had 1,450 young men and women studying in training colleges that had cost over a million pounds to build and which were taking £81,490 annually to maintain, the average cost of training a teacher being £56 5s. a year.[68]

These costs, almost negligible as they were when compared with costs in contemporary state education systems, could be kept at such a low figure only through the small salaries paid to the religious teachers. Vowed to poverty, these religious were maintained in frugal simplicity, receiving nothing more than the humble fare and sombre raiment that became their state. The cost of maintaining 9,411 religious teachers in 1935 was £470,824, the average cost of the Brothers being £130 and, of the Sisters, who were able to provide their own domestic staff, £42 6s.[69]

---

[61] Beovich, 'Catholic Education and Catechetics in Australia', p. 2. The reader should bear in mind the limitations that necessarily attach to such figures. The changing value of money, moreover, makes some of the sums that follow seem fantastically small.

[62] In 1893, for example, it was £12,536. Report on Primary Schools, Melbourne, 1893. Advocate, 16 December 1893, p. 7, a.

[63] By 1900, it was £20,987. Report on Primary Schools, Melbourne. Advocate, 8 December 1900, p. 6. Between 1893 and 1900, the figures were:
1894 £17,191 (Advocate, 8 December 1894, p. 8).
1895 £19,204 (Advocate, 14 December 1895, p. 10).
1896 £17,275 (Advocate, 12 December 1896, p. 7, a).

[64] A.C.D., 1900, p. 162; A.C.D., 1951, p. 455.

[65] Corrigan, The Achievements of Catholic Education in Australia, p. 7.

[66] The total number of children in Catholic schools in 1949 was 222,260. Of this number, 159,362 were in the parochial primary schools. Beovich, op. cit., p. 3.

[67] Some idea of the cost of Catholic education up to the end of the nineteenth century can be had from Dr Carr's address, 'The Progress of the Church in Australia', Australasian Catholic Record, 1899, p. 217.

[68] Corrigan, op. cit., p. 17. [69] Ibid., p. 12.

The responsibility of meeting these costs fell directly on the parish—its pastor and its people.[70] Just as it was the obligation of every parish to have its parochial primary school maintained 'out of the ordinary revenues of the parish',[71] so it became an obligation on the part of Catholics to support these schools.[72]

Usually the funds were raised by 'school money', the time-honoured custom of collecting the sixpence, ninepence or even a shilling a week[73] from the pupils being the usual way of gathering in the money.[74] But very frequently even this small contribution could not be made without hardship to some families; in which case no charge at all was made, and the parish undertook to make up from other sources what was lacking in the teachers' salaries. Usually such details were arranged when an order took over a school and the 'conditions' were ratified in the form of a contract between the religious community and the diocese. When the Marist Brothers, for example, took over St Mary's in Sydney in 1882, the conditions guaranteed that

As salary the Brothers shall receive the school fees which shall be fixed at sixpence, ninepence, and one shilling per week for each child according to the classification. Should the school fees not amount to £60 per annum for each Brother the Board shall make up the deficit. Should the school fees exceed this amount, the excess shall be handed over to the Board.

In addition, the Brothers were to 'be provided with a dwelling-house suitable to the community requirements free of rates and taxes and were to receive forty pounds for each Brother to provide furniture'. School expenditure 'such as furniture, fittings, maps, diagrams and other school requisites and all rates, taxes and repairs' were to be 'at the expense of the Board'.[75]

In the secondary or private schools, on the other hand, neither the parish nor the diocese incurred any financial responsibility. In some cases, it is true, a bishop would persuade a religious order to establish a college within his diocese by holding out to them some tempting gift such as the site on which to build[76] or even a tract of land as a small endowment.[77] Since neither of these was sufficient to cover the cost of

[70] Beovich, op. cit., p. 3. In addition to the school the parish generally provided a home for the nuns and Brothers who taught the children.

[71] 'Ex reditibus ordinariis paroeciae.' *Conc. Plen.*, IV, 1937, decr. 606; I, 1885, decr. 240; II, 1895, decr. 302; III, 1905, decr. 325.   [72] *Cod. Iur. Can.*, can. 1379.

[73] Catholic Education Board, Minute Book, p. 3.

[74] See letter, Fr Corbett to Superioress of Presentation Convent, Limerick. St Kilda, 28 January 1873 (copy in Archives, Presentation Convent, Windsor, Victoria).

[75] These conditions were signed on behalf of the diocese by Archbishop Vaughan, and on behalf of the Brothers by Br John, Provincial. Catholic Education Board, Minute Book, p. 6.

[76] For example, in the case of the Christian Brothers' Colleges in Ballarat, Nudgee, and Perth. *Christian Brothers' Educational Record,* 1894, p. 620.

[77] For example, the endowments conferred on the Sisters of Mercy in Queensland by Dr James Quinn. See 'Nomination of Trustees', 8 September 1869 (Register of Titles Office, Q'ld.).

running a college, the orders were obliged to charge fees[78] which were generally beyond the means of the working classes.[79]

Once the schools were established the orders and the parishes resorted to various ways of supporting them. There were no secret sources of revenue. Asked by a special deputation in Melbourne how the Catholic schools were supported, Archbishop Carr replied: 'In two ways—by fees and by collections, concerts and the like.'[80] Every conceivable device was pressed into service. 'Bazaars, lotteries, raffles, Fancy Fairs, and what not', complained the Anglican Archdeacon Wollaston in the West, were 'all bringing fish to the net'.[81] In many cases the religious themselves turned mendicants and went on collecting tours.[82] Such tours were popular among the Irish Christian Brothers and many trips were made by them in all colonies, from Queensland[83] to the West, particularly around the goldfields where they found 'money was so plentiful'.[84] Another source of income, especially in the convents, was the teaching of music. In the private schools conducted by nuns, fees from such tuition made a substantial contribution towards the building of convents and classrooms; while in the parochial schools, music lessons given after school hours were generally the means of eking out the existence which poorer parishes often failed to provide.[85] It was a question either of keeping themselves by their music lessons or, as the nuns themselves put it, throwing themselves 'upon the kindness of the Bishops in order to pay their way'.[86]

The present century brought with it a slight alleviation. With the extension of social services in favour of the family and, as mentioned above, the extension of the scholarship system, the burden on parents was eased somewhat and Catholic education benefited as a whole. In one or two instances fees were lowered. In the diocese of Sandhurst, for example, the income from what became known as the Backhaus estate,[87] together with annual collections,[88] made it possible to dispense with

[78] Letter, Fr Corbett to Presentation Sisters in Ireland, Limerick. 28 January 1873.

[79] See statement made at opening of the Marist Brothers' School, Norwood, S.A., in 1901. *Adelaide Observer*, 9 November 1901, p. 44, e.

[80] In answer to a deputation from the National Scripture Education League, Melbourne. *Advocate*, 29 December 1894, p. 10, b.

[81] Burton, Canon A. (ed.). Wollaston's Diaries, vol. iii. (WA-A).

[82] See letter from Vaughan authorizing Brother Ludovic to begin a collecting tour in order to pay off the debts that still remained. *Freeman's Journal*, 18 July 1874, p. 9, c.

[83] Annals of Christian Brothers' College, Gregory Terrace, Brisbane, p. 5 (Archives, Christian Brothers' College, Gregory Terrace, Brisbane).

[84] *Christian Brothers' Educational Record*, 1898, pp. 38-83.

[85] Ignatius, Sr M., 'The Sisters of Mercy in Victoria', chapter on Seymour, p. 3 (Archives, Convent of Mercy, Geelong).

[86] Catholic Education Association, *Teachers' Conference*, 1911, p. 45.

[87] The Rev. Dr Backhaus, originally a priest on the South Australian mission, had followed his men from Adelaide to the Bendigo goldfields. There Dr Backhaus invested in real estate and, at his death in 1882, left £250,000 worth of property. Ignatius, Sr M., op. cit., chapter on Bendigo, p. 2.

[88] These were necessary to supplement the income from the estate.

fees in the parochial schools. But such instances were rare, and most dioceses were obliged to rely on the traditional means of raising funds.

By the forties of the present century such means had fallen into disrepute and other ways began to be recommended. The Second National Catholic Education Conference, for example, considered 'on educational grounds that immediate steps should be taken to find means of financing . . . teachers in parochial schools other than by the collection of school fees'. The obligation of financing the schools, the Conference urged, 'should be distributed over [the] entire Catholic population' and not be such that it 'penalizes Catholic parents who have children of school age'. The existing system, moreover, was admitted to be 'a waste of school time' and 'a source of discontent among teachers'.[89] By way of constructive suggestion the Conference instanced the case of Wellington, New Zealand, where the diocese, having built up an education fund, was able to pay the salaries of all parochial teachers from the interest alone. But this scheme remained unique: up to the middle of the century no other diocese had been able to adopt it.

EXPANDING THE SYSTEM

Whilst this work of reorganization was going ahead, the whole system of Catholic education was being gradually expanded. Not only was it extended at the pre-school and university levels, but means were being found whereby it could reach out to Catholic children not attending Catholic schools.

University Education

One of the earliest of these developments was at the university level. A system of primary and secondary schools without a university training would remain incomplete. From the fifties of the last century, therefore, when the Universities of Sydney and Melbourne were established, the Church manifested a desire to play its full part in them.[90]

At this level of education, as Polding said, the Church began at 'some worldly disadvantage'. For 'three hundred years of disqualification and hindrance' Catholics in British dominions had been 'considered as men to whom intellectual culture was unwelcome'.[91] But disadvantage or no disadvantage, Polding was not going to allow the past to prevent Catholics from accepting the invitation to a 'freer career in acknowledged equality' with the other denominations which the New South Wales legislature was offering them.[92] Apart from the inherent advantages of higher learning,[93] Catholics were to embrace this opportunity as a

[89] *Report of Second National Catholic Education Conference*, 1939, p. 6.
[90] This is obvious from Polding's Pastoral on the matter in 1857. Quoted in Birt, *Benedictine Pioneers in Australia*, 1911, vol. 2, pp. 239 ff.
[91] Ibid., p. 240.   [92] Ibid., p. 239.   [93] Ibid., p. 242.

means of vindicating their 'name as Catholics from the vulgar slander' that they were opposed to the spread of knowledge.[94] The later bishops were far more positive. Stimulated by the forthright policies of Leo XIII, they desired 'to see the Catholic youth . . . not only instructed in their religion but perfected in every highest branch of Science'. They hoped therefore that the 'honours . . . emoluments and every advantage' of the university might 'be thrown open alike to all' and that Catholics might attend 'without any sacrifice of religious principle'.[95]

That was in 1885. As yet neither Queensland nor Western Australia had a university. In both colonies, however, Catholics were actively engaged in canvassing for one. In 1890, the Catholics of Queensland, believing that the time had come 'to establish a University' in the colony, petitioned parliament to that effect. Such a university, they admitted, need not be, for a number of years at all events, any more than an examining body which should have power to award degrees and honours to successful candidates, irrespective of where they had studied or by whom they had been taught.[96] This plan did not eventuate, however, and when early in the present century the University of Brisbane was founded it followed the pattern already established in the other states.

This meant a non-denominational university, affiliated with colleges which, although incorporated in the university, belonged to the various denominations. For such a college in Sydney the Catholics were offered a site of eighteen acres, together with £6,000 towards building costs, provided they were able to meet the grant with an equal sum. In addition they were to receive an allowance of £500 a year towards the maintenance of their professors.[97] Polding accepted the offer and St John's was incorporated in 1857 and opened in 1860. In the following year Dr Goold made application to the government in Victoria that portion of the seventy-five acres that had been set apart for similar colleges around the University of Melbourne should be made over to the Catholic body 'for the purpose of erecting thereon a College'.[98] It was not until the second decade of the present century, however, that the proposed college was erected and dedicated to the memory of John Henry Newman.[99] In 1917 St Leo's College, within the University of Queensland, was established;[1] and, in 1949, Aquinas, in the University of Adelaide.[2] The Sydney and Brisbane Colleges were eventually placed under the

94 Ibid., p. 241.
95 Pastoral Letter from First Plenary Council, 1885, p. 34.
96 Petition from the Revs. John O'Reilly, Andrew Horan, and Denis Fouhy, on behalf of Bishop Dunne. P.P.(Q'ld.), II, 1890.
97 Birt, op. cit., ii, p. 239.
98 Report from Chancellor of University, Redmond Barry, 31 May 1861; see also Letter of Colonial Sect., 9 November 1853. P.P.(Vic.), 1861-2, p. 447.
99 A.C.D., 1920, p. 95.   1 Ibid., p. 152.   2 Ibid., 1951, p. 312.

direction of the Vincentian Fathers; Melbourne and Adelaide under the Jesuits. Subsequently the Jesuit Fathers also assumed control of the Brisbane College as well as that of the new College in the University of Western Australia.[3] These colleges were for men, but St Mary's Hall, under the Loreto Sisters, was established to serve as a residential hall for women students of Newman.[4] In 1929 Sancta Sophia, under the religious of the Sacred Heart, was incorporated in Sydney as a sister college to St John's;[5] and later, under the same religious, Duchesne was established for women students in Brisbane.[6]

The Sydney precedent of a non-denominational university with affiliated denominational colleges met with general approval. This solution of the religious difficulty appeared to Archbishop Vaughan, who for a time was himself rector of St John's, as 'fair and equitable a compromise as could have been expected'. Such an arrangement, he believed, served as a valuable link with the Christian tradition in education. The planners of Sydney University, he said, 'would not hear of a godless education, or of godless colleges: they were too deeply imbued with genuine Christianity for that'.[7] The scheme also earned the approval of Archbishop Mannix who came to Australia not only as the retiring President of Maynooth College, but as a man whose knowledge of university affairs in Ireland at the time was more intimate and profound, perhaps, than that of any other man alive. To him it was a scheme that would bring not only profit to the Catholic body, but stability to the universities themselves, which, he said, 'should profit by the leavening of live active Catholicism'. At the same time the Archbishop was by no means blind to the 'difficulties to be surmounted and the dangers to be guarded against'. These were inevitable; but 'the greatest danger of all would be if Catholics were to stand aloof from the Universities' and 'exercise no influence in shaping [their] thought and ideas'.[8]

This, then, became the official mode of university education for Catholics in Australia—a Catholic college within a non-denominational or secular university. Upon this pattern subsequent ecclesiastical legislation on universities was based.[9] But between the time of the First Plenary Council in 1885 and the Fourth in 1937 the whole pattern of university attendance had changed. In 1885 there was but one university college

[3] Ibid., 1955, pp. 358, 384.   [4] Ibid., 1920, p. 95.
[5] Ibid., 1930, p. 48.   [6] Ibid., 1940, p. 325.
[7] Vaughan, *Higher Education*. Inaugural Address at St John's College, within the University of Sydney, p. 102.
[8] Archbishop Mannix in reply to address of welcome to Melbourne, 1913. *Advocate*, 29 March 1913, p. 23, b.
[9] In laying down this legislation the bishops bore in mind the directions given by Rome concerning Queen's College, Ireland. (Rescripta S. Congregationis ad Episcopos Hiberniae, 9 Octobris 1847; 11 Octobris 1848; 18 Aprilis 1850) and the Universities of Oxford and Cambridge (Rescriptum S. C. ad Episcopos Angliae, 3 Februarius 1865). *Conc. Plen.*, I, 1885, pp. 79-84. See also decr. 250, 251.

—St John's; by 1937 there were five. But even three or four times this number would have been insufficient to deal with the large numbers of Catholic students. As it was, the existing colleges made practically no contact with the great bulk of them. Accordingly, a new and more relevant set of regulations were laid down.

Superiors of secondary schools were bound, at the end of each year, to send to the chaplain of the university[10] the names of all students intending to enrol at the university the following year.[11] Before students left their own secondary schools, moreover, they were to be given an instruction setting forth the dangers of university life;[12] they were to be seriously (*graviter*) urged to reside in Catholic colleges;[13] or, failing that, at least to assist at the special conferences on Catholic doctrine,[14] and to become members of Catholic societies,[15] such as the Newman Society.[16]

Notwithstanding the fact that these ecclesiastical regulations seemed to cover most of the eventualities that might arise in university life, the bishops remained uneasy. The capacity of the Catholic colleges, in the first place, was inadequate. The few existing colleges could accommodate only a fraction of the total Catholic university population; the assembling of students for special lectures, moreover, though sound and simple enough in theory, was singularly difficult in practice. Plainly, the system was not the ideal; yet, until a Catholic university could be established, it was the best substitute.[17] Some, on the other hand, considered the lay university better for Catholics: it helped them, they said; their faith would be strengthened, so to speak, by 'seeing the other side'. This idea, however, had been entirely rejected by Leo XIII.[18] Canon law, moreover, decreed that, if the public university was not imbued with Catholic doctrine and sentiment (*doctrina sensuque catholico*), a Catholic university was to be founded.[19] In the years following World War II an attempt was made in Sydney to establish a Catholic university;[20] but owing to formidable opposition on the part of the non-Catholic Churches and the consequent failure of parliament to pass the enabling legislation, the attempt was frustrated.

[10] *Conc. Plen.*, IV, 1937, decr. 648.   [11] Ibid., decr. 642.
[12] Ibid., decr. 641: 'Specialis instructio detur in qua periculis in vita universitaria expositis . . .'   [13] Ibid., decr. 641, 646.
[14] 'Collationes speciales in re apologetica . . .' *Conc. Plen.*, IV, 1937, decr. 650.
[15] Ibid., decr. 641 (b).   [16] Ibid., decr. 652.
[17] Ibid., decr. 645: 'Cum Universitas catholica nondum constitui possit, Concilium omnino commendat ut quam primum infra septa Universitatis laicalis collegia catholica aedificentur, vel saltem hospitia prope Universitatem aperiantur, cui iuvenes catholici resideant . . .'
[18] In his encyclical letter, 'Militantis Ecclesiae'. *Acta*, vol. xvii, p. 257.
[19] *Cod. Iur. Can.*, can. 1379.
[20] A site had actually been purchased in the Mona Vale district north of Sydney. The University was to be conducted by the Congregation of the Holy Cross, the same order that conducts Notre Dame University in America.

For some Catholics this failure was a happy one. Notwithstanding the warm support of Cardinal Gilroy and his Auxiliaries and without impugning the views of Rome, there were many in Australia who considered that the time was not ripe for the establishment of a Catholic university. Chief among those who held this view was Archbishop Mannix in Melbourne. His view was that the establishment of a Catholic university, say, in Melbourne, or, for that matter, anywhere in Australia, would be a 'very gross and grievous error'.[21] First, there was the colossal financial responsibility: that was serious enough. But there was another reason, equally grave: for Catholics to withdraw from the existing universities would be equivalent to handing them over completely to the secularists.[22] This, His Grace thought, would not 'be a wise move for the Catholic body'. Neither would it 'benefit the community' nor even be 'fair' to the universities themselves.[23] Catholics could give their 'best service' to the Church 'and the whole community and the universities . . . by holding [their] places in the existing universities'. That done, they should use the 'wide opportunities' given 'to christianize [their] environment'.[24]

Special Schools

At the other end of the Catholic school system came the kindergarten and nursery school movement. At this level there had been some awakening before 1900. Yet, according to the 1900 Report for the archdiocese of Melbourne, there were 'some people—happily few' who still clung to the 'erroneous idea that infants do not require, on the part of their teachers, the ability and attention which are required in the instruction of more advanced pupils'. These 'antiquated ideas' were described as 'at variance with the authority of modern educational experts', who rightly held that infants, to be properly taught, required the services of the 'ablest teachers available'.[25] The difference between infant schools conducted under the new system and those conducted under the old was strikingly obvious. In the one type, reported the Inspector,[26] were to be found children who were 'drowsy and lethargic', in the other those who were 'full of mental and physical activity'.[27] The efficacy of the kindergarten methods, reported the same Inspector earlier, 'for fixing the attention and stimu-

21 In address to ninth Annual Catholic University Conference, at Newman College, Melbourne, 9 January 1951. *Advocate*, 11 January 1951, p. 3.   22 Ibid.
23 This, actually, was the argument advanced by leading Protestant authorities in Sydney at the time. See *Sydney Morning Herald*, 2 November 1949, p. 2; 3 November 1949, p. 2; 15 November 1949, p. 2; *Sydney Diocesan Magazine*, December-January 1950, p. 203; *Catholic Weekly*, 10 November 1949, p. 1.
24 *Advocate*, 11 January 1951, p. 3, c.
25 Report on the Catholic Primary Schools of the Archdiocese of Melbourne, 1900. *Advocate*, 8 December 1906, p. 6, b.
26 The Inspector was the Rev. J. McCarthy, later Bishop of Sandhurst.
27 Report for 1900.

lating the intelligence of very young children' was shown by the number of infant schools which, upon inspection, had been 'awarded the maximum percentage'.[28]

Actually, kindergarten methods had been adopted in some of the schools of the Victorian Department of Education 'years' before[29] but, owing to retrenchment during the time of economic depression, they had been given up.[30] But some of the religious orders of women had been quick[31] to realize the advantages offered by the new techniques, and Mother Gonzaga Barry of the Loreto Sisters came to be recognized as one of the pioneers of kindergarten work in Australia. Having observed the kindergartens at work in Europe, Mother Gonzaga introduced the idea at Mary's Mount, Ballarat. Later, in 1912, she established a free kindergarten in conjunction with the Loreto Convent at Albert Park, Melbourne, and brought out an expert from England to initiate the work.[32] The kindergarten was staffed by volunteers from among the Loreto 'Old Girls', under a Sister who directed the work. The project, Mother Gonzaga considered, besides providing a useful service for the people of Albert Park, would save her past pupils from the dangers of spending their lives in 'amusement or self-indulgence'.[33]

Gradually the movement spread. In the early stages it was a question merely of applying the more acceptable of the kindergarten principles to the first grades of the primary school. Separate kindergartens, such as Mother Gonzaga's, were a later development. In Melbourne, for example, by 1930, there were only six such kindergartens;[34] by 1938 there were eleven;[35] and, by the beginning of the second half of the century, seventeen.[36]

This multiplication of kindergartens is a further illustration of how Catholic education has in many respects been influenced by educational developments at large. Dr Beovich, the Director of Catholic Education in Victoria in the thirties, saw in the 'continued growth of secular kindergartens' a positive 'danger to the Catholic school system'.[37] Accordingly he laid down plans for the formation of a Catholic Kindergarten Union with a model kindergarten to be attached to the Mercy Sisters' Training

28 Report on Catholic Primary Schools of the Archdiocese of Melbourne, 1896. *Advocate,* 12 December 1896, p. 7, d.
29 *Final Report of Royal Commission on Technical Education,* 1899-1901. Minutes of evidence: evidence of Mr Frank Tate, q. 1289.   30 Ibid., q. 1290.
31 *Customs and Directory of the Sisters of Mercy,* p. 14.
32 Loreto Free Kindergarten, *Second Annual Report,* 1913-14, p. 3.
33 I.B.V.M., *Loreto Jubilee Magazine,* p. 17.
34 The first six were: St Brigid's, North Fitzroy; St John's, East Melbourne; Manresa, Hawthorn; St Mary's, East St Kilda; Sts Peter's and Paul's, South Melbourne; and St Joseph's, Fitzroy. Report on Primary Schools of Archdiocese of Melbourne, 1930. *Advocate,* 11 December 1930, p. 18, c.
35 Beovich, Report on Number of Catholic Children in State Schools, 1938, para. 2 (files, Catholic Education Office, Melbourne).   37 Beovich, op. cit.
36 *Advocate,* 2 February 1952.

School at Flemington. In the proposed scheme, furthermore, there were to be 'voluntary workers' to assist the already trained kindergarten teachers. Such workers, the Director pointed out, were essential. Other kindergartens had them and it was not uncommon to find them 'calling for Catholic children at their homes and bringing them to the Protestant or secular kindergartens passing *en route* the Catholic kindergarten'.[38] Another factor encouraging the development of Catholic kindergartens was that after 1943 they had been able to share in the annual grant made for denominational kindergartens by the Victorian government.[39]

On the question of pre-school, or nursery school, education the Catholic authorities held other views. Towards the movement in general they were sympathetic, but 'strongly condemned' the manner in which the government had set up in the 1930s what they termed a 'quasi-medical, quasi-educational' bureau at Canberra to control and advise the pre-school child centres in the capital cities of the Commonwealth.[40] The Third National Catholic Education Conference, in 1944, considered it 'impossible to establish nursery schools as a part of [the] Catholic school system'. Well-equipped, well-staffed kindergartens, it was thought, would serve the purpose just as well.[41] Yet, as in the case of the kindergartens, it is possible that the Church's practice in regard to nursery schools will eventually change.[42]

Another development which pre-dated even that of the kindergarten movement was the provision of schools for handicapped children. The bishops assembled at the First Plenary Council had deplored the fact that there should be some Catholics who handed over their deaf and dumb children to non-Catholic institutions with consequent great danger to their faith. Pastors, accordingly, were urged to remind these parents of their grave obligation of bringing up their children, even though they were deaf and dumb, in the principles of the Catholic faith.[43] To this end the Dominican Sisters had already established an institution at Waratah for the education of deaf mutes.[44] Later in the present century a similar school for smaller children was opened by the same Sisters at Portsea, Victoria,[45] and one for boys was opened under the Christian Brothers at Castle Hill, New South Wales.[46] Later still came

[38] Ibid.   [39] *Advocate*, 13 May 1948, p. 41, c.

[40] The government had appointed under the Federal Medical Officer a Director from the U.S.A., who was to be assisted by a small committee elected by a body styled the 'Australian Association for Pre-School Child Development'. In 1936, the association represented only a small section of the community and, said the Catholic authorities, should have 'no authority to speak for any one but that section'. *Report of Second National Catholic Education Conference*, pp. 5-6.

[41] *Report of Third National Catholic Education Conference*, 1944, p. 5.

[42] The author has it on reliable authority that one diocese has already given serious thought to the matter of developing them.   [43] *Conc. Plen.*, I, 1885, decr. 242.

[44] This was before the 1890s. A.C.D., 1888, p. xxii.

[45] St Mary's School for the Deaf, established in the 1940s. A.C.D., 1951, p. 266.

[46] St Gabriel's School for Deaf Boys, established in the 1920s. A.C.D., 1930, p. 52.

schools for the blind: St Lucy's, for girls, at Homebush[47] and St Edmund's, at Wahroonga, for boys.[48]

In 1944 a step in yet another direction was taken. The Third National Catholic Education Conference of that year recommended that 'in each capital city there should be established, and completely staffed, a day and boarding school for mentally deficients'.[49] As a result, Marillac House under the Daughters of Charity was established in Melbourne for the education of mentally deficient girls[50] and a similar institution for boys under the Hospitaller Brothers of St John of God at Morriset, New South Wales.[51] In all these institutions the design of the Church was that, besides receiving a religious education, these children might learn some art or craft whereby they might be useful to themselves and to society.[52]

Children Not in Catholic Schools

Having established a wide variety of educational institutions, the Church then turned its attention to the large number of Catholic children who still remained outside Catholic schools. That number varied considerably, not only from time to time but from place to place. In New South Wales in the eighties, for example, it was estimated at somewhere between half and one-third.[53] In Victoria over the same period it was given by the Royal Commission of 1881-4 merely as 'a large number'.[54] In the closely settled areas the figure was naturally lower. In the archdiocese of Melbourne, for example, it had been reduced, by the mid-1930s, to about a ninth of the total number of Catholic children of school age.[55] Of the 334,000 such children in the whole of Australia, however, 113,000, or one third, were still in state schools.[56] By the end of the forties it was claimed that this ratio had been reduced to about one fifth.[57]

47 Established in the 1930s. A.C.D., 1940, p. 153.
48 Established in the 1940s. A.C.D., 1951, p. 170.
49 Report of Third National Catholic Education Conference of Directors and Diocesan Inspectors of Schools, 1944, p. 7.
50 Established in the 1940s at Brighton. A.C.D., 1951, p. 265.
51 Established in the 1940s. A.C.D., 1951, p. 170.
52 'Sibi et societati utiles.' Conc. Plen., IV, 1937, decr. 630.
53 Report of Catholic Education Board (Sydney), 1884. Freeman's Journal, 11 October 1884, p. 15, c.
54 Report of Royal Commission on Education (Vic.), 1881-4, p. 10.
55 In 1935, the estimated total of Catholic children in state schools of all types—primary, secondary, technical, domestic science, special schools for mentally deficients, etc.—was 4,294. Beovich, Report on Number of Catholic Children in State Schools (files, Catholic Education Office, Melbourne). The total number of children in Catholic schools in the archdiocese was about 41,000. A.C.D., 1940, p. 491.
56 See O'Connor, Rev. T. J., 'Religious Instruction in State Schools in Cities and Towns where there are Catholic Schools', Catholic Education Congress, 1936, p. 360. Of the Catholic children receiving instruction in the early 1930s 34.66 per cent were in state schools. Of the other denominations 86.84 per cent were receiving instruction in

But even with this figure the Church found little room for complacency. In round numbers it meant that over 60,000 Catholic children —a number equivalent almost to the number of Catholic children in Queensland and Western Australia put together—still remained without adequate religious instruction. The implications thus involved in the potential cutting-off from the Church of what amounted to the Catholic population of a whole state[58] drove the ecclesiastical authorities to search for some means of overcoming the problem.

The first problem was that of the bush child. One answer to this was found in the various religion-by-correspondence schemes that sprang up. The first of these was the religion-by-post scheme organized by the Reverend Dr J. T. McMahon in the archdiocese of Perth early in 1923.[59] From there the idea spread to other parts. In Melbourne, as a result of the mission section of the National Eucharistic Congress held in that city in December, 1934, the National Correspondence Course was launched under the direction of the Reverend Dr James Hannan. The first lessons were despatched in the middle of the next year to 7,000 children in the dioceses of Melbourne, Sandhurst, Ballarat, Sale, and Goulburn. By the end of that year 14,000 children were enrolled, the scheme having been extended to the dioceses of Port Augusta, Adelaide, Hobart, and Toowoomba. Later the dioceses of Rockhampton, Lismore, and Darwin joined in.[60] Most of the New South Wales dioceses entered another scheme inaugurated in Sydney in 1936. Later still the dioceses of Adelaide, Maitland and Hobart set up their own. In July 1945, when the work had been successfully taken over by these smaller units, the National Course was allowed to terminate.[61] Within another three years Melbourne had launched its own diocesan scheme.[62]

---

state schools. Figures based on 1933 census. *Official Year Book of the Commonwealth of Australia*, no. 37, 1946-7, p. 228.

[57] This claim was made by Archbishop Beovich in a special report, 'Catholic Education and Catechetics in Australia', p. 1, drawn up by him at the request of the Hierarchy for submission to Rome. The details were:

No. of Catholics in Australia	1,569,726
No. of Catholic children attending school	261,620
No. of children in Catholic schools (of these, 16,884 were non-Catholics)	226,260
No. of Catholic children in Catholic schools (i.e., 80 per cent of possible number)	209,376
No. of Catholic children in state schools	54,244

Thus the percentage of Catholic children remaining in state schools was approximately 20 per cent. This figure was more or less uniform in all states. In South Australia, for example, the number of Catholic children in state schools was 2,740, and the number of Catholic children in Catholic schools was 10,394 (figures from Catholic Education Office, Adelaide). See also *A.C.D.*, 1951, p. 314.

At the present day, owing to the fact that Catholic schools are unable to keep pace with the increased population, this percentage is much higher.

[58] O'Connor, op. cit., p. 363.   [ence.
[59] McMahon, Rev. John T., *The Perth Plan for Teaching Religion by Correspond-*
[60] Hannan, Rev. T., 'The National Catholic Correspondence Course', *Australian Catholic Education Congress*, p. 345.   [61] *Advocate*, 31 December 1947, p. 14, a.
[62] The new plan began in January 1948. *Advocate*, 31 December 1947, p. 14, a-e.

The various schemes were conducted, in most cases, by nuns. The National scheme in Melbourne was conducted by two Loreto Sisters who had been released specially for that purpose; the Maitland scheme, by the Dominican Sisters;[63] the Adelaide scheme, by the lay association, the Legion of Mary,[64] and the Tasmanian scheme by the Home Missionary Sisters.[65]

An important adjunct to the Western Australian scheme was the religious holiday school, or 'bushie', as it came to be called. Experience there showed that the correspondence course worked best when preceded by a 'bushie'. The friendships there made between the teachers and their future correspondents gave both parties a personal interest in one another. The idea of such schools[66] found a precedent in the Church extension movements in America and was introduced into Perth at the Christmas of 1925; it was developed in many centres throughout the archdiocese and subsequently spread to dioceses in other states.

The third element developed in conjunction with the 'bushies' scheme in Western Australia and which later spread to other dioceses was the 'adoption movement'. This movement aimed at developing a sort of spiritual parenthood among the more fortunate Catholics of urban areas. Each isolated family living in the bush was to be 'adopted' by a city family for the circulation of Catholic literature—magazines, books, and periodicals. In addition to that, various sodalities and confraternities, such as the Sacred Heart, the Holy Name Society, the Holy Family Confraternity, the Children of Mary, and so on, were to adopt various districts and thus to aid the Sisters conducting the correspondence classes.[67]

But the Catholic education of the bush child was not the only problem. A far greater one was that of the Catholic child attending the state school even in areas where a Catholic school was provided. More than half the Catholic children in state schools were found in the urban areas where lack of Catholic schools could not be pleaded as an excuse.[68] The reasons for this apparent neglect were many: mixed marriages, Catholic schools inaccessible through traffic hazards, parents unable to make the voluntary offering and unwilling to accept charity, and parents who, having been educated in state schools themselves, were ill-instructed in their religion

63 'Religious Instruction by Correspondence: Archbishop Sheehan's Letters', by a Dominican Sister. *Australian Catholic Education Congress*, p. 357.
64 Information supplied to author at Legion headquarters, Catholic Education Office, Adelaide. 65 *A.C.D.*, 1951, p. 477.
66 For full account see McMahon, 'Religious Instruction of country children where there are no Catholic Schools', *Australian Catholic Education Congress*, pp. 333-6.
67 Ibid., p. 342.
68 Of the 20 per cent of Catholic children said to be in state schools, 9 per cent were in country areas where no Catholic schools existed, and 11 per cent were in urban areas where Catholic schools did exist. Beovich, 'Catholic Education and Catechetics in Australia', p. 1.

and saw no particular reason for sending their own children to any but state schools.[69] Whatever the cause, the children themselves could hardly be held responsible. Something therefore would have to be done towards providing special instruction for them.

In this matter the policy of the bishops underwent considerable modification over the years. In New South Wales and Western Australia it was legal for clergymen or other accredited persons to enter the state schools once a week to instruct children of their own denomination. To this, however, the bishops were opposed on principle lest by exercising their right and giving such instruction they might appear to approve of the state school system for Catholic children.[70] They objected to 'sending clergymen to the public schools, whether within class rooms or without, to join', as Vaughan had explained, 'in the jar of tongues and the contradiction of creeds which is abhorrent from all our instincts of reverence and religion'.[71] Besides, the idea of aggregating children of all ages in a single classroom for a common instruction had little to recommend it and was regarded by the Knibbs and Turner Commission as a 'most imperfect scheme'.[72] The Church, accordingly, preferred other arrangements whereby children were gathered together for special instuction either before or after Mass on Sundays.[73]

But this arrangement did not last. Satisfactory though it might have been for conditions existing in the nineteenth century, it proved quite inadequate in later times. Greater and greater numbers were receiving no instruction at all. In 1937, therefore, the Fourth Plenary Council introduced a change. Without abrogating the prohibition against parents sending their children to state schools,[74] it instructed the parish priest to help the children in the best way he could.[75] If, with the bishop's permission, they attended a state school, then the pastor was to make special provision for their religious instruction: besides providing for their catechism lesson every Sunday in the Church, he was to visit the state school personally, or through others, once a week or more often.[76]

But the labour involved in all this instruction was arduous and exacting, demanding more time than the average parish priest in the city or

[69] O'Connor, op. cit., p. 362.

[70] O'Brien, 'Uniformity of Method in the Teaching of Christian Doctrine', *Austral Light*, March 1911, p. 325.

[71] In an address delivered on the occasion of laying the foundation stone of the school at West Balmain, 9 November 1879. *Pastorals and Speeches on Education*, p. 29.

[72] *Interim Report on Primary Education*, p. 27.

[73] Promulgated in 1885 Synod: reprinted with *Statuta Synodalia* of 1888. *Statuta Synodalia pro Diocesi Goulburnensi*, 1888, c, iv, statutum B. *Pastoral Letter of the Cardinal Delegate and of the Archbishop and Bishops of Australia, in Plenary Council assembled*, 1895, p. 19.

[74] *Conc. Plen.*, I, 1885, decr. 238; and *Conc. Plen.*, IV, 1937, decr. 628: 'confessarius poenitenti pertinaciter renuenti utpote rite non disposito absolutionem denegat.'

[75] 'Meliore quo fieri potestmodo.' *Conc. Plen.*, IV, 1937, decr. 627.

[76] Ibid., decr. 626: 'Saltem semel in hebdomada vel saepius.'

suburban areas could devote to it. To assist them, therefore, lay helpers were co-opted. In the eastern suburbs of Sydney this became the special work of the Theresian Club;[77] and in other dioceses, one of the chosen activities of the Legion of Mary.

Notwithstanding the devotedness and competence of many of these lay helpers, nobody pretended that the system as a whole was very effective.[78] One result, it is true, was that numbers of Catholic children in state schools returned to Catholic schools; but from those who did not little could be expected. However, the movement spread, Victoria being the last to come into line. There, after the legislation of 1950,[79] it was taken up not only in the country districts but even in the metropolitan area of Melbourne itself. Without meaning to give the impression that one hour per week was in any way adequate, Archbishop Mannix nevertheless wished to take full advantage of the opportunities offered by the new conditions and instructed each parish priest to 'get in touch . . . immediately . . . with the head teacher of any school in his parish and inform him that he wish[ed] to give religious instruction to the Catholic children enrolled'.[80]

Thus, by the mid-century mark, this practice of providing religious instruction for Catholic children in state schools had become more or less general throughout the whole of Australia.[81]

REACTION

This more liberal trend in Catholic policy was accompanied by a corresponding change of attitude in the community as a whole, not only to religious instruction but also to government grants to non-state schools.

The change itself began as a reaction against the solution of the religious question that had been arrived at in the secular Acts of the seventies. Even before the turn of the century Protestant denominations had risen, not, it is true, in sympathy with the claims of the Catholic school system, but in protest against the extreme secularism that had invaded several of the state school systems. Reaction was inevitable and it took just such a form as Archbishop Vaughan and the Anglican Dr Moorhouse had prophesied—a resurgence of Christian sentiment. 'Absolute secularism', Vaughan had declared in 1880, 'was inevitable. No man [could] stop the current; it [would] flow and finish flowing; and, then, the great reaction would set in . . .'[82]

77 For a full account of the activities of this organization see A.C.D., 1940, p. 155.
78 See O'Connor, op. cit., p. 362.
79 See Act, 15 Georgii VI, no. 5521, 1950.
80 Letter, Rev. A. F. Fox (V.G.), to priests of archdiocese of Melbourne, 15 February 1951 (copy in files, Catholic Education Office, Melbourne).
81 Beovich, op. cit., p. 5.
82 Vaughan, Lecture on Education in the Pro-Cathedral, 11 January 1880. *Pastorals and Speeches on Education*, p. 104.

It was already setting in, even in the eighties, when the Royal Commissions in Victoria and Tasmania revealed the extent to which this
absolute secularism would go.[83] In Victoria, for example, not only was
every trace of denominationalism being systematically eradicated from
the schools, but even Christianity itself. Within five years of the passing
of the 1872 Act, for instance, ministerial consent had been obtained for
the expurgation[84] of every Christian reference from the Royal Readers
then in use.[85] In Tasmania the process had gone further and the Deity
itself was being evicted. In the School Readers, to take but one instance,
Longfellow's poem, 'Psalm of Life', was minus a verse—because a line in
that verse contained a reference to God.[86] Protestant religious sentiment
was outraged.

But that was not all. When it was realized that the wedge that Wilberforce Stephen claimed to have inserted in 1872 might actually be split-
ting Protestantism itself, alarm became widespread. Secularism of this
aggressive type, it appeared, was proving far more inimical to Protestantism than it was to Catholicism. Obviously it had to be arrested
before its depredations went too far.

The *Zeitgeist* was plainly changing. Earlier it had found expression
in the demands for secular education and the complete withdrawal of
government grants from denominational religious teaching of any kind.
Now it was beginning to be expressed in a new key—in the clamour for
the reintroduction of the Bible in schools or for some form of non-
denominational instruction.[87]

Amendments in Education Acts

This clamour was heard on all sides. In Victoria, for example, within
ten years of the passing of the Secular Act, strong expressions of dissatisfaction began to be made, not only in the state school Boards of Advice[88]
but also in the evidence and reports of the two big Royal Commissions
of 1881[89] and 1899,[90] and of course in the press. Similar observations

83 This term 'absolute secularism' was frequently used by Vaughan.
84 Report of Royal Commission on Education (Vic.), 1881-4. P.P.(Vic.), 1884, III,
p. 449.
85 Campbell, Rev. Colin, *The Education Question: Its Present Position and the Roman
Catholic Claims*, p. 16.
86 *Report of Royal Commission on Education* (Tas.), 1883, p. xxiv.
87 The form most frequently suggested was that of the New South Wales Public
Instruction Act of 1880 (Act, 43 Vic., xxiii).
88 Campbell, op. cit., p. 10. These boards advocated the introduction of the Irish
National scripture lessons.
89 This Commission recommended the introduction of a 'general religious teaching
of a non-sectarian character'. Report of Royal Commission on Education (Vic.), 1881-4.
P.P.(Vic.), 1884, III, p. 33.
90 This report drew attention to the fact that the purely intellectual aspect of education
was in danger of being over-emphasized at the expense of the 'moral and religious'.
Final Report of Royal Commission on Technical Education (Vic.), 1899-1901, p. 260.

were made in the Knibbs and Turner report in New South Wales;[91] but there, as in Victoria, the commissioners themselves could do no more than make observations. Action was required. This came in the form of vigorously conducted campaigns organized by the variously named Bible in School leagues that sprang up in Queensland,[92] Victoria,[93] and South Australia[94] in the early 1900s. Each of these leagues, as a part of its campaign, drew up and published in the form of a manifesto,[95] a statement of its plan of action and its demands.

Though the details varied from state to state, the substance of these demands was the same. What the leagues wanted was to have the Bible[96] read in the state schools by the ordinary teachers as a part of the normal course of studies. What they did not want was anything that savoured of a return to the denominational system—separate grants to denominations or dogmatic religious instruction.

The leagues derived their backing from the Protestant denominations generally, the Lutherans in South Australia being the only body of any consequence to withhold their support.[97] The Anglicans, who by this time had come to regret their remissness in letting their own denominational schools slip through their fingers and to admit that the stand taken by the Catholics had been the right one,[98] saw in the leagues a chance of restoring at least some form of religious instruction. In Queensland, for example, Bishop Webber went so far as to assert that 'unless Scripture reading was admitted to State schools within a reasonable time', the Anglicans would have to face up to the 'question of planting Church day schools' wherever they could.[99] Sunday schools, he said, were practically useless, because only a few of the children ever went to them.[1] Webber's successor, Bishop St. Clair Donaldson, was even more emphatic. Proud of the fact that one of his own clergymen, the

---

[91] Knibbs, G. H. and Turner, J. W., *Interim Report on Primary Education*, p. 148. Speaking of the moral element in education, they said: 'It alone possesses the necessary unifying and controlling influence.' See also their suggestions on the teaching of ethics, pp. 27, 74.

[92] *Church of England Year Book* (Q'ld.), 1902-3, p. 31. The official title in this state was 'The Bible in State Schools League'.

[93] See *Bible Instruction in State Schools*, 1906. In Victoria the league was sometimes known as the National Scripture Education League.

[94] Here there were two societies: (1) Society for promoting the Religious Education of the Young (*Adelaide Observer*, 22 February 1896, p. 29, c; and Petition from Bible in Schools Society. P.P.(S.A.), 1882, IV, paper 3); and Religious Education in State Schools League (*Adelaide Observer*, 15 August 1903, p. 40, b).

[95] See *Church of England Year Book* (Q'ld.), 1909, p. 48; *Adelaide Observer*, 15 August 1903, p. 40, b.

[96] Or failing the Bible, the Scripture extracts used in the Irish National Schools. They wanted also a conscience clause exempting conscientious objectors. See review of South Australian manifesto in *Adelaide Observer*, 25 October 1890, p. 25, c.

[97] Report of the Lutheran Synod (S.A.), 8 April 1896, in *Adelaide Observer*, 18 April 1896, p. 15, a.   [98] Reported in *Advocate*, 28 July 1894, p. 8, a.

[99] *Church of England Year Book* (Q'ld.), 1901, p. 44.

[1] Ibid. (Q'ld.), 1890, pp. 61-2.

Reverend D. T. Garland, was the great organizing power in the Queensland League, he urged his flock to throw their whole weight behind it.[2] Similar encouragement came from the Anglican bodies in Victoria[3] and South Australia.[4]

Support from the non-Anglican groups was no less strong, but it was less consistent. Now that the possibility of a return to denominational instruction seemed more remote,[5] the Wesleyans in these three states[6] strongly supported the leagues; whereas the Presbyterians still entertained a doubt. In Victoria the latter were in favour of undenominational scripture reading,[7] but in South Australia and Queensland, fearing that the granting of their request might give the Catholics a stronger claim to a share in the state grant,[8] they were in two minds over the matter: some wanted the New South Wales system of religious instruction,[9] others simply the Bible.[10]

The Independent groups were even more uncertain and at first stood cautiously apart. Ardent supporters of secularism for over thirty years, they were still reluctant to depart from it. In the 1880s they had even gone so far as to decline sending witnesses to the Royal Commission set up in Victoria to consider the matter. By the nineties, however, the Congregational Union was admitting that it had been remiss in its duty, and had swung over in support of religious instruction in school.[11]

Catholics, on the other hand, were quite opposed to the idea.[12] It was not the Bible as such that they objected to,[13] but the fact that the state schools 'for which they were taxed heavily', were to be used to 'teach a form of religion which they could not conscientiously accept'.[14] Permitting this 'reading of the Bible without note or comment', explained Dr Carr, meant 'introducing the Protestant principle of private judgment'

[2] Ibid. (Q'ld.), 1909, pp. 48, 59; 1911, p. 33.

[3] See P.P.(Vic.), 1900, I, p. xxxviii.

[4] See report of Anglican meeting in St Augustine's School, Unley, 10 March 1896. *Adelaide Observer*, 21 March 1896.

[5] Methodist Conference, *Minutes of Annual Conference* (Q'ld.), 1902, p. 52.

[6] For South Australia see Report of Wesleyan Methodist Conference, 1896. *Adelaide Observer*, 14 March 1896, pp. 42-3. For Victoria, see P.P.(Vic.), 1900, I, p. xxxviii. For Queensland, see *Minutes of Annual Conference*, 1902, p. 63.

[7] See petition to parliament, P.P.(Vic.), 1900, I, p. xxxviii.

[8] This was revealed by the Rev. W. Gray in the Presbyterian Assembly debate, 12 March 1896. *Adelaide Observer*, 21 March 1896, p. 43, c.

[9] *Minutes of Assembly of Presbyterian Church* (Q'ld.), 1906.

[10] In the 1909 Assembly a motion was moved supporting the Bible in State Schools League, but after some discussion the previous question was again moved and the matter dropped. *Minutes of Assembly of Presbyterian Church* (Q'ld.), 1909.

[11] According to a statement made by Dr Bevan at Annual Conference of Congregational Union, Melbourne, 1893. See *Age* (Q'ld.), 11 November 1893, p. 2.

[12] *Pastoral Letter of the Archbishop and Bishops of the Province of Melbourne*, 6 December 1907. See also *Church of England Year Book* (Q'ld.), 1890, p. 59.

[13] Knibbs and Turner, by quoting evidence from Catholic Schools in Germany, had dispelled any notion that it was the Bible as such to which Catholics objected. Knibbs and Turner, *Interim Report on Primary Education*, 1903, p. 154.

[14] Words of Archbishop Duhig, reported in *Argus*, 25 October 1910, p. 6.

and would be equivalent to 'Protestantizing' the state schools. This, he maintained, would constitute a double injustice: an injustice to Catholic children who still had to attend the state schools and an injustice to Catholics who had to pay taxes to support these schools in addition to their own.[15] To Archbishop Duhig it seemed inconsistent for a government to turn round and suddenly 'recognize the principle of religion in education, and not give a penny . . . to the schools that had stood for that principle for thirty years'.[16] To Dr Carr it was more than inconsistent, it was quite irrational—merely a sop 'to save the parsons'.[17]

But Catholics did not stand alone in their opposition. In Victoria the movement was opposed also by a group known as the Education Defence League,[18] under the presidency of Henry Giles Turner and the secretaryship of J. G. Latham.[19] This new league objected to the introduction of the Bible on the same grounds as the Catholics had done, namely, that it would be tantamount to Protestantizing the state schools,[20] a case of 'teaching the religion of some at the expense of all'.[21] This, the Defence League maintained, would be manifestly unjust, but no more unjust than resorting to a referendum as a means of bringing this about. 'Majority rule on matters of religion', they maintained, would, for the minority, amount to nothing short of 'religious persecution'.[22]

[15] *Advocate*, 24 December 1894, p. 10, c.

[16] Reported in *Argus*, 25 October 1910, p. 6.

[17] *Advocate*, 30 June 1904. Ten years later Dr Carr explained 'The object aimed at by the referendum in regard to scripture instruction in State schools was to have Protestantism taught in the schools—to hold a Protestant service in school every day.' Address at opening of Korumburra Convent, *Argus*, 30 June 1914, p. 5. See also E. J. Corder, in his answer to what Protestants termed the 'dog in the manger attitude' policy of Catholics ('Church and School in Australia', *Dublin Review*, vol. 173, 1923, p. 44).

[18] Education Act Defence League, a pamphlet in Education Act Defence League Correspondence (ML).

[19] The object of the League was ' . . . the defence of the present system of free, secular, and compulsory education. It is not formed in the interests of, or in antagonism to, any creed or denomination, but in the interest of the people'. No. 1 article in the platform, Education Act Defence League Correspondence, p. 1.

[20] For example, Mr Higgins, in the 1899 debates on introducing the Bible, said in answer to Alfred Deakin's motion (P.P.(Vic.), 1899): 'I regard its proposals as the thin end of the wedge to protestantize the State schools, and, although a Protestant myself, I think it would be a gross injustice to many to allow it to be done.' See also letter by J. G. Horne to H. G. Turner. He points out that when the campaign was beaten in efforts to introduce the Bible, it shifted its ground to scripture lessons of a non-sectarian character. 'The Church party,' wrote Horne, 'never losing sight of their ultimate goal, viz., to protestantize the State schools—with Jesuitical subtlety—clouded the issue by proposing Scripture Lessons of a non-sectarian character.' Letter, J. G. Horne to H. G. Turner, 7 March 1907. Education Act Defence League Correspondence, p. 15.

[21] Education Act Defence League Correspondence, p. 3.

[22] Ibid., p. 4. The idea of resorting to a referendum they attributed to Bishop Webber. To act on the result of a referendum in this matter would, in their opinion, be a gross misappropriation of political power. Draft of a proposed letter from Education Act Defence League to Members of Parliament in Victoria, 25 July 1907. Education Act Defence League Correspondence, p. 22.

See also *Southern Cross*, 21 February 1896, p. 94; *Adelaide Observer*, 25 October 1890, p. 25, c, d.

Despite the opposition of the Defence League, however, the idea caught on and several referenda were held—in South Australia in 1896,[23] in Victoria in 1904,[24] and in Queensland in 1910—but only in the last state was a 'yes' vote obtained. Even then it was only a fifty-three per cent majority.[25] Nevertheless, legislation was put through and scripture reading in state schools became law.[26] The Bible Leaguers in that state were satisfied.

But in South Australia they were not satisfied. Defeated in the referendum,[27] they tried other means of enlisting the support of public opinion.[28] But this failed also. Finally they resorted to direct legislation. The first of a series of Bills was introduced in 1921, but it got nowhere. Neither did the four others that followed at intervals[29] between that year and 1934.[30] A sixth, introduced some six years later, eventually succeeded and religious instruction once more became permissible in state schools.[31]

Similar attempts made in Victoria after the defeat of the referendum in 1904[32] likewise failed.[33] Finally, in 1945, the Council of Public

[23] The motion was moved by Mr Calwell, 18 September 1895. Referendum was finally agreed upon, 16 December 1895. P.P.(S.A.), 1895, I, p. 344. The actual form of the referendum was proposed by Mr Homburg, 16 December 1885. Parl. Deb. (S.A.), 1895, p. 2860.

[24] The referendum was held on 1 June 1904. Advocate, 28 May 1904, p. 16, a, b.

[25] The referendum was held on 13 April 1910. The results, given in the Church of England Year Book (Q'ld.), 1910, p. 41, were:

For religious instruction	74,226
Against religious instruction	56,672
Informal religious instruction	7,651

[26] Act, 1 Geo. V, no. 5. See particularly clause 22A.

[27] The referendum paper put three questions to the voters: 'Do you favour (1) the continuance of the present system of education in the state schools? (2) the introduction of scriptural instruction in the state schools during school hours? (3) the payment of a capitation grant to denominational schools for secular results?'

The answer, in each case, was to be a direct 'yes' or 'no'. P.P.(S.A.), 1895, I, p. 344; see also Adelaide Observer, 22 February 1896, p. 29, c. The Observer considered that there was 'unquestionably a latent inconsistency' in the ambiguity of those questions. Observer, 25 April 1896, p. 24, d.

The results (Adelaide Observer, 30 May 1896, p. 15) were:

Question	Yes	No	Silent
1	51,824	17,855	21,174
2	19,299	34,951	36,603
3	13,428	42,002	35,423

[28] For instance, Governor Le Hunte presided at the centenary meeting of the Bible Society on 9 March 1904, and commented disapprovingly on the absence of the Bible in state schools (Adelaide Observer, 12 March 1904, p. 34, b). This gave rise to another outburst of feeling on both sides and to a reply from the Register, which the Catholic paper, the Southern Cross, described as 'dignified, weighty, and unanswerable'. Observer, 26 March 1904, p. 34, b; Southern Cross, 18 March 1904.

[29] That is, in 1924, 1927 and 1928. Parl. Deb. (S.A.), 1925, p. 576; 1928, pp. 639-41. [30] Parl. Deb. (S.A.), 1934, pp. 337-42. [31] Act, 4 Geo. IV, xxxviii, 1940.

[32] In 1905 a Scripture Lesson Bill was introduced by Mr Watts. This was to implement the findings of the Commission which in 1900 had prepared a set of scripture lessons for schools. These had been issued on 13 September 1900. Report of Royal Commission on Religious Instruction (Vic.), 1900, under the chairmanship of Ven. Henry Archdall Langley.

[33] The Scripture Lesson Bill failed and was rejected by a vote of 45 to 6. See Votes and Proceedings of Leg. Assembly for 23 August 1905. This 'overwhelming blow',

Education intervened. It made the majority recommendation that the secular instruction provision of the Act[34] be deleted, and that 'the Education Department be asked to invite the co-operation of church-bodies with a view to providing a religious basis for education in the State schools'.[35] The upshot was the Act of 1950,[36] which removed the offending clause and made religious instruction once more possible.

By this Act Victoria, from being the first Australian colony to adopt a purely secular system of education, became the last state to relinquish it and move back to a form of religious instruction which, among Protestants at least, found general acceptance.

Changing Views of Political Parties

This predominantly religious reaction, which expressed itself in an attempt to redeem the situation created by the secular movement of the nineteenth century and which culminated in the 1950 Act in Victoria, was accompanied by certain parallel developments in other, non-religious, spheres. Whereas in the past, for example, much breath had been expended on the question of 'government aid to *denominational* schools' people now began to speak of 'government aid to *private* [or independent] schools'. The change in terminology is significant and can be accounted for in many ways.

Schools originally established as religious institutions came to enjoy (so it was believed) advantages that the ordinary state school could not enjoy. Their relative independence was supposed to leave them freer to experiment with new courses and thereby contribute to the improvement of educational methods generally. Then there were social advantages: the high fees charged in some of these schools had made them exclusive and the preserve of the well-to-do; for the latter therefore the schools became a sort of vested interest, but an interest which rising costs and mounting taxation made increasingly difficult to maintain. Furthermore, because of the alarming trends in educational control in totalitarian and Communist countries there was a genuine return to a fuller appreciation of the educational rights of parents conferred by the natural law. In short, the original notion of denominational schools was practically lost, and what had hitherto been regarded as a religious question came to be looked upon as an educational and social problem. Henceforth,

---

commented the *Austral Light*, 'has practically shattered the agitation conducted for some years past to make the State a teacher of the Protestant religion in its schools' (September 1905, p. 681, b). This defeat is surprising in that the Bible League had claimed that more than fifty members of the Leg. Assembly had promised their support. See Campbell, *The Education Question: its Present Position and the Roman Catholic Claims*, p. 5. Obviously the time was not ripe, for within another five years the Assembly had rejected a proposal for a second referendum—by 34 to 26. See *Advocate*, 31 December, 1910, p. 15, a-d; *Austral Light*, October 1910, p. 844.

[34] That is, sec. 21 of the Education Act.

[35] Council of Public Education (Vic.), *Report on Educational Reform and Development in Victoria*, 1945, p. 25.   [36] Act, 15 Geo. VI, no. 5521, cl. 2.

then, the matter of state aid to non-state schools was to be judged according to the principles of ordinary economics and social justice,[37] religion itself being regarded as merely accidental and more likely to obscure rather than clarify the real issues. But this development belongs almost entirely to the twentieth century.

The Knibbs and Turner Commission, for example, favoured the extension of government grants to non-state schools, not out of any consideration for religion, but solely on the grounds that it would secure greater efficiency in the teachers, develop a healthy rivalry between the two types of schools, and bring about a unification of the education system in all its essential particulars.[38] But because no political party was strong enough to endow it with statutory authority the recommendation was lost. The Labour Party, which was the growing power throughout the last decade of the nineteenth century, was still committed to the 'free, secular and compulsory' platform[39] and there was to be no early departure from that principle.[40] To many this attitude was difficult to understand, especially since Labour professed to be, as Dr O'Reilly of Adelaide said, 'the friend of the working man', and most Catholics were working men.[41]

But the views of Labour gradually changed. Though still opposed to the claims of Catholic schools as such, Labour, in the early part of the present century, found itself in the equivocal position of having already extended to non-state schools the various scholarship schemes[42] and other advantages, reserved, until then, exclusively for state schools.[43]

That was the turning-point. During World War I Catholic Labour men in Victoria made several attempts to have the principle of aid to non-state schools included on the agenda for the annual state conferences; and, although they repeatedly failed, it was observed that Labour sympathies were gradually veering round: in 1918 there were 84 to 51 against state aid, whereas in the previous year the ratio had been 94 to 42.[44] By 1950, the majority had swung the other way: 49 were against

---

[37] This view was advanced by the *Sydney Morning Herald*, 7 August 1950, p. 2, a, b.
[38] These recommendations of the Commission were quoted by Dr Carr in an address at the opening of a school in Fitzroy, January 1904. *Advocate*, 30 January 1904.
[39] See Labour platform (Vic.), 1910, under heading 'Education', sec. 19. Quoted in T. Tunnecliffe, 'The Labour Party and Education', *University Review*, August 1914, pp. 25-30.
[40] The Labour Party (Vic.) rejected the proposals made by the Australian Catholic Federation in 1914. *Argus*, 28 October 1914, p. 10, d. The Labour Party in New South Wales, at the same time, was actually extending its programme. Evatt, H. V., 'Liberalism in Australia' (Beauchamp Essay, University of Sydney, 1915, p. 70).
[41] This statement was made by Archbishop O'Reilly in Adelaide in 1899. *Southern Cross*, 3 February 1899, p. 75. See also *Southern Cross*, 21 April 1899, p. 250; and Archbishop J. Duhig in Lenten Pastoral, 1919. *Argus*, 25 March 1919, p. 5, b.
[42] In Queensland, New South Wales, and Victoria.
[43] Advantages such as the use of state school equipment for sloyd, cookery and dressmaking. *Argus*, 28 October 1914, p. 10, d.
[44] At this period the question was not even admitted on the agenda, but the Catholic

and 142 in favour[45]—just seventeen short of the two-thirds majority, required before it could be accepted as a plank of the party platform.

In New South Wales, the same year, the Annual Conference of the Party resolved that the expected federal grants for education should be shared among all schools, state and non-state alike, on a strictly *per capita* basis,[46] a resolution which was endorsed the following year at the Interstate Australian Labor Party Conference at Canberra.[47] The one remaining doubt—whether the term 'non-state' could be interpreted as including 'denominational' schools—was cleared up the following year by a statement from the Federal Executive of the Party in Canberra, affirming that such an interpretation 'would not be in conflict with the Australian Labor Party Constitution'.[48]

Meanwhile the initiative had passed from Canberra to Tasmania, where a Joint Committee of both Houses of Parliament, appointed by a Labour government at the end of 1951, reached a 'unanimous . . . conclusion' favouring government assistance to non-state schools.[49] The same principle had been admitted by the Tasmanian branch of the Australian Labor Party a few weeks previously.[50]

Similar changes occurred in the policy of the Liberal Party. In his budget speech to the federal parliament in August, 1952, the Treasurer, Sir Arthur Fadden, announced a Commonwealth scheme for assisting those who chose to send their children to private schools. The scheme was in the nature of a concessional deduction in taxable income for education expenses.[51] The request for such deductions had actually been brought before the Commonwealth Advisory Committee some years earlier, and strong support for the idea from the secular press of

---

Workers' Association, resorting to indirect means, was able to sound the party feeling on the matter. *Argus*, 3 April 1918, p. 6.

[45] Report of Easter Conference of Victorian branch of the Labour Party, Melbourne, 1950.   [46] *Sydney Morning Herald*, 18 July 1950.

[47] Federal Conference, March 1951. Quoted in *Sydney Morning Herald*, 19 June 1951, p. 2.   [48] *Sydney Morning Herald*, 19 June 1952, p. 2.

[49] Report of Joint Committee of Both Houses of Parliament (on aid to private schools), 1952. P.P.(Tas.), 1952, paper 12, p. 8. See also *Catholic Weekly*, 10 April 1952, p. 1.

[50] At the state conference at Ulverstone, on the motion of Senator McKenna. The motion was carried on a division by 125 to 51. *Sydney Morning Herald*, 22 February 1952, p. 3, h.

Further developments have occurred since this was written. In 1953, at the Federal Conference in Adelaide, the principle of 'financial aid for all forms of education' (denominational included) was inserted in the party platform. At the 1957 Federal Conference in Brisbane, however, the aid to denominational schools plank was definitely rejected. As an alternative the party pledged itself to the 'promotion of secondary and higher education by way of bursaries, scholarships, exhibitions and benefits of like nature, payable direct to the students'. *Sydney Morning Herald*, 16 March 1957, p. 1, a.

[51] This meant that education expenses up to a maximum of £50 for each dependent child under 21 years could be deducted from taxable income. In addition, full exemption from sales tax in respect of all goods for educational use was to be granted. *Sydney Morning Herald*, 7 August 1952, p. 10, d.

Victoria early in 1952 had revived the issue.[52] For Catholics, however, the concession meant little. In the first place, it was altogether inadequate for the purpose; in the second, it would bring scarcely any alleviation to those in the lower income groups, who most felt the burden of educating their children in non-state schools.[53] For such a policy of tax remissions, admitted Archbishop Mannix, 'a good case' could be made; but it was 'a very feeble and timid approach to a very big problem' and left 'the real problem of the survival of the independent schools untouched'.[54] Nevertheless, the policy itself indicated a pronounced shift of opinion.

In this general change of view, which had been taking place over the greater part of the present century, it will be noticed that the decisions in favour of government grants to non-state schools appear to have been reached quite independently of any appreciation of the religious motive, which in fact seemed entirely irrelevant. Nowhere is this brought out more clearly than in the reasons given by the Tasmanian Committee: 'the financial burdens', it said, 'and other problems associated with the conduct of non-State schools' were such that 'they should receive some measure of financial assistance'.[55] Parents sent their children to non-state schools for a variety of reasons; as parents they had a perfect right to do so;[56] and that right, without any questioning of motives, would be respected. According to the *Sydney Morning Herald*, the matter had become purely 'an economic issue and [would have] to be approached as such'.[57]

Changing Views of Protestants and Catholics

To these more recent views of press and political party the religious denominations gradually accommodated themselves—with varying degrees of readiness or reluctance. Among Protestants generally there still lingered a suspicion of the educational demands of Catholics.[58] It was this suspicion and the fear that Catholic schools also might benefit that helped to defeat the Bible in Schools referenda in two of the states concerned.[59] In the 1920s, for example, Catholic schools were still being

52 *Catholic Weekly*, 14 August 1952, p. 4, a, b.
53 Evidence of Mr Andrews (Lab., Vic.), in debate on tax concessions for education, 1952. *Catholic Weekly*, 2 October 1952, p. 1, a, b.
54 *Catholic Weekly*, 14 August 1952, p. 4, a, b.
55 Report of Select Committee on State Aid to non-State Schools. P.P.(Tas.), 1952, paper 12.
56 This right was championed by the United Nations Organization. See *Catholic Weekly*, 31 July 1952, p. 3, f.
57 7 August 1950, p. 2, a, b. See pp. 463-4.
58 Letter to editor from 'South Australian' in *Adelaide Observer*, 18 January 1896, p. 27, c. See also Report of Presbyterian Assembly debate, 12 March 1896. *Adelaide Observer*, 21 March 1896, p. 43, c.
59 See numerous letters to the press warning against Catholic attempts to 'break up . . . [the] splendid education system'. *Adelaide Observer*, 15 April 1896, p. 14, b;

accused of openly fostering disloyalty. Even as late as the mid-century mark the reply of the New South Wales Council of Churches to Labour's decision on a *per capita* distribution of the federal education grant was based on a veiled charge of divisiveness. 'In the interests of a united people', said the Council, it was desirable 'to lay the foundations of our common agreements', and the means *par excellence* to this end was 'the education of the great bulk of the children in a common school with certain well defined principles of loyalty'.[60]

But none of these charges against the Catholic schools had ever been successfully sustained,[61] with the result that, in the interests of consistency, the Council was obliged to make certain concessions which robbed its objections to the Catholic demands of much of their force. In the first place, while advocating the 'common school', the Council recognized the value of a 'certain number of Church schools supported without State aid'. In the second, it admitted even as late as 1950 that the most that could be expected of the state was that it 'should not impose penalties on those who [found] themselves unable to adopt the system provided by the State'.[62]

By 1952 Protestants in Tasmania and Victoria were prepared to go even further. In Tasmania, the leaders of the main Protestant groups were in full accord with the recommendations of the Select Committee of 1952. The only exceptions were the Baptist Union, the Protestant Federation, and the Seventh Day Adventists, but the grounds of their objections were exposed by the Committee itself and shown to be either

---

see also 11 April 1896, p. 12, c, 18 April 1896, p. 25, b. The columns of the *Observer* 'teemed with letters'. *Observer*, 25 April 1896, p. 24, c. See also *Australian*, 10 February 1883.

'Their suspicions of the Church's intentions,' the bishops said, were 'likely to preclude from the thoughts of Australian statesmen any change in the actual systems.' Pastoral Letter of the Cardinal Delegate. Printed in *Austral Light*, October 1905, p. 704. See also *Age* (Q'ld.), 16 September 1893, p. 5, a.

[60] *Sydney Morning Herald*, 19 August 1950, p. 3. The Churches represented were: the Church of England, by the Most Rev. Dr. H. Mowll; the Presbyterian, by the Moderator, the Rt Rev. H. Harrison; the Methodist, by the President, the Rev. B. T. Butcher; the Baptist, by the Rev. E. Clatworthy; the Church of Christ, by the President, Mr N. H. Matthews; and the Society of Friends, by Mr Syd. Wright. Later, however, Mr Wright withdrew his signature, there having been no authorization given by him for its use under this statement. *Sydney Morning Herald*, 20 August 1950.

[61] See, for example, letter in *Adelaide Observer*, 18 April 1896, p. 14, b; *Advocate*, 28 July 1894, p. 8: 'The Catholic clergy and the Catholic body do not desire to interfere in any way with those who are content with the public school system'; Pastoral Letter of the Cardinal Delegate, 1905 (*Austral Light*, October 1905, p. 711), declared that the seeming disloyalty would one day be seen in its true light—the only loyalty. 'We are confident . . . that the guardians of the public welfare will find it a good and necessary policy to assist in her educational policy an institution which devotes itself as the Catholic Church does, to the inculcation of the principles of Christian morality. In the interests of our country, we would wish that the neglect of Christian training for the children of a Christian people may not be carried so far as to exclude all hope of preserving their Christianity.'

[62] Reported in *Sydney Morning Herald*, 20 August 1950. See also Pastoral Letter of Cardinal Delegate, 1905, *Austral Light*, October 1905, p. 711.

inconsistent with their own practice[63] or based on 'sectarian antagonism'.[64] In Victoria later the same year, the members of the Anglican Synod, while still opposed to government aid, submitted as their only objection the fact that the Catholic Church, owing to the existence of its own teaching orders, would be placed at an enormous advantage.[65] Otherwise they were quite in favour. In fact, arguing purely from principles of social justice and parental right,[66] and without any reference to religious or sectarian issues, the Archbishop-in-Council put the case in terms very similar to those of the report of the Tasmanian Committee and practically identical with those used by the Catholics themselves.[67] 'Every citizen,' he said, 'is bound by law to have his child educated. He has the right for the cost of this education to be defrayed by the Government. If the citizen chose an alternative method to the Government school, he saved the Government money and should in fairness receive assistance.'[68]

This approximation between Catholic and Protestant thought on the question of social justice in education had taken the better part of eighty years to achieve. The process had been long drawn out and had passed through many vicissitudes. Earlier, in the hope of eventually winning aid, the Catholic authorities had worked in close co-operation with the state in connection with the various Teachers' Registration Acts, Bursary Acts, and the like.[69] This means failing, they tried the political approach through the Catholic Federation which was developed in the early years of this century.[70] But this also failed.[71] Opposition remained as strong as ever, with a great deal of bitterness on both sides.

[63] Report of Select Committee on State Aid to non-State Schools, P.P.(Tas.), 1952, paper 12, p. 6.   [64] Ibid, p. 7.   [65] Reported in *Advocate*, 17 July 1952, p. 6, b.
[66] See *Christian Education in a Democratic Community*. Social Justice Statement, 1949. Published with the authority of the Archbishops and Bishops of the Catholic Church in Australia, p. 13.
[67] See, for example, Sheehan, 'The Official Pronouncement of the Catholic Hierarchy of Australia'; Rumble, *Catholics Ask for Justice*, p. 22; see remarks of Archbishop O'Reilly in *Adelaide Observer*, 11 October 1890, p. 25, b; Cathrein, Rev. Victore (S.J.), *Philosophia Moralis*.   [68] *Catholic Weekly*, 15 May 1952, p. 1, b.
[69] See *Advocate*, 30 January 1904, p.14, b. See also letter, Rev. J. W. Gleeson, Inspector of Catholic Schools, to the Hon. S. W. Jeffries, Minister for Education, 24 September 1949; letter, Fr Russell, Director of Catholic Education, to Mr N. M. Grattan, Headmaster of Scotch College, Adelaide, 30 November 1948 (both letters in Archives, Catholic Education Office, Adelaide).
[70] In 1912. The need for an organized Catholic laity had been felt for some time. Articles appearing in the *Austral Light*, 1905, from the pen of Rev. M. P. Malone, advocated the adoption of the American scheme, 'American Federation of Catholic Societies', founded in 1902 with the approval of the Apostolic Delegate and the Hierarchy. 'The time', said the writer, was 'at hand for such a movement in Australia. The necessities and opportunities all about us invoke a closer union of pastors and people. By unity we can make our impress upon the work of the Commonwealth and reflect Catholic thought and action in regard to vital questions affecting the social, moral, and intellectual life of our country'. Malone, Rev. M. P., 'Australian Catholic Federation', *Austral Light*, 1 July 1905, p. 509. See report of meeting of the Federation in Melbourne in 1913. *Argus*, 20 January 1913, p. 4.
[71] *Austral Light*, November 1914, p. 824, a. See also Doyle, B. T., and Morley, J. A., *The Catholic Story*, p. 35.

Dropping the political line, therefore, the Catholics adopted more conciliatory measures. 'Though we demand the redress of a grievance,' declared the bishops in their 'Official Pronouncement' in 1936, 'we do so in the spirit of kindness, and with the desire to serve the true interests of civil government in every part of the Commonwealth.'[72] For that reason they preferred to avoid using such terms as 'denominational grants', 'aid to private schools', 'aid to religious schools', and the like, regarding them as 'confusing and misleading'. 'The education problem', they said, 'was not basically a religious one': those directing private schools 'were not seeking "aid" or "grants" or concessions from anyone', but simply a right in social justice.[73] For that reason the Fourth Plenary Council had merely affirmed the principle of a *pro rata* share in the education grant without adding anything by way of detail on the way such share was to be made available.[74]

That became clear only after the events and changes in public opinion outlined above. According to a scheme worked out by the bishops and announced by Bishop Lyons in May 1952, the ideal approach appeared to be to extend the then existing social services system to make it include education.[75] In this way the government would need to have in mind simply the child itself, 'without thought for where or to whom it [went] to school',[76] the sum needed for its education being 'worked out actuarially'.[77] Ample precedent for this sort of procedure, said the Bishop, already existed. Under the hospital benefit scheme, for example, if a person were ill, he was allowed to choose his own hospital, public, intermediate or private, irrespective of whether that hospital was conducted by secular or religious bodies.[78] Each child, 'like the hospital patient', would then carry with him to the school selected by his parents, whether state or non-state, the amount granted for his education. Such a plan, concluded the Bishop, had the added advantage that it 'could be enacted without the introduction of, or need to vindicate, any new principle, since no new principle would be involved'.[79]

[72] Sheehan, 'Official Pronouncement of the Catholic Hierarchy of Australia on the Education Question', *Australasian Catholic Record*, vol. xiv, January 1937.
[73] Statement made by Bishop Lyons. Reported in *Catholic Weekly*, 15 May 1952, p. 1.
[74] 'Patres solemniter affirmant ius esse scholis catholicis ad proportionatum pro rata summam ex aerario publico tribuendam.' *Conc. Plen.*, IV, decr. 631.
[75] This idea had previously appeared in the Report of Select Committee on State Aid to non-State Schools. P.P.(Tas.), 1952, paper 12, p. 6.
[76] Reported in *Catholic Weekly*, 15 May 1852, p. 1.
[77] This, according to the Bishop, would present no difficulty. It is known, for example, what it costs for an average child in the state school. On the basis, then, that 68 per cent of all children are in state schools, the cost for the average child could be calculated.
[78] This suggestion actually appeared earlier in the Report of Select Committee on State Aid to non-State Schools. P.P.(Tas.), 1952. See *Catholic Weekly*, 10 April 1952, p. 19, a.
[79] *Catholic Weekly*, 15 May 1952, p. 1.

12

Retrospect

THE FOREGOING chapters attempt to lift out from the matrix
of historical events and cultural determinants the principles
underlying the development of Catholic education in Australia.
In the course of its history that education has appeared under a variety
of forms, but the principles on which it is based remain unchanged and
emerge with sufficient clarity to justify this particular approach.

Actually these principles are based on the Catholic philosophy of life,
which ultimately is derived from that concept of man—his nature, origin,
and destiny—as determined by reason and revelation.[1] From this position
—the natural law and the positive divine law—the Church defines her
role in education and those of the family and the state as well. Nothing
in these definitions, however, suggests that a separate system of Catholic
education independent of the state is essential or even desirable. The
fact that such a system does exist in this country is an indication that
circumstances have demanded it.

But the circumstances themselves have been subject to a great deal
of misunderstanding. It has been contended, for instance, that in this
country the state has interfered too much in education. This view has
been widely held, perhaps with some justification; yet, given the circumstances and the obstacles confronting education in the nineteenth
century (see chs. 1-3), it would be interesting to speculate on the
parlous condition in which education would have found itself had it
not been for government intervention. So far as official Catholic opinion
is concerned, the state has a definite right and duty to intervene; the
only grievance is that it has not intervened enough: it has not extended
to Catholics the same freedom of conscience that it has extended to
members of other denominations; while giving equal rights in all other
social services, it withholds them in the matter of education.

Another mistaken view not infrequently met, especially among Catholics, is that the Catholic schools were squeezed out of the old denominational system either because of sectarian jealousy on the part of the other
denominations, or because it suited the policies of certain political groups
or the personal ambitions of a few political careerists. The name of Sir
Henry Parkes, for instance, is not held in high regard among Catholics
in New South Wales owing to the part he played in administering the

[1] See *Advocate*, 5 December 1885, p. 9, a.

Public Schools Act of 1866 and in the passing of the 1880 Act. But Parkes' position has not always been understood. The provisions of his 1880 Act surpassed those of any other piece of educational legislation before his time, on which account he is with some justice looked upon as the founder of the present system of education in New South Wales. Moreover, he must be held as a benefactor by those who feared a strictly secular education, for he stood as a bulwark against it until it was finally headed off by his Public Instruction Act of 1880.[2] The introduction of this measure late in 1879 was timely; it is hardly conceivable that New South Wales could have stood apart from the general trend of development and accepted a system of national education different from the pattern that was working itself out in the other Australian colonies and in so many other parts of the world as well. Parkes or no Parkes, the Act would have come—perhaps even ten years earlier, when Vaughan would not have been there to parry it nor the teaching orders prepared to step into the breach. To that extent Catholics are indebted to him. But any genuine admiration is tempered by the fact that in his treatment of them in the late seventies he put himself in the class of those who would put expediency before principle, or would not scruple to stir up religious bigotry to save a portfolio. The Catholics as a voting power had been gradually isolated: Parkes had juggled with them up to 1876; from then on he could do without them.[3] Towards the end of his life he is reported to have 'regretted that State aid had been withdrawn'[4] and to have expressed the desire to rectify the matter if he were returned to power.[5] But that was not to be. The 1880 Act remained— a vindictive reprisal, some thought, on the whole Catholic body. Actually it was not, but it suited Parkes to let it appear so at the time.[6]

Parkes did not stand alone in this attitude towards Catholics. Though there is evidence that the ruling idea in some political circles was to

[2] It would be quite misleading to suggest that at any period of his career Parkes was a firm believer in denominational schools. In his speeches and writings, he made it clear that he defended them, not as a matter of educational or religious principle, but as a matter of political necessity or expediency (*Fifty Years in the Making of Australian History*, vol. 2, pp. 1-8). Nevertheless, he was no friend of the secularists. He resisted their 'all-out' attempts in the Assembly (*Parl. Deb.* (N.S.W.), 2, 1879-80, p. 1121), and was congratulated by Professor Smith in the Council for the 'firm stand' he had taken on the matter (ibid., p. 1467). For an appreciation of Parkes' work in education from another angle, see Sir Thomas Bavin, *Sir Henry Parkes: His Life and Works*, p. 45.

[3] Earlier Parkes had regarded them as 'a disturbing agency of mischief and little else'. Letter, Parkes to James F. Maggar, 21 August 1869. Parkes' Correspondence, vol. 45, p. 113 (ML).

[4] Report of visit to Convent School and Orphanage, Bathurst, 22 October 1895. *National Advocate*, Bathurst, 23 October 1895, p. 2.

[5] See statements of Cardinal Moran (*Freeman's Journal*, 11 August 1906, p. 25), and A. J. Riley (*Sydney Morning Herald*, 17 August 1906, p. 9).

[6] See *Parl. Deb.* (N.S.W.), 1879-80, 1, pp. 260-7, and the opinions of other members of the Assembly (p. 453).

See also P. S. Cleary, 'Secular Education in New South Wales—An Appeal to History', *Australasian Catholic Record*, 1911, p. 194.

'dish the R.C.s'[7] it is no stronger than the evidence found for similar motives among a great number of Protestant clergymen. Just as Bishop Broughton had rallied Protestant opposition to Governor Bourke's educational proposals in the eighteen-thirties on the grounds that by giving Catholic schools equal opportunity with Protestant they were 'prepar[ing] the way for the ultimate establishment of popery',[8] so a great many Protestant clergymen were induced to close their denominational schools in the eighteen-seventies on the grounds that by keeping them open they were, as the ex-Baptist minister Greenwood suggested, only 'serving to keep the Roman Catholic schools in countenance'.[9] But not all were actuated by such motives.[10] Sectarianism was only one factor: the schools themselves suffered from many defects. Among other things, they had failed to outstrip their rivals in educational achievement and could no longer command the respect they had formerly enjoyed.[11] It is unlikely, therefore, that they would have lasted much longer than they did, even if the sectarian issue had never been raised.

Moreover, any justification there may have been in the past for the existence of denominational schools on purely religious grounds was now fast disappearing. Initially, Catholic and Protestant practice in the matter of religious education had been the same, but under the impact of liberal and rationalistic thought, which had grown critical of dogmatic belief, Protestants had veered away from their earlier practice and the need for denominational instruction was no longer widely felt. In increasing numbers, the Protestant groups were becoming satisfied with the general, non-denominational type of instruction or even with none at all.[12] The result was that the Church school was fast losing its real significance. No longer a place where a thorough religious education was given, it was coming to be looked upon as a preserve of the privileged classes and therefore quite out of place in a liberal, democratic society which accorded privileges to none and equal opportunity for all.

But to Catholics this opportunity was not equal. In their eyes the so-called non-sectarian or secular schools that replaced the denominational schools were in fact Protestant—not in the sense that they taught positive Protestant doctrine but in the sense that what was done in them was acceptable to Protestants and in no way prejudicial to their conscience.

[7] Observation of Presbyterian clergyman, the Rev. Andrew Harper, in his *The Honourable James Balfour*, p. 176.

[8] Letter, Broughton to Marsden, 25 September 1835. Marsden Papers, vol. 1 (ML).

[9] *Freeman's Journal*, 19 September 1874, p. 8, b.

[10] See particularly the work of the Anglicans, Bishop Moorhouse and Bishop Barker, and of the Presbyterian, Dr Whyte, of Singleton, who did what they could to restrain sectarian outbursts.

[11] See letter, Polding to Chairman, D.S.B., 29 July 1861. D.S.B. (N.S.W.) Report, 1862, p. 7.

[12] Cf. Professor Manning Clark, *Select Documents in Australian History, 1851-1900*, p. 662.

Educational legislation, it appeared, had followed the trend in Protestant practice, not preceded it.

To these developments a great number of Protestants, no doubt, remained quite indifferent. A few looked upon them as retrograde and regrettable, the rest as perfectly natural. 'When two religions,' they said, '(i.e. Catholic and Protestant) adopt different rules on matters in which the State, within its own sphere, is called upon to act, its decision is, and must necessarily be, in accordance with the principles of Protestant Christianity.'[13] Whether or not any of the colonial governments, while giving adherence to a more liberal creed, did in fact accept this line of reasoning, even in the later referenda (pp. 458-63), is immaterial here; the result was the same: national education took a direction which Catholics claimed they were not able in conscience to follow. Had they been able to do so, the separate Catholic system as it exists in Australia today might never have developed—certainly not to the extent it has.

This new, separate system called for the introduction of the religious orders. Coming mainly from Europe, these teaching communities spread throughout the colonies, taking over schools formerly taught by lay teachers and establishing new ones of their own. Then followed a period of acculturation. With the orders had come the educational traditions of Western Europe. Centuries old, these traditions had to be adapted to new conditions, and in the process of adaptation certain practices were considerably modified.

By the turn of the century the chief characteristics of the present system were already clearly defined. But at the beginning there had been no clear pattern; a system independent of the state had then seemed impossible. The chief difficulty was finance: Catholics might desire such a system, but they would never be able to maintain one. That was the view commonly held among Protestants and, it appears, among a number of Catholics as well. Even some of the clergy doubted; and, although the bishops eventually made the decision to stand alone, they did so with certain well-founded doubts as to what the future would bring. This they revealed in their pastoral letter of 1885:

Within the last ten or fifteen years, State grants have been withdrawn from all Christian education in these colonies. The general feeling at the time was that its days were numbered. Some said it was foolish of Catholics to contemplate keeping up a system for themselves; some, that it was despotic of the clergy to 'force' the laity into the manifold self-impoverishment it would entail. 'For a while,' such people said, 'they will not complain; but by degrees and with one excuse or another, the call for funds will be grumbled at, and finally, not responded to, and the schools will imperceptibly disappear.'[14]

[13] Queensland Evangelical Standard, 20 July 1878, p. 30, c.
[14] Pastoral Letter of the Archbishops and Bishops of Australasia in Plenary Council Assembled, 1885, p. 28.

And, admitted the bishops, 'all human likelihood appeared to support these foreboders of evil'.[15] To many, in fact, the uncompromising attitude of Catholics to state education seemed extravagant and far-fetched, and the decision of the bishops rash and unnecessarily provocative. Both, however, can be explained in part.

Rightly or wrongly, state education for most Catholics became synonymous with secular education, and on that point the Catholic mind was already made up. Its attitude had been determined, or rather predetermined, by the attitude of the Church in Europe. In England and Australia there had never been serious question of excluding religion; the real problem was how to include it;[16] secular education had been put forward mainly as a way out of the difficulty. In Europe, on the other hand, particularly in France and Italy, the idea of secular education had proceeded from another motive—that of straight-out infidelity and hatred of all revealed religion in general and of Catholicism in particular. No wonder then that to Catholics secular education appeared in such a dangerous light. To Vaughan it was the dreaded offspring of liberalism, 'the main instrument of the great apostasy',[17] 'the solvent of Christianity', 'the rack, the gibbet, and the thumbscrew all over again'.[18]

Obviously, Vaughan was overwrought—unnecessarily so, thought Parkes.[19] Yet the position confronting the Archbishop called for just such a policy of 'reasonable alarm'.[20] His was the particularly difficult task of rousing to a sense of apprehension and responsibility a laity (and to some extent a clergy) whom state aid had for so long lulled into a false security.

In this the archdiocese of Sydney was a particular case, and over-concentration on it has exaggerated the importance of Vaughan's role in the general story and distorted the oral tradition that has grown up round his name. On this account the attitude of the Australian bishops as a whole has been generally misrepresented, both in Australia and abroad. In Hans' study of comparative education,[21] for example, the author perceives, as a result of the 1864 Encyclical and *Syllabus* of Pius IX, a

---

[15] Ibid., pp. 26-7.

[16] Inspector Childers in Victoria spoke of the problem as one of 'more or less religion'. Childers, H. C. E., Report on General System of Education, 1851, p. 3. P.P.(Vic.), 1851.

Governor Denison in New South Wales spoke of the religious problem simply as 'the difference of opinion as to [its] character and extent'. Governor's minute in Proceedings of the Executive Council on Commission Report, 1855, p. 4. P.P.(N.S.W.), 1855, I, p. 1017.

[17] Vaughan, 'Address in Reply to Opponents on the Education Question', delivered in the pro-Cathedral, 14 December 1879. *Pastorals and Speeches on Education*, p. 41.

[18] Vaughan, *Pastoral 3* (on Education), 7 September 1879, p. 3.

[19] See Parkes, Sir Henry, *Fifty Years in the Making of Australian History*, vol. 2, p. 15.   [20] See policy advocated by Polding, p. 251.

[21] Hans, Nicholas A, *Comparative Education: a Study of Educational Factors and Traditions*.

general stiffening on the part of Catholic leaders throughout the world. This stiffening, he claims, was nowhere more apparent than in their attitude towards governments over the education question. In Ireland he ascribes it to Cardinal Cullen, in Canada to Charbonnel, and in Australia to Vaughan. But Vaughan did not set foot in Australia until 1873, whereas the 'stiffening' noted in the Australian bishops is quite apparent in the pastoral of the 1869 Synod. Besides, the stand taken by the bishops on that occasion (see chs. 5, 6) was not one whit firmer than that taken by Dr Geoghegan as Bishop of Adelaide in 1860, or even as a simple priest in Melbourne in 1852.[22]

The crowning of Archbishop Vaughan, therefore, as the hero of Catholic education in Australia is quite inaccurate. There were warriors in plenty before his time, though none, admittedly, so eloquent, none so majestic, none who so drew the fire of their opponents or captured the imagination of their contemporaries as he did.

One reason for this inaccuracy, which still lingers and distorts the picture, may be the fact that the only authoritative work on Catholic education in Australia is that of Brother Urban Corrigan.[23] Vaughan is the hero of that work; but the conclusions reached by the author apply only to New South Wales, and even then they fail to do justice to Vaughan's contemporaries in the Hierarchy. The situation that Vaughan faced in 1879 had already been faced by James Quinn five years earlier in Queensland, earlier still by Goold in Victoria, and even before that by Geoghegan and Sheil in South Australia. With such examples behind him, therefore, and the obvious determination of his suffragans in Bathurst, Maitland, and Goulburn before him, the Archbishop could not but act as he did.

Vaughan was a leader, not an innovator. For the real architects of the present system of Catholic schools it is necessary to go further back—to Geoghegan, Serra, James Quinn, Sheil, and especially to Tenison Woods. Despite the clouds of misunderstanding that hung over the later part of his life, Woods stands out as a significant figure in the development of Catholic education in Australia. Of greater significance still is the figure of Mary McKillop who, as Mother Mary of the Cross, was co-foundress with Woods of what is today Australia's largest single teaching congregation under central control. Woods, it is true, was the architect who conceived the first sketchy outlines of the new congregation and assisted at its foundation, but Mother Mary was the builder. She it was who stood by it in the first precarious years of its early development, and imparted to it a spirit which seems constantly to renew itself and which has made the congregation such an important instrument in the Church's educational programme.

22 Report of Select Committee on Education, P.P.(Vic.), 1852, II, p. 639.
23 Catholic Education in New South Wales.

The idea of using religious teaching congregations in Catholic schools was not wholly Woods' or Mother Mary's. In this they had been anticipated by all the early bishops: by Polding in 1839, Willson in 1847, Brady in 1848, Goold in 1857, and James Quinn in 1861. But with one or two exceptions these religious had concentrated on superior schools for the children of the middle and upper classes. Here and there they staffed a parochial school for the poor, but that was all. New South Wales, apparently, was not the only colony where the view existed that it was the well-to-do who needed the schools of the religious (and who, incidentally, could afford to pay for them) and that the children of the poor could be well accommodated in the government denominational schools.

It was in diverting religious to the schools of the poor, therefore, that Woods and Mother Mary have attracted most attention. Not only did they demonstrate that small religious communities could exist in comparative isolation, but also that subjects for the religious life could be recruited from among the poor they served. In addition, they showed conclusively that state aid could be done without.

Regarded somewhat sceptically at first, the plan Woods outlined for South Australia at the end of the sixties came to be accepted a decade or so later as practically the only one capable of meeting the Church's needs. At the time of the first three Plenary Councils, 1885-1905, it had become quite general, the sole remaining problem being that of finding more religious. New communities had been brought out from Europe and those already in Australia induced to interest themselves in staffing the parochial schools. In addition, the religious had superimposed on the parochial primary system a secondary system of their own, thus doubling the field of their apostolate to youth.

But their influence was not restricted to the school. The significant contribution they were making to society in general and to the Church in particular was becoming increasingly apparent, and the passing years only confirmed the bishops in the decision they had made in the eighteen-seventies. Even before the end of the century, results showed that, though the struggle had been 'hard and costly', they had acted wisely and in the best interests of their people and their Church. For that God was to be thanked, but 'particularly for two blessings'—'the singular unity by which [the] Bishops [were] united with their people, and the uncompromising spirit of Faith which [had] filled and sometimes sustained the heart of Catholic Australia'. Both these blessings, they felt, had resulted from the stand they had taken.[24]

In this respect Catholic education in Australia had anticipated most of the later pronouncements from Rome. The directives and exhorta-

[24] Pastoral Letter of the Cardinal Delegate, 1905. Printed in *Austral Light*, October 1905, p. 705.

tions of Leo XIII and later Popes,[25] were not without their effects, but they had little to add to the ideas and principles enunciated with astonishing clarity by Geoghegan[26] and Serra[27] in the fifties and repeated by Vaughan with magnificent eloquence in the seventies. This is hardly surprising, for, in their eyes at any rate, they were defending not only the Catholic position but truth itself. Moreover, their objective notions on man and society, the family and the state, together with their clear-cut distinctions between what is from nature and what is from will,[28] strongly suggest a common thomistic source. External evidence points in the same direction: Vaughan's huge work on St Thomas Aquinas[29] appeared in the same decade as Leo XIII's emphatic recommendation of thomistic philosophy, and Serra and Geoghegan had been educated in the great schools of Spain and Portugal where the thomistic tradition had never really disappeared.

Such was the proximate source of the ideas that gave rise to the present-day system of Catholic education. Besides adhering closely to these traditional principles, the system absorbed much that was useful from the cultural environment of the age in which it developed. In the matter of technique, for example, it has borrowed judiciously from the so-called secular pedagogy of the day, only to realize in the end that it had been re-adopting methods that were traditionally its own. From the influence and competition of the state systems, moreover, especially in the matter of standards and organization, it has profited immensely. It has also benefited from the improved social and economic position of Catholics of the middle and working classes, finding in the bursary and scholarship systems particularly not only a way of adding incentive and purpose to the whole primary course, but of assuring a much higher percentage of pupils staying on in the secondary classes.

The system, however, has not been without its defects. The low standards and lack of organization consequent upon the haphazard growth of the system have not entirely disappeared, despite the fact that the basic outline of a satisfactory organization has existed (on paper) since the nineteen-thirties (see pp. 437-42 and Fig. 20). More recently felt weaknesses, such as the need for a greater variety of non-academic courses in the secondary schools, have already been noted. Yet another difficulty has been that of working with a syllabus prescribed by an outside non-Catholic authority. This, it is claimed,[30] has resulted in

[25] See Fleming, Rev. Brian (S.J.), 'Leo XIII and Catholic Education' (unpublished M.A. thesis, University of Melbourne, 1952).

[26] In particular, Geoghegan's explanations given in evidence before the Select Committee on Education in Victoria, 1852, referred to on pp. 171, 475.

[27] In particular, Serra's letters to Governor Kennedy, referred to on p. 168.

[28] The distinction here is between the *ius naturale* and the *ius positivum* (*etiam divinum*). [29] This was Vaughan's *Life and Labours of St Thomas of Aquin*.

[30] O'Brien, Rev. A. E., 'Uniformity in the Teaching of Christian Doctrine', *Austral Light*, March 1911, p. 325, a.

the development of a defensive mentality among Catholics, who seem to have been far better equipped to adopt negative and protective measures against error and non-Catholic prejudice than they have been to appreciate the positive riches of their own faith. This mentality, however, is disappearing. Seen in its proper perspective, it would appear to have been a characteristic of the Irish Catholic population, which, from occupying a distinctly inferior position in the early part of the nineteenth century, has, largely as a result of the present system of Catholic education, risen to occupy a position little inferior to that of others. But this introduces a broader social question quite beyond the scope of this work.

One more point, relevant at the close of this book, is the uncertainty concerning the future of the system. Constant pressure from diocesan authorities for more and more schools has strained staff to the utmost; and in the past decade the increase in candidates for the teaching orders has not been commensurate with the increase in the Catholic school population.[31] Whether this gap will continue to widen, or prove to be merely a passing phase and close again after the steep rise in population has levelled out, it is difficult to say.[32] Should it not close and Catholics desire to preserve their independent system intact, lay teachers will have to be employed in increasing numbers until a point is reached where the structure of the system could eventually change, reversing the whole order of its development: the religious could gradually withdraw into a smaller number of select schools, leaving the parochial and diocesan schools in the hands of lay teachers.

Such a possibility lends support to the opinion that the present system is no more than a temporary measure which was hastily designed to meet the crisis of the eighteen-sixties and seventies but which, having outlived its usefulness, should now be abandoned.[33] Such abandonment, however, would be generally regarded as retrograde. Though in no way incompatible with Catholic principles,[34] it would be out of harmony

[31] *Report of the Third National Education Conference of Directors and Inspectors of Schools*, Sydney, 1944, p. 3.

The members of the Fifth Conference noted 'with dismay the alarming shortage of vocations to the Religious Teaching Orders'. Report of the Fifth National Education Conference of Directors and Inspectors of Schools, Hobart, 1951, p. 1 (Archives, Catholic Education Office, Melbourne).

[32] From figures that have since been made available it seems that the gap has been widening during the 1950s. It was 'conservatively estimated' that the number of children having to be refused admission to Catholic schools was increasing, having jumped by 50,000 over the years 1953-6. 'The Catholic School in Australia', *Current Affairs Bulletin*, August 1958, p. 138.

It has also been estimated that between the years 1946-64 the number of Catholic children seeking admission to Catholic schools will have risen from 211,000 to 433,000. This means, in effect, that over those 18 years the Catholic school system will have to double itself in size. *Holy Name Monthly*, October 1957, p. 4.

[33] This view arises from a mistaken interpretation of a remark made by Bishop Lanigan in the 1880s. *Catholic Standard*, April 1884, p. 57, a. See also Vaughan, *Pastoral 1* (on Education), p. 11.

[34] This is demonstrated by the fact that, since these lines were written, some dioceses,

with the cherished Catholic conception of education and opposed to the express wish of ecclesiastical authority.[35] Moreover, the mature deliberation and prolonged effort entailed in establishing and maintaining the system indicate that most Catholics regard it as much more than an expedient.[36]

No longer regarded as a rival in the broad national scheme of education, the Catholic system has emerged today as the state's *de facto* partner, educating more than twenty per cent of the children of the state, and still upholding, in an impenitent spirit of loyalty, the principle over which Catholics and the state separated more than eighty years ago. The fact that in recent times the state[37] and other denominations[38] have shown a readiness to return to this principle by attempting to provide a more thorough religious foundation in education only accentuates the importance of this Catholic contribution which, as a factor in the survival of Christian education in this country, remains unique.

Conspicuous from the beginning as the Church's uncompromising protest against the liberal tendencies of the nineteenth century, this system stands today as her considered and sustained criticism of the prevailing ideologies and socializing pressures of the twentieth. Besides giving great satisfaction to the ecclesiastical authorities and to the Catholic laity, it has rendered valuable service to society as a whole, buttressing by its relative independence a precarious pluralism, enriching by its insistence on ultimate values an age of spiritual impoverishment.

---

notably Melbourne, Perth, and Adelaide, have established schemes for training lay teachers, if not to take over Catholic schools, at least to supplement the work of the religious. See *Advocate,* 13 January 1955, p. 3; 25 September 1958, p. 10, c.

[35] *Conc. Plen.,* IV, decrs. 606, 607.

[36] Since this was written strong measures have been taken in several dioceses to ensure financial backing for Catholic school projects: for example, the Catholic Schools Mutual Provident Funds in Melbourne, Wagga, Perth, and Hobart. *Advocate,* 25 September 1958, p. 10, c; 2 October 1958, p. 10, c.

[37] See pp. 462-3 and *Curriculum for Primary Schools,* Department of Education, N.S.W., p. viii.

[38] Since this was written a significant development has taken place in the Anglican Church in Victoria. Realizing the need for religious education, the members of the Melbourne Synod in 1958 adopted a motion which asserted 'the natural right of parents to obtain, if they so desire, a Church School education for their children' without (it was understood) being penalized financially for exercising this right. *Advocate,* 9 October 1958, p. 5, a.

Appendices

	NEW SOUTH WALES	TASMANIA	VICTORIA
1830			
	1836 Bourke's Church Act	1836 Report of Board of Inquiry 1838 Franklin's scheme 1839 Franklin's modified scheme	
1840	1839 Gipps's scheme		
	1844 Select Committee 1848 National and Denominational Boards established	1847 Denominational schools permitted by Denison	1848 Denominational Board established
1850			1851 National Board established
	1854 Select Committee 1855-6 Commission of Inquiry 1857 Non-vested schools admitted by National Board	1853 Select Committee	1852 Select Committee
1860		1860 Commission on Education	
	1866 Public Schools Act	1867 Royal Commission 1868 Public Schools Act	1862 Common Schools Act 1866-7 Royal Commission 1867 Higinbotham's Bill 1869 Proposals of T. H. Fellows
1870			1872 Education Act
1880	1880 Public Instruction Act		
		1882 Select Committee 1883 Royal Commission 1885 Education Act	1884 Royal Commission
1890			
1900			1899-1901 Fink Commission
	1903 Knibbs and Turner Commission (Report on Primary Schools) 1904 Knibbs and Turner Commission (Report on Secondary Schools)	1906 Registration of Teachers and Schools Act	1905 Registration of Teachers and Schools Act
1910	1912 Bursary Endowment Act		
1920			
1930			
1940			
1950			1950 Act allowing Religious Instruction in schools

SOUTH AUSTRALIA	WESTERN AUSTRALIA	QUEENSLAND	
			1830
			1840
1847 Public Education Act	1847 Board of Education established 1848 Separate grant to Catholic schools		
1851 Select Committee 1851-2 Education Act	1855-6 Withdrawal of separate grant to Catholic schools		1850
1861 Select Committee 1868 Select Committee		1860 Education Act Grammar Schools Act 1861 Select Committee	1860
1875 Education Act	1871 Select Committee 1871 Elementary Education Act	1874-5 Royal Commission 1875 State Education Act	1870
1881-3 Royal Commission			1880
1891 Education Act			1890
	1893 Education Act 1894 Joint Select Committee 1895 Education Act		
			1900
		1910 Act introducing Scripture reading	1910
			1920
			1930
1940 Act allowing Religious Instruction in schools			1940
1947 Act amending the above			1950

483

APPENDIX II

FOUNDATION OF CATHOLIC DIOCESES AND SUCCESSION OF BISHOPS

Time scale: 1830 – 1950

Sydney: POLDING · VAUGHAN · MORAN · [M.] KELLY · GILROY

Maitland: DAVIS · [J.J] MURRAY · [P.J] DWYER · GLEESON

Canberra and Goulburn: GEOGHEGAN→ · LANIGAN · GALLAGHER · [J.J] BARRY · McGUIRE

Bathurst: [M.J] QUINN · [J.P.] BYRNE · O'FARRELL · [J.M.] DUNNE · [J.F.J] NORTON

Armidale: O'MAHONY · TORREGGIANI · [P. J.] O'CONNOR · COLEMAN · DOODY

Lismore: DOYLE · CARROLL · FARRELLY →

Wilcannia-Forbes: [J.J] DUNNE · HAYDEN · FOX

Wagga Wagga: [J.J] DWYER · HENSCHKE

Hobart: WILLSON · [J.J] MURPHY · DELANY · [W.] BARRY · [W.] HAYDEN · SIMONDS · TWEEDY

Perth: BRADY (SERRA. Adm. Ap.) · GRIVER · GIBNEY · CLUNE · PRENDIVILLE

New Norcia: Mission established · Vicariate · SALVADO · TORRES · CATALAN · Pallotine Fathers

Kimberley: COPPO · RAIBLE

Geraldton: [W. B.] KELLY · CLUNE (A. A.) · [R.] RYAN · O'COLLINS · GUMMER

Chart of Roman Catholic bishops and archbishops by diocese, c. 1830–1950.

Diocese	Succession of bishops (earliest → latest)
Melbourne	GOOLD · CARR · MANNIX
Ballarat	[M.] O'CONNOR · MOORE · HIGGINS · FOLEY · O'COLLINS
Sandhurst	CRANE · REVILLE · McCARTHY
Sale	CORBETT · PHELAN · [R.] RYAN
Brisbane	[J.J.] QUINN · [R.] DUNNE · DUHIG
Rockhampton	CANI · HIGGINS · DUHIG · SHIEL · HAYES · TY-NAN
Toowoomba	[J.J.] BYRNE · ROPER
Townsville	McGUIRE · [H.J.] RYAN
Cairns	HUTCHINSON · [J.D.] MURRAY · HEAVEY · CAHILL →
Adelaide	[F.] MURPHY · GEOGHEGAN · SHEIL · REYNOLDS · O'REILLY · SPENCE · BEOVICH
Darwin	SALVADO / SERRA · *(European settlement abandoned 1849)* · GSELL · O'LOUGHLIN →
Port Augusta	O'REILLY · MAHER · [J.H.J.] NORTON · KILLIAN · GIL-ROY · McCABE

Time scale: 1830 · 1840 · 1850 · 1860 · 1870 · 1880 · 1890 · 1900 · 1910 · 1920 · 1930 · 1940 · 1950

APPENDIX III

The following is the outline presented by Father Tenison Woods at the inaugural meeting in 1867 and reported in the *South Australian Register,* 29 April 1867.

Catholic education shall in future be carried out by a Director-General, a Central Council, and Local Boards, under the respective local pastors.

All school property shall be vested in Trustees, to be appointed by the Bishop.

The Director-General shall inspect and report on schools, and regulate the mode of instruction to be given therein. He shall, in conjunction with the local pastor, submit to the Bishop the names of five persons as a Local Board of Management for each separate school in the diocese; but where the distance between the schools is not great two may be managed by one Local Board, if the Director General think it desirable. He shall certify to the fitness of teachers, and no person unless certified by him shall be eligible for appointment by the Central Council. He shall visit and examine all the schools of the diocese, or in very remote districts delegate others to the office. He shall report on sites for the purpose of school buildings, and all plans must be approved by him before being passed by the Council. He shall personally visit all school buildings, and approve of them before they shall be licensed as schools by the Council. He shall, in fine, be charged with all the details of the department of education in the diocese, and be its responsible head, appointed by the Bishop, and removable at his good pleasure.

The Bishop will also appoint a Central Council of Education, to consist of the Vicar-General, the Director-General, three clerical members, and five lay members. The Bishop, or in his absence the Vicar-General, shall be *ex officio* President. Three to form a quorum. The duties of the Central Council shall be:

1st. To frame general regulations for the distribution of money for education purposes.

2nd. To determine upon the localities in which schools receiving aid shall be maintained.

3rd. To frame general regulations for the inspection of schools, the examination and classification of teachers, to determine on the course of instruction to be adopted in the schools, and to fix, from time to time, the fees to be charged to parents of children, and generally to do everything that may be necessary to carry into effect the intentions of the Bishop to give to the children of the whole of his diocese a good religious training in the doctrines and practices of the Holy Catholic Church, with a sound secular instruction to fit them for their position in life, and their social duties to their fellow-colonists in the land of their adoption.

4th. To recommend to the Bishop, for appointment or removal, such officers as shall be deemed requisite for carrying out the regulations.

5th. To see that the moneys collected for the purposes of education be properly applied.

The Council shall meet once a month at the time and place they shall choose. An extraordinary meeting can be at any time convened by the Director-General. A Secretary can be appointed as an officer; the Director-General shall be the Treasurer, but orders for payment must be made by the President, the Treasurer, and one lay member of the Council.

Local Boards shall have power over their respective schools as far as visitation and supervision, as well as the admission of poor children; but any alteration in the teachers' methods of instruction or the established regulations can only be made with the consent of the Central Council; their members may, however, attend and speak at the Central Council, or formally delegate one of their number to do so, but without a vote. Local Boards shall also superintend the collection of local funds for educational purposes, which shall be lodged in the hands of their Treasurer, who will make payments only on the order of the Director-General; the local pastor may be the Treasurer, but shall be *ex officio* the President of every Local Board. The Local Board shall meet once a month, and appoint for the ensuing month one of their number to visit the schools once in the month together with the local pastor. They shall also, every six months, visit and examine the school, and report to the Central Council on the attendance, religious and secular instruction, etc.; and this visit shall not be made at the time of the visit of the Director-General, but be totally distinct from it.

A sermon in aid of education shall be preached morning and evening on one Sunday in every year throughout the diocese, and the moneys derived therefrom shall go into the general fund at the disposal of the Central Council.

By order of His Lordship,

J. E. Tenison Woods, *Secretary*

APPENDIX IV

RULES AND REGULATIONS OF THE CATHOLIC ASSOCIATION FOR THE PROMOTION OF RELIGION AND EDUCATION, NEW SOUTH WALES, 1867

These 'Rules and Regulations' were presented by the Reverend E. Luckie at a Public Meeting of Catholics in St Mary's Cathedral, 5 November 1867, and reported in the *Sydney Morning Herald*, 6 November 1867.

The object of this Association is to raise funds for the purpose of promoting the interests of religion and education in the Archdiocese of Sydney. The means of obtaining this object shall be:

1. The formation of local committees in each district consisting of the clergy and as many lay gentlemen as may be deemed advisable.

2. The establishment of a central council for the general management of the affairs of the Association, to consist of one priest and one lay member from each local committee in the city and suburbs.

3. The appointment by the local committee of a certain number of collectors to receive weekly subscriptions from one penny upwards.

4. Meetings of the central committee to be held on the first Thursday in each month at 8 p.m. in St. Mary's committee room.

5. The appointment of treasurers to the funds of the Association who shall be a priest who shall be named by His Grace the Archbishop and two lay gentlemen to be elected by the Central Council.

6. The funds shall be applied by His Grace the Archbishop, with the advice of the Central Council for the following purposes in the first instance:

   (i) To aid in the establishment of new Catholic primary schools as they may be required.

   (ii) To the assistance of existing schools where the provision made by the Government is inadequate.

   (iii) To establish and maintain a Catholic Training School for teachers.

   (iv) To invite from Europe and to aid in establishing here, competent teachers of religious congregations to take charge of the said training school, and also to conduct primary schools where provision can be made for them.

7. The monthly remittance to the treasurers of the Association of the amount raised in each district, which amount shall be recorded in the books or register of the Association.

8. The Central Committee shall elect two honorary secretaries, namely, one clergyman and one layman with a paid clerk (if necessary).

APPENDIX V

The following 'Minute of Committee' was issued by the Catholic Education Committee in Victoria, 1863. The accompanying letter to the clergy explains its purpose.

St. Francis',
Melbourne,
31st July, 1863.

Dear Rev. Sir,

As some of the schools in your district have already been deprived of Government assistance through their not having the average attendance required by the Board of Education, and as it is of the greatest importance not to allow them to be closed, I am directed by his Lordship the Bishop to forward to you the subjoined minute made at a meeting of the Catholic Education Committee yesterday.

(Signed) J. I. Bleasdale

Minute of Committee

In order that those schools which have been deprived of Government aid since 1st July, in consequence of not having had the required average attendance, may not be closed, the committee advise the clergy to adopt the following plans:

1. To obtain, where possible, married couples of which one is able to teach, while the other pursues his or her usual avocations.

2. To use their influence to induce Catholic parents to send their children to Catholic Schools, and to pay their school fees weekly, since the teacher has now to depend almost solely upon them for subsistence.

3. To make a collection once in each quarter, the proceeds to be given to the teacher at the end of each quarter as a subsidy, if the school has been conducted to the satisfaction of the local pastor.

4. To induce the charitably disposed, particularly the wealthy and those who have no families, to give their subscriptions in aid of local Catholic Education.

5. To lay before the Catholics of the school district accurate returns, every half-year, of all receipts and disbursements for the above purpose.

6. To keep rolls of attendance as nearly as possible in the usual form, and to make a return of the total number and average attendance, as well as the amount received from fees and subscriptions to this office at the end of each quarter.

7. Wherever there is a chance of establishing a new school, to do so without delay on the above plan; and in all cases to locate it in such a position as to leave Catholics the least pretence for sending their children to the Common School.

(Report of Royal Commission on Education (Vic.), 1867, evidence of Dr Goold, Appendix K, P.P.(Vic.), IV, p. 640.)

APPENDIX VI

School Regulations—Infant School

Opens at Nine O'Clock in Summer and at half-past Nine O'Clock in Winter.
No Child to be absent after that time.

Every Child to have clean Skin and Hair.

Clothes very tidy, and if old to be well mended.

No Child having Pock, Hooping Cough, or other infectious Disorder to be kept in School.

No Child to be kept kneeling for punishment longer than five minutes, or slapped on the right Hand.

Any Child knowingly putting out the Right Hand for punishment to get two slaps.

Corporal punishment is not prohibited for experience proves that over certain characters, it must be held *in terrorem* and occasionally inflicted. It should however be considered a bad sign when much punishment is required—a sign that either through the neglect of former Masters the proper spirit of discipline has been lost, or that the present are unfit for their situation. Let Corporal punishment even in a mitigated Form be seldom used.

Any Child not joining in the Exercises, Singing, etc., to be placed on a Seat before the Gallery until induced to imitate the rest.

Boys and Girls to sit apart.

Hats and Bonnets to be carefully deposited in the place appointed. A General Rule theoretically and practically to be inculcated is this: "Let there be a place for every thing, and every thing in place."

Memorandum

All assemble (in this Room) to Prayers. After Morning Prayers the Exercises, Singing, etc., are proceeded with. Instructions on Catechism and Tablets are given to the Children on their Seats. The Alphabet, Spelling and Reading Lessons are taught from the Tablets against the Wall. The Children being formed into Classes. Girls are taught Sewing. The Elder Children are sent into the Class Room during the time of Instruction on any subject intelligible to them, as Simple Arithmetic, Natural History, etc.

Class Room

1. Opens at Nine O'Clock in Summer, and half past Nine O'Clock in Winter. Any pupils absent at that time to lose their play for that day. As time allowed for recreation between the morning and evening classes is short, it is recommended that a Task be given, to be performed at Home, in case of absence.
2. Personal Cleanliness will be enforced.
3. Boys and Girls to sit apart.
4. Hats and Bonnets to be left orderly in their proper Place.
5. Any Pupils absent without leave to lose their play for one day.
6. Any Pupils staying from School without the knowledge of their Parents, after the third offence, and admonition to the Pupil and Parent or

Guardian shall be expelled, unless circumstances justify a departure from the Rule. On this as in every case of doubt and difficulty the Master or Mistress will consult with the Pastor and follow the directions given.

7. No boy to approach the Water Closets while the girls are in the play Ground. As a general Rule to be most religiously enforced only one Pupil is to be allowed to be absent for necessary purposes at a time. Let there be in each School a pass-board about four inches square. Let this be ordinarily on the Master or Mistresses' Desk; when a Pupil asks to retire let the Board be presented and the Master will absent or not as may be thought proper. In the absence of the Pass-Board leave will not be granted. But the habit of retiring from the School during study hours except in case of young children, is an idle habit ordinarily speaking which ought not be encouraged.

8. Silence to be observed in Classes, Halls and Passages, and when forming for Departure in the Evening.

9. All playthings, Knives, etc., in use during School Hours to be forfeited for a week, month, or three months according to circumstances.

10. Any Pupils absent from Mass on Sunday or Holyday of Obligation to lose their Play for three days.

11. Any Pupils leaving their Seats or otherwise disorderly when kept in for punishment to lose another day's play.

12. School Rooms to be swept every afternoon. Two girls to take the Duty in turn for a week.

Order of School Business

Nine O'Clock	Bell rings. Children assembled in the Play Ground come into School. Slates, etc., are given out, and arrangements made for the day.
Half past Nine	Prayers—The Lord's Prayer, Hail Mary, Apostles' Creed, Acts of Faith, Hope and Charity and Contrition. Prayers for the Archbishop, Queen, Faithful Departed, etc.
Quarter to Ten	Spelling Classes.
Half past Ten	Catechism Classes.
Eleven O'Clock	Arithmetic.
Twelve O'Clock	Angelus Domini, then Reading Classes.
One O'Clock	Recreation.
Two O'Clock	School called in. Grammar and Geography. The business of next day studied.
Quarter past Three	Prayers—The Lord's Prayer, Litany of the Blessed Virgin, etc. Scholars now dismissed for the day.

The Pastor or some one duly authorised by the Archbishop to give Religious Instructions for half an hour twice in each week.

Vacation

A Fortnight to be allowed at Christmass.
Two days at Easter.
At midwinter from the fifteenth of June to the first of July.

(Enclosure in letter, McEncroe to Chairman of Denominational Schools Board, 1848. D.S.B. (N.S.W.), Letters Inwards, no. 48/38, ML)

APPENDIX VII

STATEMENT OF 1866

(1) That as the principle of religious liberty and equality has been established in the constitution of this colony, we are entitled to expect the application of that principle in all measures regarding a general system of education.

(2) That the principle of religious liberty and equality would be violated if the Roman Catholic community was not adequately represented at the Central Board of Education and among the inspectors by Catholics enjoying the confidence of the Bishops.

(3) That as the Roman Catholic members of the Central Board and also the Roman Catholic inspectors are entrusted in the degree required by their office, with a certain representation and guardianship of Catholic faith and morals, their nomination to office should depend upon the Bishops of the Colony who are the guardians of faith and morals.

(4) That in Catholic schools attended by at least twenty-five children, conducted by an approved teacher, the patrons consist of the Catholic clergyman, and two of his congregation, and that these three shall have the right of recommending to the proper authority the removal of such teacher, and that in such schools the selection of the books rest with the Bishops.

(5) That in order to secure proper teachers, according to Catholic faith and morals, there should be a Catholic training school, approved for the purpose by the Bishops.

(6) The school lands shall be vested in the local patrons in trust.

(7) That the Government should determine and examine the qualifications of inspectors and teachers in secular subjects and satisfy itself of the proper application of the public money, should direct its equitable adjustment and also inspect all teaching in secular matters, the methods and the results in all the schools.

(8) That in mixed schools the formal religious instruction should be at appointed hours when only those are present for whom it is especially intended.

(9) That the function of the Central Board should be to see that the system is carried out according to certain defined rules and to the principles involved in such rules.

(*Resolutions of the Roman Catholic Clergy of the Archdiocese of Sydney,* forwarded to parliament, 16 July 1866.)

STATEMENT OF 1867

(1) The Roman Catholic Bishops of New South Wales beg to submit to the Government the following statement of their views on Primary Education in this colony.

In doing this they are influenced by no hostility to the present or any other Government. They are simply discharging a conscientious duty which they owe their flocks, whose faith they are bound to protect.

In order to avoid the possibility of a misunderstanding respecting what they require, they beg to state that they do not object to the Government satisfying itself as to the competency of the teachers, and ascertaining by inspection, that they discharge their duties efficiently. Neither do they object to the strictest supervision over the expenditure of public funds.

In places thinly populated they do not require separate schools.

They are satisfied with one Board, provided it be properly constituted.

What they require is:

1. Wherever the Roman Catholic children amount to the normal number to constitute a public school, the Roman Catholics may establish a separate school which shall be entitled to all the aid granted to public schools.

2. That in all schools the property of Roman Catholics, the right of appointment and dismissal of teachers shall belong to the managers of such schools.

3. That in mixed schools the Roman Catholic children shall not receive religious instruction, *moral* or *doctrinal*, in common with children of other denominations, nor in any case from a teacher not of their creed; and that no class books objectionable to Catholics shall be used in such schools.

4. That aid be granted for the training of Catholic teachers.

(2) The Roman Catholic Bishops cannot co-operate with any system of education that does not recognise the preceding principles. Moreover, they feel assured that a liberal Government will admit the justice of what they subjoin, namely:

1. A fair representation of the Catholic body in the Council of Education.

2. That school books of acknowledged merit as to secular knowledge, and approved by the Roman Catholic Bishops, should be provided by the Council of Education for Roman Catholic schools, on the same terms as class books are provided for other schools.

3. That to remove the suspicion of proselytism no child be allowed to attend religious instruction given in a school belonging to a religious denomination different from that of the child, except at the express request of its parent or guardian.

4. That the power of the Board should be executive, and not legislative, and thus the question of education be removed from the arena of politics.

From what has been stated, it is apparent that the Roman Catholic Bishops claim nothing for their co-religionists which they do not advocate for every section of the Community.

(*Views of the Roman Catholic Bishops of New South Wales on Primary Education*, as stated in a paper handed to the Colonial Secretary, Mr Parkes, on 21 July 1867.)

APPENDIX VIII

PROGRAMME AND METHOD FOLLOWED IN THE FIRST SCHOOLS OF THE SISTERS OF ST JOSEPH

The popularity of the schools of the Sisters of St Joseph in the first years of their existence is to be attributed largely to their improved organization. Some idea of this organization may be had from the original *Directory or Order of Discipline,* published between 1867 and 1869.

In the second lowest grade of the school the subjects were 'Reading (Part Second of the First Book), Hymns, Small Letters on Slates, Figures, and Prayers' (p. 84). In the second highest grade, the fourth, the pupils were to read English history, and 'learn same'; they were also to do ancient history, spelling by dictation, writing in copy-books, and arithmetic as far as proportion. Parsing was to be 'nicely entered in books according to the rules of syntax', and in addition to grammar. The pupils were to do Latin and Greek roots and 'Write easy essays'. Geography, which was to include mapping, was to be taken from the fourth class lessons as prescribed in the geography text. While the girls did plain and fancy needlework, the boys were to be taught 'Book-keeping by single entry'; double-entry, the first book of Euclid and mensuration were to be added in the top grade (p. 84; see details for 4th and 5th classes). The programme, which varied from day to day, was set down in detail for Monday, Tuesday, Wednesday, and Thursday, the Fridays being reserved for repetition in all classes. Thus, for the fifth class, the Monday's programme included grammar, Greek roots, ancient history, and poetry; the Tuesday's, geography, Latin roots, English history, and Irish history; the Wednesday's, grammar, spelling, ancient history, and prose; and the Thursday's, mathematical geography, English history, and Irish history (p. 85). The morning programme, the same for each day, was as follows (p. 86):

9.15   Hymn to St. Joseph, Morning Prayers and Dictation.
9.30   Writing.
10.00   Arithmetic.
11.00   Tasks.
12.00   Examination of Conscience, Angelus, Calling the Roll, and Catechism.
12.30   Recreation and Dinner.
1.30   Children Re-assemble.

The afternoon programme varied from day to day and from class to class as set out in the accompanying table.

The conduct of small schools on such time-tables was made possible by the use of a modified monitorial system, the details for the working of which were also set down in the *Directory.* The monitors were to be selected 'from the most advanced, orderly, and punctual of the children' (p. 81). Those appointed to this office were to endeavour by 'earnest attention, cheerful patience, and tidy, regular habits', to merit not only the approbation of their teachers but the love of their companions as well. One part of their duty was to be in attendance half an hour before the school opened in order to have the slates distributed and ruled. They were to maintain order, especially when marshalling pupils in small groups (p. 81) before the teacher for recitation (p. 82). To distinguish themselves from the rest the monitors were to wear a 'distinguishing cross of blue or red ribbon' (p. 82).

Besides relying on the help of monitors the Sisters were to cultivate a spirit

1.30	Children take their places, singing a hymn as they do so.					
	First Class		*Second Class*	*Third Class*	*Fourth Class*	*Fifth Class*
1.30 to 2.00	Little girls sew, boys copy on slates	1.00 to 2.00	TUESDAYS, WEDNESDAYS, AND FRIDAYS			
			Reading	Parse on slates	Reading	Parse, and enter same in books
2.00 to 2.15	Object Lesson	2.00 to 2.30	Copy from grammar or geography	Reading	Parse, and enter same in books	Reading
2.15 to 2.45	Make figures and letters on slates	1.30 to 3.30	MONDAYS AND THURSDAYS			
			Plain and fancy needlework. Boys — Book-keeping, etc.			
2.45 to 3.15	Spelling and reading lessons	2.30 to 3.00	TUESDAYS, WEDNESDAYS, AND FRIDAYS			
			Lecture or gallery lesson — that is, explanation of either maps or science charts, globes, etc.			
3.15 to 3.30	Exercises	3.00 to 3.30	TUESDAYS AND WEDNESDAYS			
			Mapping lessons			
		3.00 to 3.30	FRIDAYS			
			Darning and patching. Boys — Book-keeping, etc.			
3.30	Afternoon attendance marked and children dismissed, singing as they go out.					

Afternoon programme for the first schools of the Sisters of St Joseph, South Australia

of industry and application by fostering emulation: coercive methods were frowned upon. The best child of the week in each class was to wear a special ribbon, medal, or rosette. The ribbons themselves were to be of different colours, or of different widths, and were to be awarded, not for any particular phase of school work, but on the aggregate of regularity, obedience, tidiness, catechism, merit, and singing (pp. 81-2). Elaborate regulations for awarding marks in each of these areas were laid down. Thus, for regularity, two marks, morning and afternoon, were awarded to each child who attended or was ready to enter school when the bell sounded. Those who were late lost their marks, and, if late through their own fault, they received a bad mark, which was equivalent to losing five good ones (p. 83).

Other recommendations in the *Directory* referred to minor points on order and administration (p. 88). Those dealing with religion were the most detailed: they referred to religious instruction (p. 84), to the prayers to be said and the hymns to be sung at various periods throughout the day (p. 88, Art. 20), to preparation for the Sacraments (p. 88, Art. 9), to retreats for children, and to special devotions proper to certain feast days (p. 89).

Bibliography

The bibliography is arranged under manuscript and printed sources. These major divisions are further subdivided according to the following plan:

I. MANUSCRIPT SOURCES

    A. Official   *page* 497

    B. Educational   498

    C. Religious   501

    D. General   503

    E. Theses and Papers   504

II. PRINTED SOURCES

    A. Statutes   506

    B. Parliamentary Papers   507

    C. Religious   510

        I. Catholic

            (a) Acts and Decrees of Councils and Synods
            (b) Addresses and Speeches
            (c) Circulars, Notices, Reports
            (d) Pastoral Letters and Bishops' Official Statements
            (e) Roman Documents
            (f) Rules, Directories, etc., of Religious Orders

        II. Non-Catholic

            (a) Anglican
            (b) Congregational
            (c) Lutheran
            (d) Presbyterian
            (e) Wesleyan
            (f) Protestant Missionary Societies

    D. Newspapers and Journals   521

    E. Books and Pamphlets   526

    F. Bibliographies, Indexes, Directories   589

1. MANUSCRIPT SOURCES

Reference is made to specific documents in the footnotes. In the bibliography it has been impossible to include any more than a list of the sources and collections from which the documents in question are drawn.

A. OFFICIAL

Included under this heading are those sources relating to early colonial administration: colonial returns, colonial secretaries' correspondence, governors' duplicate despatches, etc.

New South Wales

Bigge, J. T., Commissioner. Appendix to Report. B. T. (ML)

Colonial Secretary's Correspondence, 1828-32 (ML)

Governor's Duplicate Despatches, 1818-41 (ML)

Petitions and Papers, Legislative Council, N.S.W.

Returns of the Colony (corresponding to the Blue Books in other colonies), 1825 (ML)

Tasmania

Blue Books and Returns for the Blue Books, 1826-55 (T-A)

Colonial Secretary's Files (T-A)
  a. Letters Inwards, 1832-61
  b. Letter Books (Clerical and Educational), 1830-44
  c. Index to Letters Inward (Arthur), 1824-36, M-Z
  d. Register Book (Arthur and Denison)
  e. Reports, in particular:
     1. Report of the Board of Inquiry upon the State of Government Schools in Hobart Town, 31 December 1835
     2. Report of Chief Magistrate on Schools in Hobart Town, 1836
     3. Report of Colonial Treasurer on schools in Hobart Town, 1836 (Arthur, 17847)

Governor's Duplicate Despatches, 1846-53 (T-A)

Minutes of Legislative Council, 1828-39 (T-A)

Victoria

Chief Secretary's Correspondence (V-A)
  a. Register Book, 1866
  b. Index to Letters Outwards, 1864-70
  c. Index to Letters Received, 1851-70

Colonial Superintendent's Correspondence (V-A)

Gipps—La Trobe Correspondence (v-A)

Returns from Port Phillip (Archives of Government Statist, Melbourne)

School Returns, 1842-7 (Archives of Government Statist, Melbourne). These returns were despatched each year to the Colonial Secretary's Office, Sydney. In 1858, W. H. Archer, the Registrar-General for Victoria, visited Sydney and brought back with him many of the earlier documents relating to Port Phillip. Among these were the School Returns in question.

South Australia

Colonial Secretary's Records (SA-A)
  Letters Inwards, 1836-51
  Letters Outwards, 1837-51

Governor's Duplicate Despatches, 1840-3 (SA-A)

South Australian Year Books (Blue Books), prepared for the Colonial Office, 1838-9 (SA-A)

Western Australia

Blue Books, 1837-95 (Registrar-General's Office, Perth)

Colonial Estimates of the Revenue and Expenditure, 1852, 1857, 1859-69 (WA-A)

Colonial Office Despatches, 1847-76 (WA-A)

Colonial Secretary's Office Records (WA-A)
  Index to Letters Inwards, 1839-43, 1849-78
  Index to Letters Outwards, 1829-37, 1849-78
  Letters Inwards, 1846-69
  Letters Outwards, 1849-56

Legislative Council Papers, 1868 (WA-A)

Returns for the Blue Books, 1867-71 (WA-A)

Queensland

Nomination of Trustees, 1869 (Registrar of Titles Office, Brisbane)

Register of Arrivals of Immigrants arriving in Moreton Bay, 1848-1923 (Registrar-General's Department, Brisbane)

B. EDUCATIONAL

In this section are included documents relating to the public boards, committees and councils administering education before the establishment of full government departments of education. The boards within each colony are listed chronologically.

New South Wales

Denominational Schools Board, 1848-66 (Records in Mitchell Library, Sydney)
  Inspectors' Reports, 1855-66
  Letters Inwards, 1848-66
  Letters Inwards Register, 1861
  Minute Books, 1856-63
  Rough Minute Books, 1861-6
  Queries from the Educational Board, 1847

National Board of Education, 1848-66 (Records in Mitchell Library, Sydney)
  Answers to Circulars, 1859, 1866
  Chief Inspectors' Outward Letters, 1859-62, 1865
  Letters Inwards, Miscellaneous, 1848-66
  Letters from District Inspectors, 1862-3
  Letters to Chief Inspector, 1855-7, 1859-62
  Letters from Colonial Secretary, 1848-51, 1859-63
  Minute Books, 1848-58, 1863-6
  Rough Minute Books, 1848-67
  Secretary's Outward Letters, 1861-2

Council of Public Education, 1866-79 (Records in Mitchell Library, Sydney)
  Index to Letters Inwards, 1867-9
  Index to Minute Books, 1867-76
  Inspectors' Reports on Roman Catholic Schools, 1873-5
  Inspectors' Reports, 1872-3, 1875, 1877
  Letters Inwards, 1867-76
  Letters Inwards, Miscellaneous, 1867
  Letters Outwards, 1868-1880
  Letters Outwards (Department of Justice and Public Instruction), 1873-80
  Matters dealt with by President, 1873-5
  Minute Books, 1868-9, 1871-8
  Rough Minute Books, 1874-80
  Secretary Wilkins' Private Letter Book, 1867, 1879

Tasmania

Board of Education, 1838-84 (Records in State Archives)
  Inspectors' Reports, 1850-3 (Reports of Thomas Arnold)
  Letter Books, 1848, 1857-85
  Rules and Regulations (later published in *Hobart Town Gazette*, 7 February, 1854, p. 153)

Victoria

Denominational Schools' Board, 1848-62 (Records in State Archives, Public Library of Victoria)

General Letter Book, 1857

Inspectors' Reports (Journal of Inspection), 1851

Letters Inwards Register, 1860-2 (volumes diversely labelled)

Letters Inwards, 1848-50 (answers to circulars)

Letters Outwards (Department of Justice and Public Instruction), 1873-80 visits, applications for aid, etc.)

Minute Books, 1848-62

Register of Teachers, containing lists of teachers and teachers' examination results, 1859-62

Reports of Examination of Teachers, 27 vols.

Board of National Education, 1851-62 (Records in State Archives, Public Library of Victoria)

Inspectors' Reports, 7 vols.

Minute Books, 1852-62

Special Returns relating to National Schools, 1851-62

Board of Education, 1862-72 (Records in State Archives, Public Library of Victoria).

Agenda Books, 7 vols.

Application for Aid to New Schools, 9 vols.

Common School Committees, vol. 3

Inspectors' Reports, 1863

Letters Inward, 1863, 1869

Letter Registers, 1862-72

Minute Books, 1862-72 (the last volume of this series becomes, on p. 202, the 'Orders and Decisions of the Minister of Public Instruction')
School Statistics, 1862-72

Education Department, from 1872 (Records in State Archives, Public Library of Victoria)

Minister's Order Book, vols. 2-4 (vol. 2 contains decisions on schools receiving capitation grant)

South Australia

South Australian School Society (Records in Archives Department, Public Library of South Australia)

First London Report of South Australian School Society, A 22, B 1,

Papers relating to South Australian School Society (9476)

Central Board of Education, 1852-75

Minute Books, April 1852—November 1875

Board of Education, after 1875
  Minute Book

Teachers' Guild of South Australia
  Minute Book, 1893-1904. After 1893 the Guild became 'The Collegiate Schools Association' (1224)

Western Australia

Committee of General Education, 1846-7 (Records in Archives Department, Public Library, Perth)
  Minute Book. (This becomes, after September 1847, the Minute Book of the General Board. Book 1 extends to 1856 and contains copies of outward correspondence up to September of that year.)
  Letter Book

General Board of Education, 1847-71 (Records in Archives Department, Public Library, Perth)
  Index to Correspondence, 1869-71
  Letters and Reports addressed to Colonial Secretary
  Letter Book, 1868-9
  Minute Book

Central Board of Education, 1871-93 (Records in Archives Department, Public Library, Perth)
  Albany District Board of Education, Minute Book, 1871-81
  Busselton District Board of Education, Minute Book, 1871-5
  Central Board Minute Books, 1873-93

Queensland

Board of General Education, 1860-75 (Records in John Oxley Memorial Library, Brisbane)
  Letter Books, vols. 1-7, 1870-5

C. RELIGIOUS

Included in this section are papers and documents found in ecclesiastical and religious institutions. The location of the document is given only in those cases where it cannot be inferred from the title.

New South Wales

Annals of Presentation Convent, Mt Erin, Wagga
Annals of Sisters of Mercy, Bathurst
Annals of St Patrick's College, Goulburn
Annals of Ursuline Convent, Armidale
Annals of the Marist Brothers, Mittagong
Benedictine Letters (St Mary's Cathedral Archives, Sydney)

Circulars to Clergy, 1883-6 (St Mary's Cathedral Archives)

Diocesan Correspondence, 1837-56 (St Mary's Cathedral Archives)

Minute Book of Catholic Education Board, Sydney (St Mary's Cathedral Archives)

Minute Book of the Conferences of the Clergy, Archdiocese of Sydney, 1872 (St Patrick's College Archives, Manly)

Rogers, J. W., Reports on Catholic Schools, 1883-4 (St Mary's Cathedral Archives. The 1883 report is in galley proof form.)

South Australian Letters, 1859-62 (St Mary's Cathedral Archives. These letters, of the Geoghegan-Sheil period in Adelaide, were taken to Sydney by Cardinal Moran when writing his *History of the Church in Australasia*. They still remain there. Duplicate copies have been made and may now be consulted in the Catholic Church Archives of South Australia.)

'State of the Mission' Reports, 1870-7 (St Mary's Cathedral Archives)

Therry Papers (Archives of Canisius College, Pymble)

Woods, Rev. Julian E. T., Rules for the Institute of Saint Joseph for the Catholic Education of Poor Children, 8 October 1867 (Archives of St Joseph's Convent, Mount Street, Sydney)

————Statement made by Father Woods on the Institute of the Sisters of St Joseph and his connection with it (Archives of St Joseph's Convent, Mount Street, Sydney). This statement is sometimes referred to as the 'Memoir'.

Tasmania

Annals of St Joseph's Convent, Hobart

Letters in Archives of Presentation Convent, Launceston

Victoria

Annals of St Patrick's College, Ballarat

Beovich, Archbishop M., 'Catholic Education and Catachetics in Australia'.

Report compiled for Conference on Education and Catachetics, Rome, 1950 (Catholic Education Office, Melbourne).

'Catholic Education.' Information Service, June 1951

Correspondence, Frayne to Goold, 1885 (Archives of St Patrick's Cathedral, Melbourne)

Letters and documents in files of the Catholic Education Office, Melbourne, 1943-51

Letters in Archives of Presentation Convent, Windsor

Minutes and Correspondence of Catholic Education Board, no. 2, 3 January 1860-May 1872 (St Patrick's Cathedral Archives)

Minute Book, Catholic Education Committee (same body as above, but books are labelled differently, finishing at 1866)

School Ledger, from 1860 (St Patrick's Cathedral Archives)

Minute Book of the General Council of the Sisters of St Joseph of the Sacred Heart, 1947 (Archives of St Joseph's Convent, Mount Street, Sydney)

South Australia

Annals of Christian Brothers' College, Wakefield Street, Adelaide

Documents and Letters in files of Catholic Education Office, Adelaide

Geoghegan, Bishop P. B., Correspondence 1860-2 (CCSA-A)

Kranewitter, letter to secretary, Missionary Society, Munich, 24 September 1853 (Archives of St Aloysius' College, Sevenhill)

Western Australia

Annals of Christian Brothers' College, Perth

Annals of the House, Sisters of St Joseph of the Apparition, Fremantle

Frayne, Mother Ursula, Recollections (typescript, Archives of Convent of Mercy, Victoria Square, Perth)

Sketches of the Mission (typescript, Convent of Mercy, Victoria Square, Perth)

Queensland

Annals of All Hallows' Convent, Brisbane

Annals of Christian Brothers' College, Gregory Terrace, Brisbane

Duhig, Archbishop James. Notes for a History of Catholic Church in Queensland (Archives of Archbishop's Palace, 'Wynberg', Brisbane)

Letters and other documents, 1861 (Archives of Archbishop's Palace, Brisbane)

Register of All Hallows' Convent, beginning at 1860

D. GENERAL

Documents in general collections. The location is given in each case.

Autograph Letters of Notable Australians, A 62, 68, 70 (ML)

Bonwick Transcripts: Bonwick Biography
                  Fulham Papers
                  Missionary Papers (ML)

Boucaut Papers (Education) 1876-7 (99) (SA-A)

Burton, Canon (ed.). Wollaston's Diaries, vol. iii (WA-A)

Deas Thomson Papers, A 1531-3 (ML)

Donaldson Ministry, Letters of, A 731 (ML)

Education Defence League of Victoria, Correspondence (ML)

Education, Papers on, A357 (ML)

Kirby Papers, 614/10 (ML)

Lang, Rev. J. Dunmore, Letters of, A 2227, vol. 7 (ML)

————Papers of, A 2221, vol. 1; A 586 (ML)

Marsden Papers, A 1992, C244 (ML)

Miscellaneous Papers re New South Wales, A 01, A 030, A 285, A 2146 (ML)

Parkes, Henry (Sir), Correspondence, A 911, A 915, A 919, A 924-6, A 929; vols. 12, 45 (ML)

————Papers on Education, A952 (ML)

Perry, Rt Rev. Charles, Address at Prize-giving, Melbourne Diocesan Grammar School, 1849 (V-A)

Redall Papers (ML)

Rusden Papers (V-A)

Society for the Repeal of the Fifty-Third Clause in the Victorian Constitution, Minute Book of the General Board (V-A)

School Register of Melbourne Diocesan Grammar School (V-A)

Spence, Catherine H., Notes of Sermons (in Unitarian Church) (SA-A)

Unitarian Church, Miscellaneous Circulars, 1880-1935. 1352, S.G., A1 (SA-A)

Wentworth Papers, A 753 (ML)

E. THESES AND PAPERS

Included in this section are theses submitted by graduate students at various universities and papers read before learned societies.

(a) Theses

Brown, Henry, 'The Development of the Public School System in South Australia, with special reference to the Education Act of 1851', University of Adelaide, 1940.

Burns, A. L., 'Historical Explanation', M.A. thesis, Schools of History and Philosophy, University of Melbourne, 1944.

Child, A. C., 'John Dunmore Lang—Some Aspects of His Work and Character' (ML).

Evatt, H. V., 'Liberalism in Australia', Beauchamp Essay, University of Sydney, 1915.

Fleming, Brian (S.J.), 'Leo XIII and Catholic Education', Master's thesis, University of Melbourne, 1952.

Gregory, J. S., 'Church and State in Victoria, 1851-1872', Master's thesis, University of Melbourne, 1951.

Ignatius Sr M., 'The Sisters of Mercy in Victoria'. (MS., Archives of Convent of Mercy, Geelong).

Jordan, Rev. Henry J. (M.S.C.), 'de Structura Juridica Paroeciarum Australiæ', Dissertatio ad Lauream in Facultate Juris Canonici, Pontifica Universitas Gregorina Romae, 1939.

Ingham, S. M., 'Some Aspects of Victorian Liberalism', Master's thesis, University of Melbourne, 1949.

McKenna, K. C., 'Progressivism and the Roman Catholic Schools', B.Ed. Investigation, University of Melbourne, 1951.

Morris, George, 'The Nature of the National Tradition', B.Ed. Investigation, University of Melbourne, 1945.

Nicholas, R. J., 'The Growth and Development of State Secondary Schools in South Australia', B.Ed. Investigation, University of Melbourne, 1949.

O'Brien, Eris M., 'The Early History of Education in New South Wales', Master's thesis, Irish National University, Dublin.

O'Donoghue, E. M. (Sr M. Xaverius), 'The Development of Catholic Schools in Queensland', Dip.Ed. Dissertation in University of Queensland, 1940.

Whitfield, L. F., 'The Age and Public Affairs', Master's thesis, University of Melbourne, 1950.

Wyeth, E. R., 'A History of Education in the Moreton Bay District of New South Wales and Queensland', M.Ed. thesis, University of Melbourne, 1943 (3 vols.).

(b) Papers

Australian Catholic Historical Society, Sydney (these records remain unpublished in the keeping of the Society's Secretary).

Aloysius, Rev. Brother, 'St John Baptist de la Salle and his Institute in Australia', 1951

Clare, Sr M., 'The Story of the Institute of the Good Samaritans', 1945

Cleary, P. S., 'Catholic Journalism', 1941

Corder, F. J., 'Church and State in Australia', 1944

Dennet, Rev. F. (S.J.), 'Riverview College', 1946

Dunstan, Wilson, Sr M., 'The Sisters of Charity in Australia', 1941

McCay, Rev. Mother, 'History of the Sacred Heart Convent, Rose Bay, 1944

McGrath, Brian J., 'William Augustine Duncan', 1948

McMahon, Rev. J. J. (M.S.C.), 'The History of Catholic Secondary Education in New South Wales', 1950

O'Brien, Eris M., 'Inaugural Address at the Society's Foundation', 1940

Regis, Rev. Mother, 'The Sisters of Mercy in Australia', 1942

Rupert, Rev. Brother, 'St Joseph's College', 1945

————'National Education in New South Wales', 1948

Scholastica, Rev. Mother, 'Origins of Catholic Education in Australia', 1942

Dunlop, E. J., 'Education in the Early Days of Queensland', Records of Queensland Historical Society, 1943, paper 148

Kiddle, J. Beacham, 'Melbourne Church of England Grammar School— Foundation Date' (prepared for Old Melburnians' Association), 1932

Morrison, Rev. R. A., 'The Story of Catholic Education in South Australia', 1844-64 (Catholic Church of South Australia Archives, Adelaide)

Suttor, T. L., 'The Position of Catholicism in Australia, 1840-1900' (paper read before the Research School of Social Sciences, The Australian National University, August 1958)

II. PRINTED SOURCES

A. STATUTES

Great Britain and Ireland
Act, 4 and 5 Gulielmi IV, c. 95, 1834
Act, 5 and 6 Victoriae, c. 76, 1842
Act, 13 Victoriae, c. 50, 1850

New South Wales
Act, 7 Gulielmi IV, no. iii, 1836
Act, 11 Victoriae, no. xlviii, 1848 (Incorporating the National Board)
Act, 30 Victoriae, no. xxii, 1866 (Public Schools Act)
Act, 43 Victoriae, no. xxiii, 1880 (Public Instruction Act)
Act, 2 Georgii V, 1912 (Bursary Board Act)

Tasmania
Government Notice, no. 247, 1838 (Appointing Board of Education)
Act, 32 Victoriae, no. xiv, 1868 (Public Schools Act)
Act, 49 Victoriae, no. xv, 1885
Act, 6 Edwardii VII, no. xv, 1906 (Registration Act)

Victoria

Act, 15 Victoriae, no. vii, 1851 (Incorporating National Board)
Act, 16 Victoriae, no. xxviii, 1853 (Aid to Ministers of Religion)
Act, 25 Victoriae, no. cxlix, 1862 (Common Schools Act)
Act, 32 Victoriae, no. xiv, 1868 (Public Schools Act)
Act, 36 Victoriae, no. cccxlvii, 1872 (Education Act, 1872)
Act, 43 Victoriae, no. xxvii, 1880 (Public Instruction Act)
Act, 49 Victoriae, no. xv, 1885 (Education Act, 1885)
Act, 5 Edwardii VII, no. 2013, 1905 (Registration Act)
Act, 15 Georgii VI, no. 5521, 1950 (Religious Instruction Act)

South Australia

Ordinance no. 10, 1847 (Church and Chapels)
Ordinance no. 11, 1847 (Schools)
Ordinance no. 20, 1851
Act, 15 Victoriae, no. xx, 1852
Act, 38 and 39 Victoriae, no. xi, 1875
Act, 41 and 42 Victoriae, no. cxxii, 1875
Act, 4 Georgii VI, no. xxxviii, 1940 (Religious Instruction)
Act, 11 Georgii VI, no. xxviii, 1947 (Religious Instruction)

Western Australia

Act, 35 Victoriae, no. xiv, 1871 (Elementary Education Act)
Act, 38 Victoriae, no. v, 1874
Act, 57 Victoriae, no. xvi, 1893
Act, 59 Victoriae, no. xxvii, 1895 (Abolishing Assisted Schools)

Queensland

Act, 24 Victoriae, no. vi, 1860 (Primary Education Act)
Act, 24 Victoriae, no. vii, 1860 (Grammar School Act)
Act, 39 Victoriae, no. xi, 1875
Act, 1 Georgii V, no. v, 1910 (Scripture Reading Act)

B. PARLIAMENTARY PAPERS

Great Britain and Ireland

Bigge, John Thomas, *Report on the Colony of New South Wales,* House of Commons, 1822 (First Report)

————*Report of the Commissioner of Inquiry on the Judicial Establishments of New South Wales and Van Diemen's Land,* 1823 (Second Report)

————Report of the Commissioner of Inquiry on the State of Agriculture and Trade in the Colony of New South Wales, 1823 (Third Report, dealing with ecclesiastical and educational matters.)

Colonial Office: Copies of extracts from despatches relative to the establishment of episcopal see in Australia. (December 1834-August 1849.) Bound as Parliamentary Documents, 1850, vol. 57, no. 6.

Correspondence relative to South Australia, 1841.

Report of the Select Committee on Transportation, 1812, Parliament of Great Britain and Ireland.

Report of the Select Committee on the State of Gaols, 1819, House of Commons: Parliamentary Documents, Great Britain and Ireland, 1819, II.

Report of the Select Committee on South Australia, with minutes of evidence, 1841, Parliament of Great Britain and Ireland, 1841.

Report of the Select Committee on Transportation, 1837-8. Parliament of Great Britain and Ireland, 1838.

Reports of the Commissioners of National Education in Ireland, 1835-9 (copies in General Library of the University of Melbourne).

Australian Colonies

Government Gazette

Parliamentary Debates

Parliamentary Papers, which comprise Votes and Proceedings, Journals, and Printed Papers.

In addition to addresses, motions and petitions submitted to parliament the above papers contain the regulations (Gazette), annual reports and statistical returns (Papers) of the various boards, councils, committees and departments of education. Only special reports, such as those of frequently quoted select committees, royal commissions and enquiries, are listed separately below.

New South Wales

Knibbs, G. H., and Turner, J. W., Interim Report of the Government Commissioners on certain parts of Primary Education, Sydney; Government Printer, 1903.

————Report of the Commissioners, mainly on Secondary Education. Sydney, Government Printer, 1904.

Report of the Select Committee on Education, with Appendix and Minutes of Evidence, 1844, P.P.(N.S.W.), 1844, II, p. 449.

Progress Report of the Select Committee on Education (N.S.W.), 1854, P.P.(N.S.W.), 1854, II, p. 221.

Report of the Select Committee on Education, with Minutes of Evidence, 1855, *P.P.*(N.S.W.), 1855, I, p. 1017.

Report (Final) of School Commissioners, 1856, *P.P.*(N.S.W.), 1856, II, pp. 87-118.

Report of the Sydney University, 1879, *P.P.*(N.S.W.), 1879-80, pp. 463ff.

State of Schools in New South Wales, 1858, *P.P.*(N.S.W.), 1859, IV, p. 543.

Statistics of Schools in New South Wales, 1859, *P.P.*(N.S.W.), 1859, IV.

Statistics of Schools in New South Wales, 6 March 1861, *P.P.*(N.S.W.), II, p. 751.

Tasmania

Report of the Board of Inspection of the State of the Public Schools of the Island, 1852.

Report of the Select Committee appointed to take into consideration the question of Public Education, 1853, *P.P.*(Tas.), 1853, paper 72.

Report of the Southern Board of Education, 1860.

Report of Commission on Superior Education, 1860. *P.P.*(Tas.), 1860, no. 18.

Report of Royal Commission on Education, 1867. *P.P.*(Tas.), 1867, paper 31.

Report of Select Committee on Education, 1882. *P.P.*(Tas.), 1882, paper 106.

Report of Royal Commission on Education, 1883, *P.P.*(Tas.), 1883, paper 70.

Technical Education in Tasmania—Report of the Commission appointed by the Premier and Minister of Education, 1916, *P.P.*(Tas.), 1916, paper 48.

Report of Royal Commission on the Education Department (Tas.). Interim Report, 1907, *P.P.*(Tas.), paper 49. Final Report, 1909, *P.P.*(Tas.), 1907, paper 1.

Report of Joint Select Committee of Both Houses of Parliament (on State Aid to Non-State Schools), 1952, *P.P.*(Tas.), 1952, paper 12.

Victoria

Report of Select Committee on Education, 1852, *P.P.*(Vic.), 1852, II, p. 639.

Return of the Number of Schools in operation in the Port Phillip District during 1850, *P.P.*(Vic.), 1851-2.

Report of Royal Commission on Education, 1866-7, *P.P.*(Vic.), 1867, IV, p. 257.

Report of Royal Commission on Education, 1881-4, *P.P.*(Vic.), 1884, III, p. 449.

Report of Royal Commission on Religious Instruction, 1900, *P.P.*(Vic.), 1900.

Report (Final) of the Royal Commission (Theodore Fink) on Technical Education, 1899-1901. Melbourne, Government Printer, 1901.

Report (of the Council of Public Education) on Educational Reform and Development in Victoria, Government Printer, 1945.

Report of the Council of Public Education, 1948, Melbourne, Government Printer, 1948.

Tate, Frank, *Preliminary Report upon observations made during an official visit to Europe and America, with recommendations referring to state education in Victoria.* Melbourne, Government Printer, 1908.

South Australia

Report of Select Committee of Legislative Council appointed to consider the propriety of bringing in a general educational measure, *P.P.*(S.A.), 1851, paper 14.

Report of Select Committee on Education, 1861, *P.P.*(S.A.), 1861, paper 131.

Report of Select Committee on Education, 1868, *P.P.*(S.A.), 1868, II, paper 56.

Report of Royal Commission on Education, 1881-4. Interim Reports 1881-2, *P.P.*(S.A.), paper 27; 1883-4, III, paper 27A.

Report of Competition between Government and Private Schools, *P.P.*(S.A.), 1890, IV, paper 152.

Report to the Minister of Education from the Inspector General of Schools on Scripture-reading in the schools of New South Wales (*Adelaide Observer,* 4 March 1893).

Western Australia

Report of Select Committee on Education, *P.P.*(W.A.), 1871.

Royal Commission on Education, 1887, *P.P.*(W.A.), 1887-8, paper 13.

Return of Lands granted to Religious Bodies between 1880 and 1891, *P.P.*(W.A.), 1890-1, paper A8.

Technical Education, Report of Committee, 1890-1, *P.P.*(W.A.), 1891, paper 40.

Report of Joint Select Committee of the Legislative Council and the Legislative Assembly appointed to consider the terms and conditions equitable to abolish the Assisted School System of Public Education, August 1895, *P.P.*(W.A.), 1895, II, paper A10.

Queensland

Primary School Statistics, 1869. *P.P.*(Q'ld.), 1869, I, p. 573.

Report of Select Committee on Education, 1861, *P.P.*(Q'ld.), 1861, I, p. 661.

Report of Royal Commission on Education, 1875, *P.P.*(Q'ld.), 1875, II, p. 83.

C. RELIGIOUS

I. CATHOLIC

(a) Acts and Decrees of Australian Councils and Synods

Acta et Decreta concilii primi provinciae Australiensis a Reverendissimo Archiepscope Sydneinsi una cum praesulibus provinciae suae suffraganeis, anno Domini MDCCCXLIV Pontificatus Gregorii Papæ XVI. A sancta sede approbata. Sydn., ex typis F.A. Row.

Acta et Decreta concilii primi provinciae Australiensis, 1844. Sydn., ex typis F. Cunninghame, 1847.

Acta et Decreta secundi concilii provincialis Australiensis, Diebus xviii-xxv, Aprilis, 1869. Printed with *Acta et Decreta* conciliorum Primi et secundi provincialium australiensium, etc. Melbourne, Advocate Office, 1891.

Acta et Decreta primae synodi diocesanae Melbournensis, Diebus x et xi Martii, 1875. Melbourne, Advocate Office, 1891.

Acta et Decreta secundae synodi diocesanae Melbournensis, Die Decimanona Melbournensis, Die Decimanona Maii, 1885. Melbourne, Advocate Office, 1891.

Acta et Decreta secundae synodi diocesanae Melbournensis, Die Decimanona Maii, 1885. Melbourne, Advocate Office, 1891.

Acta et Decreta tertiae synodi diocesanae Melbournensis, Die Decimasexta Novembris 1887. Melbourne, Advocate Office, 1887.

Acta et Decreta conciliorum primi et secundi provincialium Australiensium et synodorum primae, secundae, tertiae, quartae, quintae, et sextae, Diocesanarum Melbournensium. Melbourne, Advocate Office, 1891.

Acta et Decreta synodi provincialis Melbournensis primae apud Melbourne habitae 17-24 Novembris 1907. Melbourne, Advocate Office, 1907.

Acta et Decreta concilii plenarii australasiae, I, habiti apud Sydn., 1885. Sydney, F. Cunninghame, 1887.

Acta et Decreta concilii plenarii australiensis, II, habiti apud Sydn., 1895. Sydney F. Cunninghame, 1898.

Acta et Decreta concilii plenarii australiensis, III, habiti apud Sydn., 1905. Sydney, William Brooks, 1907.

Concilium Plenarium IV Australiae et Novae Zealandiae, habitum apud Sydn., 1937. Sydney, Manly Daily Press.

Decrees of the Fourth Plenary Council, which concern Religious and Catholic Schools. Published by the authority of the Archbishop of Sydney on Behalf of the Hierarchy of New South Wales. Sydney, St Vincent's Boys' Home Press.

Decrees of the Diocesan Synod of Sydney, 1891. Sydney, Finn Bros., 1891.

Decrees on Education adopted by the Archbishop and Bishops assembled in

Provincial Council at Melbourne, April, 1869. Printed in *Acta et Decreta secundi concilii provincialis Australiensis,* 1869. Reprinted by Advocate Office, 1891.

Diocese of Bathurst, Synodal Decrees on Education. *Record* (Bathurst), 16 January 1883, p. 38.

Statuta Synodalia pro Diocesi Goulburnensi, lecta, approbata, et promulgata a Reverendissimo D. Gulielmo Lanigan, Goulburnii, 1888.

Supplementum. Observanda quae addita fuerunt decretia primi concilii provincialis a Reverendissimo Archiepiscope et Episcopis Congregatis, 1 November 1862. Printed with *Acta et Decreta* primi concilii provincialis Australiensis.

Synodus Diocesana Maitlandensis, in Ecclesis Cathedrali S. Joannis Baptistae, in civitate Maitlandensi, Die 8a Augusti, 1888. West Maitland, T. Dimmock, 1888.

(b) Addresses and Speeches

Much useful and important documentation on the Catholic viewpoint and policy in the educational crises of the nineteenth century is to be found in the addresses and speeches delivered by members of the Hierarchy and other Catholic spokesmen of the time. Faced with the problem of keeping Catholics informed of their duties, sustaining morale and arousing enthusiasm for Catholic education, the Bishops made use of occasions such as the laying of the foundation stones or the openings of new schools to deliver their message to the people orally. Owing to the great number of these addresses, however, and to the fact that they have been fully documented in the footnotes, they have not been separately listed here.

(c) Circulars, Notices, Reports

Valuable documentation on the early development of the independent Catholic school system is to be found in these circulars and notices, and especially in the reports of individual colleges and the diocesan inspectors of schools. Most of these reports are to be found in the various Catholic newspapers of the time and are too numerous to list separately in the bibliography. Reports from the diocesan inspectors of the dioceses of Bathurst and Goulburn, for example, are to be found in the Bathurst *Record;* of the Victorian dioceses in the *Advocate;* of the archdiocese of Sydney in the *Freeman's Journal.* Likewise reports of the monthly meetings of the short-lived but important Central Council of Catholic Education in Adelaide are to be found in the monthly publications of the *Southern Cross and Catholic Herald* between the years 1867 and 1869. Except in a few cases, only those reports that were published as independent documents are listed separately in the bibliography.

Archdiocese of Sydney, Letter to the Clergy from Very Rev. S. J. A. Sheehy (v-G), 24 August 1867, *Sydney Morning Herald*, 24 November 1869, p. 5.

Archdiocese of Sydney, *Second Annual Report of the Catholic Association for the Promotion of Religion and Education*, 1869. Sydney, J. G. O'Connor, 1869.

Board of Registration, *Regulations for the Training and Registration of Catholic Primary Teachers, New South Wales*. Sydney, Lionel Flynn, 1931.

Catholic Education Association, *Reports of Teachers' Conferences*, 1927, 1928, 1933.

Catholic Education Board, *Annual Report*, Sydney, 1884. *Freeman's Journal*, 11 October 1884, p. 15, c.

Catholic Education Conference of New South Wales, 17-20 January 1911, *Statement, Resolutions, Proceedings*. Sydney, William Brooks, 1911.

Catholic Primary Schools, Reports, 1913-15. Sydney, William Brooks.

Catholic Secondary Schools Association of New South Wales, Constitution. Sydney, St Vincent's Boys' Home Press, 1947.

Dwyer, Rev. P. V., *Reports on the Primary Schools*, 1882-7, West Maitland, T. Dimmock.

Half-Yearly Report of St Mary's Seminary, Hobart, June 1874. Hobart Town, W. Fletcher, 1874.

Maher, Bishop of Port Augusta, *Circular to Clergy*, 3 April 1899. *Southern Cross*, 14 April 1899, p. 234.

Pronouncement of the Central Education Committee (S.A.), *Southern Cross*, 7 April 1899, p. 218 a, b.

Report of First National Catholic Education Conference of Catholic School Inspectors (Adelaide), 1936. Reprinted in Third Report.

Report of Second National Catholic Education Conference of Directors and Inspectors of Schools, Melbourne, 1939. Melbourne, Advocate Press, 1939.

Report of Third National Catholic Education Conference of Directors and Diocesan Inspectors of Schools, Sydney, 1944. Sydney, Verity Press, 1944.

Resolutions of the Catholic Clergy of the Archdiocese of Sydney forwarded to Parliament, 16 July 1866 (St Mary's Cathedral Archives).

Resolutions of the Clergy of the Archdiocese of Sydney on school texts, 13 June 1867. Printed in *Progress Report* of Council of Education, 1867.

Resolutions extracted from the Pastoral Address of the Archbishop and Bishops to the Catholic Clergy and People of Ireland, 1860 (document in St Mary's Cathedral Archives, Perth).

Statement of Priests of South Australia to Bishop Sheil, 1871. Printed in Byrne, Frederick, Rev., *History of the Catholic Church in South Australia*. Melbourne, E. W. Cole, 1896, pp. 217-18.

Views of the Roman Catholic Bishops of New South Wales on Primary Education as stated in a paper handed to the Colonial Secretary, Mr H. Parkes, 21 June 1867 (ML).

Woods, J. E. T., Rev., Report on Catholic Education read before Provincial Council, Melbourne, 1869. Published in *Southern Cross and Catholic Herald,* 20 June 1869, p. 337, b.

(d) Pastoral Letters and Bishops' Official Statements

Christian Education in a Democratic Community. Social Justice Statement, 1949. Published with the authority of the Archbishops and Bishops of the Catholic Church in Australia. Carnegie, Renown Press, 1949.

Corbett, Bishop, J., Lenten Pastoral, 1904. *Advocate,* 27 February 1904, p. 16, a, b.

Duhig, Archbishop James, Lenten Pastoral, 1919. *Argus* (Melbourne), 25 March 1919, p. 5, b.

Gallagher, Bishop John, Lenten Pastoral on Teaching Christian Doctrine, *Freeman's Journal,* 4 March 1904, p. 29.

Geoghegan, Bishop P. B., *Pastoral Letter to the Clergy and the Laity of the Diocese on the Education of Catholic Children.* Adelaide, G. Dehane, 1860.

Goold, Bishop James Alipius, Pastoral Letter, 1869. *Advocate,* 13 February 1869, p. 6.

————Pastoral Admonition, 1872. *Age,* 24 June 1872, p. 3, a.

————Pastoral Letter, 1879. *Advocate,* 17 February 1879, p. 6.

(Joint) Pastoral Letter of the Archbishop and Bishops exercising Jurisdiction in New South Wales, 1879. Sydney, Edward F. Flanagan, 1879.

Kelly, Archbishop Michael, *Pastoral Letter on Religious Education,* 3 December 1911. Sydney, William Brooks, 1911.

Lanigan, Bishop William, Pastoral Letter, 1879. *Record* (Bathurst), 15 April 1879, p. 180, a.

————Pastoral Letter, 13 August, 1879. *Record* (Bathurst), 1 September 1879, p. 404.

————Lenten Pastoral, 1884. *Catholic Standard* (Tas.), April 1884, p. 57, a.

Manning, Cardinal Henry Edward, *National Education and Parental Rights.* Melbourne, Catholic Book Depot, 1872. (This is a reprint of the London work.)

Murray, Bishop James, *Pastoral Letter to the Catholic Clergy and Laity of the Diocese of Maitland.* West Maitland, Henry Thomas, 1867.

————Pastoral Letter, 1873. *Freeman's Journal,* 20 December 1873, p. 11.

————Pastoral Letter, 1875. *Freeman's Journal,* 3 July, 1875, p. 14.

————Pastoral Letter, 1879. *Freeman's Journal*, 6 September 1879, pp. 17-18.

————Pastoral Letter, 1884. *Record* (Bathurst), 1 May 1884, p. 209.

Murphy, Bishop Daniel, *Pastoral Letter for Lent*, 1872. Hobart: Mercury Press, 1872.

————Pastoral for Lent, 1884, *Catholic Standard* (Tas.), 1884, pp. 1-3.

O'Reilly, Bishop John, *Pastoral Letter on Education*. Port Augusta: D. Drysdale, 1889.

Pastoral Letter of the Most Reverend the Archbishop and the Right Reverend the Bishops of the Province of Australia, in Council Assembled, 1 November 1862. Melbourne, Wilson and Mackinnon, 1862.

Pastoral Letter of the Archbishop and Bishops of the Province, assembled in the Second Provincial Council of Australia, 1869. *Advocate,* Supplement, 8 May, 1869.

Pastoral Letter of the Archbishops and Bishops of Australasia in Plenary Council Assembled, 1885. Sydney, F. Cunninghame, 1886.

Pastoral Letter of the Cardinal Delegate and of the Archbishops and Bishops of the Australian Commonwealth in Plenary Council Assembled, to the Clergy and Laity of their charge, 8 September 1905. *Austral Light,* October 1905, p. 704.

Pastoral Letter of the Archbishop and Bishops of the Province of Melbourne (First Provincial Council of Melbourne), 6 December, 1907. Australian Catholic Truth Society, Melbourne, Advocate Press, 1907.

Polding, J. B., Archbishop, *A Report containing the Pastoral Address of the Rt Reverend Bishop J. B. Polding.* Sydney, A. Cohen, Australasian Office, 1836.

————Pastoral Letter, 1839. *Australasian Chronicle,* 2 August 1839.

————*The Pastoral Letter of John Bede Polding,* Archbishop of Sydney and Metropolitan, to the Faithful Clergy and Laity of the Archdiocese, July 1860 (ML, 042, p. 206).

————*The Pastoral Letter of John Bede Polding, By Divine Grace, and Favour of the Holy Apostolic See . . . on the threatened amalgamation of the Catholic and Protestant orphan school.* Sydney, F. Cunninghame, 1873.

————*The Pastoral Letter of John Bede Polding, Apostolic See, Archbishop of Sydney,* 1876. Sydney, F. Cunninghame, 1876.

Quinn, Matthew, Bishop, Pastoral Letter of the Bishop of Bathurst to the Catholic Laity of the Diocese of Bathurst, 1867. *Times* (Bathurst), 20 March 1867, p. 2, e, f.

————Pastoral Letter to the Clergy and Laity of the Diocese of Bathurst, 1878. *Record* (Bathurst), Supplement, 1 July 1878.

————*Pastoral Letter to the Clergy and Laity of the Diocese of Bathurst.* Record Office, 1882.

Reville, Bishop, Lenten Pastoral, 1904. *Advocate,* 27 February 1904, p. 15, a.

Second Provincial Council, *The Pastoral Letter of the Archbishops and Bishops of the Province.* Melbourne, Clarson, Massina, 1869.

Sheehan, Archbishop M., 'The Official Pronouncement of the Catholic Hierarchy of Australia on the Education Question'. *Australasian Catholic Record,* xiv, January 1937, pp. 11-18.

Sheil, Bishop L., Pastoral Letter (written from Ireland). *Southern Cross and Catholic Herald,* 20 November 1867, pp. 37 ff.

————*Pastoral Letter of 1871. Irish Harp,* 14 October 1871, p. 6, a.

Vaughan, Archbishop Roger B., *Pius IX and the Revolution, A Pastoral Letter to the Clergy and the Laity of the Diocese of Sydney,* 1877.

————*Pastoral Letters on Education,* published by Edward F. Flanagan in Sydney:

No. 1,	10 August 1879	No. 4,	28 September 1879
No. 2,	24 August 1879	No. 5,	12 October 1879
No. 3,	7 September 1879		

————*Pastorals and Speeches on Education.* Sydney, Edward F. Flanagan, 1880.

————Lenten Pastoral, 1883. *Freeman's Journal,* 10 February 1883, p. 18.

Willson, Bishop R. W., *Pastoral Letter for Lent,* 1862. Hobart Town, William Fletcher, 1862.

————*Pastoral Letter for Lent,* 1865. Hobart Town, William Fletcher, 1865.

(e) *Roman Documents*

Christian Education of Youth (American edition of the Encyclical of Pius XI. 'Divini Illius Magistri'). New York, Paulist Press, 1929.

Codex Iuris Canonici (ed. Petro Cardinal Gasparri). Romae, Typis Polyglottis Vaticanis, 1917.

Codex Iuris Canonici (iussu digestus Benedicti Papae XV). New York, P. J. Kennedy and Sons, 1918.

Corpus Iuris Canonici. Pars Prior, Decretum Magistri Gratiani; Pars Secunda, Decretalium Collectiones. Editio Lipsiensis secunda. Lipsiae, ex Officina Bernhardi Tauchnitz, 1922.

Instructio ad supremos moderatores et moderatrices religiosarum laicarum familiarum de obligatione subditos in doctrina christiana rite imbuendi. Acta Apostolicae Sedis, 28 January 1930, p. 28.

Leonis XIII, Pontificis Maximi, *Acta*. Romae ex Typographia Vaticana (up to 1903, 23 vols.):

'Aeterni Patris', 4 August 1879.

'Affari Vos', 8 December 1897.

'Caritatis Studium', ad Archiepiscopos et Episcopos Scotiae.

'Constanti Hungarorum', ad Episcopos Hungariae, 2 September 1893.

'Epistola Apostolica' (review of his pontificate) ad patriarchos primates Archiepiscopos et Episcopos Orbis Catholici, 19 March 1902.

'Humanum Genus', 20 April 1884.

'Inscrutabili', 24 April 1878.

Letter to Cardinal Valetta, I.

Letter to Hungarian Bishops, 28 May 1896.

'Libertas Praestantissimum', 1888.

'Militantis Ecclesia.'

'Mirae Caritatis', 28 May 1902.

'Sapientiae Christianae', 10 January 1890.

Leonis XIII, Sanctissimi Domini Nostri, *Allocutiones, Epistolae, Constitutiones Aliaque Acta Praecipua*. Brugis et Insulis, Typis Societatis Sancti Augustini, Desclée, de Brouwer et Soc., 1887:

'De Augenda Re Christiana In Brazilia.'

'Immortale Dei', 1 November 1885.

Letter to Bavarian Bishops, 22 December 1887.

Mansi, Joannes Dominicus, *Sacrorum Conciliorum*. Paris, H. Welter, 1902 (editio iterata, facsimile, of the Antonium Zatta edition, Venice, 1749).

Pius IX, *Encyclical Letter of Our Holy Father the Pope*. Hobart Town; William Fletcher, 1865 (English translation of the 1864 Encyclical, and Syllabus).

————'Gravissimos inter', ad Gregor. Archiep. Mor. et Frising., 11 December 1862.

The Papal Encyclical and Syllabus (1864). London, Bradbury, Agnew and Co., 1875.

Pius X, 'Acerbo nimis', 1905.

Pius XI, 'Divini Illius Magistri', 31 December 1939. *Acta Apostolicae Sedis*, Romae, Typis Polyglottis Vaticanis, 1930.

————Ep. encyc. 'Casti Connubii', 31 December 1930. *Acta Apostolicae Sedis*. Romae, Typis Polyglottis Vaticanis, 1930, pp. 545 ff.

Pius XII, Allocution to First International Congress of Teaching Nuns, Rome, 1951. *Catholic Weekly,* 4 October 1951, p. 2, c.

Pius XII, Allocution on Education of the Conscience. *Advocate,* 10 April 1952, p. 5, a.

Pope and the People, The. Select Letters and Addresses on Social Questions—Popes Leo XIII, Pius X, Benedict XV, and Pius XI. London, Catholic Truth Society, 1932.

Sacra Congregatio Concilii, 'Decretum de Catechetica institutione impensius curanda et provehenda'. *Acta Apostolicae Sedis,* 1935, pp. 145-54. Sacred Congregation for the Propagation of the Faith, 'Instructions': 23 November 1845, n. 8; 7 May 1860, n. 1 (ad Archiep. Hiberniae); 25 May 1868; 8 September 1869, n. 37 (ad Vic. Ap. Ind. Orient); 18 December 1883, n. xi, 5, 6 (ad Ap. Sin.).

Sacred Congregation of the Holy Office, Instructiones ad Ep. Stat. Foeder. Americae Septentrion., 24 November 1875; 10 May 1884, n. 6.

Wynne, Rev. John J., *The Great Encyclicals of Pope Leo XIII.* New York, Benziger Bros., 1903.

(f) Rules, Directories, etc., of Religious Orders

CHRISTIAN BROTHERS OF THE SCHOOLS OF IRELAND

Directory and Rules of the Congregation. Dublin, 1927.

DE LA SALLE BROTHERS

Circulaires instructives et administratives. Romae, Maison Saint Joseph.

Management of the Christian Schools. New York, De La Salle Institute, 1887.

Règles Communes des Frères des Écoles Chrétiennes, Lembecq-Lez Hal, Maison Mère, 1923.

DOMINICAN SISTERS

Rule of Saint Augustine and the Constitutions of the Congregation of the Dominican Sisters of New South Wales, 1941.

INSTITUTE OF THE BLESSED VIRGIN MARY

Constitutions of the Institute of the Blessed Virgin Mary for the Houses dependent on the General Mother House, Rathfarnham, Dublin. Browne and Nolan, 1938.

Exhortations on the Rules of the Institute of the Blessed Virgin Mary, Melbourne, Advocate Press, 1910.

Usual Customs and Observances. Dublin, Browne and Nolan, 1914.

JESUITS

Constitutiones Societatis Jesu, 1858. London, J. G. and F. Rivington, 1858.

MARIST BROTHERS OF THE SCHOOLS

Calendrier Religieux. Saint Genis-Laval. Maison Mère des Frères Maristes, 1952.

Common Rules of the Institute of the Marist Brothers of the Schools (based on 1947 revision). Tournai (Belgium), Society of St John the Evangelist. Desclée & Co.

Constitutions et Règles du Gouvernement de l'Institut de Petits Frères de Marie. Lyon, Imprimerie X. Jevain. 1889.

Constitutions of the Institute (based on the revision approved by Rome in 1822). Dumfries, Courier and Herald Press, 1923.

Guide des Écoles. Lyon, Perisse Frères, 1853.

Guide des Écoles (2nd edition). Lyon, Librairie Catholique Emmanuel Vitte, 1923.

Guide des Écoles. Société de Saint Jean l' Evangéliste. Paris, Desclée et Cie, 1932.

Frère, Jean Baptiste, *Sentences, Leçons, Avis du Vénéré Père Champagnat.* Lyon, Imprimerie de V. J. Nicolle, 1868.

The Teachers' Guide of Principles of Education. Grugliasco, Mother House of the Marist Brothers, 1931.

RELIGIOUS OF THE SACRED HEART

Plan d'Études des Pensionnats de la Société du Sacré Coeur de Jesus. Tours, Maison Alfred Name et Fils, 1922.

Plan of Studies of Boarding Schools of Society of the Sacred Heart. Roehampton, Roehampton Press, 1931.

—————*The Society of the Sacred Heart* (4th edition). Chicago, Convent of the Sacred Heart, 1923.

SISTERS OF MERCY

Constitutions of the amalgamated houses of Victoria and Tasmania. Melbourne, J. Roy Stevens, 1918.

Customs and Directory. Dublin: (part of title page missing), 1865. In Archives of Convent of Mercy, Victoria Square, Perth.

The Rule and Constitutions of the Religious called Sisters of Mercy. Dublin, James Duffy (n.d.).

SISTERS OF SAINT JOSEPH OF THE SACRED HEART

McKillop, Mary (Mother Mary of the Cross). *Statement in Rome.* (This document is printed, but bears no date or title. It is recognized, however, as the document Mother Mary prepared on her first visit to Rome (1873). It was meant to appraise the Roman authorities of the conditions in Australia and of the measures taken by her Sisters to meet them.)

Customs and Practices. Sydney, The Mother House (printed by C. G. Meehan, Melbourne, 1950).

Directory of Order of Discipline, 1867-9. (This is only a fragment: the title page is missing, as also are several pages at the back. The present Secretary-General of the Institute places it before 1871, probably 1867-9. The fragment remains in the Archives of the Mother House of the Sisters of Saint Joseph of the Sacred Heart, North Sydney.)

URSULINES

Les Constitutions des Ursulines de la Congrégation de Paris. Clermont, Imprimerie de Thibaud-Landriot, 1840.

Rules and Constitutions of the Roman Union of Saint Ursula.

II. NON-CATHOLIC

(a) Anglican

Anglican Synod, 1865 (Tas.), 'Charge of the Bishop'. *Mercury*, 29 March 1865.

Barry, Bishop Alfred, *Three Sermons on Religious Education.* Sydney, Joseph Cook, 1884.

Broughton, Rev. W. G. *A letter in vindication of the Principles of the Reformation, addressed to Roger Therry, Esq., Commissioner of Court of Requests in New South Wales in consequence of a speech delivered by him in the Catholic Chapel at Sydney on July 29th, 1832.*

————*Pastoral Letter,* with declaratory protest in resistance to certain acts of the See of Rome, 1843. (Also in MS. form in N.S.W. Governor's Despatches, vol. 42, 1843, pp. 555-7, A1231. ML.)

————*Speech delivered to the Committee of Protestants,* 3 August 1836. Sydney, Stephens and Stokes, 1836, p. 4.

————*Speech in the Legislative Council upon the resolutions for establishing a system of general education,* 1839.

————*Take Heed,* a sermon preached in the female factory at Parramatta, June 1844.

Campbell, Rev. C., *Speech delivered in the Provincial Synod of the Church of England in N.S.W. on denominational education,* 1879.

Church of England, Proceedings of the First General Synod of the Dioceses of Australia and Tasmania. Sydney, Joseph Cook, 1873.

————*Digest of Acts and Resolutions passed in the Diocesan Synod of Tasmania.* Hobart Town, William Fletcher, 1868, 1871, 1876.

Gordon, A. and Stuart, A. *Speeches in the Provincial Synod of New South Wales on denominational education* (Church of England).

Minutes and Proceedings of a meeting of the Australian Bishops (Anglican) at Sydney, October 1850. Reported in *South Australian Register,* 8 February 1851, p. 3, c.

Moorhouse, Bishop James, Address to Church of England Synod (Melbourne), September 1878. *Age*, 19 September, p. 39; *Argus*, 18 September 1878, p. 6, c, d, e.

Nixon, Bishop F. R., *A Charge delivered to the Clergy of the Diocese of Tasmania*, April 1846. Hobart Town, William Gore Elliston, 1846.

Perry, Bishop Charles, *The School and the Schoolmaster*. Melbourne, George Robertson, 1860.

Proceedings of the Church of England Synod (Melbourne), 1878. *Age*, 28 September 1878, p. 7, b, e.

Proceedings of the Church of England Provincial Synod (Sydney), 1879. *Sydney Morning Herald*, 19 September 1879.

Reports of the Adelaide Diocesan Synod, 1855-61. In *Church of England Year Books*.

Report of the Diocesan Synod appointed to inquire into the existing state of education. *Church of England Synod Report of 1857*, p. 7.

Report of the Select Committee appointed by the Synod on the working of the Education Act in the Diocese of Newcastle, April 1869. West Maitland, Henry Thomas, 1869.

Report of Anglican Diocese of Perth (Bishop Hale), 1871. *Herald* (Fremantle), 3 June 1871.

Report of Anglican Synod, Melbourne, 19 November 1872. Supplement to the *Argus*, 5 December 1872, p. 2.

Report of the Church of England Diocesan Synod, Sydney, 1879. *Freeman's Journal*, 25 June 1879, p. 19, b.

Report of the Church of England Synod (Melbourne), September 1879, p. 6.

Report of the South Australian Church Society. Adelaide, Henry Hussey, 1849-50, 1852.

Report of the South Australian Diocesan Assembly for 1853. Adelaide, Hussey and Shawyer, 1854.

Rules for the Church of England Schools of the Middle District. Sydney, Kemp and Fairfax, 1850.

Short, Bishop A., Pastoral Letter of 1871. *Church of England Year Book*, 1871.

————Pastoral Letter of 1872. *Church of England Year Book*, 1872, p. 126.

(b) Congregational

Congregational Union, Victoria. Annual Conference, 1893. *Age*, 11 November 1893, p. 2.

Report of the Congregational Board of Education, 1848-9. London, Tyler and Reed, 1849, p. 7.

(c) *Lutheran*

Report of Lutheran Synod, S.A., 8 April, 1896. *Adelaide Observer*, 18 April, 1896, p. 15, a.

(d) *Presbyterian*

Minutes and Proceedings of the General Assembly (N.S.W.). Sydney, John Hutton, 1875-87.

Presbyterian Assembly, 1896, Debates. *Adelaide Observer*, 21 March 1896, p. 43, c.

Presbyterian Church, Queensland. *Minutes of Assembly*, 1906, 1909.

Proceedings of the Commission of the General Assembly of the Presbyterian Church of Victoria, May 1866.

Proceedings of the Commission of the General Assembly of the Presbyterian Church, 1869.

Proceedings of the General Council of Presbyterians, 1879. *Sydney Morning Herald*, 7 November 1879, p. 6, c.

Proceedings of the Presbyterian Assembly (Vic.), 12-21 November 1872. *Argus*, 5 December 1872, Supplement p. 2.

Proceedings of the Presbyterian Assembly (Q'ld.), 5-7 May 1873. See also *Brisbane Courier*, 20 March 1873.

Proceedings of the Presbyterian Assembly (Q'ld.), 1-11 May 1900.

(e) *Wesleyan*

Methodist Conference, Queensland. *Minutes of Annual Conference*, 1902.

Petition from Wesleyan Committee of Education, 23 September 1872.

Wesleyan Committee of Education, *Statement and Correspondence with the Government relative to Wesleyan Day Schools in Victoria*. Herald Office, 1856.

(f) *Protestant Missionary Societies*

A General View of the Origin and Objects of the Society for Promoting Christian Knowledge. (Extracts from the Society's Report, 1833.) Sydney, Stephens & Stokes, 1834.

Report of the Diocesan Committee of the Societies for the Propagation of the Gospel in Foreign Parts and for Promoting Christian Knowledge, 1837; and 1838. Sydney, the Society's Depositary, St James's Church, 1837, and 1838.

Report of the Society for Promoting Christian Knowledge. Hobart Town, James Ross, 1833.

Rules and Regulations of the District Committee of the Society for Pro-

moting Christian Knowledge, Established in New South Wales, 1826. Sydney, R. Howe, Government Printer, 1826.

Second Annual Report of the Van Diemen's Land Committee of the Societies for Promoting Christian Knowledge and for Propagating the Gospel in Foreign Parts. Hobart Town, William Gore Elliston, 1840.

D. NEWSPAPERS AND JOURNALS

I. NEWSPAPERS

New South Wales
Australian
Australian Banner
Australasian Chronicle
Australian Churchman [Anglican]
Australian Free Religious Press [Rationalist]
Catholic Press
Catholic Weekly
Chronicle
Church of England Messenger
Empire
Evening Post (Goulburn)
Express [Catholic]
Freeman's Journal [Catholic, not officially]
Gleaner
Liberal
Liberator
Record (Bathurst)
Stockwhip (in October 1876 it became the *Stockwhip and Satirist* which, in November of the same year, became the *Satirist*. All were Rationalist publications.)
Sydney Gazette
Sydney Morning Herald
Times (Bathurst)
Weekly Register
Weekly Times

Tasmania
Catholic Herald
Catholic Standard
Colonial Times
Cornwall Chronicle
Hobart Town Courier

Hobart Town Gazette
Mercury
Monitor (Launceston)
Morning Star
Tasmanian Messenger [Protestant]

Victoria

Age   Presbyterian Messenger
Argus   Victorian [Catholic]
Advocate [Catholic]   Independent [Congregationalist]
Port Phillip Gazette

South Australia
Adelaide Observer
Advertiser
Catholic Monthly
Chaplet and Southern Cross
Christian Weekly and Methodist Journal
Church Chronicle [Anglican]
Churchman [Anglican]
Irish Harp [Catholic]
Irish Harp and Catholic Herald
Irish Harp and Farmers' Herald
Methodist Journal (became, in 1881, the Christian Weekly, which, in
1901, became the Christian Commonwealth)
South Australian
South Australian Gazette and Colonial Register
South Australian Register
South Australian Wesleyan Magazine
South Australian Tablet
Southern Australian
Southern Cross

Western Australia
Australian Advertiser (Albany)
Catholic Record, from 1875
Church of England Magazine Newspaper
Daily News
Herald
Inquirer and Commercial News (1840-1901; incorporated in Daily News,
July 1901)
Perth Gazette (1833-54, 1856-74; incorporated in Western Australian Times,
July 1874)
Swan River News and Western Australian Chronicle (London, Edward
Colyer, ed. Alexander Andrews)
West Australian
Western Australian Journal
Western Australian Times (after 1879 the West Australian)

Queensland

Age [Catholic]	*Moreton Bay Courier*
Australian [Catholic]	*Queensland Evangelical Standard*
Brisbane Courier	*Queensland Guardian*
Catholic Leader	

II. JOURNALS

Austral Light

Cleary, D. J., 'The Marist Brothers of the Schools', February 1917, p. 70.

Cullen, Rev. J. H., 'The Early Days of the Church in Australia—Father Therry in Tasmania', February 1917, p. 13.

Hoare, Benjamin, 'Twenty Years of Catholic Education', 1907, p. 621, a.

————'Catholics and Politics', November 1914, p. 818.

Magner, Therese, 'The Education of our Girls', July 1903, p. 485, a.

Malone, Rev. M. P., 'Australian Catholic Federation', 1905, p. 501, 621.

'News and Notes', March 1911, p. 245, a.

O'Brien, Rev. A. E., 'Uniformity of Method in the Teaching of Christian Doctrine', March 1911, pp. 233, 323, 364.

Australasian Catholic Record

Carr, Archbishop Thomas, 'The Chuch and the Bible', 1895, p. 541.

————'The Progress of the Church in Australia', 1899, p. 217.

Cleary, P. S., 'Religious Instruction in National Education', January 1912, p. 53.

————'Secular Education in New South Wales', April 1911, p. 189.

Directions of the Sacred Congregation of the Council, 12 January 1930, vol. vii, no. 3, July 1930, p. 198.

Dwyer, Bishop P. V., 'The Marist Brothers and their Work in Australia', 1906, p. 461.

Forster, Marie, 'Lyndhurst and Benedictine Education', vols. xxiii-xxiv, 1946-7.

Hanrahan, Br M. B., 'The Teaching of Catechism', vols. i-ii, 1924-5.

'Letter of Pope Leo XIII to the Superiors General of Orders and Religious Institutes, 29 June 1901', 1901, p. 595.

McGovern, Rev. J., 'John Bede Polding' (series of biographical articles extending from 1934 to 1936).

McMahon, Rev. J. T., 'A Liturgical Programme for Schools', vol. viii, no. 4, October 1931, p. 297.

————'The Irish Renaissance in Christian Doctrine', vol. vi, no. 3, July 1929, p. 222.

————'Archbishop Sheehan's Book of Religion—A short commentary', vol. xii, no. 2, April 1935, p. 180.

————'Solving the Bush Problem in Australia', vol. viii, no. 1, January 1931, p. 42.

Moore, Rev. John (S. J.), 'Catholic History for Catholic Schools', vol. xxiv, no. 1, January 1947, p. 35.

McNamara, Rev. M., 'Father J. E. T. Woods and the Bathurst Foundation of the Sisters of St Joseph', vol. vii, no. 1, January 1930, p. 23.

O'Brien, Rev. A. E., 'The Practical Aim of Religious Teaching', vol. iii, no. 2, April 1926, pp. 125-8; and vol. vi, no. 2, April 1929, p. 130.

O'Brien, Rev. E. M., 'Catholic Church in Queensland, some McEncroe Letters', vol. vii, no. 3, July 1930, p. 204.

————'Catholic Emancipation applied to Australia', vol. vii, no. 1, January 1930, p. 32.

Pius XI, Motu Proprio, *Orbem Catholicum* (trans.), 'On the teaching of Christian Doctrine throughout the World', vol. ii, no. 1, January 1925, p. 5.

Power, A. (S.J.), 'Classics in Education', January 1901, p. 14.

Sacred Congregation of the Holy Office: on Sex Education, 21 March 1931 (trans.), vol. viii, no. 3, July 1931, p. 190.

Australian Quarterly

Gamba, C., 'A Papal Consul-General in Western Australia, 1846', vol. xxi, no. 4, December 1949, pp. 101-5.

Australian School Review (published monthly by J. J. Brown, Yass, N.S.W., 1873-4).

Christian Brothers' Educational Record

'A Few Notes and Observations on Mental Instruction', 1895, p. 171.

'Catechism, The', 1887, p. 10.

'Catholic Education in Australia', 1889, p. 188.

'Colonial Notes', 1895, p. 519.

'Education in South Australia', 1898, p. 6.

'Enactments of the School Committee' (Australia), 1892, p. 129.

H. B. O'H., 'State Education in Queensland', 1895.

'Is the Intermediate a Success in our Schools?', 1889, p. 165.

J. B. L. and J. P. O'M., 'A Short Sketch of the Christian Brothers' Institute, Australia', 1892, p. 101.

J. J. B., 'Educating versus Teaching', 1895, p. 188.

P. J. H., 'The Intermediate Examination System', 1893.

————'A Bit of Forgotten History', 1919, p. 52.

'Some Notable Incidents in Australia', 1919.

Spence, Archbishop, 'Australian Jubilee, 1868-1918'.

'University Examinations' (Australasia), 1898, p. 14.

Christian Brothers, *Our Studies*. Published in May and October by the Christian Brothers. Vol. i, no. 1, published from Nudgee College, Queensland, April 1929. Later published from Strathfield, New South Wales.

Current Affairs Bulletin, ed. J. L. J. Wilson. Sydney, Department of Tutorial Classes, vol. 22, no. 9, 25 August 1958.

Education Society Records (Sydney).
Spaull, G. T., 'Educational Aims and Work of Sir Henry Parkes', no. 43, 1920.

Historical Records of Australia. Series I, vols. vii-xxi; Series III, vol. vii. Individual documents referred to are not listed separately in the bibliography.

Historical Records of New South Wales, vols. i-vii. Individual documents referred to are not listed separately in the bibliography.

Holy Name Monthly. Melbourne, October 1957.

Journal and Proceedings of the Royal Australian Historical Society
Barker, S. K., 'Gipps and Education', vol. 16, 1930, p. 231.

Goodin, Vernon W. E., 'Public Education in New South Wales before 1848', vol. 36, 1950, pts. i-iv.

McGuanne, J. P., 'Early Schools of New South Wales', vol. 2, 1906, pts. iii-iv, p. 70.

————'Early School Days in New South Wales.' Paper read before R.A.H.S., 10 October 1906 (ML).

Smith, S. H., 'William Timothy Cape and other Pioneers of Secondary Education in Australia', vol. 5, 1919, pt. v, p. 201.

Wood, F. L., 'Some Early Educational Problems and W. C. Wentworth's Work for Higher Education', vol. 17, 1931, pt. vi, p. 268.

Journal and Proceedings of Western Australian Historical Society
Ewers, John K., 'John Kennedy and the Board of Education', new series, vol. 9, December 1947, p. 10.

Marist Brothers of the Schools, *Bulletin de l'Institut* (published quarterly in French at Mother House of the Institute in France).

————*Bulletin of Studies* (published annually at Mittagong, N.S.W.).

Melbourne Review

'Those Catholic Claims', vol. x, 1885, p. 66.

Schooling (Sydney Teachers' College)

Hirst, E., 'The Church and School Corporation', vol. vii, no. 5, July 1924.

Lynch, M. L., 'Education under Macquarie', vol. viii, 1925, pp. 150-3, 193-5.

Victorian Review

Blair, David, 'A Last Word on the Education Question', 1879, p. 13.

Clarke, Marcus, 'Civilisation without Delusion', November 1879—April 1880, p. 65.

Hogan, J. F., 'The Collapse of the Bible League', vol. viii, no. xl, February 1883.

Pearson, Professor Charles, 'The Education Question', vol. iii, no. xiv, December 1880, p. 141.

Perry, Bishop Charles, 'Civilisation without Delusion: a Reply', December 1879, p. 242.

E. BOOKS AND PAMPHLETS

Address delivered in Connection with the opening of the New Unitarian Church, Melbourne. Melbourne, George Robertson, 1887.

Anderson, Francis, *Tendencies of Modern Education with some Proposals of Reform.* Sydney, Angus and Robertson, 1909.

————*The Public School System of New South Wales.* Sydney, Angus and Robertson, 1909.

Annals of the Propagation of the Faith, vols. v-vi. London, 1844-5 (published for the Institution).

Anselm, Sr M. (O.P.), *Catholic Evidence Guild in Secondary Schools.* Sydney, E. J. Dwyer, 1939.

All Hallows' Convent School Magazine, *The Arches of the Years,* 1933.

Arithmetic for Secondary Schools. Strathfield, the Christian Brothers, 1929.

Arnold, Thomas, *Passages in a Wandering Life.* London, Edward Arnold, 1900.

Australian Labor Party—Constitution and Platform. Carlton, according to the amendments of the Annual Conference, 1927.

Badham, Charles, *Primary Education—A Letter to Mr Bede Dalley.* Sydney, Gibbs, Shallard (n.d.).

Baierl, Joseph J., Bandas, Rudolph G., and Collins, Joseph, *Religious Instruction and Education.* New York, Joseph F. Wagner, 1938.

Bandas, Rudolph G., *Catechetics in the New Testament*. Milwaukee, the Bruce Publishing Co., 1935.

Barnard, H. C., *A Short History of English Education*. London University Press, 1947.

————*Little Schools of Port Royal*. Cambridge University Press, 1913.

————*The Port Royalists on Education*, Cambridge University Press, 1918.

Battersby, Rev. W. J., *De La Salle, A Pioneer of Modern Education*. London, Longmans Green, 1949.

————'Educational Work of the Religious Orders of Women', *The English Catholics* (ed. Rt Rev. G. A. Beck). London, Burns Oates, 1950, pp. 337-64.

Battye, J. S., *Western Australia—A History from its Discovery to the Inauguration of the Commonwealth*. Oxford, Clarendon Press, 1924.

Bavin, Sir Thomas, *Sir Henry Parkes: his Life and Works* (John Murtagh Macrossan Lectures for 1940, University of Queensland), Sydney, Angus and Robertson, 1941.

Beechinor, Rev. Michael, *Memoir of Archbishop Murphy*. Launceston, Tabart Bros., 1916.

Beovich, Archbishop Matthew, 'Religious Instruction: its place in the Catholic Schools', *Australian Catholic Education Congress, 1936*. Melbourne, Advocate Press, 1937.

Bible Instruction in State Schools. Melbourne, the Bible in State Schools League, 1906.

Birt, Rev. Henry Norbert (O.S.B.), *Benedictine Pioneers in Australia*. 2 vols., London, Herbert and Daniel, 1911.

Blacket, Rev. John, *A South Australian Romance: How a Colony was founded and a Methodist Church was formed*. London, Charles H. Kelly, 1899.

Bleasdale, Rev. J. I., *Practical Education: A Survey of Its Present Conditions on the Continent of Europe and in Great Britain*. Technical Commission of Victoria. Melbourne, Mason and Firth, 1869.

Board of Education, *Curriculum and Examinations in Secondary Schools* (Report of the Committee of the Secondary School Examinations Council appointed by the President of the Board of Education, 1941). London, His Majesty's Stationery Office, 1943.

————*The Education of the Adolescent*. (Report of the Consultative Committee.) London, H.M. Stationery Office, 1926.

————*Grammar Schools and Technical High Schools* (Report of the Consultative Committee). London, H. M. Stationery Office, 1938.

————*The Primary School* (Report of the Consultative Committee). London, H.M. Stationery Office, 1931.

Bonwick, James, *Australia's First Preacher, the Rev. Richard Johnson.* London, Sampson Low, Marston and Company, 1898.

————*Curious Facts of Old Colonial Days.* London, Sampson Low, Son and Marston, 1870.

————*First Twenty Years of Australia.* London, Sampson Low, Marston, Searle and Rivington, 1882.

Boyce, Rev. F. B., *Letters in Defence of Denominational Schools.* Sydney, Geo. Loxton.

Brodrick, Rev. James (S.J.), *The Progress of the Jesuits, 1556-79.* London, Longmans, Green & Co., 1946.

Browne, G. S., *The Case for the Curriculum Revision.* Melbourne University Press, 1932.

Browne, Spencer, *A Journalist's Memories.* Brisbane, the Read Press, 1927.

Brubacher, John S., *A History of the Problems of Education.* New York, McGraw-Hill, 1947.

Burgmann, Bishop Ernest Henry, *Education of an Australian.* Sydney, Angus and Robertson, 1944.

Burke-Savage, Rev. Roland (S.J.), *Catherine McAuley.* Dublin, M. H. Gill and Son, 1949.

Burton, Canon A., *Hale School, Perth* (published privately). Perth, 1939.

Burton, Judge William, *The State of Religion and Education in New South Wales.* London, J. Cross and Simpkin and Marshall, 1840.

Byrne, Rev. Frederick, *History of the Catholic Church in South Australia.* Melbourne, E. W. Cole, 1896.

Cam, Rev. A. B., *Phases of Unitarianism, Orthodoxy, and Freethought in Sydney.* Sydney, Robert Bone, 1885.

Campbell, Rev. Colin, *History of Public Education in Victoria.* Melbourne, Melville, Mullen and Slade, 1896.

————*The Education Question: Its Present Position and the Roman Catholic Claims.* Melbourne, Melville, Mullen and Slade, 1898.

————*Remarks on National Education* (with reference to the Colony of Victoria). Melbourne, B. Lucas, 1853.

Carey, Rev. P., *Christian Doctrine Notes.* Sydney, E. J. Dwyer, 1941.

Catechism, The. Approved by the Plenary Council of Australasia. Dublin, M. H. Gill, 1886.

Catechism, The. Sydney, Finn Bros., 1891.

Catechism, The. Dublin, M. H. Gill, 1902.

Catechism, The. Approved by the Cardinal delegate, Archbishops, and Bishops of the Australian Commonwealth in Plenary Council assembled. Sydney, Catholic Book Depot, St Mary's Cathedral, 1905.

Catechism, The. Sydney, Louis Gille, 1920.

Catechism of Christian Doctrine (adapted for Australia by 2nd and 3rd Plenary Councils). Sydney, St Vincent's Boys' Home Press, 1939.

Catechism (issued with Episcopal Authority on the Occasion of the 4th Plenary Council, 1937). Melbourne, Australian Catholic Truth Society, 1938.

Catholic Faith, The. Sydney, E. J. Dwyer, 1942.

Catholic History Readers. Melbourne, Catholic Education Office, 1951, pts. i-vi.

Catholic Schools of Victoria, *Syllabus of Religious Instruction.* Melbourne, Advocate Press, 1950.

Cathrein, Rev. Victore (S.J.), *Philosophie Moralis.* Friburgi Brisgoviae, Sumptibus Herder, Typographi Editoris Pontificii, 1900.

Century of Charity in Tasmania, A. Hobart, Sisters of Charity, 1947.

Christian Brothers, *Souvenir cf Golden Jubilee in Australasia,* Sydney, W. Brooks and Co., 1918.

Clark, C. H. M., *Select Documents in Australian History, 1851-1900.* Sydney, Angus and Robertson, 1955.

Cleary, P. S., 'The Obligation of the State to Catholic Schools', *Australian Catholic Education Congress.* Melbourne, Advocate Press, 1936.

Cole, E. W., *In Defence of Mental Freedom.* Melbourne, E. W. Cole, Book Arcade, 1917 (first edition, 1868).

————('Edwic'), *Mental Freedom Necessary to the Welfare of Man.* Melbourne, Robert Bell, 1869.

————('Edwic'), *The Real Place in History of Jesus and Paul.* Melbourne, E. W. Cole, 1860.

Coleridge, Rev. Henry James (S.J.), *St Mary's Convent, Micklegate Bar, York.* London, Burns, Oates, and Washbourne, 1887.

Concilii Plenarii Baltimorensis II, Acta et Decreta. Baltimore: Excudebant Johannes Murphy, 1868.

Connell, W. F., *The Educational Thought and Influence of Matthew Arnold.* London, Routledge and Kegan Paul, 1950.

Conway, Rev. James, 'Catholic Education in the United States', *Second Australasian Catholic Congress.* Melbourne, 1915.

Corrigan, Rev. Br Urban, *Catholic Education in New South Wales.* Sydney, Angus and Robertson, 1930.

————*The Achievements of Catholic Education in Australia.* Sydney, E. J. Dwyer, 1937.

Cubberley, Ellwood P., *The History of Education.* Cambridge, Houghton Mifflin, 1920.

Cullen, J. H., *The Australian Daughters of Mary Aikenhead: A Century of Charity, 1838-1938.* Sydney, Pellegrini, 1938.

Curriculum for Primary Schools, Department of Education, N.S.W. Sydney, Government Printer, 1952.

Curtis, S. J., *History of Education in Great Britain.* London, University Tutorial Press, 1948.

Davitt, Arthur, *National Education.* Melbourne, Wilson, Mackinson and Fairfax, 1856.

Deharbe's Catechism of the Catholic Religion (for use in the Schools of the Diocese of Adelaide). Adelaide, Advertiser General Printing Office, 1882.

De Sales, Mother, M., 'Teaching of Religion in Primary Schools', *Australian Catholic Education Congress, 1936.* Melbourne, Advocate Press, 1937, pp. 420-31.

Dewey, John, *Democracy and Education.* New York, Macmillan, 1916.

————*Reconstruction in Philosophy.* University of London Press, 1921.

Digby, Everard (ed.), *Australian Men of Mark.* Sydney, Charles F. Maxwell, 1889.

Donnelly, Rev. Francis P. (S.J.), *Principles of Jesuit Education in Practice.* Chicago, P. J. Kennedy and Sons, 1934.

Drinkwater, Rev. F. H., *Teaching the Catechism.* London, Burns, Oates and Washbourne, 1939.

Duffy, Sir Charles Gavan, *My Life in Two Hemispheres.* London, T. Fisher Unwin, 1898.

Duncan, W. A., *Lecture on National Education.* Brisbane, James Swan, 1850.

Dwyer, Bishop P. V., *What steps may be taken to advance the interests of our religious primary and higher schools?* (Paper read before the Catholic Congress at St Patrick's College, Manly, 1901.) Privately printed.

Echoes from St Stanislaus', Bathurst, vol. i, no. 1, December 1889, and vol. viii, no. 9, December 1912.

Edmund Ignatius Rice and the Christian Brothers (by a Christian Brother). Dublin, M. H. Gill and Son, 1926.

Education Act Defence League (Victoria). Pamphlet found among Education Act Defence League Correspondence (ML).

Elliott, W. J., *Secondary Education in New South Wales.* Melbourne University Press, 1935.

Emilie de Vialar, Fondatrice de la Congrégation de Soeurs de St Joseph de l'Apparition. Marseille, l'Oratoire Saint-Léon, 1901.

English Reports, The, vol. 24. London, William Green, 1903.

Essays and Reviews. London, Longmans, Green and Roberts, 1861 (8th ed.).

Farrell, Rev. Allen (S.J.), *The Jesuit Code of Liberal Education.* Milwaukee, the Bruce Publishing Co., 1938.

Fitzpatrick, Rev. E. A., *St Ignatius and the Ratio Studiorum.* New York, McGraw-Hill, 1933.

Fitzpatrick, Kathleen, *Sir John Franklin in Tasmania.* Melbourne University Press, 1949.

Fraser, Rev. James, *The Common School System of the U.S.A. and Canada* (Report to the Commissioners appointed by Her Majesty to inquire into the education systems of Great Britain). Sydney, Thomas Richards, Government Printer, 1868.

'Garryowen' (Edmund Finn), *The Chronicles of Early Melbourne.* Melbourne, Ferguson, Mitchell, 1888.

Gollan, Kenneth, *The Organization and Administration of Education in New South Wales.* Sydney Teachers' College Press, 1924.

Goulter, M. C., *Schoolday Memories.* London, Burns, Oates and Washbourne, 1922.

Greenwood, Rev. James, *New South Wales Public School League, for Making Primary Education National, Compulsory, Secular and Free—Summary of Facts and Principles.* Sydney, F. Cunninghame, 1874.

————*Speech in reply to the Hon. Henry Parkes,* 4 December 1874 (reprint from *Sydney Morning Herald,* 5 December 1874). Sydney, F. Cunninghame, 1874.

Guérin, Bella, 'Higher Education for Women', *Loreto Eucalyptus Blossoms.* Ballarat, F. W. Niven, 1886, p. 7.

Hall, Rev. John, *History of St Stanislaus' College, Bathurst.* Bathurst, St Stanislaus' College, 1944.

Halloran, Laurence, *Proposals for the Support of a Public Free Grammar School in the Town of Sydney, N.S.W.* Sydney, R. Howe, Government Printer, 1825.

Handbook of Public and Matriculation Examinations, University of Melbourne, 1948.

Hanley, Br A. B., 'Catholic Technical Schools in Australia', *Australian Catholic Education Congress.* Melbourne, Advocate Press, 1937, pp. 308-16.

Hannan, Rev. James, 'The National Catholic Correspondence Course', *Australian Catholic Education Congress, 1936.* Melbourne, Advocate Press, 1937, pp. 345-58.

Hans, Nicholas, *Comparative Education: a Study of Educational Factors and Traditions*. London, Routledge and Kegan Paul, 1949.

Harper, Rev. Andrew, *The Honourable James Balfour*. Australia, Critchley Parker, 1918.

'Herald and Education, The.' *A Century of Journalism*. Sydney, John Fairfax and Sons, 1931.

Herment, Jules, *Les Idées Pédagogiques de Saint Jean Baptiste de la Salle*. Paris, P. Lethielleux, 1932.

History of Australia and New Zealand for Catholic Schools. Australia, the Christian Brothers, 1932.

Hovre, Rev. Francis de, *Le Catholicisme: ses Pédagogues et sa Pédagogie*. Bruxelles, Librairie Albert Dewitt, 1930.

How Shall the State Promote Education? (Reprint from the *Tasmanian Church Chronicle*, August 1852). Tasmania, H. and C. Best, 1852.

I.B.V.M., *Annual Magazine of the Australian Loreto Convents*. Ballarat, John Fraser, 1901.

I.B.V.M., Loreto Convent, Mary's Mount, Ballarat. *A Retrospect*. Programme of Concert and Prize List. Ballarat, James Curtis, 1885.

John Baptist, Rev. Brother, *Life of Marcellin-Joseph-Benedict Champagnat*. Paris, Society of St John the Evangelist, Desclée and Co., 1947.

Jose, Rev. G. H., 'Religion'. *The Centenary History of South Australia*. Adelaide Royal Geographical Society of Australasia, South Australian Branch, 1936.

Jeffries, Rev. J. T., and Canon Smith, *The Roman Catholic Church and the Education Question*, being Archbishop Vaughan's Pastoral and Replies thereto. Brisbane, William Rowney, 1879.

Kandel, I. L., *History of Secondary Education*. Cambridge (U.S.A.), Riverside Press, 1930.

Kenny, Rev. Dean, *A History of the Commencement and Progress of Catholicity in Australia up to 1840*, Sydney, 1886.

Kelsh, Rev. Thomas, *Personal Recollections of the Rt Rev. R. W. Willson*. Hobart, Davies Bros., 1882.

La Nauze, J. A., *Political Economy in Australia*. Melbourne University Press, 1949.

Lang, Rev. John D., *An Historical and Statistical Account of New South Wales*. London, Sampson Low, Marston, and Searle, 1875 (4th ed.).

————*Historical and Statistical Account of New South Wales*. London, Cochrane and McCrone, 1834.

————*Popery in Australia and How to Check It*. Edinburgh, 1847.

————*Public Schools Act and its Romish Recusants.* Sydney, Robert Downing, 1868.

Leach, A. F., *Educational Charters and Documents.* London, Cambridge University Press, 1911.

————*English Schools at the Reformation.* London, Archibald Constable and Co., 1894.

————*History of Winchester College.* London, Duckworth and Co., 1899.

Lemire, C., *L'instruction publique nationale, laïque, obligatoire, et gratuite en Australie.* Paris, Challamel, 1885.

Life of Mother Mary, Foundress of the Sisterhood of St Joseph of the Sacred Heart. (By a Sister of St Joseph.) Sydney, St Vincent's Boys' Home Press, 1916.

Linz, C. C., *The Establishment of a National System of Education in New South Wales,* Educational Research Series, no. 51. Melbourne University Press, 1938.

Loch, John D., *An Account of the Introduction and Effects of the System of General Religious Education Established in Van Diemen's Land.* Hobart Town, J. C. MacDougall, 1843.

Loreto Abbey, *Prospectus* (undated). Archives of Loreto Abbey, Ballarat.

Loreto Eucalyptus Blossoms, December 1886. Ballarat, F. W. Niven, 1886.

Lowndes, G. A. N., *The Silent Social Revolution.* London, Oxford University Press, 1937.

Lynch, Rev. P. J., *Liturgical Catechism.* Sydney, E. J. Dwyer, 1940.

Macarthur, James, *New South Wales—Its Present State and Future Prospects.* London, D. Walker, 1837.

McCay, Mother (gen. ed.), *Early and Mediaeval History.* Sydney, E. J. Dwyer, 1947.

McGucken, Rev. William J. (S.J.), *The Jesuits and Education.* Milwaukee, the Bruce Publishing Co., 1932.

MacInerney, Rev. M. P. (O.P.), *Liberalism in Religion.* Melbourne, Australian Catholic Truth Society, 1910.

Mackenzie, T. Findlay, *Nationalism and Education in Australia.* London, P. S. King and Son, 1935.

McKiernan, Mother Justin, *The Order of Saint Ursula.* New York, Ursuline Provincialate, 1945.

Mackle, Francis, *The Footprints of Our Catholic Pioneers.* Melbourne, Advocate Press (n.d.).

McMahon, Rev John T., *Liturgy for the Classroom,* 1934.

————*The Perth Plan for Teaching Religion by Correspondence*. Dublin, Browne and Nolan, 1928.

————*Pray the Mass*. Sydney, Pellegrini, 1951.

————'Religious Instruction of Country Children where there are no Catholic Schools', *Australian Catholic Education Congress, 1936*. Melbourne, Advocate Press, 1937, pp. 332-44.

————*Some Methods of Teaching Religion*. London, Burns, Oates and Washbourne, 1928.

McSorley, Joseph, *An Outline of the History of the Church by Centuries*. New York, Herder, 1948.

Mahoney, E. J., 'Christian Marriage', *The Teaching of the Catholic Church* (ed. G. Smith). London, Burns, Oates and Washbourne, 1948.

'Marist Brothers' Centenary Year Celebrations', *Cerise and Blue and St Joseph's College Magazine*, 1917.

Maritain, Jacques, *Education at the Cross Roads*. New Haven, Yale University Press, 1944.

Martin, Marie de Saint Jean (O.S.U.), *Ursuline Method of Education*. New Jersey, Quinn and Boden, 1946.

Mary's Mount, *Annual Magazine*. Ballarat, John Graser, 1901.

Mayer, Mary Helen, *The Philosophy of Teaching of St Thomas Aquinas*. Milwaukee, the Bruce Publishing Co., 1928.

Mennel, Philip, *The Dictionary of Australasian Biography*. London, Hutchinson, 1892.

Mercy Centenary Record. Melbourne, Advocate Press, 1931.

Mercy, Sisters of, *Brief History of the Goulburn Foundation*. Goulburn, R. Johnstone, 1931.

Michie, Sir A., *Observations of the Working of the Victorian Education Act and on the Alleged Roman Catholic Grievance*. Melbourne, George Robertson, 1885.

Monica, Sister M., *Angela Merici and Her Teaching Idea*. New York, Longmans, Green, 1927.

Monroe, Paul, *A Brief Course in the History of Education*. London, Macmillan, 1925.

Monahan, M., *Saint Madeline Sophie*. London, Longmans, Green, 1925.

Montmorency, J. E. G. de, *National Education and National Life*. London, Swan Sonnenschein, 1906.

————*State Intervention in English Education*. Cambridge University Press, 1902.

Moran, Cardinal Patrick F., *History of the Catholic Church in Australasia*. Sydney, the Oceanic Publishing Co.

Morgan, J. A., and Price, A., *Architecture for Intermediate Students*. Sydney, Shakespeare Head Press, 1949.

Morris, Edward E., *A Memoir of George Higinbotham*. London, Macmillan and Co., 1895.

Murtagh, Rev. James G., *Australia, The Catholic Chapter*. New York, Sheed and Ward, 1946, 2nd edition, Sydney, Angus and Robertson, 1959.

Neville, Rev. W. P. (ed.), *Addresses to Cardinal Newman with his Replies, 1879-81*. London, Longmans, Green, 1905.

Newman, J. H., *Apologia pro vita sua*. London, Oxford University Press, 1913.

'Nonconformists and Primary Education', *The Christian Witness*. London, 1868.

Nudgee College Jubilee, Queensland, 1941.

O'Brien, Archbishop Eris M., *Life and Letters of Archpriest John Joseph Therry*. Sydney, Angus and Robertson, 1922.

————*The Dawn of Catholicism in Australia*. Sydney, Angus and Robertson, 1928.

————*Foundation of Australia, 1786-1800*: a study in English Criminal Practice and Penal Colonization in the Eighteenth Century. London, Sheed and Ward, 1937.

O'Connor, J. G., *A Brief History of the Sacred Heart Presentation Convent, Wagga*. Sydney, J. G. O'Connor, 1881.

O'Connor, Rev. T. J., 'Religious Instruction in State Schools in Cities and Towns where there are Catholic Schools'. *Catholic Education Congress, 1936*. Melbourne, Advocate Press, 1937, pp. 359-64.

O'Hanlon, Sister Assumpta. *Dominican Pioneers in New South Wales*. Sydney, Australian Publishing Co., 1949.

O'Leary, Margaret, *Education with a Tradition*. London, University of London Press, 1936.

O'Neill, Rev. George (S.J.), *Life of Mother Mary of The Cross*. Melbourne, Pellegrini, 1931.

————*Life of the Reverend Julian Edmund Tenison Woods, 1832-1889*. Melbourne, Pellegrini, 1929.

Parkes, Sir Henry, *Fifty Years in the Making of Australian History*, 2 vols. London, Longmans, Green, 1892. (This appears as a 2-volume edition and a single-volume edition, with different pagination. The 2-volume edition has been used in this work.)

————*Irish Immigration* (speech in Legislative Assembly, opposing second reading of 'A Bill to authorize and regulate Assisted Immigration'). Sydney, S. E. Lees, 1869.

————*Mr Gladstone and English Liberalism from an Australian Point of View.* Sydney, Lee and Ross, 1878.

————*Speech Delivered in the Legislative Assembly,* 18 June 1875. Sydney, Gibbs, Shallard, 1875.

————*Speeches.* Melbourne, George Robertson, 1876.

Perry, Bishop Charles, *Science and the Bible.* Melbourne, Samuel Mullen, 1869.

Plan of a company to be established for the purpose of founding a colony in South Australia. London, Ridway and Sons, 1831.

The Political Platform of Mr A. Michie for Election, 1856 (Victorian Pamphlet, vol. 33, Public Library of Victoria).

Portus, G. V., *Free, Compulsory, and Secular—A Critical Estimate of Australian Education,* Studies and Reports, no. 11. University of London, Institute of Education. London, Oxford University Press, 1937.

Presentation Convent, Wagga. *Souvenir of Golden Jubilee, 1874-1924.*

Rankin, D. H., *The History of the Development of Education in Victoria.* Melbourne, The Arrow Printery, 1939.

Reeves, Clifford, *A History of Tasmanian Education,* Educational Research Series, no. 40. Melbourne University Press, 1935.

Refresher School in Christian Doctrine. Melbourne, Advocate Press, 1950.

Reilly, J. T., *Reminiscences of Fifty Years' Residence in Western Australia.* Perth, Sands and MacDougall, 1903.

Replies to Essays and Reviews. Oxford and London, John Henry and James Parker, 1862.

Report of Council of Public Education, Victoria. Melbourne, J. J. Gourley, Government Printer, 1948.

Robertson, Rev. Andrew, *Letter to the Hon. James McCulloch on the Education Question.* Melbourne, 1868.

Robertson, Charles, *Objections to a System of Free Education for the People.* London, for the Congregational Board of Education, John Stow (n.d.).

Rowland, E. C., *A Century of the English Church in New South Wales.* Sydney, Angus and Robertson, 1948.

Rumble, Rev. L., *Catholics Ask for Justice.* Melbourne, Australian Catholic Truth Society, 1937.

Rusden, G. W., *History of Australia.* London, Chapman Hall, 1883.

————*National Education.* Melbourne, the *Argus,* 1853.

Rusden, H. K., *Inquest into the Death of Christianity as a Practical Force.* Melbourne, J. Wing, 1884.

————('Hokor'), *Morality and Theology* (essay read before the Sunday Free Discussion Society, 5 November 1871). Melbourne, Robert Bell, 1871.

————*Moral Responsibility* (read before the Royal Society, 24 February 1868). Kew, Stillwell and Knight, 1868.

————*Paul* (read before the Sunday Free Discussion Society). Melbourne, Robert Bell, 1870.

————*Piety and Pilfering* (read and debated at the Free Discussion Society's Meetings on Sunday, 4 December 1881). Melbourne, J. Wing, 1881.

————*Selection: National and Artificial* (lecture delivered in Wangaratta, 26 October 1874). Beechworth, Richard Warden, 1874.

————*Science and Theology* (essay addressed to the Rev. A. M. Henderson). Melbourne, Robert Bell, 1870.

————('Hokor'), *Sin* (essay read before the Sunday Free Discussion Society, Sunday, 23 April 1871). Melbourne, Robert Bell, 1871.

————('Hokor'), *The Bishop of Melbourne's Theory of Education*. Melbourne, Robert Bell, 1871.

————('Hokor'), *The Person, Character, and Teaching of Jesus* (lay sermon read to the Sunday Free Discussion Society, 6 October 1872). Melbourne, H. Thomas, 1872.

————*The Power of the Pulpit* (lay sermon delivered before the Sunday Free Discussion Society, 28 January 1877). Melbourne, E. Purton, 1877.

————(Prometheus Unbound), *The Only True and Effective Moral Sanction*. Melbourne, A. H. Massina, 1903.

Ryan, T., *Educational Ideals of the Labour Party of South Australia*. Adelaide, the *Daily Herald*, 1910.

Ryan, Rev. Wilfrid (S.J.), 'The Story of Catholic Education in South Australia'. *Australian Catholic Education Congress*. Melbourne, Advocate Press, 1936.

St Ignatius' College, Riverview. *Prospectus*. Sydney, F. Cunninghame, 1887. *St Joseph's College Annual*, Hunter's Hill, N.S.W., 1951.

St Thomas Aquinas, *Summa Contra Gentes* (English translation). London, Burns, Oates and Washbourne, 1923.

————*Summa Theologica* (trans. by English Dominicans). London, R. and T. Washbourne, 1914.

————*Quaestiones Disputatae*. Parmae, Typis Petri Fiaccadori, 1859.

South Australian Bible Christian Magazine. Adelaide, 1867-84.

Sharp, John K., *Aims and Methods in Teaching Religion*. New York, Benziger Bros., 1929.

Sheehan, Archbishop Michael, *A Child's Book of Religion*. Dublin, M. H. Gill, 1934.

Sketch of the Life and Labours of the Rt Rev. Dr O'Quinn, First Bishop of Brisbane. Brisbane, the *Australian* Printing Office, 1881.

Smeaton, Thomas Hyland, *Education in South Australia from 1836 to 1927*. Adelaide, Rigby, 1927.

Smith, S. B., *Elements of Ecclesiastical Law*. New York, Benziger Bros., 1895.

Smith, S. H., *Brief History of Education in Australia, 1788-1848*. Sydney, Angus and Robertson, 1917.

Smith, S. H., and Spaull, G. T., *History of Education in New South Wales, 1788-1925*. Sydney, George B. Philip and Son, 1925.

Spencer, Herbert, *Education: Intellectual, Moral and Physical*. London, Williams and Norgate, 1891.

Stephens, John, *The History of the Rise and Progress of the New British Province of South Australia*. London, Smith, Elder, Cornhill, 1839.

Stuart, Janet Erskine, *The Education of Catholic Girls*. London, Longmans, Green, 1911.

Sweetman, Edward, Long, Charles R., and Smyth, John, *A History of State Education in Victoria*. Melbourne, Critchley Parker, 1922.

Sweetman, Edward, *Victoria's First Public Educationist*, Educational Research Series, no. 55. Melbourne University Press, 1939.

Subiaco, Benedictine Sisters, Rydalmere.

Supreme Court of Victoria, *The Australian Jurist Report* (ed. P. S. Davis). Melbourne, J. and A. McKinley, 1873.

Symons, Rev. John C., *Education for Victoria*. Melbourne, George Nichols, 1857.

Therry, Roger, *Explanation of the Plan of the Irish National Schools, showing its peculiar adaptation to New South Wales*. Sydney, A. Cohen, 1836.

——————*Reminiscences of Thirty Years' Residence in New South Wales and Victoria*. London, Sampson Low, Son and Co., 1863 (2nd ed.).

Thorpe, Fr Osmund (C.P.), *Mary McKillop*. London, Burns Oates, 1957. 1957.

Tyerman, J., *Hidden Springs Uncovered* (three lectures delivered by Mr John Tyerman in the Victoria Theatre in reply to Archbishop Vaughan's Pamphlet, *Hidden Springs*). Sydney, John Ferguson, 1876.

Ullathorne, Archbishop W. B., *From Cabin Boy to Archbishop* (autobiography). London, Burns and Oates, 1941.

——————*Memoir of Bishop Willson*. London, Burns, Oates, and Washbourne, 1887.

————'Mission de l'Australie.' *Annales de le Propagation de la Foi.* A Lyon, chez l'Editeur des Annales. Juillet 1838, no. lix, pp. 419-78.

————*Reply to Judge Burton of the Supreme Court of New South Wales on 'The State of Religion in the Colony'.* Sydney, W. A. Duncan, 1840.

————*The Catholic Mission in Australia.* Liverpool, Rockliff and Duckworth, 1837 (2nd ed.).

Ursulines, The. London Catholic Truth Society, 1917.

Vaughan, Archbishop Roger B., *Hidden Springs: Or Perils of the Future and How to Meet Them* (address by Vaughan at the opening of the Catholic Guild Hall, Sydney, 1876). Sydney, Edward F. Flanagan, 1876.

————*Higher Education* (inaugural address at St John's College within the University of Sydney). Sydney, J. J. Moore, 1875.

————*The Life and Labours of St Thomas of Aquin.* London, Longmans, Green, vol. i, 1871; vol. ii, 1872.

Wentworth, W. C., *A Statistical, Historical and Political Description of the Colony of New South Wales.* London, G. and W. B. Whittaker, 1819.

————*A Statistical Account of the British Settlements in Australasia.* London, Geo. B. Whittaker, 1824.

Whateley, E. J., *Life and Correspondence of Richard Whateley, D.D.* London, Longmans, Green, 1866.

White, Rev. James S., *Lecture on Education: National, Secular, Compulsory, and Free.* West Maitland, Henry Thomas, 1875.

————*Lecture on Education: National, Secular, Compulsory and Free* (reply to the Rev. Dr McGibbon). West Maitland, Henry Thomas, 1875.

————*Lecture on Education.* Singleton, Thomas B. Boyce, 1876.

Whitington, Rev. F. T., *Augustus Short: First Bishop of Adelaide.* Adelaide, E. S. Wigg and Son, 1887.

————*William Grant Broughton.* Sydney, Angus and Robertson, 1936.

Wight, Rev. Geo., *Congregational Independency: Its Introduction to Queensland.* Brisbane, Gordon and Gotch.

Wilkins, W., *National Education: and Exposition of National System of New South Wales.* Sydney, Alexander W. Douglas, 1865.

Wollaston, Rev. John Ramsden, *Wollaston's Picton Journal* (ed. Canon Burton and Rev. Percy U. Henn). Perth, C. H. Pitman and Sons, 1948.

Wood, Norman, *The Reformation and English Literature.* London, George Routledge, 1931.

Woods, Rev. Julian E. T., *A. Guide to Confession and First Communion.* Sydney, Louis Gille, 1875 (a 'new' edition bearing the imprimatur of Bishop D. Murphy of Tasmania).

————St Joseph's School Series, *Grammar for Catholic Children*. Brisbane, S. Pole, 1874.

Yeo, Mary E. J., *The Early Days of Yass* (collection of a series of articles appearing in the *Yass Evening Tribune*, 1920, ML).

Young Catholic Students' Movement, *Handbook*. Melbourne, Y.C.S. Movement Headquarters, 1949.

————*In Manibus Tuis, Bulletin for Religious Assistants,* no. 3, December 1948. Melbourne, Y.C.S. Movement Headquarters, 1948.

————*Leaders' Bulletin,* no. 5, July 1949. Melbourne, Y.C.S. Movement Headquarters, 1949.

————*Programme—1951.* Melbourne, Y.C.S. Movement Headquarters, 1951.

F. BIBLIOGRAPHIES, INDEXES, DIRECTORIES

I. BIBLIOGRAPHIES AND INDEXES

Ferguson, John Alexander, *Bibliography of Australia*. Sydney, Angus and Robertson, 1945.

Hawley, L. P., *General Index to the Printed Papers, 1890-1946*. Perth, William H. Wyatt, Government Printer, 1948.

Index to the Parliamentary Papers of the Legislature of South Australia, 1857-81. Adelaide, E. Spiller, Government Printer, 1882.

Index to the Papers laid before Parliament and Printed Petitions, from 1901 to 1915 Inclusive (prepared by the Clerks of the Legislative Council). Adelaide, R. E. E. Rogers, Government Printer, 1916.

Index to Papers laid before Parliament and Petitions presented to both Houses, 1916-37 (prepared by Clerks of the Legislative Assembly). Adelaide, Government Printer, 1939.

Index to Public Acts and Ordinances of the Province of South Australia to 1893. Adelaide, C. E. Bristow, Government Printer, 1894.

Index to Sydney Morning Herald's Reports of the Parliamentary Debates in New South Wales (extends throughout 1849, then 1851-4).

Mayo, M. Penelope. *Index to Miscellaneous Information and Advertisements contained in South Australian Almanacks and Directories, 1839-72*. Adelaide, 1947.

Van der Wall, Charles W. J., *A Consolidated Index to the Government Gazette, from 1836 to 1890*. By authority, Wm Clowes and Dons, London, 1903.

Western Australian Parliamentary Handbook, The. Perth, Robert H. Miller, Government Printer, 1944.

II. DIRECTORIES

(a) General

Archer, W. H., *The Statistical Register of Victoria*. Melbourne, John Ferres, Government Printer, 1854.

Australian Almanack and General Directory. Sydney, G. Howe, R. Mansfield, and Sydney Gazette, 1834, 1835.

Australian Pocket Almanack, 1822-6.

Boothby, Josiah, *The Adelaide Almanack and Town and Country Directory*. Adelaide, E. S. Wigg and J. Howell.

Brisbane Directory. Brisbane, J. U. McNaught, 1878, 1879.

South Australian Almanack (Thomas), 1839.

South Australian Almanack and Country Directory (Bennet), 1845.

South Australian Almanack and Town and Country Directory (Murray), 1847.

South Australian Almanack and General Directory. Adelaide, J. Stephens, 1847.

Walch's Tasmanian Almanack. Tasmania, J. Walch and Sons.

Western Australian Almanack. Perth, Arthur Shenton.

(b) Ecclesiastical

Australasian Catholic Directory. Sydney, published by different publishers: Cunninghame, William Brooks, James J. Lee, Pellegrini, 1888, 1895, 1900, 1910, 1920, 1930, 1940, 1951.

Catholic Almanac and Directory of Divine Service in the Archdiocese of Sydney and the Diocese of Maitland. Sydney, J. Moore, 1854.

Catholic Almanac and Directory of Divine Service. Sydney, J. Moore, Wm Dolman, 1855.

Catholic Almanac and Directory of Divine Service in the Archdiocese of Sydney. Sydney, Wm Dolman, 1862.

Catholic Directory of Australasia. Melbourne, Michael T. Gason, 1858 (a note in the preface claims that this is the first Australasian Catholic Directory).

Catholic Home Annual and Directory of Australasia, 1892.

Church of England Year Book (S.A.), 1888, 1896.

Church of England Year Book (Q'ld.), 1890, 1895, 1901-3, 1909-11.

Coghlan, Timothy, A., *New South Wales Handbook of The Statistical Register, 1885-8*. Sydney, Government Printer, 1888.

Commercial Directory and Almanac (Young's), 1856.

Jesuit Year Book and Directory. Melbourne, 'Messenger' Office, 1950.

Melbourne Almanac and Port Phillip Directory (compiled by William Kerr). Melbourne, Kerr and Holmes, 1840, 1841.

New South Wales Pocket Almanack. Sydney, George Howe, 1813-16, 1818-21.

Official Year Book of the Commonwealth of Australia. Canberra, Government Printer, nos. 37-8.

Ordo Divini Officii Recitandi. Sydneii, Typis F. Cunninghame, 1876.

Ordo Divini Officii Recitandi. Sydneii, Edward F. Flanagan, 1878.

Ordo Divini Officii Recitandi. Sydneii, Typis F. Cunninghame, 1881.

Port Phillip Almanac and Directory (compiled by J. Mauritz). Melbourne, the Herald Office, 1847.

Index

Academy of Mary Immaculate, *ii* 344
Accrediting systems and Catholic schools: possibilities, *ii* 412-13; Tasmania, 412; Victoria, 412
Acerbo nimis, ii 391; *see also* Pius X
Acta et Decreta, see Decrees
Activity methods in the teaching of religion, *ii* 397
Acts of Parliament, *see* Parliament
Adaptation in religious orders, *see* Religious
Adult education, *ii* 387
Advocate: on secondary education, *ii* 320; on the Woods-Sheil scheme, *i* 225
Age (Vic.): and a Romish plot, *i* 164; and David Syme, 162; on clerical interference, 164; support for secular education, 162
Age of pupils, *see* School leaving age
Aikenhead, Mary, foundress of Sisters of Charity, *ii* 301
Albury, *i* 113
Allanby, Rev. C. G., *i* 142n.
All Hallows' Convent, *ii* 298n., 347, 413
Allpass, Inspector, *i* 106n.
Aloysius, Rev. Brother, F.S.C., *ii* 266, 271n., 374n.
Amalgamation of religious communities, *see* Religious
Amphion, Rev. Brother, F.S.C., *ii* 271
Anderson, Professor Francis, *ii* 352, 429
Anglicans and Bible in School Leagues, *ii* 459
Anglican Churchman, and distrust of Rome, *i* 146
Anti-denominationalism, *i* 155
Apostleship of Prayer, *ii* 414
Apprenticeship Commission, *ii* 375
Aquinas, St Thomas: on natural law, *i* 180, 181n.; on the oneness of the Church's doctrine, 191n.; on vital activity of the learner, *ii* 398
Aquinas College, University of Adelaide, *ii* 447
Archdiocese of Sydney, educational achievements in 1870s, *i* 245, 249
Archer, W.H., *i* 40n., 48
Argus (Vic.): and sectarianism, *i* 164; support for secular education, 162; under Higinbotham, 162
Arnold, Thomas: Inspector of schools in Van Diemen's land, *i* 67n.; on abuses in appointment of teachers, 83; on training colleges, 85n.

Arithmetic, *ii* 353, 354
Arthur, Governor Sir George: and Board of Inquiry, *i* 35; on separate grant for Catholics, 34
Assisted schools (W.A.): Catholic attitude towards, *i* 74; established, 64; Protestant attitude towards, 74n.
Associate of Arts Degree (Tasmania), *ii* 366
Association of the Sacred Heart, *i* 226
Assumptionist Fathers, *ii* 266, 269, 319
Atchison, W.C., *ii* 323
Atmosphere in religious education, *ii* 398
Augustinian Fathers: and education, *ii* 269, 341; arrival in colony, 270
Australian: ii 320
Australian Bible Society, *i* 6
Australian Broadcasting Commission, *ii* 437
Australian School Society, *i* 6

Backhaus estate, *ii* 445
Backhaus, Rev. Dr, *ii* 445n.
Badham, Professor Charles, *ii* 361n.
Balfour, James, *i* 141, 203
Balmain, *i* 113
Baptist Union, *i* 122n., *ii* 467
Baptists, *i* 122-3
Barat, St Madeleine Sophie, *ii* 301
Bar Convent, York, *ii* 301
Barker, Bishop Frederic, *i* 146
Barr, Rev. Father, *ii* 280n.
Barry, Mother Gonzaga: and teacher training, *ii* 436; pioneering kindergarten movement, 451
Barry, Sir Redmond, *ii* 447n.
Barry, Rev. Zachary, *i* 124, 143, 146
Bathurst, diocese of: first Sisters of Mercy, *ii* 261; replacement of lay teachers by religious, 279-86
Bavin, Sir Thomas, *ii* 471n.
Beechinor, Rev. Michael, *i* 84n., *ii* 263n.
Bell, Barbara, and training of teachers, *ii* 436
Bell, Margaret, and training of teachers, *ii* 436
Bell system: and the Church of England, *i* 13; in Catholic schools, 101n.; in wide use, 34, 101; opposition to, 22n.
Benedict XV, Pope, and the teaching of religion, *ii* 399
Benedictines: and education, *ii* 325; and Polding's aspirations, 299; first community in Australia, 269; influence in Australia, 301

Benedictine nuns, *ii* 261, 271-2, 334, 381
Benedictinism, *i* 244-8
Benson, Sister Hilda, and Loreto Training College, *ii* 432
Benziger Brothers, publishers, *ii* 410
Beovich, Archbishop M.: and kindergarten movement, *ii* 451; and training of teachers, 430, 434; and organization of Catholic education, 440; on teaching religion, 394; report to Rome, 1950, *Catholic Education and Catechetics in Australia*, 440
Bible in school: and Protestants, *ii* 459-61; Anglican attitude to, *i* 45; Catholic attitude to, 46, 115, 190-1, 214, *ii* 460-1; Douay version permitted, *i* 70; in South Australia, 70; leagues, *ii* 459-63; legislation on, 462-3; opposition of Education Act Defence League, 461; referenda, 461n., 462
Bible-reading, *see* Bible in school; *see also* Carr, Archbishop Thomas, and Moorhouse, Bishop James
Bigge, Commissioner J. T.: Catholic petition to, *i* 12-20; reports of, 11, 13
Bills, education: New South Wales, *i* 66, 159; South Australia, *ii* 430, 462; Tasmania, 427, 430; Victoria, *i* 65, 66, 121n., 125, *ii* 333, 430, 462n.
Birmingham, Rev. P., *i* 84n.
Bishops, Catholic: and a national system, *i* 207; and central government for religious, *ii* 290, 294, 295; and citizenship, 415; and Public Instruction Act of 1880, *i* 253-4; and school boards, 180; and secondary education, *ii* 320; and state aid, *i* 173; attitude to Irish National System, 169; attitude to liberalism, *ii* 422; attitude to the state system, 456-7; authority in education, *i* 180, 238, *ii* 437, 442; diversity of views, *i* 170-1, 221; economic independence, 181; increase in numbers, 176, *ii* 421; increasing Irish element, *i* 176; influenced by events overseas, 176, 177, *ii* 383; on importance of Catholic education, 305, 310; preference for schools under religious, 267-8; problems confronting, *i* 171; report to Rome on Catholic education, 1950, *ii* 440; request state inspection of Catholic schools, 426-7; responsibilities in education, *i* 105, 180, 196; Standing Committee on Education, *ii* 440; statements in N.S.W., 492; stiffening of attitude on education question, *i* 176; succession of, *ii* 484-5; support for public examinations, 373
Blair, David, *i* 201
Blanch, George E., *ii* 362
Bleasdale, Rev. John Ignatius: and Catholic Education Committee (Vic.), *i* 79, 218, *ii* 438, 489; and examining

board for teachers, *i* 90n.; and local boards, 76, *see also* Local boards; and training establishment in Melbourne, 89
Blessed Eucharist, devotion to, *ii* 419
Bligh, Governor William, *i* 7
Board, Peter, Director of Education, New South Wales, *ii* 423
Boarding allowances, *see* State grants for education
Boarding schools, *ii* 304, 322, 323, 329, 344, 346
Boards of education: and Catholic schools, *i* 175, 203, 207; central, 27, 67; general board (W.A.), 37, 125; North and South (Tas.), 67; Vaughan's Catholic School Board, *ii* 438; *see also* Denominational Schools Boards and National Board of Education
Board of examiners for classification of teachers, *i* 90
Board of Inspection (V.D.L.), 1852, *i* 35, 62
Board of Registration for Catholic Training Colleges, *ii* 434
Bond, Rev. William, *ii* 316, 321
Boniface, Rev. Brother, P.B., *ii* 412
Borgia, Rev. Brother, F.M.S., *ii* 349n.
Bothian, Rev. Brother, F.S.C., *ii* 271
Bourke, Governor Sir Richard: and grants for Catholic schools, *i* 21, 42; attitude to Church control of education, 28; Church Act, 31, 40, 170; educational plans opposed by Protestants, 29; educational plans supported by Catholics, 30; on motives of Dr Broughton, 141; proposals for general system, 27-8, 66
Bourke, Mary, early teacher, Q'ld., *i* 39
Bourke, Rt Rev. Monsignor Anselm (W.A.), *i* 78, 207
Boyce, Rev. F. B., on motives of Protestants, *i* 147
Bradley, James, and Marsden, *i* 11
Brady, Bishop John: and Catholic secondary schools, *ii* 314; and religious teachers, 266; educational schemes, *i* 37, 39, 46; petition to Queen Victoria, 47; teachers from Europe, 86
Breen, Rev. J. B., and St Kilian's College, *ii* 329
Brennan, Bishop W., *ii* 440n.
Brisbane, Archdiocese of: distribution of orders, *ii* 275-6; replacement of lay teachers by religious, 279
Brisbane Courier, support for secular education, *i* 161
Brisbane, Governor Sir Thomas, Orphan School policy, *i* 8, 16
British and Foreign School Society system of education, *i* 31, 41, 122, 126
Bromly, Rev. J. E., *i* 151
Broughton, Bishop W. G.: address

before Legislative Assembly on Gipps' plan (1839), *i* 129-30; and control of education, 1n.; and Irish National System, 141; on Catholic difficulty, 141; on common Christianity, 130; on nondogmatic instruction, 129; on role of schools, 181, *ii* 310n.; opposition to general system of education, *i* 27, 29

Brown, Inspector W. G., proposals on pupil-teachers, *i* 85

Brunn, Rev. Father, *ii* 266, 319

Budd, R. Hale, *i* 89

Buenos Aires, *ii* 264

Building materials for schools, *i* 55

Burch, Augustine, *i* 102n.

Burgess, Rev. H. T. (Independent), *i* 124n.

Burton, Judge William, and Clergy and Schools Corporation, *i* 14n.

Bush child, Catholic education of: correspondence schemes for, *ii* 454-5; religious holiday school, 455; 'Adoption movement', 455; work of Rt Rev. J. T. McMahon, 454

Butcher, Rev. B. T., *ii* 467n.

Butler's *Catechism*, *i* 115

Byrne, Rev. J. P., inspector of schools, Bathurst, *ii* 237, 295

Byrne, Thomas, teacher employed by Father Therry, *i* 21

Cabra (Ireland), *ii* 264

Cadet corps in primary schools, *ii* 356

Cahill, Rev. Father, s.j., evidence before Royal Commission, 1884, *i* 184n.

Cam, Rev. A. B., *i* 186n.

Cameron, J., *ii* 259n.

Campbell, Colin, Sec. D.S.B. (Vic.), *i* 97n.

Campion Society, *ii* 416

Cana conferences, *ii* 387

Cani, Bishop John, *ii* 329

Canon law: codification, *ii* 384; on religious instruction, 389-90

Caporelli, Nicola, Pontifical Consul-General in Australia, *ii* 314

Carey, Rev. P., *ii* 396, 440n.

Carnarvon (Tas.), *ii* 331

Carr, Archbishop Thomas: and amalgamation of religious, *ii* 290; and educational reform, 421; and training of teachers, 436; influence of Leo XIII on, 422; on Bible in schools, *i* 193n., *ii* 460; on education of women, 382; on effect of Catholic education on Church, 303; on sex instruction, 406; quest for religious, 266; significance of a Catholic school, 303, 305, 427; standards in Catholic schools, 352, 353, 356, 421

Carr, Rev. R. J., inspector of Catholic schools, Goulburn, *ii* 424, 429

Cartwright, Rev. Robert, *i* 10, 11

'Case' method of teaching religion, *ii* 397

Casey, William P., inspector of Catholic schools, *i* 80

Catechism: Deharbe, 393; objections to, *ii* 393-4; teaching, 393-5; the 'penny' catechism, 393; uniform, 391

'Catechisms and formularies', *i* 154

Catholic Action, *ii* 414, 415, 416

Catholic Association: Tasmania, *i* 218; Western Australia, 218

Catholic Boys' School, Perth, *i* 96

Catholic children in state schools: change of attitude of bishops to, *ii* 456-7; numbers, 453-4, 455n.; reasons for, 455; Vaughan on religious instruction of, 456

Catholic Church: educational resources of, *ii* 258; morale heightened by Catholic education, 303; sacrifice on behalf of Catholic education, *i* 255; unity effected by Plenary Councils, *ii* 274

Catholic difficulty in education: Broughton on, *i* 141; Moorhouse on, 141

Catholic education: and modern philosophies of education, *ii* 392; Australian notion of, *i* 209, 268; contribution to Church, *ii* 303-5; ends of, *i* 25, 181, *ii* 415, 417; of the poor, 291, 292; role in society, *i* 255

Catholic education associations
diocesan boards, *ii* 438
in New South Wales: Catholic Association for the Promotion of Religion and Education (Catholic Education Association), *i* 218-19, 220, 246, *ii* 488; Central Council of the Society for Promoting Catholic Education, *i* 79, *ii* 267; Council of Education, 438; proposed Central Committee, 438; Vaughan's Catholic Schools Board, 421, 438
in South Australia: 'School Fund', *i* 223; Central Council, 225-6
in Victoria: Catholic Education Committee, 78, 79, 218, *ii* 489

Catholic Education Committee (Vic.), *see* Catholic education associations

Catholic Education Congress, Adelaide, *ii* 438

'Catholic evidence' method, *ii* 397

Catholic Federation, *ii* 337

Catholic Metropolitan Model and Training school, *i* 88

Catholic schools: and modern developments, *ii* 423-4; and science teaching, 368; as part of the government system, *i* 209; associated with parishes, 54; charge of divisiveness, *ii* 467; competition from state schools, 356; defects in the system of, 423, 477; development of, *i* 53-4, 75; early, 17, 38-40; independent of government, 208, 224, 238, 239; need for efficiency, *ii* 425; new era for, 423; not termed 'Catholic' schools, *i* 209; numbers, 38, 53-4, 74-5, 224, 238-9, *ii* 304; organization in early schools of Sisters of St Joseph, *i* 232; pressures against, 220; pupils in, *ii* 305; spirit of, 409-10; standards of proficiency, *i* 107-8, 111-12, 208-9, *ii* 259, 356; support for public examinations, 369; under central boards, *i* 194; under the Woods-Sheil scheme, 231

Catholic school texts, *ii* 410

Catholic Secondary Schools Association, N.S.W., *ii* 435

Catholic Teachers' Association of New South Wales, *ii* 374

Catholic Training School, *see* Catholic Metropolitan Model and Training School

Catholic University, *see* University education

Catholics: adherence to religious instruction, *i* 139; and politicians, *ii* 471-2; attending public schools, *i* 211-13, 251, 253; attitude to secular education, 183; deluded by government schools, 210; enervated by state aid, 217; greater proportion in labouring classes, 59, 210-11, *ii* 307-8; liberal, *i* 215, 255; loss in social prestige, *ii* 334; support for Bourke's educational plans, *i* 30; support for own schools, 216-17, 219; *see also* Laity

Central Boards of education, *see* Boards of education, central

Central Council of the Society for Promoting Catholic Education, *see* Catholic education associations

Chanel, Sister, *ii* 293n.

Character training, *see* Formation

Charcoal Creek, *i* 114

Charity, Sisters of: difficulties under Polding, *i* 245; educational work hampered, 246; first community in Australia, *ii* 261, 269; invitation from bishops, 264; refuge in Tasmania, *i* 246, *ii* 262; secondary schools, 340; take up teaching, 271; visiting schools for religious instruction, *i* 114

Childers, Hugh C. E., *i* 65, 91, 111, *ii* 474

Child's Book of Religion, A, ii 396

Christian Brothers, Irish: and boarding schools, *ii* 330; and Catholic school texts, 410; and Irish Hierarchy, 267; and Select Committee of 1852, 264; and technical education, 375; and science teaching, 368; and teaching of Greek, 361; arrival in Perth, *ii* 266; central government, 295; early secondary schools, 326; evolution of middle class curriculum, 371-2; in Sydney in 1840s, *i* 101, 245, 246, *ii* 261, 263; influence of De La Salle, *ii*

302; invited to Tasmania, 262; 'pay' schools, 289; requests for, 261; role in education in Australia, *i* 244, 246; schools and colleges, 266, 326, 327, 328-9, 372; second arrival in Australia, 246, *ii* 271; *see also* Text-books

Christian doctrine, refresher school in, *ii* 435-6

Christian mentality: means of developing, *ii* 409-17; Tenison Woods on, 409

Christian Education in a Democratic Community, Social Justice Statement, *ii* 385n.

Christian Education of Youth, The, ii 385; *see also* Pius XI

Christ's College (Tas.), *ii* 330

Chronicle, i 101

Church Act, *see* Bourke

Church of England: and British and Foreign School Society system, *i* 129; and denominational schools, 129, 136, 147; and dogmatic religious instruction, 14; and Irish National System, 129; and non-dogmatic instruction, 129, 130, 131-2; and secular education, 145-6; changed views in second half of century, 131; children in Catholic schools, 140; collapse of resistance in Queensland, 133; divided on educational issues, 133-4; Higinbotham on indecision among Anglicans, 132; influence of other Protestant groups on, 132; influence of, 128-9; influence of laity, 134; Moorhouse and non-dogmatic instruction, 131; schools under Clergy and Schools Corporation, 24; social justice and parental rights, *ii* 468

Church of England Defence Association, *i* 133, 144n.

Church schools, early, *i* 3

Church, the: responsibilities in education, *i* 180; views of education, 181

Citizenship, an objective in Catholic schools, *ii* 415

Clarendon Commission (England), *ii* 362, 366

Clarke, Marcus, *i* 150n.

Classics in education, *ii* 325, 362; *see also* Curriculum

Classification of teachers: board of examiners for, *i* 90; courses for, 90n., *see also* Teachers; grades of, 90n.; Sisters classified under Council of Education, 90n.

Clatworthy, Rev. E., *ii* 467n.

Cleary, P.S., *i* 190n.

Clergy: role in education, *i* 12; *see also* Education

Clergy and Schools Corporation: and Church of England, *i* 14; attitude of Dissenters, 16; Catholic attitude to, 16, 20; charter of, 14; Dr Ullathorne on, 15, 16; John Dunmore Lang on, 15;

Judge Burton on, 14n.; opposition to, 22; revocation of charter, 27; *Sydney Morning Herald* on, 15

Clergy, Catholic: doubts on Catholic education system, *ii* 473; state grants, *i* 235-6

Co-education: avoided in denominational schools, *ii* 408; bishops encourage legitimate association of sexes, 409; Catholic views on, 408-9; Knibbs and Turner on, 408

Coffey, Mrs. Catherine, *i* 107n.

Cole, E. W., *i* 150n.

Collège des Hautes Études des Carmes, *ii* 323

Collège Stanislaus, *ii* 323

Commercial subjects, *see* Curriculum

Commission of Inquiry (N.S.W.), 1855-6, *i* 62, 66, 91, 99

Commissions on education, Royal:
New South Wales (1903-4, Knibbs and Turner), *ii* 366, 368, 402, 429, 459, 464
Queensland (1875), *i* 122, 126, 128, 140, 188
South Australia (1913), *ii* 333
Tasmania (1867), *i* 190; (1883), *ii* 458
Victoria (1867), *i* 77n., 93; (1881-4), *ii* 458; (1899-1901, Fink), 362, 366, 458; (1900), 462n.

Committee of Protestants (in opposition to educational plans of Bourke), *i* 29, 31

Committee on General Education (W.A.), *i* 37

Common Christianity; Broughton's views on, *i* 130

Companion to the Catechism, ii 396

Composition, teaching of, *ii* 354

Comprehensive system, *see* General system

Condition of schools, *see* Schools

Conduite des Écoles, ii 303

Confraternity: of the Divine Child, *ii* 414; of the Holy Childhood, 414

Congregation of the Holy Cross, *ii* 449n.

Congregational Union and secular instruction, *i* 122

Congregationalists: and aid to education, *i* 119, 120; and aid to religion, 119, 120; and Bible in School leagues, *ii* 460; and general system, *i* 120; and non-dogmatic religious instruction, 120-1; and secular education, 121, 122; and the denominational system, 120; and the voluntary principle, 120; influence in education, 119; influence in secularist leagues, 123-4; influence in South Australian Society, 119; influence on the press, 160

Connelly, Rev. Philip, *i* 38n.

Conquest, Rev. D. J., Director of Catholic Education, Victoria, *ii* 412n., 440

Continuous education, the problem of, *ii* 420

Convent schools: and good breeding, *ii* 299; centres of culture, 297; education provided in, 382; musical traditions, 297

Corbett, Bishop James, *i* 186n., *ii* 265, 384n.

Corcoran, Rev. P. T., *ii* 438n.

Corder, E. J., *ii* 461n.

Corporal punishment, *see* Punishment

Corporate life of the school, *ii* 388

Correction in moral formation, *ii* 403-5

Correspondence schemes for teaching religion, *ii* 454

Cost of education: amounts spent, *i* 216-17, 249, *ii* 443; cost per child, *i* 58-60, *ii* 443; problem of Catholics supporting own schools, *i* 216-17; *see also* Finance for Catholic Schools

Council, National of Ireland, 1875, *ii* 393

Council of Baltimore, *ii* 357, 383

Council of Churches (N.S.W.), attitude to state grants to education, *ii* 467

Council of Education (N.S.W.): and teachers in Catholic schools, *i* 205; interfering in ecclesiastical affairs, 206; Plunkett on, 206

Council of Education (Tas.), *ii* 322, 331

Council of Lateran: Third, *i* 2; Fourth, 2

Council of Public Education (Vic.): and registration of Catholic teachers, *ii* 435; on deletion of secular instruction clause, 462-3

Council of Rome, *i* 2

Council of Vaison, *i* 2

Councils of Australia
Plenary: First (1885), *i* 176, *ii* 274, 309, 310, 324, 384, 391, 410; Second (1895), 274, 303, 309, 357, 384, 391, 410, 426; Third (1905), 274, 384, 391; Fourth (1937), 309n., 385, 387, 389, 391, 395n., 407, 409, 414, 424, 426, 456
Provincial: Sydney (1844), *i* 167, *ii* 309, 424; Melbourne (1862), *i* 170, 175, 178, 196; Melbourne (1869), 175, 178, 234, 238, 240, *ii* 320

Cowper, Rev. William, *i* 10

Cox, Rev. F. W., *i* 124n.

Crane, Bishop Martin, o.s.a., *ii* 265

'Creation versus Development', *i* 151

Cremen, David, 'Mathematical and Mercantile Academy', Adelaide, *ii* 324

Cross, Rev. John, *i* 19

Cullen, Paul Cardinal, *i* 86n., *ii* 475

Culture class, Mary's Mount, Ballarat, *ii* 378

Curr, Edward, Catholic representative on first D.S.B., Victoria, *i* 48n.

Curriculum
Boys' secondary: agriculture courses,

ii 375-6; and social aspirations of Catholics, 357, 369; bookish and academic, 357; claims of industry and trade competition, 367; classics, 359-63; commercial subjects, 359, 363-5; determined by social conditioning Catholic body, 358; English, 363; French, 371, 498; influence of public examinations, 357; in schools for middle classes, 370-1; mathematics, 363; non-classical, 357; science, 357, 365-9; technical branches, 367-8, 374-5

Girls' secondary: 'accomplishments and amiability' programme, *ii* 376; art, 376, 377, 378; dancing, 377; 'English education', 377; foreign languages, 376-7; gradual change in, 382; handicrafts, 377; influence of public examinations, 379-382; music, 376-7, 379; needlework, 376; organization of classes, 378; bishops' appraisal of, 382

Primary: arithmetic, *ii* 353-4; composition, 354; crafts, 355; defects, 352-3; domestic economy, 355; drill and gymnastics, *see* Physical education; elementary mechanics, 355; elementary science, 355; English, 355; geography, 354, 355; geometry, 355; grammar, 355; history, 353-5, 358; improvement in standards, 354; Irish history, 355; needlework, 355; object lessons, 354, 355; reading, 352-3, 355; science, 354; shorthand and book-keeping, 355; spelling, 353; typing, 355; vocal music, 355; writing, 355

Daly, J. G., *i* 226n.
Darcy, Rev. T., *ii* 438n.
Darling, Governor Sir Ralph, *i* 23
Darlinghurst Boys' school, *i* 114
Daughters of Charity, *ii* 453
Davis, Bishop C. H., o.s.b.: first president of Lyndhurst, *ii* 313; on senate of University of Sydney, 313; plans for Lyndhurst, 313
Dawson Street Training College, *ii* 432
Deaf, schools for, *ii* 452
Deakin, Alfred, *ii* 461n.
Decrees: from Provincial Council (1869), *i* 176, 196; *Official Pronouncement*, 197n., *ii* 422; of Plenary councils, 383, 422, *see also* Councils; of synods, 309, 384; of Third Plenary Council of Baltimore, 310n.; on recruiting religious, 287
Deharbe, Rev. Joseph, *ii* 393
Delane, W., *i* 226n.
Delaney, Bishop P., *i* 78, *ii* 427, 436
De La Salle Brothers (Brothers of the Christian Schools): and Catholic school texts, *ii* 410; early schools in

W.A., *i* 102, *ii* 271; influence in conduct of schools, *i* 102; invitations from bishops, *ii* 262, 266
De La Salle, St John Baptist, *ii* 302, 372
Democratic liberalism, *i* 152
Denison, Governor Sir William Thomas, *i* 45, 107n., 108
Denominational schools: attitude of central boards, *i* 202-3, 240; Catholic, 27, 240, 250, 253; comparison with others, 111-12; condition of, 61; course of instruction in, 69; duplication of, 61; for Catholic poor, *ii* 292, 476; mixed population in Protestant schools, *i* 137-8; phases in development, 26; Protestant, 27; unable to meet requirements of boards, 111, 204
Denominational Schools Boards: Catholic attitude to, *i* 52; composition of, 48; functions of, 49, 50; origin, 47; policy of, 54; regulations, 50; unification with National Board, 62, 66-7
Denominational system: attitude of society to, *i* 118; defects associated with, 61; disabilities for Catholics, 64; dissolution of, 60; redundancy of, 62; supported by conservative elements, 152
Denominations, mutual jealousies, *i* 123
Devotional practices in Catholic schools: and liturgical life of parish, *ii* 420; educational significance of, 418-20; examples of, 418-20; in honour of Blessed Virgin Mary, 419
Dewey, John, and Catholic education, *ii* 392, 397, 398
Director of Catholic education, *see* Organization of Catholic education system
Discipline: defective, *i* 93; disciplinary measures, 94-5; 'free', *ii* 405; mental, through classics, 362; preventive, 403; role in moral and religious formation, 402
Dissenters: early missionaries, *i* 11-12, *see also* Nonconformists; grievance of, 142; influence in secularist leagues, 123
Divini Illius Magistri, *ii* 385, *see also* Pius XI
Dixon, Rev. James, *i* 17, 18
Dogmatic religious instruction: attitude of central boards, *i* 195; attitude of Church of England, 14; necessity of positive dogma, 184n., *ii* 392; role of, *i* 71, 186-7; under Clergy and Schools Corporation, 14
Domestic economy, *ii* 355
Dominican Sisters: and religious instruction by correspondence, *ii* 455; and sodalities, 414; arrival in S.A., 386; first communities, 262, 264; secondary schools, 344; traditions, 301

Douay version of Bible, use in South Australia, *i* 192, 193
Downside Abbey, *ii* 261
Doyle, Bishop Jeremiah, episcopal committee on standards in school subjects, *ii* 356
Drawing, not taught in denominational schools, *i* 99
Drinkwater, Father, editor of Sower Series, *ii* 396
Duchesne College, University of Brisbane, *ii* 448
Duffy, Gavan, *i* 145n., 162
Duncan, W. A.: and the Marist Brothers, *i* 247; favoured Irish National System, 154, 215; on Select Committee of 1844, 43; teacher, writer, public servant, 153; views on teaching of religion, 189
Duhig, Archbishop James: on Bible in school leagues, *ii* 461; variety in religious orders, 276
Dunne, Alicia, *i* 86n.
Dunne, Archbishop Robert, *ii* 276, 329
Dunne, Rev. P., *ii* 316
Dunne, Rev. W. J., *i* 76n., 190
Durkheim, Émile, *ii* 398
Dwyer, Bishop P. V.: inspector of Catholic schools, *ii* 424; on replacement of lay teachers by religious, 279; president of Sacred Heart College, Maitland, 326; requests state inspection of Catholic schools, 426; standards in Catholic schools, 357

Eagar, Edward, and evidence before Bigge Commission, *i* 11
Eardley-Wilmot, Governor Sir John, *i* 44n.
Ecclesiastical colleges, *ii* 304
Education: and state responsibility, *i* 43; as ecclesiastical function, 1, 2, 4, 14, 20, 23, 47-9, 52, 77, 123, 152; bishops on importance of, 108, 181; control of, 67; 'free, secular and compulsory', (and Baptists), *i* 122, (and Congregationalists), 122, (and secularist leagues), 123; low standard of, 108; social role of, *ii* 308; state rights in (Catholic view), 470
Education Acts, *see* Parliament
Education, Catholic system of: defects in, *ii* 477; established, 257; financial support, *see* Finance for Catholic schools; underlying principles, 384n., 470, 477
Education Defence League (Victoria), *ii* 461
Education League (South Australia), *i* 124
Education of women, *see* Women
Educational writers, *i* 153; *see also* Duncan, W. A.; Hanrahan, Rev. Br M.

B.; McMahon, J. T.; O'Brien, A. E.; Rusden, G. W.; Wilkins, W. A.
Elizabeth I, Queen, *i* 4
Elley, S. M., Most Rev. Dr, and founding of Sisters of St Joseph, *ii* 293
Elliot, J., *i* 142n.
Emulation, in Catholic schools under religious, *ii* 404
English, teaching of, *ii* 355, 363
Episcopal committee on standards in school subjects, *ii* 356, 391
Equipment in schools, *see* Schools
Eugenius II, Pope, *i* 2, 3
Europe, educational traditions of, *ii* 257, 473
Evatt, H. V., *i* 252n., *ii* 464n.
Experimentalists and Catholic education, *ii* 392

Faithful Companions of Jesus, *ii* 436
Family, the role of, *i* 171
Fees: in schools of religious, *ii* 289; under the boards, *i* 54, 59-60, 71
Fiddes, M. J., *i* 142n.
Finance for Catholic schools: difficulties in, *ii* 473; endowments, 445; fees from music lessons, 445; means of raising funds, 444; parochial schools, 443; recommendations on abolition of fees, 446; 'school money', 444; secondary schools of the orders, 444-5; supporting religious communities, 443
Fink, Theodore, *ii* 366; *see also* Commissions on education
First Fleet, *i* 5
Fitchett, Rev. W. H., *i* 125n.
Fitzgerald, Rev. Brother Ambrose, *ii* 361
Fleming, Rev. Brian, s.j., *ii* 477n.
Fleury's *Historical Catechism of the Old and New Testament*, *i* 114
Flynn, Julia, *ii* 412n.
Foran, Rev. M., *ii* 438
Forest Lodge, Catholic School at, *ii* 289
Formation, moral and religious: Catholic practice, *ii* 401-20; character training, 402; co-education, 408-9; correction, 403-5; discipline, 402; in state schools, 402; Pius XII on, 402; self-government, 405; surveillance, 403-5; training in purity, 406-8; true liberty, 403
Forrest, Rev. Dr, rector of St John's, University of Sydney, *i* 247, *ii* 369n.
Forrest, Sir John, *i* 200
Fort Street Model School (N.S.W.), *i* 67, 88, 211
Fortitude Valley, Brisbane, *i* 113
Fouhy, Rev. Denis, *ii* 447n.
Fox, Bishop A. F., *ii* 457n.
Fox, Bishop Thomas, and abolition of the select school, *ii* 350
Franciscan Teaching Brothers, *ii* 270, 271, 374
Franklin, Governor Sir John: attitudes

of denominations to, *i* 35, 44-5, 122; education scheme, 41

Frayne, Mother Ursula, *i* 46n., *ii* 263

Free education, *i* 71

Freehill, F. B., *ii* 299n.

Freeman's Journal and secondary education, *ii* 321

'Free, secular and compulsory', *see* Education

Freethought, *i* 166

French, teaching of, *ii* 363

Gallagher, Bishop John: and the classical tradition, *ii* 361; Bishop of Goulburn, 421; first president of St Patrick's College, Goulburn, 321

Ganly, Rev. Father, inspector of Catholic schools, Melbourne, *ii* 354, 424, 429

Garland, Rev. D. T., *ii* 460

Gawler, Governor George, *i* 36

Geary, Inspector, proposals on pupil-teachers, *i* 85n.

General system of education: Anglican attitude to, *i* 45; Catholic attitude to, 46, 173-4, 196; desirability of, 66-7; favoured by Nonconformists, 46; general Protestant attitude to, 118; Polding's proposals on, 170; trend towards, 27, 66-7

Geoghegan, Bishop Patrick Bonaventure: attitude to Irish National System, *i* 169; basic philosophy and theology of, *ii* 383; Bishop of Adelaide, *i* 170, 222, *ii* 475; educational policy in S.A., *i* 222; evidence before Select Committee (Vic. 1852), 169, 171, 182n., *ii* 264, (S.A. 1861), *i* 223; natural law as basis of parental rights in education, 180; on non-dogmatic instruction, 190-1; on state rights in education, 196; Pastoral (1860), 168, 184n., 188n., 223; proposed non-denominational secondary institution, *ii* 316; quest for religious, 263; (Vicar-General, Melbourne), *i* 38, 52; withdrawing Catholic schools from Board, 239

Geography: Catholic school texts in, *i* 229; the teaching of, *ii* 354

Geometry, in the primary school, *ii* 355

Gibbons, Peter, *ii* 271n.

Gibbons, Sister Scholastica, *ii* 288n.

Gibney, Bishop Matthew: and Subiaco House, Perth, *ii* 322; and system of assisted schools, *i* 207; and the Christian Brothers, *ii* 266; and the *West Australian*, *i* 163; on cost of Catholic education, 217; on 'schools before churches', 311; quest for teaching Brothers, 266; replacement of lay teachers by religious, 281

Gilroy, Norman Cardinal, support for idea of a Catholic university, *ii* 449

Gipps, Governor Sir George: and aid from missionary societies, *i* 6n.; and the religious denominations, 32; proposals for general scheme of education, 27, 31-2

Gladstone, William Ewart, *i* 45, 190

Gleeson, Bishop J. W., *ii* 468n.

Glenelg, Lord, and Bourke's plan, *i* 29

Gold rushes and education, *i* 55, *ii* 264

Good Samaritan, Sisters of the: Australian foundation, *ii* 269; Benedictine influence in, 301; diversion to teaching, 288; founded by Polding, *i* 245; 'Rosebank' Convent, *ii* 348

Goodin, Vernon W. E., on early education in New South Wales, *i* 4

Goold, Archbishop J. A.: and development of Catholic schools, 54; and founding of Sisters of St Joseph, *ii* 293; and liberalism, 422; and Royal Commission of 1867, *i* 93n.; and scientists, *i* 97; and secondary schools, *ii* 315; and the D.S.B., *i* 51; and the University of Melbourne, *ii* 447; diary of 264; on Common Schools Act, 1862, *i* 172; on defective discipline, 92-3; on Secular Bill, 1872, *i* 196n.; on teachers' salaries, 83; opposed to religious leaving his diocese, *ii* 290n.; Pastoral Admonition of 1872, 164; quest for religious, *ii* 263, 264, 265

Gospel discussion, *ii* 414

Goulburn, Diocese of: first Sisters of Mercy in, *ii* 259; replacement of lay teachers by religious, 280

Government aid, *see* State grants for education

Government participation in education, *see* State sponsorship of education

Gräber, Rev. Dr, inspector of Catholic schools, Melbourne, *ii* 424

Grace: Joint Pastoral on, *i* 181; role of in Catholic education, *ii* 417-18; means of, 417-18

Grace, Rev. Brother, *i* 104n.

Grammar, *i* 229n., *ii* 355

Grammar School Act (Q'ld), controversy over, *ii* 317-18

Grants of land, *see* Land grants for schools

Grants, separate, to Catholics, *i* 47

Gratton, N. M., *ii* 434n., 468n.

Gray, Rev. R. G., *i* 120n.

Greenwood, Rev. James, Congregationalist leader in N.S.W., *i* 122, 147

Gregory, Abbot: educational secretary to Polding, *i* 78; on need of secondary education, *ii* 312; and the religious orders, *i* 245-6

Gregory, John (Colonial Treasurer, Van Diemen's Land), *i* 35

Gregory, J. S., *i* 141n.

Gregory XVI, Pope, *ii* 300

Gregory, Rev. Brother, F.S.C., *ii* 271n.
Grenfell school case, *i* 204
Grievances in education, *i* 142
Griffith, Sir Samuel, *i* 121, 202
Griver, Bishop Martin: and De La Salle Brothers, *ii* 271; and Subiaco House, Perth, 322; quest for religious, 266
Guardian, Queensland: and non-dogmatic religious instruction, *i* 160; and sectarianism, 163; Congregationalist influence in, 160; support for secular education, 161
Guide des Écoles, *ii* 303, 406
Gunson, J. M., *i* 226n.

Hackett, Winthrop, *i* 161, 163
Half and half system, *i* 40, 57
Hall, Rev. John, educational secretary to Bishop Willson, *i* 78, 115n., 178n., *ii* 262
Hand, Rev. P., *ii* 438
Handicapped children: ecclesiastical legislation on education of, *ii* 452; schools for, 304, 452
Hanley, Rev. Brother A. B., *ii* 374
Hanly, Rev. J. (Q'ld), *i* 38n.
Hannan, Rt Rev. J., organizer of National Catholic Correspondence Course, *ii* 454
Hanrahan, Rev. Brother M. B., *ii* 394n., 400
Hans, Nicholas A., *i* 178n., *ii* 474
Harker, George, *i* 203
Harold, Rev. Father, *i* 18
Harper, Rev. Andrew, *i* 141n.
Harrison, Rt Rev. H., *ii* 467n.
Hart, Sr Mary Agnes, *ii* 288n.
Hartley, *i* 113
Hassall, Rev. J. S., *i* 133
Hassall, Rowland, Nonconformist missionary, *i* 10
Hay, Rev. Alexander, *i* 126, 128
Headmasters' Association, Great Public Schools, *ii* 437
Heales' Bill, *i* 66n.
Healy, Rev. J., *ii* 440
Healy, Monsignor, founder of Brothers of St John the Baptist, *ii* 271
Hearn, Professor W. E., *i* 145
Hedebough, Rev. F., *ii* 266
Henderson, Rev. A. M., *i* 122n.
Heptonstall, Rev. Father, *i* 169
Herbart, J. F., *ii* 399
Heydon, J. K., *i* 214n., 219
Higgins, Bishop Joseph, episcopal committee on standards in school subjects, *ii* 356
Higher branches of study in elementary schools, *i* 97
Higher education, *i* 56
Higinbotham, George: and secular education, *i* 157; and role of Church in education, 155; and role of state in education, 155; attitude to denomina-

tional system, 121; editor of the *Argus*, 162; interest in Unitarianism, 156; liberalist views in religion, 156; on Catholics and religious instruction, 139; on inconsistency in Anglican views, 132; on distrust of Rome, 143; on school attendances, 108n.; on the Protestant conscience, 198; on Protestants and religious instruction, 139
Hill, Rev. Richard, *i* 10
History: Catholic text-books in, *ii* 411; in the primary school, *ii* 353, 354, 355, 358
Hobart Town Courier, *i* 81
Hogan, J. F., *i* 164n.
Holy Family Confraternity, *ii* 455
Holy Ghost College, Ballarat: and teaching of science, *ii* 367; and the Christian Brothers, 327; foundation, 327
Holy Ghost Fathers, *ii* 269
Holy Name Society, *ii* 455
Holy Week, *ii* 418
Home Missionary Sisters: adaptation to Australian conditions, *ii* 291; Australian foundation, 269; foundation, 297
Horan, Rev. Andrew, *ii* 447n.
Horne, J. G., *ii* 461n.
Hospitaller Brothers of St John of God, *ii* 453
Hostility between Catholic authorities and Boards of education, *see* Boards
'Howl against Rome', *see* Rome, distrust of
Hughes, Rev. Brother J. G. *ii* 337n.
Hughes, Rev. Father, S.J., *ii* 361n.
Hunter, Governor John, *i* 5
Hutchins College (Tas.), *ii* 330
Hutt, Governor James, *i* 37n.
Huxley, Thomas, *ii* 365

Independent (Victoria), *i* 121
Independents: and Bible in School leagues, *ii* 460; attitude to educational plans of Bourke and Gipps, *i* 31; *see also* Congregationalists
Individual method, *i* 100
Industrial schools planned, *i* 54
Industry and trade, influence on education, *ii* 367
Ingham, S. M., *i* 155n.
Inquirer and Commercial News (W.A.), *i* 161
Inspection of schools: an obligation of pastors, *ii* 424; appointment of laymen as inspectors, 425; bishops request state inspection, 426-7; ecclesiastical legislation on, 424, 425; friction over, *i* 204; importance after withdrawal of government aid, *ii* 426; in religion, 389-90; objections to state inspection of Catholic schools, 427
Inspector-General of Catholic Education, *see* Sheil

Inspectors of schools: of Catholic schools,
i 80, 81, ii 425; dissatisfaction over, i
80; limited functions at beginning, 42;
no rights in religious instruction, 50;
under central boards, 81; under Denominational Board, 50, 79-80
Ireland, National Synod of, see Synods
Ireland, source of religious teachers, ii
265
Irish National System: and attitude of
Irish bishops, i 176; opposition to, 31;
proposed use in New South Wales,
27, 33; teachers trained under, 86;
texts used in Australia, 70
Irwin, Governor Frederick Chidley, i 37

Jackson, Cyril, Director of Education,
Western Australia, ii 423
James, Mr and Mrs (early teachers, Adelaide), i 39
Jeffries, Rev. J., i 124n.
Jeffries, S.W., ii 468n.
Jesuit Fathers: admission of commercial
subjects, ii 364; and commercial training, 364; and sodalities, 413-14; and
the classics, 361; and Australian university colleges, 448; educational work,
i 144, ii 269; first community in Australia, 270; organization within colleges, 442; schools and colleges, 259,
265, 325, 327, 330, 341; in South
Australia, 270, 316
Jocist movement, ii 417
John, Rev. Brother, first provincial of
the Marist Brothers, ii 438
Johnson, Rev. Richard, first chaplain, i
9
Joint Pastoral: and the press, i 250, 252;
appearance in 1879, 250; condemna-
tion of secular principle, 250; on parental responsibilities, 180; purpose of,
253; response of Catholics, 251; role
of grace in education, 181
Joostens, Rev. J., i 46n., ii 315
Jordan, Rev. E., ii 440n.

Kane, B. F., Secretary to Board of Edu-
cation (Vic.), i 140
Kane, Caroline, teacher in Lonsdale
Street Catholic School, i 107n.
Kelby, Rev. John F., and Catholic His-
tory Readers, ii 411
Kelsh, Rev. Thomas, and St Mary's
Seminary, Hobart, ii 321
Kennedy, Governor Sir Arthur Edward,
i 63, 168
Kenny, Rev. Dean, i 247
Kent Street North Model School, i 87,
102, ii 279; see also Model Schools
Kindergarten movement: Beovich on
need for Catholic kindergarten, ii 451;
development of, 304, 451-2; early
stages in Catholic school, 450-1; pion-

eering work of Mother Gonzaga
Barry, 451
King, Philip Gidley: and Orphan
Schools, i 5, 7, 8; attitude to convict
priests, 17; school finance at Norfolk
Island, 6
Kissing Point, i 10; see also Missionary
activities
Knibbs, George Handly, ii 366n., see
also Commissions on education
Knibbs and Turner Commission, see
Commissions on education
Kranewitter, Father, s.j., ii 261n.

Labor Party, and grants to non-state
schools, ii 464-5
Laity, the Catholic: deluded by government schools, i 210; educational responsibilities, ii 309; ill-informed, i
209, 213, ii 314; interference in ecclesiastical affairs, i 168; means of en-
lightening, 179; mentality of, 210,
249-50, ii 478
Lancastrian System, i 13, 101
Land grants for schools, i 54
Land, opening up of, i 152
Lane, Rev. M., ii 440n.
Lanigan, Bishop William: and the Joint
Pastoral, i 254; founder of St Pat-
rick's College, Goulburn, ii 321; quest
for teaching Brothers, 262; requests
state inspection of Catholic schools,
427
Lang, Rev. Dr John Dunmore: on
Clergy and Schools Corporation, i 15;
attitude to general system, 28n.; on
Romish plans, 143
Langley, Ven. Henry Archdall, ii 462n.
Langsford, J. W., i 142n.
Latham, J. G., and Education Act De-
fence League (Vic.), ii 461
Latin in Catholic schools, ii 363, 371
La Trobe, Lieut.-Governor, C. J., i 65
Lauriston school case, i 203
Law, natural and rights of parents, i
180
Lay teachers in Catholic schools: being
replaced by religious, i 224, ii 279,
280-1, 284-5; difficulty in retaining,
i 244; employed in early secondary
schools, ii 321; high cost of, 259; ratio
to religious, 284, 286, 478; used by
Bishop Willson, i 221
Leach, A. F., i 3
Leadership in Catholic schools, ii 415
Legion of Mary, ii 455, 457
Leo XIII, Pope: and liberalism, ii 422;
and the spirit of a Catholic school,
410; encyclicals of, 383, 384; need
for efficiency in Catholic schools, 399,
424; on importance of the teacher,
387; on the regeneration of society,
415; social teachings of, 308, 385
Leonard, Rev. Dean, ii 438n.

Levinge, Thomas, inspector of Catholic schools, *i* 80, 94n.
Liberal, i 166
Liberalism: and Pius IX, *ii* 385; and politics, *i* 152; and scepticism, 150n.; Archbishop Polding on, 148; Archbishop Vaughan on, 186; Bishop Broughton on, 148; Bishop Moorhouse on, 150; Bishop Perry on, 150; Catholic attitude towards 186, 215, *ii* 422; described by John Henry Newman, *i* 149; identified with non-dogmatic principle, 149; in educational policies of 19th century, 148; influence in the press, 165-6; influence on Protestantism, 150, 186, *ii* 472
Liberty for the child, *ii* 403
Libraries in convents, *ii* 298
Lilley, Sir Charles, *i* 121
Liturgy, as a pedagogical instrument, *ii* 400-18
Local boards: and the clergy, *i* 76, 77; Catholic objection to mixed boards, 77; composition of, 49; failure of, 77; functions of, 50; regulations of, 68; role of clergy on, 76; under Catholic education association, 219; under Woods-Sheil scheme, 77, 225, 228
Local committees, *see* Local boards
Local subscription, *i* 55
Loch, J. D. (Van Diemen's Land), *i* 45
London Missionary Society, *i* 6
Long, J. W., headmaster of St James's Catholic School, Brisbane, *i* 86n., 98n.
Loreto Annual, ii 381
Loreto Sisters (Institute of the B.V.M.): adaptation, *ii* 291; and public examinations, 381; and religious instruction by correspondence, 455; and sodalities, 414; central government, 290; invitations to Australia, 263, 266
Loreto Training Colleges: Albert Park, Melbourne, *ii* 433; Dawson Street, Ballarat, 432
Louch, Rev. Canon, *i* 134n.
Lovat, Rev. Charles, first president of St Mary's Seminary (N.S.W.), *ii* 312
Love, Rev. A., *i* 126n.
Lucerne House Collegiate School, *ii* 323
Luckie, Rev. E., *i* 204n.
Ludovic, Rev. Brother, F.M.S., *i* 247, *ii* 287
Lutheran support for Bible in School leagues, *ii* 459
Lynch, Thomas, *i* 38
Lynch, Very Rev. Dean, *i* 113
Lyndhurst, St Mary's College: academic success of alumni, *ii* 314; beyond humbler class, 326; closed, 325; curriculum, 325, 359, 360, 364; Davis's plans, 313; internal examination system, 369; origin, 313; purpose of,

358-9, 369; success of, 369; unpopular, 325
Lyons, Bishop Patrick, on Catholic Educational claims as social services grant, *ii* 469

Macarthur, James, *i* 32
Macartney, Rev. H. B., *i* 144n., 146
Mackie, Rev. George, *i* 141n.
Mackinson, Rev. Thomas, inspector of Catholic schools, *i* 80
Macmillan's Magazine, ii 299
Macrossan, James M., *i* 202
Macquarie, Governor Lachlan: and Dissenters, *i* 11; and Irish priests, 18, 23; and Marsden, 11; and Nonconformists, 12, 13; dissatisfaction with schools, 12; educational policy, 8; on Sunday schools, 11
Madden, R. R., Colonial Secretary (W.A.), *i* 47n.
Madras System, *i* 101; *see also* Bell system
Maggar, James F., *ii* 471n.
Maguire, Mother Xavier, *ii* 272n.
Maintenon, Madam de, *ii* 301
Maitland, Diocese of, *ii* 278
Maitland, West, *i* 113
Malone, Rev. M. P., *ii* 468n.
Mannix, Archbishop Daniel: and the scholarship scheme, *ii* 338; on Catholics and secondary education, 334; importance of Catholic education, 304-5; on religious instruction of Catholic children in state schools, 457; on tax remissions for education, 466; on the Catholic college within the university, 448; on training in purity, 406-7; views on a Catholic university in Australia, 449-50
Mannix, Michael, *ii* 271n.
Marillac House, *ii* 453
Marist Brothers: and Archbishop Polding, *i* 247; and Archbishop Vaughan, 246; and Australian recruits, *ii* 287; and science teaching, 368; and technical education, 375; Brother Ludovic, first superior, 287; and Catholic school texts, 410; evolution of middle class curriculum, 371; *Guide des Écoles,* 406; influence of De La Salle, 302; invitation to Australia, *i* 246; requests for openings, *ii* 262, 264, 265, 266; St Mary's High School, Sydney, 326-7; schools and colleges, 326, 328, 330; secondary schools for middle classes, 325-6; subjected to close examination, *i* 144n., 247; subsequent foundations, *ii* 276
Marist Fathers: educational work, *ii* 269, 375; proposed Mission to Chinese in Australia, 264
'Marks' days, *ii* 404
Marryat, Ven. Archdeacon, *i* 131

Marsden, Rev. Samuel: and establishment of schools, *i* 9; and Macquarie, 11; and Sunday school conflict, 11

Mary, the Blessed Virgin, *i* 69n., *ii* 419

Mary of the Cross, Mother: and central government, *ii* 294, 295; and education of the poor, 292; as a teacher, 293; co-foundress of Sisters of St Joseph, *i* 232, *ii* 292; excommunicated, *i* 236-7; significance in Catholic education, *ii* 475; spiritual formation of, 302; standards in Catholic schools, 357

Mary's Mount, Ballarat, *ii* 378, 381

Mass, assistance at, *ii* 419

Mathematics, teaching of, *ii* 363

Matthews, Rev. M., first president of Sacred Heart College, Maitland, *ii* 321

Matthews, N. H., *ii* 467n.

McCarthy, Bishop John, formerly inspector of Catholic schools, Melbourne, *ii* 424

McCay, Mother, and Catholic school texts, *ii* 411n.

McClean, James, principal of Victoria College, East Melbourne, *ii* 324

McCredie, Inspector J., *i* 106n, 205n.

McCristal, Thomas, proprietor of private secondary schools, Benalla and Mentone, *ii* 324

McCusker, Rev. J., *ii* 440n.

McEncroe, Rev. John: bringing teachers from Ireland, *i* 85; Director of Catholic schools in New South Wales, 52, 78; inspector of Catholic schools, 80; and Irish National System, 169; and the Marist Brothers, 246; quest for religious, *ii* 260, 265

McGavin, Rev. M., *i* 128n.

McGirr, Rev. James, first president of St Stanislaus', Bathurst, *ii* 321, 361

McGirr, Michael, teacher at St Stanislaus', Bathurst, *ii* 321

McGovern, Rt Rev. J., *ii* 418n.

McGrath, Daniel, early teacher, Q'ld, *i* 39

McGuire, Archbishop Terence, *ii* 376

McHale, Bishop John (of Tuam), *i* 177

McKay, Rev. J., *ii* 440n.

McKillop, Mary, see Mary of the Cross

McMahon, Rev. P. J., *ii* 438n.

McMahon, Rt Rev. J. T.: protagonist for improved methods of teaching religion, *ii* 396, 400; reforms in Catholic schools, 421

McMullen, M., *i* 226n.

Meagher, Rev. P., *ii* 438n.

Mechanics, elementary, in the primary schools, *ii* 355

Meditation, *ii* 419

Melbourne, Archdiocese of: distribution of orders, *ii* 275; replacement of lay teachers by religious, 281

Melbourne Education Exhibition, *ii* 352

Memorizing, over-emphasis on, *ii* 353, 354, 394

Mentone College, *ii* 324

Mercury (Hobart), *i* 160

Mercy, Sisters of: accompany Bishop J. Quinn, *i* 222; amalgamation, *ii* 290-1, 433; and the Argentine, 274n.; arrival in Western Australia, *i* 37, 39; Brisbane, *ii* 272n., 275; Broken Hill, 276; daughter communities, 276; early communities in Australia, 261, 266, 276-7; from South America, 264; Gunnedah, 276; independent groups, 290n.; Monte St Angelo, Sydney, 272n.; New Zealand, 276; not relying on state grants (Q'ld), *i* 222; 'pension' schools, *ii* 289; role in Bathurst scheme, *i* 237, 243, *ii* 271; secondary schools, 342-3; Singleton, 276; training colleges, Geelong (Vic.) and Nudgee (Q'ld), 431

Method of teaching religion, see Religious instruction

Methods of teaching: collective, *i* 100; monitorial, 100 (see also Monitorial system); mixed, 100; Scotch parochial, 100; simultaneous, 104

Michie Bill, see Bills

Michie, Sir Alexander, *i* 65, *ii* 264n.

Miller, Henry, *i* 65

Military drill, see Physical education

Mistress of schools, office of, *ii* 442

Missionary activities: Kissing Point, *i* 10; Toongabbie, 10; Windsor, 10

Missionaries, Nonconformist, used as teachers, *i* 10

Missionaries of the Sacred Heart: and education, *ii* 269, 341; first community in Australia, 270

Missionary Societies, *ii* 263; see also Propagation of the Faith

Mitchell, Sir Thomas L., Surveyor-General, *i* 54

Mitchell, T., *ii* 330n.

Model Schools: and proposals for training, *i* 80, 85; Catholic, 80, 87; common to all denominations, 89; short courses in, 88

Monasticism: and Presentation Convent, Wagga, *ii* 300; civilizing power of, 300; traditions of, 299-302

Monitorial system, the: illustrated from time-table, *i* 102; widely used, 100, 101n.

Monitors, *i* 48, 88n.

Monitum Pastorale, 1858, *i* 168; see also Decrees

Moon, Misses, Girls' School, Yass, *ii* 344

Moore, Bishop James, *ii* 327

Moore, W. S., *i* 189n.

Moorhouse, Bishop James: on distrust of Rome, *i* 145; on Protestants and the Bible, 131; on the Catholic position, 141, 198; on secular education, 250n.

Moran, Patrick Cardinal: and education committees, *ii* 438; and educational reforms, 423, 438; and Christian Brothers, 267; on convent education, 382; and De La Salle Brothers, 266; education of the poor, 308-9; influence of Leo XIII, 308, 422; on Catholic education in Queensland, *i* 75; on school and society, *ii* 358; plans for reorganization of Catholic School system, 421, 432; succeeds to see of Sydney, 421, 424

Morely, George, first teacher employed by Father Therry, *i* 21

Moreton Bay, *i* 39

Moreton Bay Courier, and Grammar School Act (Q'ld), *ii* 317

Morris, Rev. W. E., *i* 131

Morrison, Alexander, and the Fink Commission, *ii* 362

Motivation in girls' schools, *ii* 378-9

Month of May devotions, *ii* 419

Mowll, Most Rev. H., *ii* 467n.

Munich method, *ii* 399; *see also* Religious instruction

Murphy, Bishop Daniel: proposed college at Carnavon, *ii* 330-1; quest for teaching Brothers, 262-3; replacing lay teachers by religious, *i* 239; withdrawing Catholic schools from under the Board, 239

Murphy, Rev. E., *ii* 440n.

Murphy, Bishop Francis: and first Catholic school in Adelaide, *i* 39; and Provincial Council of 1844, 167; and state sponsorship of education, 53; evidence before Select Committee, 1851, 171; on social role of education, *ii* 308; quest for religious, 263

Murphy, Mother Ignatius, *ii* 272n.

Murray, Archbishop Daniel (Dublin), *i* 85, 176

Murray, Bishop John: debarring parents from sacraments, *i* 206, 215; purpose of Joint Pastoral, 253; use of religious, *ii* 262

Music: in convent schools, *ii* 297-8, 377, 379, 445; in denominational schools, *i* 100; instrumental, *ii* 377; vocal, 377

Nagle, Nano, foundress of Presentation Sisters, *ii* 301

Naturalism and Catholic education, *ii* 392

Natural law and parental rights in education, *i* 180, *ii* 463

Natural Science: special courses approved by Dr Goold; *i* 97; views of Dr Polding and Dr Goold on, 97

National Board of Education (N.S.W.): Model School, Fort Street, *i* 88; origin, 47; and non-vested schools, 67

National education before Reformation, *i* 3

National outlook, emergence of, *i* 43

National schools, increase of, *i* 135

Normal schools and safeguards for Catholic students, *i* 87

National Catholic Education Conference (of Directors and Inspectors): and select schools, *ii* 351; and Young Catholic Students movement, 416; encourages legitimate association of the sexes, 409; on accrediting systems, 412; on corporal punishment, 404; on danger of regimentation, 405; on nursery school movement, 452; on schools for handicapped children, 453; on teacher-training, 430; on the Catechism, 396; on uniform syllabus of religious instruction, 392; triennial meetings of, 440

National education, problems of, *i* 24-5; influence of press, 162-3

'National' System, *i* 101; *see also* Bell

National system, Catholic schools a part of, *ii* 257

Nealon, Rev. T., *ii* 438n.

Needlework, teaching of, *ii* 355

Neutral Schools and Catholics, *i* 179

Nevin, Rev. Bernard, first president of St Francis Xavier's Seminary, Adelaide, *ii* 322

Newman College, University of Melbourne, *ii* 447

Newman, John Henry: on liberalism, *i* 149; on Unitarianism, 151

Newman Society for Catholic university students, *ii* 449

New South Wales Sunday School Society, *i* 6

New South Wales Public Schools League, i 123n.

Nixon, Bishop Francis Russell, *i* 45

'No Popery', *i* 148n.

Nonconformists: and Clergy and Schools Corporation, *i* 16; and educational plans of Bourke, 29, 31, 33; educational schemes in South Australia, 35; influence in press, 161; *see also* Missionaries, Sunday schools

Non-dogmatic religious instruction: Catholic attitude to, *i* 190-1; Congregationalist attitude to, 120-1; support from educational writers, 154; support from press, 160

Non-vested schools, *i* 64, 66, 112

Norfolk Island, *i* 5, 6

Normal Schools, *i* 48, 50, 87

Nursery school movement, *ii* 452

Obedience, vow of, *ii* 442

Object lessons, *ii* 354

O'Brien, Rev. Dean, *ii* 438n.

O'Brien, Archbishop Eris M., *i* 4n., 5, *ii* 435

O'Brien, Rev. A. E.: American and German influence on, *ii* 400; and traditional catechetical methods, 400; protagonist for improved methods in teaching of religion, 393n., 394n., 395n., 399

O'Brien, Sister M. Anselm, o.p., and 'Catholic Evidence' method, *ii* 397

Observer, Adelaide, i 161

O'Connor, J. G., letter from Vaughan, *i* 255

O'Connor, Bishop Michael, *ii* 266

O'Connor, Rev. T. J., Inspector of Schools, *ii* 400, 453n.

O'Donovan, Denis, *ii* 323

O'Farrell, Bishop Michael, *ii* 350

Official Pronouncement of the Australian Hierarchy, ii 385

O'Flynn, Rev. Jeremiah, *i* 17n., 18, 20

Ogg, Rev. C., *i* 192n.

O'Grady, Michael, *i* 203n.

O'Haran, Rev. Denis, *ii* 268n.

O'Neale, Rev. Peter, *i* 17

O'Reilly, Archbishop J.: on Catholics and liberalism, *i* 215; on Catholics and the Bible, 193; on policy of Australian Labor Party, 152n.; on Protestant influence in Education Acts, 197

O'Reilly, Rev. John, *ii* 447n.

O'Reilly, Rev. Maurice, c.m.: and Bursary Board (N.S.W.), *ii* 339; need for more pupil responsibility, 405; president of St Stanislaus's College, Bathurst, 405

Organization of Catholic education system: and Archbishop M. Beovich, *ii* 440; bishops' standing Committee on Education, 440; Fourth Plenary Council on, 439; little organization in early schools, 437; office of Director of Catholic education, 437, 438-9; pattern of diocesan organization, 437, 439-40; recommendations of National Catholic Education Conference, 438-9; units of, 437, 441; within religious communities, 442

Organization within schools, *see* Schools

Orlebar, Inspector A. R., *i* 98n.

Orphan Schools, *i* 5, 7, 8, 20; *see also* King, Philip Gidley

Oscott House, Elsternwick, *ii* 323

O'Shannassy, Sir John, *i* 48

Oxford Movement, *i* 80

Palmer, Sir James, *i* 203n.

Palmer, Thomas, *i* 121, *ii* 360

Panico, Archbishop John, Apostolic-Delegate, *ii* 305

Parents: apathetic in regard to education, *i* 52, 77, 107, 108; debarred from sacraments, 215, 236; educational responsibilities, *ii* 324, 385-7; not fitted to give religious instruction, *i* 185; responsibilities of, 180, 195; rights of, 179-80, *ii* 468

Parkes, Sir Henry: 'aid to education not aid to religion', *i* 121; and Catholics, *ii* 470, 471; and general system, *i* 158; and religious orders, *ii* 299; and secular education, *i* 157, 159, 162; and the clergy, *ii* 260n.; and the sacramental life in Catholic education, 417; attitude to denominational schools, *i* 158; correspondence with David Syme, 162; *and Empire,* 157; on motives of Protestants in abandoning denominational schools, 146; on necessity of religion in education, 158; on influence of laity in Church of England, 134; on justice of Catholics' claim, 199-200; on the Roman bogey, 201; political somersault, 159; Public Schools Act, 1866, 67; reaction to *Joint Pastoral,* 251; 'religious instruction not at expense of state', 121; on state rights in education, 157, 200

Parliament, Acts of: effects on Catholic secondary schools, *ii* 348-9; alleged Protestant influence in, *i* 197-8, 201, 222; appear superfluous, 140, 202; Catholic attitude to, 196-7, 199; motives behind, 202, 220-1; principal education acts, *ii* 482-3

New South Wales: Bursary Endowment Act (1912), *ii* 333, 349, 379; Bourke's Church Act (1836), *i* 31, 32, 40; Denominational and National Boards (1848), *i* 47; Public Instruction Act (1880), 60, 239, 250n., *ii* 288, 471; Public Schools Act (1866), *i* 67, 81, 93, 120, 194n., 250n.; University Act (1912), *ii* 333

Queensland: Grammar School Act (1860), *ii* 317; Primary Education Act (1860), *i* 64, 67, 120, 130; State Education Act (1875), 60, 149, 249; Scripture reading in state schools (1910), *ii* 462

South Australia: Education Act (1852), *i* 60, 63, 67n., 190, 192; Education Act (1875), 197n., 249; Education Act (1878), *ii* 426; Education Act (1891), *i* 249; Public Education Act (1847), 46, 53, 56n., 57; High School Act (1915), *ii* 333; Act permitting religious instruction in schools (1940), 462

Tasmania: Registration Act (1906), 349

Victoria: Act permitting religious instruction (1950), 463; Common Schools Act (1862), *i* 66, 67n., 93, 97, 120, 125, 134-5,

172; Registration Act (1905), *ii* 290n., 349, 379, 427; Secular Act (1872), *i* 149, 248, 250, *ii* 265, 285, 458

Western Australia: Education Act (1893), *i* 249; Education Act (1895), 60, 249, *ii* 266, 426; Elementary Education Act (1871), *i* 64, 67, 68n., 194n., 207; High School Acts (1875, 1876), *ii* 332-3

Parliament, Select Committees of: New South Wales (1844), *i* 33, 43, 47, 61, 169; (1854), 66; Queensland (1861), 64, 105; South Australia (1851), 62; (1861), 183, 224; (1868), 231; Tasmania (1853), 62, 63; (1952), *ii* 466, 467, 468n., 469n.; Victoria (1852), *i* 62, 65, 85n., 171, 180, *ii* 475n.; Western Australia (1871), *i* 63; (1895), 78n.

Parochial system: factors in development, *ii* 306-9; its influence and extent, 305-6; school an essential part of the parish, 310; secondary (boys), 339-41; secondary (girls), 351

Parramatta Street Catholic Model School, *i* 87, 110

Parsons, J. Langdon, *i* 192n.

Pastoral letters: from Provincial Council, Melbourne, 1862, *i* 170, 171; from Provincial Council, Melbourne (1869), 188n., 196, *ii* 475; Joint Pastoral (1879), *i* 179; minor pastorals of 1870s, 178-9; *Monitum Pastorale* (1858), 168; of Archbishop and Bishops of the Plenary Council (1885), *ii* 473; Archbishop and Bishops of Province of Melbourne (1890), 460n.; of Cardinal Delegate, Archbishops and Bishops (1905), 303n., 467n., 476; of Geoghegan (1860), *i* 168, 223-4; of Polding (1836, 1839), 167; (1857), 167; of Sheil (1871), 178n.; of Vaughan (1879), 250-1; (1883), 253, *ii* 258

Pastors: educational responsibilities, *ii* 309; rights of, *i* 179

Patrician Brothers: invitations from bishops, *ii* 262; secondary schools, 326

Payment by results, *i* 73, 98

'Pay' schools, *ii* 289

Peake, E. J., *i* 226n.

Pearson, Professor Charles H., *i* 198n.

'Penny a day' system, *i* 46, 56, 63

Penola, *i* 223, *ii* 293

'Pension' schools, see 'Pay' schools

Perry, Bishop Charles, *i* 131

Pestalozzian system, the, *i* 101

Petitions of Catholics to parliament, *i* 78n.

Phillip, Governor Arthur, *i* 5

Phillips, Mrs, early teacher, Adelaide, *i* 39n.

Physical education, *ii* 355

Pirie Street Catholic School, Adelaide, *i* 110

Pius IX, Pope, *i* 176, 186n., *ii* 383, 385, 422, 474

Pius X, Pope: *Acerbo nimis*, *ii* 391, 399; *Quam singulari*, 399

Pius XI, Pope: and the spirit of a Catholic school, *ii* 409, 410; encyclical, *Divini Illius Magistri, The Catholic Education of Youth* (English trans.), 385, 423; *Motu Proprio*, on teaching religion, 399; on importance of the teacher, 387; on sex instruction, 406-7; on surveillance, 403

Pius XII, Pope, and the adequate training of religious, *ii* 431

Plan d'Études, *ii* 303

Pluralism, *ii* 479

Pitt Street Refuge, *ii* 288

Plunket, James, Oscott House, Elsternwick, *ii* 323

Plunkett, John Hubert: and Common Schools Act (1866), *i* 206; chairman of National Board, 67n.; proposals for two boards, 47; supporter of national education, 28, 153, 215

Pohlman, R. W., first chairman of Denominational Schools Board, Vic., *i* 48n.

Polding, Archbishop John Bede: aims of education, *i* 52; and Benedictine aspirations, *i* 245, *ii* 299; and delegation of authority, *i* 78; and Denominational Board, 52; and Irish National System, 30, 169; and secondary schools, *ii* 312-13; and St John's College, 447; and Marist Brothers, *i* 246-7; and use of liturgical ceremony, *ii* 418; at Downside, *i* 261; and education of poor, *ii* 291-2; and the classical tradition, 364; attitude to religious teachers, *i* 245, *ii* 261, 302; basic philosophy and theology of, 383; circular to clergy (1863), *i* 170; evidence before Select Committee (1844), 169, 185; on Common Schools Act (1862), 172; on Council of Education, 206, 219-20; on courses of study, 96; on defects in teachers, 88; on religious education, 187; on teachers' salaries, 83; on training local teachers, 87; pastorals (1836, 1839), 167, (1859), 167, 184; principles set before legislature, 173; proposed general scheme, 170; regulations on using text-books, 106; religious for upper classes, *ii* 292; role of dogma, *i* 186; 'School Regulations' of, 94-6, *ii* 490, see Appendix VI; social plan for education, 359, 364, 365; support for Bourke's plans, *i* 30; traditions of monasticism, *ii* 300; writer of text-books, *i* 101, 115

Post-primary schools for girls, *ii* 351

Port Phillip College, *ii* 316
Portus, G. V., *i* 4, 141n.
Powell, Rev. P., *i* 37n.
Power, Rev. Daniel, *i* 23
Practices in religious education, Catholic, *i* 183, 187; *ii* 303
Pre-Cana conferences, *ii* 387
Prefect of Studies, office of, *ii* 442
Presence of God, meditation on, *ii* 419
Priestcraft, *i* 164, *ii* 352
Premonstrants, *i* 144, *ii* 259
Prendiville, Archbishop Redmond, *ii* 281, 421
Presbyterians: abandoning denominational schools, *i* 136; and British and Foreign School Society system, 126; and educational plans of Bourke and Gipps, 31; and Irish National system, 126; and non-dogmatic instruction, 126; and secular education, 125-6; expenditure on education, 58-9; mixed views on denominational and general systems, 126-7; parents versus state in education, 127; proposed use of licentiates, 126; religious instruction from class teacher, 126; opposition on religious instruction, 124
Presentation Sisters: amalgamation, *ii* 434; daughter foundations, 277, 279; Gardenvale, 290; secondary schools, 344; Wagga Wagga, 277, 300; Windsor, 265n., 290
Press, influence of, *i* 153, 162
Priests, convict, as schoolmasters, *i* 17
Principles of Catholic education, *ii* 470, 477
Private schools: for boys, *ii* 323-4; for girls, 345
Privy Council System, *i* 106, 170
Progressives and Catholic education, *ii* 392
Propagation of the Faith, Society of, *i* 223-4
Protestants: abandoning denominational schools, *i* 134-5, 141; at convent schools, *ii* 347-8; aversion for Roman practices and beliefs, *i* 143-4; change of attitude, 118, *ii* 457, 459-63, 467-8; distrust of Catholics, *i* 143, 201, *ii* 466; drawn to secularism, *i* 148; grievance of, 142-3; Higinbotham on, 139; mixed population in denominational schools, 137-8; motives in abandoning denominational schools, 146, *ii* 472; neglect of religious instruction, *i* 139-40; opposition to general system of education, 27, 29-30
Protestant Christianity, principles of, *ii* 473
Protestant Federation and the 1952 Select Committee (Tas.), *ii* 467
Protestant Political Association, *i* 143
Provincial Councils, *see* Councils
Provisional schools, *i* 238

Prussia, *i* 163
Public examinations: and proposed accrediting system, *ii* 374, 412; disadvantages of, 411; in girls' schools, 379-82; premium on results, 374-5; resistance to, 381; support from Catholic schools, 369, 372
Public schools: Catholics attending, *i* 19, 20, 211-13, 232; Catholic attitude towards, 19, 253
Public Schools League (N.S.W.), *i* 123, 146
Punishment: corporal, *i* 94, *ii* 404; forms of, *i* 94
Pupil responsibility, need for, *ii* 405
Pupil-teacher system: as a system of training, *i* 85; condemned by Knibbs and Turner, *ii* 432; living allowances for, *i* 89; pupil-teacher centres, *ii* 431; widely used in 19th century, 431
Purity, training in: Archbishop Carr on, *ii* 406; Catholic views on, 406-8; measures taken in archdiocese of Melbourne, 407-8; Pius XI on, 406-7
'Psalm of Life', *ii* 458
Pyrmont, Catholic School at, *ii* 289

Quam non sine, *ii* 383
Quam singulari, and age for receiving Holy Communion, *ii* 399
Queensland Guardian, see *Guardian, Queensland*
Quinn, Bishop James: alleged collaboration in general system, *i* 172, 195, *ii* 318-19; alleged influence on Bishop Tufnell, *i* 145; and central government for religious, *ii* 290n., 294; and Grammar School Act, Q'ld, 317-20, 328; and plans concerning University of London, 370; and Sisters of St Joseph of Sacred Heart, 294-5; and state inspection of Catholic schools, 426, 428; evidence before Royal Commission, *i* 188; experienced teacher, *ii* 266; immigrant teachers from Ireland, *i* 86; on cost of Catholic education, 217; on secular education, 184; plans for Catholic education, 221-2, 244, *ii* 266; proposals for university, 320; support for public examinations, 370, 381; requests for school grants, *i* 65
Quinn, Bishop Matthew: and schools independent of government, *i* 238-9; and the curriculum, *ii* 364; quest for teaching Brothers, 262; scheme for Catholic education in Bathurst, *i* 237-8, 242; shaping educational policy of bishops in N.S.W., 254; use of religious, *ii* 259, 262

Rationalism, *i* 151-2
Ratio studiorum, *ii* 303
Reading in primary schools, *ii* 352-3, 355
Reddall, Rev. Thomas, *i* 13

Redemptorists, the, *i* 144

Regimentation in Catholic schools, danger of, *ii* 405

Register, South Australian: Nonconformist influence in, *i* 161; support for secular education, 161

Registration of teachers, *see* Acts and Bills

Règlements (of Ursulines), *ii* 303

Reilly, Joseph, inspector of Catholic schools, *i* 80

Religion, teaching of, *see* Religious instruction

Religious: adaptation, *ii* 288, 291; amalgamation, 290-1, 433; and professional qualifications, 388-9; and scholarships, 337; and school fees, 289; Australian foundations, 269, 271; Australian recruits, 261, 287; Church's policy on use in schools, 259, 267, 268, 387; communities from abroad, 268, 272-4, 286; contribution to culture, 257, 297-8; daughter communities, 274, 276-7; defects in training, 428; distribution in dioceses, 274-5; diversion to teaching, 288; employed in teaching the poor, *i* 233, 234; influence on Catholic people, *ii* 299; initial foundations, 272-5; in service training as teachers, 435-6; instruction from the Misses Bell, 436; in Woods-Sheil scheme, *i* 232-3; new secondary schools, *ii* 326; not accepting state grants, *i* 247; orders taking up teaching in Australia, *ii* 270; organization within communities, 441-2, *see also* Religious communities; quest for, 257, 267, 268; refresher schools for, 435-6; replacing lay teachers, *i* 238, *ii* 279-81, 284; role in Catholic education, 257, 476; sceptical approach to modern theories of discipline, 405-6; schools for upper classes, 292, 341; teaching systems of, 302-3

Religious communities, government in: central, *ii* 290, 294, 295; diocesan, 290; independent houses, 289

Religious difficulty, *i* 139-40

Religious education: atmosphere, *i* 3, 187-8; a unity, 187; Bigge's recommendations on, 13; in early institutions, 3; factors affecting, *ii* 383-5; formation as well as information, 401-20

Religious indifference in the community, *i* 137

Religious instruction: activity methods, *ii* 397; American influence on, 400; and impact of secular pedagogy, 383, 395, 397; and the boards, *i* 49-50, 69; and the class teacher, 195; and the teaching orders, *ii* 401; by correspondence, 454-5; Catholic requirements in, *i* 183-95; difficulties owing to mixed population in denominational schools, 138; ecclesiastical directives on, *ii* 389-92; ecclesiastical inspection and examination, 389-90; for Catholic children not in Catholic schools, *i* 115; given by visiting pastors and sisters, 70, 113-14; impossibility of leaving to parents, 185; interests of various groups safeguarded, 69; methods, 113-15, 116, *ii* 393-9, 400; non-dogmatic, *i* 150; obligation of religious, *ii* 389; omitted, *i* 138; parents' rights safeguarded, 50; psychological approach, *ii* 399; questionnaire on, *i* 113-14; 'released' time, 70; requirements in a teacher of religion, 188; restrictions on, 194; revival of traditional Catholic methods, *ii* 398, 400; social setting, 397, 398; standard of efficiency in, *i* 116; teacher of religion, 188, 189; textbooks, 69, 113-14; syllabus of, *ii* 390-2; uniform syllabus in Victoria, 401; voluntary principle, *i* 35-6, 120; writers on methods, 399-401; *see also* Religious formation

Reville, Bishop Stephen, *ii* 384, 427

Reynolds, Archbishop C.: and the Deharbe Catechism, *ii* 393; members of Woods' Central Council, *i* 226n.; on 'schools before churches', *ii* 311; quest for religious, 264

Riddell, C. D. (first chairman of Denominational Schools Board, N.S.W.), *i* 48n.

Rigney, Very Rev. Dean, *i* 105, *ii* 318

Robe, Governor Frederick Holt, *i* 36, 46

Robertson, Rev. A., *i* 198

Rogers, J. W.: and military drill, *ii* 355; Inspector of Catholic schools, Sydney, 323, 353, 425, 428; on religious teachers, 288n., proprietor of private secondary school, Ballarat, 323

Roman Catholic Education Society, *i* 22

Rome, distrust of: among Protestants, *i* 141-3, 164; Anglicans divided on, 145; Bishop Barker on, 144; effect of uniting Protestants, 144; motives of Public Schools League, 146; and Nonconformists, 143, 145; and Protestant Political Association, 143

Ronan, Rev. Father, *ii* 440n.

Roper, Alban, teacher at Catholic school, Launceston, *i* 86n.

Roper, Joseph, teacher at Catholic school, Hobart, *i* 86n., *ii* 330

Rosary of the B.V.M., *ii* 419

'Rosebank' Convent, *ii* 348

Ross, Rev. D., *i* 142n.

Ross, Rev. R. R., *i* 120n.

Rousseau, Jean Jaques, *ii* 392

Rowe, Rev. G. E., *i* 142n.

Royal Commission on education, *see* Commissions on education

Royal Readers, *ii* 458
Rozelle, Catholic School at, *ii* 289
Rusden, G. W.: on control of education, *i* 1n.; agent of National Board, 153; on national systems, 163; role of Church in education, 154
Rusden, H. K., *i* 150n.
Russell, Rev. Father, Director of Catholic Education, Adelaide, *ii* 434n.
Ryan, Rev. Michael, *i* 78, 183n.
Ryan, Rev. Wilfrid, s.j., *ii* 330n.

Sacraments: parents debarred from, *i* 215, 236; place in education, 181, *ii* 400, 417-18
Sacramental system as a pedagogical instrument, *ii* 400, 417-18
Sacred Congregation of the Holy Office, on sex instruction, *ii* 407
Sacred Heart, Brothers of: congregation disbanded, *ii* 269, 271; numbers, *i* 243
Sacred Heart College, Geelong, *ii* 345
Sacred Heart College, Maitland, *ii* 321, 326, 364, 366, 370
Sacred Heart, Religious of the, *ii* 290, 381
Sacred Heart Sodality, *ii* 455
St Aloysius' College, Sevenhill, *ii* 316, 361, 364
St Aloysius' Teachers' Training College, Geelong, *ii* 431
St Augustine, and *De Catechizandis Rudibus*, *ii* 399
St Benedict's School, *ii* 289
St Benedict's Catholic Model School, *i* 87
St Clair Donaldson, Bishop, *ii* 459
St Francis' School, Melbourne, *i* 89, *ii* 285n.
St Francis' Seminary, Melbourne, *ii* 315
St Francis Xavier's College, Kew: beginnings, *ii* 327; curriculum, 366; honours class, 362
St Francis Xavier's Collegiate School, Adelaide, *ii* 330
St Francis Xavier's School, Adelaide, *i* 243n.
St Francis' Xavier's Seminary, Adelaide, *ii* 321, 361, 364
St Ignatius' College, Riverview: curriculum, *ii* 366-7, 369; observatory, 368; origin, 325
St John the Baptist, Brothers of, *ii* 269
St John's College, Perth, *ii* 314, 361, 363, 366
St John's College, University of Sydney, *i* 167, *ii* 265n., 447, 448
St Joseph, Sisters of, *ii* 295
St Joseph of the Apparition, Sisters of, *ii* 266
St Joseph of the Sacred Heart, Sisters of: adaptation to Australian conditions, *ii* 291; and education of the poor, 291, 292, 296; Australian foundation, 269;

central government, 294; daughter communities, 276; early demand for, *i* 232; indiscretion of some early members, 236; organization in early schools, 232, *ii* 294; primitive spirit maintained, 296; rapid development, 293, 295; role in Woods-Sheil scheme, *i* 232; role in Bathurst scheme, 237, 242-3; schools in rural districts, 233; training of early teachers, *ii* 293
St Joseph's College, Hunter's Hill: and science teaching, *ii* 368; curriculum, 369; foundation, 326
St Joseph's College, Nudgee, *ii* 329
St Kilda House, Woolloomooloo, later St Aloysius' College, North Sydney, *ii* 325
St Kilian's College, Brisbane, *ii* 327, 370
St Leo's College, University of Brisbane, *ii* 447
St Mary's College, Lyndhurst, *i* 80; *see also* Lyndhurst
St Mary's Hall, University of Melbourne, *ii* 448
St Mary's High School, Sydney, *ii* 326-7
St Mary's Seminary, Hobart, *ii* 316, 322, 361, 364, 366
St Mary's Seminary, Sydney, *i* 80n., 312, 325
St Mary's Superior Boys' Boarding and Day School, Geelong, *ii* 316
St Patrick's, Church Hill, Catholic Model School, *i* 87
St Patrick's School, Adelaide, *i* 243n.
St Patrick's College, Goulburn: curriculum, *ii* 364, 366, 369; early staffs, 323, 326; origin, 321
St Patrick's College, Melbourne, *ii* 316, 327
St Patrick's Secondary School, Church Hill, *ii* 325
St Patrick's Seminary, Launceston, *ii* 324
St Paul, *i* 181n.
St Stanislaus' College, Bathurst: curriculum, *ii* 364, 366, 369; early staff, 323; origin, 321; Vincentian staff, 326; X-ray experiments, 368
St Stanislaus' High School, Bathurst, *ii* 321
St Vincent de Paul Society, *ii* 416
St Vincent's College, Potts' Point, *ii* 344
Salaries, teachers', *see* State grants for education
Salesian Fathers, and education, *ii* 341
Salvado, Bishop Rosendo, *ii* 300
Sancta Sophia, University of Sydney, *ii* 448
Saunders, Rev. John, *i* 31, 122n.
Scannel, Rev. Brother B. P., Irish Christian Brother, *i* 88n., 101n.
Scepticism, religious, *i* 140, 150n., 151
School attendances, *i* 108-9
School fees, *i* 54
School Fund (S.A.), *i* 223

School leaving age, *i* 108-9, 110
'School money', *see* Finance for Catholic Schools
'School Regulations', *see* Polding, Archbishop John Bede
'Schools before churches', *ii* 309, 310
Schools, Catholic boys' secondary: and public examination system, *ii* 372; competition from state secondary schools, 325; diocesan clergy replaced by religious, 326; early phase, 311-20; evolution of middle class schools, 371-2; fees, 334; fillip from scholarships, 339; for middle class, 370; fourth phase, 331-41; lack of diversity, 374; legislation, First Plenary Council, 324; numbers of, 331-2, 341; parochial, 339-41; phases in development, 311-12; proprietary schools, 323-4; second phase, 320-24; staffs, 322-3; survival of, 331; technical and agricultural, 359, 375; third phase, 324-31; under religious orders, 326; *see also* Secondary education.
Schools, Catholic girls' secondary: attended by Protestants, *ii* 347-8; contribution to secondary education, 348; disappearance of the select school, 349-50; first phase, 342-5; for middle classes, 345; for 'Young Ladies', 345; importance of, 386; motivation, 378-9; numbers, 342, 344, 346, 348, 351; organization of classes, 378; parochial, 351; phases of development, 342; post-primary, 351; private schools, 345; second phase of development, 345-8; select schools, 342, 348
Schools, state secondary: competition for Catholic schools, *ii* 325, 331, 334; development of, 331-3; difficulties of early schools, 335
Schools under the Boards: equipment, *i* 91; material conditions of, 91-3; organization, 94, 107
Scholarship system: 'Bishops' Scholarships', *ii* 337; liberalizing of, 339; promotion of secondary education, 336-7; Protestant opposition to, 337
Scholastica, Sister M., *ii* 288n.
Science in the primary school, *ii* 354, 355
Science Teachers' Association and Catholic teachers, *ii* 437
Scotch parochial method, *i* 100
Scott, Rev. H. F., *i* 145n.
Scott, Rev. Thomas Hobbes: *i* 12n.; as visitor of schools, 15; resignation, 16; jurisdiction over Catholic schools, 21
Scripture-reading in school, *see* Bible in school
Scripture, without note or comment, *i* 36
Secondary education: and lack of appreciation by Catholics, *ii* 324-5; and Provincial Council (1869), 320; and

scholarship system, 336-7; and the Catholic bishops, 320; classical bias, 325; contribution of the convent school, 348; need of society, 312
Sectarianism: in politics, *i* 201; in the press, 163-4
Sectarian jealousy among denominations, *ii* 318, 470
Secular education: and Catholic attitude towards, *i* 183, *ii* 474; interpretation of in state schools, 458; reaction from, 457-63; support from the press, *i* 160-1
Secular pedagogy: and assimilation by religious orders, *ii* 302; influence on Catholic education, 477; influence on methods of religious instruction, 383
Secularist leagues, *i* 123
Secularist motives, *i* 146
Select Committee on education, *see* Parliament
Self-government by pupils, Catholic views on, *ii* 405
Serra, Bishop Joseph M.: and religious teachers, *ii* 266; and traditions of monasticism, 300; correspondence with Governor Kennedy, *i* 63, 168; refuses place on Board of Education, 180n.
Seventh Day Adventists and the 1952 Select Committee (Tas.), *ii* 467
Sex instruction, *see* Purity, training in
Sheehan, Archbishop Michael: and improved methods of teaching religion, *ii* 400; and the 'Official Pronouncement', *i* 197n., *ii* 385; author of *A Child's Book of Religion*, 396; author of *Religion by Letter*, 396; on religious teachers, 388
Sheedy, Rev. S. J. A., Vicar-General to Polding, *i* 78, 113, 219, 247
Sheil, Bishop Laurence: and full religious instruction, *i* 194; Bishop of Adelaide, 224 and n.; debarring parents from sacraments, 215, 236; educational policy, 173; first president of St Francis' (Melbourne), *ii* 316; Inspector-General of Roman Catholic Schools, *i* 78-9; on education of women, *ii* 386; quest for religious, 264; Woods-Sheil scheme, *i* 79, *ii* 225-37
Sheridan, Rev. Father, *i* 114
Shields, Dr Thomas, and the Catholic Readers, *ii* 396
Short, Bishop Augustus, *i* 131, 147
Shorthand and book-keeping in primary schools, *ii* 355
Simonds, Archbishop Justin, and accrediting system (Tas.), *ii* 412
Simultanschulen, *i* 178
Sisters classified under Council of Education, N.S.W., *see* Classification
Sloyd, in primary schools, *ii* 355
Smith, F. L., *i* 74n, 135n.
Smith, G. V., *i* 184n.
Smyth, Rev. John, *i* 223n., 226n., 236

Specialist teachers, *i* 97
Spelling, *ii* 353
Spencer, Herbert, *ii* 365, 387, 392
Social conditions of Catholics, *i* 210
Social justice: and Catholic view of education question, *ii* 469; approximation between Catholic and Protestant thought, 468
Social services and Catholic educational claims, *ii* 469
Society of the Propagation of the Faith, *i* 223-4
Society for Promoting Christian Knowledge, *i* 6
Society for the Propagation of the Gospel in Foreign Parts, *i* 6
Sodalities: history of, *ii* 413-14; manner of operating, 413; names of, 414; recommended by Plenary Councils, 414
Somerwell, A., *ii* 298n.
Sorell, Lieutenant-Governor William, *i* 34
South Australian Register, *i* 161
South Australian School Society: and aid to religion, *i* 120; Congregationalist influence in, 119; origin, 36
'Sower' Series in teaching religion, *ii* 396
State aid to religion, *i* 120, 152
State and education, *i* 25, 171, 182, 196, 200
State before Church, *i* 140
State control in education, *i* 1; *ii* 470
State grants for education: accepted by religious, *i* 71; books and equipment, 56; Catholics claim *pro-rata* share, *ii* 469; Catholic schools relying on, *i* 73, 174, 217; conditions for, 40-2, 55, 60, 67, 70; disparity and discrimination, 59, 73; distribution, 57-9; enervating Catholics, 217; extent of, 40-1, 54-5, 57-9, 72, 72n., 73n.; for boarding, 56; for buildings, 55-6, 70-1; for salaries, 56, 62n., 71, 72
State grants to non-state schools: Knibbs and Turner on, *ii* 464; Labor Party on, 464-5; Liberal Party on, 465; 1952 Joint Select Committee (Tas.), 466; no longer a purely religious matter, 466
State schools: competition for Catholic schools, *ii* 356; protestantizing of, 461, 472; reintroduction of religion, 462-3; standards in school subjects, 356-7
State system of education embracing the Catholic system, *i* 60, *ii* 479
Standards in Catholic schools: assimilated to those of the state, *ii* 356-8, 423, 424; episcopal committee on, 356; uniform standard undesirable, 357; *see also* Catholic schools
Stanley, Lord Edward, *i* 28

Stephen, Wilberforce, and Catholics, *i* 201, *ii* 458
Stephens, John, *i* 161n.
Stow, Rev. Thomas Quentin, Congregationalist leader in South Australia, *i* 36, 120
Stuart, Sir Alexander: attitude to Rome, *i* 146; motives of Protestants in abandoning denominational schools, 146
Subiaco (N.S.W.), *ii* 376, 413; *see also* Benedictine nuns
Subiaco House, Catholic secondary school for boys, Perth, *ii* 322
Sunday schools, *i* 10, 11, 122
Sunday School Society, New South Wales, *i* 11
Supernatural in Catholic education, the, *ii* 417-20
Support for Catholic schools, *see* Catholic schools
Surry Hills (N.S.W.), Catholic school at, *ii* 289
Surveillance, *ii* 403-5
Sydney, archdiocese of: distribution of orders, *ii* 275; replacement of lay teachers by religious, 279; use of religious, *i* 245
Sydney Boys' High School, *ii* 368
Sydney Gazette, *i* 22
Sydney Morning Herald: and general system, *i* 160; and sectarianism, 165; and secular education, 160; and the *Joint Pastoral*, 252; changed attitude towards state grants to non-state schools, *ii* 466; Congregationalist influence on, *i* 160; on Clergy and Schools Corporation, 15; opposed to non-denominational scheme, 160
Syllabus errorum, *i* 176, 186n., *ii* 383, 474; *see also* Pius IX
Syme, David, *i* 162
Symons, Rev. J. C., *i* 135n., 183n.
Synods: of Bathurst (1883), *ii* 309n., 384, 424; of Goulburn (1888), 384; of Ireland (National, 1875), 267n., 393; of Maitland (1888), 267, 424; of Melbourne (diocesan, 1875, 1885, 1887), 384, (provincial, 1907), 424; of Sydney (1891), 267-8, 356, 409
Systems of Education, *see* Bell, Denominational, Irish National, Lancastrian, Madras, National systems
Swan River settlement, *i* 39

Tappeiner, Rev. J., s.j., *i* 226n.
Tasmanian Area Schools, *ii* 376
Tate, Frank, Director of Education (Vic.), *ii* 333, 398n., 423
Tax remissions for education at non-state schools, *ii* 465
Teachers: abuses in appointments, *i* 83, 84; appointments and dismissals, 50,

68, 179; brought from Europe, 52; Catholic teachers removed, 205; Catholic views on importance of, *ii* 387, 388, 424; classification, *i* 89-90; defects in training of, 88, *ii* 428; ecclesiastical licence, *i* 2, 4; extra-mural associations for, *ii* 435, 436-7; inferior teachers appointed to Catholic schools, *i* 204-5; in service training for, *ii* 435-6; lack of qualifications, *i* 81, 83-4, 208; of same religion, 68; payment of, 24; place of training, 88; Polding on training of, 88; qualifications of, 50, 60-1; refresher schools, *ii* 435; superiority of women, *i* 84n.; training of, 48, 82, 85; unsuitability of, 81, 83; teacher of religion, *see* Religious instruction

Teaching Methods, *see* Methods of teaching

Technical education: *ii* 374; *see* Curriculum

Text-books: by Polding, *i* 101; by Woods, 229; Catholic objections to, 105, 106; Catholic series of, *ii* 410-11; Christian Brothers series of, *i* 104; control of central boards, 106; diversity of, 104, 208; for use in Catholic schools, 52, 104; prescribed by central boards, 68-9, 105; produced by religious orders, *ii* 410; right of selection of, *i* 51-2; selection, 102-3

Theresian Club, *ii* 457

Therry, Rev. John Joseph: and religious, *ii* 260; and local authorities, *i* 49; arrival as chaplain, 20; attack on Scott, 23; attitude to national scheme, 191n.; establishes schools, 21; in Van Diemen's Land, 45; on necessity of Catholic schools, *ii* 309; Roman Catholic Education Society, *i* 22; suspended by Darling, 23; visiting schools for religious instruction, 113

Therry, Roger, Judge: attitude to general system, *i* 28; on poverty of Catholic community, 59

Thomistic philosophy, influence of, *ii* 477

Thompson, Rev. John, C.M., *ii* 435n.

Thomson, Deas, *ii* 313

Thornton, Rev. Brother F., *ii* 261n.

Tierney, Rev. Father, *ii* 440n.

Time-tables, *i* 102, 103

Tissot, Rev. Father, *ii* 266

Toongabbie, *i* 10; *see also* Missionary activities

Torreggiani, Bishop E., *ii* 262

Town Courier (Hobart), opposed to non-denominational plan, *i* 160

Training colleges for teachers: and impact of Registration Acts, *ii* 432; and Council of Public Education (Vic.), 435; bishops supporting Bills requiring registration of teachers, 430;

Board of Registration (N.S.W.), 434; central colleges planned, 432-4; Church's view on necessity of, 430; common training colleges tried, 433; convent secondary schools as, *i* 89; early colleges established by religious, *ii* 431-2; evolve from pupil-teacher centres, 431; numbers, 434; phases in development of, 431-7; provincial or diocesan colleges suggested, 430; recommended, *i* 85; *see* Teachers

Training, mental, through classics, *ii* 362

Tufnell, Bishop, E. W.: aid for Church schools, *i* 222; and denominational education, 64; attitude to Rome, 145; on non-dogmatic instruction, 130; on religious education, 187n.

Turner, Henry Giles, and Education Act Defence League (Vic.), *ii* 461

Turner, John William, *ii* 366n.; *see also* Commissions on education

Tunnecliffe, T., *ii* 464n.

Tweedy, Archbishop E., and Home Missionary Sisters, *ii* 297

Typing, in primary schools, *ii* 355

Ullathorne, Archbishop W. B.: and Irish National System, *i* 169; and St Mary's Seminary (N.S.W.), *ii* 312; and teachers as immigrants, *i* 85; and the Bible, 193; arrival as Vicar-General, 21; on Clergy and Schools Corporation, 15-16; quest for religious, *ii* 260

Unification of denominational and national boards, *i* 62, 66-7; *see also* Denominational Schools Board

Unitarianism: and liberalism, *i* 151; Higinbotham's interest in, 151; John Henry Newman on, 151

University Colleges, *ii* 304

University education: Catholics active in development of Australian universities, *ii* 446-7; Catholic university colleges, 447-9; precautions for Catholic students, 449; proposed Catholic university, 449-50

University Vacation Schools, *ii* 437

University of: Belgium, *ii* 320; London, 320; Melbourne, 378; Notre Dame, U.S.A., 449n.; Sydney, 313, 361

Ursuline Sisters: and the Kulturkampf, *ii* 274n.; principle of adaptation, 291; traditions maintained, 301

Vatican Council, *i* 178

Vaughan, Archbishop R. B.: and closing of Lyndhurst, *ii* 325; and his Catholic School Board, 438; and liberal Catholics, *i* 254; and the Marist Brothers, 246; and Parkes, 199, *ii* 474; and recruiting of Australian religious, 287; and replacing of lay

teachers, 259; attitude to Polding's Benedictine aspirations, *i* 246; attitude to teaching orders, 246, 248, *ii* 260, 388; educational achievements, 259-60; family background, *i* 248; foresees reaction to absolute secularism, *ii* 457; influenced by suffragans, *i* 248, 249, 254; *Joint Pastoral*, 250, 253; leadership of, *ii* 258, 475; Lenten pastoral (1883), *i* 253; minor pastorals (1879), 250-1; on liberalism, 186, *ii* 422, 474; on monasticism, 300; on secondary schools, 320-1; plans for introducing religious, *ii* 257, 259, 421; schools before other diocesan works, 310
Vicar-General, educational responsibilities, *i* 78
Victorian Catholic Education Association, *see* Catholic education associations
Victoria College, East Melbourne, *ii* 324
Victorian Education League, *i* 123
Victoria, Queen, *i* 47
Viliéglée, Père Lewis Quelen de la, French chaplain, *i* 19
Vincentian Fathers: and sodalities, *ii* 414; and teaching of science, 366; and university colleges, 448; educational work, 269; first community in Australia, 270

Wade, Owen, convict teacher, *i* 38
Wallis, Rev. John, and Home Missionary Sisters, *ii* 297
Walsh, Rev. P., *ii* 440n.
Walsh, Rev. R., *ii* 316
Walsh, W. H., *i* 202
Ward, Mary, foundress of Loreto Sisters, *ii* 301
Webber, Bishop, *ii* 459
Wesleyans: and denominational schools, *i* 124, 136; and secular education, 125; attitude to general system, 31, 125; attitude to non-dogmatic religious instruction, 124; expenditure on education, 58-9; on rights of parents, 125; on rights of state, 125; shift in opinion on religious instruction, 124; support for Bible in School leagues, *ii* 460
Wesleyan Education Committee, *i* 125
West Australian: and the Roman bogey, *i* 164; opposed to assisted schools, 161
Whateley, Dr Richard, *i* 177
White, Rev. James S., *i* 142
Wight, Rev. George, Congregationalist leader in Queensland, *i* 120n.
Wilberforce, William, and education, *i* 7
Wiles, Bridget Lucy, teacher in Parramatta Street Girls' Model School, *i* 84n., 87n.
Wiles, John Henry: head of St Bene-

dict's Catholic Model School, *i* 87n.; inspector of Catholic schools, 80
Wilkins, William A.: and Catholic teachers, *i* 204-5; views on religious education, 154, 186, *ii* 394; writer, teacher, administrator, *i* 153
Willis, J. W., Chief Magistrate, Van Diemen's Land, *i* 35
Willson, Bishop Robert: and Governor Denison, *i* 45; and lay teachers, 221; and Provincial Council (1844), 167; and state sponsorship of education, 53; attitude to religious, *ii* 262; teachers from England, 86; unable to forgo state grant, *i* 221
Wilson, Rev. B. G. (Baptist), *i* 122n.
Wilson, Sr M. Dunstan, *ii* 287n.
Wilson, Rev. W. S., *i* 144n.
Windeyer, W. C., *ii* 336
Windsor, *i* 10, 19; *see* Missionary activities
Women, education of, special care of bishops, *ii* 264, 386
Wood-carving, *ii* 355
Woodlock, Rev. Dr, President of All Hallows', Dublin, selecting teachers for New South Wales, *i* 86n.
Woods, Rev. Julian E. T.: and education of Catholic poor, *ii* 292, 296; and publicity for Catholic education, *i* 226, 231; and state rights in education, 182; and use of religious, *ii* 259; as Director-General of Catholic education, *i* 226; 'Classical and Commercial Academy', Adelaide, *ii* 324; editor of *Southern Cross and Catholic Herald*, *i* 231n.; educational schemes laid before Provincial Council (1869), 173; evidence before Select Committee (1868), 74n., 184n., 231; founder of religious orders, *ii* 271, 292, 295; Jesuit and Passionist influence on, 302; on success of local boards, *i* 77; opposition to, 234-7; significance in Catholic education, *ii* 475; writer of school texts, *i* 229; *see also* Woods-Sheil scheme
Woods-Sheil scheme: enrolments, *i* 231; examinations, 230; funds for, 227; improvement on older system, 225; influence in other colonies, 237; local boards, 77; numbers of schools, 231; opposition from clergy, 234-7, 255; organization in schools, 228; participation of laity, 226-7; placed before Provincial Council (1869), 234; policy on religious teachers, 232-3; publicity, 226, 230; role of Sisters of St Joseph, 232; structure of, 225-38, *ii* 438; textbooks, *i* 229; training of teachers, 228
Woolley, Dr John, Chancellor of University of Sydney, *ii* 313
Woolloomooloo, site of first Catholic secondary school, *ii* 312

Woolnough, Rev. G., *i* 142n.
Wright, S., *ii* 467n.
Writing, teaching of, *ii* 355
Wyatt, William, inspector of schools (S.A.), *i* 81, 244n.
Wyeth, E. R., *ii* 339n.

Xaverian Brothers, *ii* 259

Young, Archbishop Guilford, *ii* 350
Young Catholic Students' Movement (Y.C.S.): and leadership, *ii* 415, and National Catholic Secretariat, 416; history of, 416; methods, 415, 417; organization, 415-17; part of Catholic action, 414; publications, 416; purpose and objectives, 414-15